THE ACCIDENTAL PROLETARIAT

THE ACCIDENTAL PROLETARIAT

WORKERS, POLITICS, AND CRISIS IN GORBACHEV'S RUSSIA

Walter D. Connor

PRINCETON UNIVERSITY PRESS   PRINCETON, NEW JERSEY

Copyright © 1991 by Princeton University Press
Published by Princeton University Press, 41 William Street,
Princeton, New Jersey 08540
In the United Kingdom: Princeton University Press, Oxford

Library of Congress Cataloging-in-Publication Data
Connor, Walter.
The accidental proletariat : workers, politics, and crisis in
Gorbachev's Russia / Walter D. Connor.
p.   cm.
Includes index.
ISBN 0-691-07787-8
1. Labor—Soviet Union.   2. Working class—Soviet Union.
3. Working class—Soviet Union—Political activity.   I. Title.
HD8526.5.C594   1991
322'.2'0947—dc20   91-8557

This book has been composed in Linotron Palatino

Princeton University Press books are printed
on acid-free paper, and meet the guidelines
for permanence and durability of the Committee
on Production Guidelines for Book Longevity
of the Council on Library Resources

Printed in the United States of America by
Princeton University Press, Princeton, New Jersey

10 9 8 7 6 5 4 3 2 1

(Pbk.)
10 9 8 7 6 5 4 3 2 1

To Christine and Elizabeth

Contents

List of Tables

Preface

THE SOVIET UNION of 1991 is not the Soviet Union of 1985. Nor is it the Soviet Union that will exist—under whatever name and political arrangement(s)—by 1995. No doubt like many other authors who set out in the mid-1980s, at the beginning of the Gorbachev era, to write a book on the contemporary USSR, I have found the flow of events since then fascinating, gratifying (who would not be gratified as the ice of this long-frozen colossus finally began to crack?), troubling (who would not wish the peoples of the Soviet Union a smoother journey to limited government, a viable economy, a civil society than they are likely to experience?), and confusing. Who finds it easy to write a book about a moving target, even one facet thereof? Things are not what they were. Brezhnev's USSR of 1980 was, by and large, in broad outline and in many critical details, the USSR of 1975, indeed of 1970. For many years, the task of the analyst was to deal with and explicate the processes of a very stable system, to determine what, if any, were rather subtle portents of change. Boredom was a more likely occupational disease than any other. No longer.

This book, then, which attempts to explore the Soviet working class—the blue-collar majority of Soviet society—its emergence over the decades leading to the present, its social composition and characteristics, and the "politics" it has made (and is likely to make in the future) is almost bound, it seems to me, to be a failure, if by success we mean the "last word," and a long-enduring one, on the topic. Too much tumultuous change has been packed into too short a time span, too much alteration in the political architecture, too much destructuring and too little effective "restructuring" in the economy, and too much change yet impends for an author to presume to finality of conclusions. Having lifted the lid on a long-suppressed society, Gorbachev let loose social forces—class, ethnic, intellectual—that the Soviet state can no longer totally control; his reasons for doing so, and with what degree of consciousness, will remain topics of debate for a long time. Prime among those "class" forces, by virtue of their numerical weight, their central role in classic coal-and-steel economy, and their existence as the product of decades of Soviet political and economic development, are the workers themselves. This surely justifies the topic; I can only hope that the treatment here does justice to it.

Though the book is not exclusively organized on either chronological or topical bases, but on a mix of the two, it is clearly the case that earlier chapters deal with matters on which more distance, more "perspective" was achievable, while later chapters cover events that unfold very rapidly indeed. This approach is unavoidable, unless one wants to delay the final version until long after some clearly decisive event had occurred and been recognized as such. That time seems still distant. What is offered here, then, already delayed and revised several times in the face of events in the USSR, bears the marks of its uncertain times.

Organizational support and financial aid played a significant role in facilitating the research and writing of the present book—however much the accelerating changes in the Soviet Union complicated the business of arriving at the end. On the organizational side, it is a pleasure to thank my colleagues in Boston University's Department of Political Science, who were unfailingly sympathetic to a chairman engaged in a time-consuming writing project. To Harvard University's Russian Research Center, and my friends and colleagues there, it is once again a large debt of gratitude I acknowledge for an atmosphere and context of interaction from which this, as well as much of my previous work, has benefited greatly.

The writing of the first draft was facilitated immeasurably by freedom from other duties from May 1986 to September 1987—a freedom "bought" with the support of both the National Council for Soviet and East European Research and the John Simon Guggenheim Memorial Foundation. My thanks to both organizations for their support and continued interest. Later, a travel grant from the International Research and Exchanges Board allowed a brief but extremely profitable visit to the USSR in early 1988, for consultations with a broad range of Moscow-based specialists on labor and social problems and on economic reform. Both IREX and the specialists with whom I spoke in Moscow at that time and later contributed significantly to whatever merit this book possesses.

Intellectual debts are due as well to many colleagues in the Soviet field, both in academia and the government, on whom I have over the years, in speaking and in writing, tried out a number of the ideas and approaches, and refined (or abandoned!) tentative conclusions, that have been part of the work embodied here.

A writer who persists in recording his initial drafts on yellow legal pads in a high-tech age owes much to those who later take poorly typed pages and turn them into something clean and legible. Rose DiBenedetto did much of this work, and Barbara Sindriglis prepared the final version. At Princeton University Press, Alice Calaprice devoted a good deal of her time and editorial talents to the manuscript, while Gail Ullman was unfailingly sympathetic to a frequently revised schedule and to my desires to hold off the Epilogue to the last possible moment before the production process began.

Finally, my wife Eileen has, for nearly twenty-five years, borne the peculiar burden of living with an author-husband's preoccupations: my love and thanks to her once again, as well as to our daughters, Christine and Elizabeth, whose wisecracking but affectionate irreverence toward a father who frequently needs it has more than earned them the dedication page.

List of Abbreviations

The following abbreviations are used in the text. A list of abbreviations used in the notes can be found at the beginning of the Notes section.

ASSR	Autonomous Soviet Socialist Republic
AUCCTU	All-Union Central Council of Trade Unions
CPD	Congress of People's Deputies
CPSU	Communist Party of the Soviet Union
FYP	Five Year Plan
ICFTU	International Congress of Free Trade Unions
ILO	International Labor Organization
ITR	Inzhenerno-tekhnicheskie rabotniki (engineering-technical employees)
KGB	Komitet Gosudarstvennoi Bezopasnosti (Committee on State Security)
KTU	Koeffitsient trudovogo uchastiia (coefficient of labor participation)
MUPK	Mezhshkol'nye uchebno-proizvodstvennye kombinaty (interschool production-training combines)
NEP	New Economic Policy
NTS	Narodno-Trudovoi Soiuz (People's Labor Alliance)
OFTR	Ob"edinennyi Front Trudiashchikhsia Rossii (United Front of Workers of Russia)
PTU	Professzional'no-tekhnicheskoe uchilishche (vocational-technical school)
RSFSR	Russian Soviet Federated Socialist Republic
SIP	Soviet Interview Project
SLR	State Labor Reserves
SMOT	Svobodnoe Mezhprofessional'noe Ob"edinenie Trudiashchikhsia (Free Interprofessional Association of Workers)
SPTU	Srednee professional'no-tekhnicheskoe uchilishche (secondary vocational-technical school)
STK	Sovet Trudovogo Kollektiva (Council of the Labor Collective)
TU	Tekhnicheskoe uchilishche (technical school)
VSNKh	Verkhovnyi Sovet Narodnogo Khoziaistva (Supreme Council for the National Economy)
VUZ	Vysshie uchebnoe zavedenie (higher-education institution)

THE ACCIDENTAL PROLETARIAT

Introduction

IN JANUARY 1989, the economist Robert Heilbroner—hardly an unqualified cheerleader for capitalism and an unfettered market—began a *New Yorker* article thus:

> Less than seventy-five years after it officially began, the contest between capitalism and socialism is over: capitalism has won. The Soviet Union, China, and Eastern Europe have given us the clearest possible proof that capitalism organizes the material affairs of humankind more satisfactorily than socialism: that however inequitably or irresponsibly the marketplace may distribute goods, it does so better than the queues of a planned economy; however mindless the culture of commercialism, it is more attractive than state moralism; and however deceptive the ideology of a business civilization, it is more believable than that of a socialist one.[1]

If, later in his article, Heilbroner also raised doubts about the future of capitalism as we know it, this was only to stress the ubiquity of change and the pitfalls of projecting present realities into the future. But the verdict on socialism was clear enough, and accurate.

Less clear, at the time of this writing, is what will replace Soviet-model socialism as a political and economic system, where it has existed for so long. The reemergence of traditional political culture patterns and problems in Eastern Europe has made for a renewed diversity there as, for example, Czechoslovakia and Romania follow different trajectories as the Soviet bloc decays. Nowhere are matters less clear than in the case of the Soviet Union itself. From a rather slow beginning in 1985 to early 1986, Gorbachev's program of glasnost', perestroika, and democratization has picked up speed as it assumed a more definite shape. Changes in politics have been profound, even though the threadbare Soviet economy has yet to show signs of improvement, or indeed of the pains of the truly radical surgery needed before improvement can become a realistic prospect.

But along the way, various social and political forces were activated, and claiming access to power and consultation, *have* gained space in the arena of politics: the pace and direction of change are no longer determined solely by the success of Gorbachev's programs and ideas in the face of passive or bureaucratic resistance. Issues untouchable in 1985–86—the leading role of the Communist party, the permanence of the Soviet federal state within its historical boundaries, the broad definitions of socialism itself—are on the table, some already resolved in ways inconceivable only five years ago.

The Soviet system is thus in crisis—economic, political, social—on the very soil that gave it birth. It is by far a more complicated crisis than the one that befell and precipitated the wholesale collapse of Eastern Europe, where the system had been imposed "from above and abroad." Never has the ability of the political system to guide, control, and exercise authority over economy and society been so weakened. Never have social forces, developing over a long time and now unleashed, counted for so much. We will deal with one of those forces—a very major one—here.

Workers, the State, and Perestroika

This book is about Soviet workers, Soviet politics, and Soviet society. Workers—their labor, wages, morale, and general mood—have been a major preoccupation of Soviet politics, especially the "low" politics that concerns itself not with foreign affairs, military policy, and grand matters of state, but with the incremental, complicated processes of dividing national income between investment and consumption and consumption into wages and salaries versus unpaid services and subsidies, and with questions of labor force allocation, training, and so on. Workers and their families make up the majority of Soviet society. To the considerable degree that politics has sought to control society, to the near-total degree that political considerations have dictated economic policy in the socialist Soviet state, politics has been inextricably bound up with the blue-collar work force, attempting to direct it while at the same time attempting to respond to those "needs" that the leadership perceived existed and were legitimate.

In the period that concerns us here, from Stalin's death over a third of a century ago to the current period of doubt, hope, and upheaval under Gorbachev's perestroika, the USSR and its workers have experienced, until recently, a relative stabilization of society, an extended time of relative tranquility and normality—all in contrast to the dislocations and deprivations of social revolution, war, and postwar reconstruction under the conditions of severe political repression of the 1928–53 period.

Tranquility and normality do not preclude change. They only impart to it a different feel, a different character; and change aplenty there has been since 1953 in Soviet society. Some elements are directly traceable to the effects of state policy—increased educational levels as the national educational system grew more developed and socially inclusive, and increased material welfare as the economy developed and more of its output was allocated to consumption. Other changes are less matters of state intent, however traceable they may be as consequences of policy. The USSR is more urban than ever before. But the urbanity of today is not a matter of driving rural masses into existing cities, or of populating new cities with them. Increasingly, in the late Khrushchev and early Brezhnev eras, urban growth became a matter of internal reproduction, the rise of a population of second- and third-generation city dwellers with tastes, standards, and a psychology far removed from that of ex-peasants. The maturation of the Soviet economy, reflected even before the onset of Brezhnevian "stagnation" in a slowing growth rate and a stabilization of the occupational structure, reduced the opportunities for inter- and intragenerational social mobility. Stratum, or "class," boundaries hardened, and the opportunities for mobility or the contingencies that faced earlier Soviet generations were lessened for those growing to maturity in the Brezhnev era. This reduction of mobility was experienced in a society at the same time more stable—but also more complex and specialized in terms of its occupational structure—than it had been in the Stalin, or indeed the earlier Khrushchev, period.

It was a society changed in many ways by the processes that Brezhnev presided over in his last years; that witnessed the short Andropov-Chernenko interregnum; that for all *its* changes found little state recognition of those changes, no real *political* adaptation or change, until Gorbachev's accession in 1985. The period since then, to the time of writing, has been one of renewed upheaval as "politics" has come to react to, and at the same time has tried to manage, the consequences of long-term changes come to fruition only over the past twelve to fifteen years.

In their millions, Soviet workers constitute a critical part of the complicated legacy that history has presented to Gorbachev's reformers (and their opponents). Much about today's workers is unclear. Their resemblance to the workers of Stalin's, or Khrushchev's, or even of Brezhnev's earlier time cannot be assumed. Workers' attitudes and values, aspirations, and expectations were important in the late-Brezhnev period, as the regime attempted to deliver adequate material rewards and security while economic performance faltered. They will not be less important in the time of economic reform, social mobilization, and democratization ushered in by Gorbachev. If convinced of the rationale and need for perestroika, workers would be formidable grass-roots allies for the reformers. If unconvinced, or if they perceive threats to aspects of life they value, workers can hinder reform's progress and provide an important political pretext to have it modified or abandoned by a leadership that fears a broad social crisis. They are not without the resources to do so.

To make this point about workers' potential power is not to engage in an oversimplifying "socialization" of political processes in a system very different from those of Western democracies. Most of us don't need to be reminded of the power and the relevance of the Soviet *state* in the state-society relationship. The Russian, and Soviet, reality has been that of a strong state dominating a weak society, driving social and economic processes that have operated more autonomously in the West. Whether the tsarist state, the new Soviet state of Lenin's time, or the industrializing/terrorizing state of the Stalin era were "legitimate"—and to how much of the population—are interesting questions. But society's reactions did not determine the outcome in these days. Students of polity and society have been reminded in recent times that, in general, the state and its activity—*pace* traditional Marxist understanding—are not "emanations" of social process. States possess "autonomy"; in the absence of legitimacy, a state possessed of adequate coercive resources can secure itself against the society that refuses to accord it legitimacy.[2] Even if we assume that, for most of its existence, the Soviet state has been accepted as legitimate by the majority of the population (especially the Russian ethnic population), the contemporary situation presents some new issues in the relationship between what has been, historically, a strong state and a historically "weak" society.

Gorbachev the "reformer" sought, from the outset, a transformation of Soviet economy and society that would require a large element of free and active compliance and support from the population. Like all Russian reforms, the process began as "reform from above"; it broadened when political reform came to be seen as critical to the economic reform that refused, in 1985–86, to take shape. Political decompression has, however, led to a flood of participation, with a multitude of participants involved in a new, broader, but unstable politics, making guidance "from above" less and less evident or enforceable. Still, perestroika requires that people find motivation and resources to act—as producers, consumers, citizens—as if they were free, to be less dependent on the state, and to take greater responsibility for the results of their own actions.

This is unique. Earlier changes had consisted of Lenin's political revolution and the New Economic Policy, and Stalin's violent transformation. Khrushchev's liberalization had modified state control over society by a moderate and selective slackening of that control on the state's terms. Whatever Gorbachev's ultimate rationale for change—radical reform to save something called "socialism," a basic revulsion at the Soviet past, a once hidden desire to produce a strong, "modern" state that might readily dispense with the Communist

Party of the Soviet Union and its historical/ideological iconography in toto—his design would seem to require that subjects act more like "citizens." For some, this is surely no problem. Large numbers have been active politically—some in support of Gorbachev and reform, some critical of perestroika's slow pace; but some have organized in resistance, and a vast mass has remained politically passive and economically disenchanted.

With respect to the latter, one cannot force people to be "free," to compel them toward autonomy. Thus the historical strength of the Soviet state—whatever of it remains—is less of an asset now than it has been to Soviet leaders of the past. More depends on society—and much depends on the workers who make up its majority.

The interwoven processes of social change noted earlier that had, by the late Brezhnev era, changed Soviet society, if not the polity, are of the sort that are conducive to differentiation of interests, of groups tied to interests, of *classes* in a general sense. To the degree that Soviet society is not only unequal (as all societies are), but also shows signs of a class structure—and within that structure, the presence of a "working class"—the problems of a reforming leadership, the range of possible outcomes, grow more complicated and interesting.

Workers and the Problem of Class

The question of whether Soviet workers constitute a "class" or not (in a broad sense, using some of the traditional Marxian analytical criteria) runs as a continuing thread through the pages to come. Tougher-minded left-wing analysts have had to confront the rather obvious fact that the "class" their political convictions make them want to believe in has a good deal of trouble emerging under Soviet-type socialism, and an easier time under capitalist regimes. As Irving Howe asked rhetorically nearly two decades ago: "Where, to use a Marxist category, do the workers come closer to constituting 'a class for itself'—where do they have more independence, assertiveness, dignity, and a greater sense of their potential: in England, not yet visited by the revolution, or Russia, 50 years after it has occurred?"[3] It is, of course, arguable that workers nowhere satisfy the combination of analytic and mythopoeic elements that go into Marx's notion of the militant, activated class, the proletariat. As Howe put it, the working class is a "social presence," a "reality"—the proletariat a "historic potential," "an idea."[4] Ralph Miliband, also an analyst from the Left, adds that, using as a criterion consciousness of collective interests *as* a class, the rich are more class conscious than the poor, the "dominant classes have so far fulfilled [the criterion of class consciousness] a great deal better than the proletariat."[5]

If we take these as accurate observations in the context of Western capitalist-democratic systems, we can expect that in the USSR, with its very different path of historical development and its ensemble of political and economic institutions, the question of whether workers there constitute a "class" is likely to be complicated as well. Of course, if workers can define themselves only as a class, a proletariat, versus a class of capitalists on a large scale, the matter ended for the USSR in the late 1920s—along with the capitalists. But obviously, to restrict definitions so narrowly in an inquiry about Soviet political and social reality would only be a "sterile play of words."[6] We must go further.

Soviet workers, as chapter 1 will show, have been the objects of tumultuous change, of massive, violent social transformations, and not a self-regulating, self-actualizing collectivity as producers or as citizens. There has been little syndicalism, but much of the old-fashioned top-down authority relations in this brand of socialism. If Western workers have been subordinated to managers who were "capital personified," then so have Soviet workers—over the long period traced in the chapters to follow—been subordinated to managers who were "the party personified."[7] The control exercised over Soviet workers has been pervasive, the asymmetry of authority between bosses and workers immense.

Indeed, part of the argument in this book is that control has aimed at preventing the emergence of workers as a class in the USSR. But control has not been total, nor always clear in its focus. Much autonomous development has occurred over the long run, altering the face of the blue-collar Soviet world and, we shall argue, contributing to the emergence of certain class characteristics in the Soviet proletariat. Much of that development has been "accidental," in two senses. First, it did not flow from the purposes of the Soviet regime, however logically it may have followed from the policies the regime adopted and the social processes it first set in motion with the industrialization drive of the late 1920s. Second, it hardly accorded with the lines of development Marx had sketched out much earlier; but then, the course of working-class development has nowhere fit quite into Marx's framework. As a predictive enterprise rather than a political-ideological one, Marxism has run afoul of many historical accidents.

Some may have reservations about my use of the term "accidental" in this regard. Fair enough. Alternatives have been suggested to me, but I have nonetheless stubbornly opted for my original choice. "Unanticipated" seems the least objectionable among these, capturing the sense that the gradual acquisition of at least some class characteristics by the workers was not something the regimes intended or quite fore-saw as happening. But without assuming that Lenin in his years in power, or even more so, Stalin, saw things in such explicit terms, both did, in opting for tight political controls over society in general, "antic-ipate" the possibility of combination, organization, and interest artic-ulation, if it were not prevented. In the Brezhnev period, the system and its controls were already "set"—the failure to perceive, to antici-pate some of the long-term social developments was a matter of poor social intelligence. The state, for all its resources, knew little about the society; officially, it did not listen to the sociologists, economists, and others who did know a great deal, as Western observers now realize more than ever. Thus, what came upon the state came as an "acci-dent," one to which, in its limited awareness, it could not respond.

"Inevitable" proletariat has also been suggested to me—and has the virtue of expressing the notion that certain consequences "must" in a sense follow large-scale industrialization and urbanization and the settling down of a society where these processes were, at first, driven fast and furiously. But taking "inevitable" to mean that the state can only "delay," only postpone, the inevitable developments, gives rather short shrift to the differing capacities of states to resist, to delay the inevitable. There is a great deal of difference between states that "must," because of their policy, institutions, or structure, respond rather quickly to unwelcome, unanticipated developments and the stronger states that can defer such accommodation for a long time. There is more than one brand of inevitability; the pre-Gorbachev So-viet state was solid enough in its control that it never, in fact, faced many "inevitabilities." Since then, much has been recognizable as in-evitable partly because a different political process, in a political sys-tem undergoing rapid change that was not, in 1980–85, "demanded" by any broad section of Soviet society, has allowed change to "hap-pen." Thus, though I am aware that it is a far from perfect term, I remain wedded to "accidental" as the best label for the outcome of the long process we will investigate here.

To whatever degree workers have "accidentally" acquired the char-acteristics of a class, their clout in a rapidly changing, fluid political situation should be even greater. The class issue, then, sharpens but does not exhaust the question of whether workers are likely to be a force for or against the sort of social and economic changes, cutting to the core of Soviet everyday life, which are the aims of perestroika. The latter question links the outcome of decades of past developments with some of the critical and as yet undetermined prospects for the future—indeed the survival—of the Soviet system. Will workers prove a mainstay of Gorbachev's attempt to save Soviet socialism by reforming it, by moving toward the market? Or will they weigh in largely as a conservative force, claiming that much of what Gorbachev finds distorted, inefficient, or disaster-bound is the system they prefer, thereby demanding restoration of the status quo?

Our exploration, however rooted in political events and controversies that move with amazing speed, will benefit from some analytic framework. For class-analysis purposes, Michael Mann's schema, developed in the West European context,[8] for defining working-class consciousness of a "truly revolutionary sort"—that which would make "reality" of Howe's "ideas"/"historical potential"—will serve as a rather demanding test. Mann proposes four criteria, which build in serial order toward that consciousness:

1. Class *identity* (one realizes one *is* working class, like other workers, and hence different from owners).

2. Class *opposition* (the conviction that the owners are, and must be, opposed to the workers and vice versa).

3. Class *totality* (identity and opposition are understood to define the workers' total situation and to constitute the major division in society).

4. Consciousness of an *alternative* (a different society, treated as a goal that workers strive for against the owners).

In toto, these criteria constitute a tall order; their coming together would be a rare occurrence. In the Soviet context, without prejudging the question or revealing what is to come, it is reasonable to say that we have no evidence that all four elements have yet come together, or are likely to do so in the near future. Still, we can make some preliminary comments.

There seems little reason, first of all, not to expect a substantial degree of working-class identity among Soviet workers. Their place in the production process is subordinate; their subjection to a technocratic division and segmentation of labor tasks is certainly no less than that of workers in the West, and more so than in some Western cases where innovations in work organization have taken root. They are "controlled."[9] What might be said about the effects of work organization on the rank and file is generally summed up in a worker-advocate's conclusion that both "capitalism's and socialism's industrial revolutions have, in fact, been monuments to the inefficient and inhumane uses of labor."[10] Assuming that the better-documented worker life in Eastern Europe is relevant to the Soviet case, observations by Miklos Haraszti, drawn from his experience as a worker in a Budapest factory, suggest a deep-rooted sense of worker identity in the plant. Management and its agents are "them" ("nowhere, except among factory workers, have I heard this absolute *them*, peremptory, exact, and crystal clear"). Managers may use the word "us," but workers never ("either by chance, or in jest, or by slip of the tongue, or in error, and probably not even in their dreams").[11]

These attitudes underline identity. They also smack of class *opposition*. Identity and opposition grow in a hostile environment, against attempts to blunt them. As Ivan Szelenyi puts it for East European workers in general:

> Not only are the workers deprived of the opportunity to associate with their fellow workers, but their quest for identity as workers is also continuously questioned. The worker is replaced with an ideological notion, that of the proletariat—the worker who is aware of his historical mission. The worker finds himself labeled as "petty bourgeois" or "lumpen proletariat" if he tries to live up to his immediate values and aspirations, and he is accused of lacking proletarian consciousness. The empirically identifiable values, aspirations, and ways of life of the actual physical workers are confronted with the ideals of "socialist man," who socially and in class terms is a faceless creature devised by Soviet Marxist ideologues.[12]

The effectiveness of this assault is unclear—or must be treated as such at this point. It is also worth noting here that worker attitudes, oppositional as they may be, need not add up to "class" opposition, narrowly construed. We lack, for the USSR, an ethnography of the factory, like those we have for Eastern Europe. Characterizing the public consciousness in the USSR in late 1988 with respect to the central bureaucracy's core, the *nomenklatura*, the reformist sociologist and economist Tatiana Zaslavskaia suggested a "we-they" general division, rather than one of class distinction, within society: "People's awareness does not oppose the *kolkhoz* members to the workers or the workers engaged in physical labor to the intellectuals, but primarily opposes the 'administered' to the 'administrators.'"[13] Workers could thus be seen as a component of the large, controlled "we" versus the small, controlling "they." But workers who have, as a social category, acquired over time some of the attributes of class, could be a more combative, problematic "we" than their predecessors in earlier periods of Soviet history, who confronted "them" without such attributes.

At this early point it is harder to discuss questions of class totality, or of clear conceptions of an alternative social-economic reality among Soviet workers. "Totality" would require, essentially, that the worker-manager relationship of subordination be *the* central experience, that work be the context within which all social life is summarized. But, just as Mann asks about Western workers, we can certainly question whether work is "all," that it is so central to Soviet workers that other distractions or compensations, material or otherwise, may not reduce its salience for them. Given this, even alienating work may not be the prime determinant of worker attitudes. (Certainly, much in Soviet sociological literature suggests that women workers, whose pay and work conditions are often quite poor, do not necessarily exhibit high degrees of dissatisfaction with it—nor the sort of high expectations of work whose violation might contribute to a consciousness of "totality.")[14] If the social world Soviet workers inhabit is the "industrial firm writ large," then worker-"non-worker" opposition of the sort Haraszti notes in his Budapest factory might move toward totality. But if, as in West European societies, the world outside work is organized differently, then the "line of social confrontation over the distribution of spoils and the prerogatives of command"[15] may fade markedly, leaving the experience of identity and opposition linked in time and place *to* the plant but diffused outside of it, and thus consciousness is clearly short of class totality.

With respect to worker consciousness of alternatives, it goes without saying that the Soviet educational, ideological, media, and police/administrative dice here have been loaded against any such development. The claim that Soviet-type socialism *is* the "workers' state" rhetorically preempts, to a degree, the possibility of an alternative being verbalized.[16] (In the West, worker consciousness is generally less than revolutionary because systemic alternatives have been articulated, if at all, only in the context of Communist-dominated unions, as in France and Italy. The more typical "economistic" trade unionism has stopped short of systematic alternatives.)

The alternative held out to Western workers has been "socialism." The obvious alternative for Soviet-type systems is market and democracy: Soviet-model socialism has encompassed neither. Before the political landslide of 1989, it is doubtful that any political group or movement with a substantial worker base advocated this alternative. In Poland, the original Solidarity of 1980–81 moved toward democracy, certainly, but was economically ambiguous;[17] the Solidarity that now occupies critical space in the new Polish government is for the capitalist market. So, increasingly, are many Soviet economists and political actors. But there is no indication that Soviet workers, in any large numbers, have yet signed on this line. More critical at present is blue-collar perception and reaction to Gorbachev's constantly unfolding, less than totally consistent alternative. As a "class," or as groups, workers are faced with programs of change, some of whose elements they may find attractive but others repellent.

The Limits of Class Analysis

Class, and the analytic pegs on which to hang evidence for or against it, will come in and out of focus as we move through the various topics in this book. For several reasons, it is a less constant theme than it might be.

First, direct evidence of workers' class identification—the subjective dimension tapped via questionnaires that ask respondents to place themselves in a particular social class—is lacking. Soviet sociology, for all the information it yields on a number of topics, gives us very little on this matter. The emergence of empirical research on social stratification in the USSR was a very sensitive matter. Parting company from the analytically useless ideological formula of "two nonantagonistic classes" (workers and collective farmers) and one stratum (the white-collar "intelligentsia," broadly defined) required that researchers make finer cuts on skill levels, income, and so forth. Although this produced a more complex map of social inequality and diversity, it never directly addressed problems of class identification. Research on Soviet emigrés of the 1970s and 1980s has not, on the whole, been able to fill the gap.

Second, although questions of class, posed within the Marxist tradition, are important, I am a Marxist neither by analytic approach nor political persuasion. Once one goes past a certain point of analytic/ terminological complexity, the issue of whether the "something" we observe is a class or not loses its importance. If I seem to opt too readily for a general or "soft" definition of class characteristics, it is because I am convinced that this analytical level is largely appropriate to the topic. With respect to my own political persuasion, I can sympathize with the many Marxists who see the Soviet system as very different from what they have "meant" by socialism—that it violates Marxism's promise. But I have held no belief that a better, more authentic socialism was the most desirable outcome of reform, nor that the proletariat, the working class, had somehow to be the agent of that reform. Its potential role remains to be defined. My own sympathies are unabashedly pro-market, capitalist, and democratic. While these need be of little concern to the reader, they do mean that I can afford to be agnostic on any role the Soviet working class "must" play, and that I remain "broad church" in terms of the range of outcomes I would consider improvements over the system that the Brezhnev era bequeathed to the present.

Third, and more important, questions about what kind of political force workers may constitute and the directions their politics may take are part of a broader set of concerns about the nature of Soviet socio-political change, and how it reflects the cumulation of the various long-term currents of social change referred to earlier—labeled by one analyst as a "quiet revolution."[18] Recent analytic perspectives on Soviet politics and society in the Gorbachev era have offered various frameworks for understanding patterns of change. Some focus on the concept of the social contract between regime and society—that is, political quiescence and compliance by society exchanged for an economy of subsidized prices, secure (over-)employment, controls over emergent inequalities delivered by the state—as a glue that began to weaken in the late Brezhnev years as the state found it more difficult to deliver, and society, grown more complex and variegated in its group structure and array of interests, began to avoid compliance.[19] Others draw upon our understanding of the decay of authoritarian regimes in Southern Europe and Latin America, of failures of systemic performance (especially economic) leading to cleavages among the elites, opening the political system to more influence from "society";[20] or on the notion of a more autonomous, self-regulatory "civil society" both as an emergent, spontaneous development in the USSR and as a necessary desideratum for Moscow political and economic reformers seeking support for their program from critical groups in Soviet society.[21]

But inquiry into the dynamics of the state-society relationship began not with the coming of Gorbachev, but much earlier. Zbigniew Brzezinski's seminal article, "The Soviet Political System: Transformation or Degeneration?" published in 1966,[22] evoked an extended discussion on the pages of *Problems of Communism*, in which a point of rather broad agreement was that Soviet society had grown more complex, industrial, "differentiated," and less malleable than in the past, while political ideology and institutions had changed much less, were ill-fit, by their reliance on command, to manage this society, and thus were anachronistic, irrelevant, inappropriate.

These were ideas expressed at the outset of what was to become the Brezhnev era; to the degree that they were couched as predictions of near-future contingencies, they were premature. Economic performance in the USSR from 1966 to 1970 was rather good, and to some degree eroded the base from which moderate economic reformers of the time tried to defend the "Kosygin reform" of 1965 against its eventual strangulation. Nor, in the 1960s and 1970s, was the regime unwilling to apply coercion and repression to contain political manifestations of that growing societal complexity. As I wrote in early 1973, the "costs of managing a complex, differentiated society by command techniques may be mounting, but even if this is the case, one cannot predict with any certainty when the bill will come due."[23]

It came due over a decade later, in 1985. Until then, albeit with declining effectiveness, the regime absorbed the cost, deferred the bill. But an active, cantankerous society did not force the Politburo to elect Gorbachev. The declining economic performance, the decreasing efficacy of the social contract, and the demoralization of segments of the elite fed the developing cleavages that made for policy struggles, and policy change, after 1985. As the new regime, via glasnost' and democratization, conceded more room to society, those who sought to participate openly in the public sphere found voice to do so: mainly, at first, the intelligentsia. The emergence of more elements of a civil society—of a public realm of discussion and debate, the interplay of interests and groups in which the state is one actor among many—remains at the time of writing a development that simultaneously supports a reformist leadership in many ways, while also threatening its degree of central control over policies and their execution. It was such control that Gorbachev sought, throughout 1990, by way of a new office of president, and the later addition of special powers to that office.

It is within this context as well that we must seek to understand the role of worker politics. The weakening of the control capacities of central party and state institutions has meant freedom not only to voice one's support for political reform and economic perestroika, but also to criticize them or to advocate their modification—attacking, under a guise of perfecting, refining, and "achieving" reforms. (It has also allowed new politically mobilized groups to put on the table a whole set of critical national-ethnic concerns Gorbachev had barely anticipated in 1985.) The complexity of the current situation—as well as the complexity of the blue-collar milieu itself—suggests that we should be ready to see a variety of directions in politics. The slow acquisition of some class characteristics by the workers has been part of their social evolution; even if this has been an incomplete process, the broader social activization of groups, occupational strata, and so on gives workers the opportunity to advance aspirations and claims.

These may be, on the whole, pro-reform in both the political and the economic sense. But equally likely is anti-reform mobilization, especially in the economic sphere. Worker resistance that might appear to be purely a "class" struggle could arise; it would be closely related to the world of work, wherein workers are subordinated to the bosses in the plant, and to the bosses' superiors in the ministries. Perestroika's innovations in wage scales, quality control, and conditions of employment have all made for a worker experience that may be quite different from that of the intelligentsia, managers, and collective or state farmers. Or, worker disaffection might instead focus on less work-related economic and social issues, where their sense of grievance could be shared with other elements of society. Persistent shortages, creeping inflation, the extraordinarily volatile prospect of retail price reforms are all possible points of contention. So, too, is the "justice issue" reflected in the high incomes earned by the new cooperative entrepreneurs compared to the lower incomes of many workers and employees. Such tensions could define an "us" of which workers would be only one component, and a "they" including not only the old bosses, but new groups seen to profit disproportionately under the new rules. Workers might also present themselves more broadly as a significant part of a generally socially and culturally "conservative" coalition. Here not economic grievance but symbolic politics might be critical. In 1989 Seweryn Bialer offered a characterization of workers along this line that, even if it turns out to be somewhat overdrawn, is rather widely accepted:

> As in other industrial countries, so in the Soviet Union the working class is by and large anti-intellectual, deeply patriotic, and traditional in its values. In part at least, whether they are members of the Communist Party or not, workers provide a ready-made constituency for the values and sentiments that are being expressed by the conservative opposition. The workers, for example, hate the bureaucrats and call them *bumazhnye dushi* (paper souls) but like the predictability of the old order. Workers are egalitarian not so much in their dislike of the perquisites and privileges of the *nachalstvo* (bosses) as in their support of equality at the lowest common denominator within their own class—not unlike the solidarity of the peasant *mir* (collective) against the *khutor* (the individual farm) at the time of the Stolypin reform during the decade before the October Revolution. Workers hate the instant affluence of the *deltsy* (entrepreneurs) in the cooperative enterprises and regard profits made by individual efforts as "dirty money," although this does not prevent them from making money through collective stealing from state enterprises or through work *na levo* (under the table), done either after work or during official working hours. Workers have a deep-seated and instinctive dislike of intellectuals and the media and are jealous and critical of the newfound freedom of such groups. The older workers are against the Western mass culture adopted by the younger generations. They glorify the Soviet past and the role of their class in it. In the final analysis, they are the conservative opposition's greatest source of power, and their vocal opposition to *glasnost'* and democratization is the greatest danger to Gorbachev.[24]

The workers' role in the unfolding drama, then, is likely a complicated one: one in which many of them might act as blue-collar producers, or as consumers; as a distinctive class, or as a component of a broader, agitated mass, whose shared long-term evocations of a better Soviet life for all may conflict with its perception that, over the short run, reform makes too many harsh demands and imposes its real costs disproportionately on common folk. Worker militancy will be as interesting and important an empirical phenomenon as will be the analytical question of class. Much, then, remains to be seen.

The Plan of This Book

My original intent was to develop the themes in each chapter (chapters 2–6), up to the coming of Gorbachev, and reserve the period beginning in 1985, the impact and meaning of perestroika, for the final chapter. But too much has happened since I began writing this book for a final chapter to comfortably contain the relevant points. Thus the reader can generally expect to find, in chapters 2 to 6, penultimate sections that summarize some of the important policy changes that came in roughly the first three years since Gorbachev's accession, and a final section in each chapter that relates that chapter's content to "class" and other questions dealt with earlier in this introduction. Chapter 7 deals with the increased political and economic tensions of 1989–90, including the rise of unprecedented labor militancy. The Epilogue revisits the issues of "class" and class politics, in the context of the growing systemic crisis of 1991, and offers some thoughts on the indeterminacy of the outcome.

What follows, follows in this order. Chapter 1 attempts to lay down a historical base, in pre-1953 development, for our consideration of workers over the past three to four decades. It begins in the social and economic context of late nineteenth-century tsarist industrial development, continues through the rupture and disorder of World War I and the revolution, into the New Economic Policy period, and finally the social-economic upheaval of Stalin's industrialization of the 1930s. The chapter, then, is the chronicle of the development of a small working "class" in pre-Soviet times, and of the Stalin-period dissolution of the remnants of this old working class in a new, vastly expanded *mass* of workers recruited from the peasantry.

Chapter 2 traces the emergence of new patterns, as in the postwar years the mass gradually changes its shape, as change comes in the sources of recruitment to the blue-collar work force, and in its levels of education. These processes, gathering strength through the Khrushchev and Brezhnev eras, again build the elements of a "class." Chapter 3 considers the patterns and problems of recruitment to blue-collar work. It examines the significance of both the academic and vocational education systems in directing young people toward, or diverting them from, the working class, and the difficulties of matching a changing structure of aspirations and expectations to the needs of the Soviet economy, as understood by the bosses.

In chapter 4 material aspects of the workers' lives—wage levels, differentiation within and outside the blue-collar ranks, the value of wages in terms of one's standard of living—form a base for discussing evidence of the satisfaction or dissatisfaction of workers' lives. Chapter 5 extends this inquiry to look at the work process itself, and how it is reflected by contentment or discontentment with work. The nature of jobs the economy makes available, their intrinsic attractions or repulsions for workers, and the structures of authority (and evasion thereof) within the factory all form part of this picture of the world of work.

Chapter 6 examines party organization and activity in the blue-collar milieu, and the functioning of official Soviet trade unions as modes of channeling and controlling worker behavior, while defending the worker interests that successive regimes have come to recognize. Beyond this, it treats at some length the record of labor militancy in the post-Stalin era, examining the incomplete but revealing record of strikes in the USSR and the attempts to give some organizational expression, via (unofficial) free trade unions, to what their founders have perceived as worker needs and demands.

At a time of such heightened interest in Soviet affairs, it is possible that a work like this one may attract more and a greater variety of readers than in the slow and steady Brezhnev period. Readers whose main interest is in the current scene may thus find it useful to read chapter 7 and the Epilogue first. Preceding chapters then can supply background for tracing particular concerns through the post-Stalin period to the early stages of perestroika, and among these the reader can pick and choose as seems best. Because some conclusions may be rather outdated by the time the book is in the reader's hands, I can only plead that writing *finis* to any work on contemporary Soviet affairs has become as difficult and frustrating, on the one hand, as following those affairs is fascinating and exciting, on the other. What was a standing target in the Brezhnev era has been moving rapidly since March 1985, and shows no signs of slowing down on its trajectory toward a very uncertain terminus.

1

Workers and Society:
From Tsarism to Socialism

Our proletariat—is the proletariat of a huge
peasant country.
  (*D. Manuilskii, 1928*)

THE DEVELOPMENTS that concern us in this book are deeply rooted in
the past, despite the revolutionary transformations that gave first
birth, then shape, to the USSR. The focus here is the period from
Stalin's death in 1953—a benchmark for so many facets of Soviet life—
to these, the twilight years of the system in the "Gorbachev era." But
an appreciation of some of those roots, both tsarist and Soviet, is essential to an understanding of the issues raised by the emergence and
growth of today's Soviet working class, in the context of the decline of
the 1970s and the tumult since 1985.

This chapter abounds in generalizations and may give pause to
those deeply steeped in the social history of late tsarist and early Soviet Russia. In defense, I must say, first, that the present work aims at
the concerns of political science and sociology, and second, that this
chapter could only have been written on the base of the increasingly
rich social historiography of the working class[1] upon which it has
drawn. What is known today was largely *tabula rasa* yesterday. This
progress is what makes it possible at all to get to the post-1953 period
in a useful historical context. This chapter, moving from tsarist nineteenth-century roots through war, revolution, and the New Economic
Policy (NEP) interlude of the 1920s to the great industrialization and
collectivization drives—the "great break," the "second revolution" of
1928 onward—draws heavily, if concisely, on the wealth of fact and
interpretation that history has provided.

"Prehistory": Workers under the Tsar

Pre-1861 imperial Russia's subjects, in their vast majority, were
serfs—legally unfree and tied, by law and by varying degrees of real
dependence, to the land. Serfs as well were the first souls employed

in factories, in the "industries" of the Muscovite state, and in growing numbers in the metalworks, mines, and armament factories of the "modernizing" Peter the Great. Yet concern for the labor supply preceded the wholesale 1861 liberation of the serfs under Alexander II. A law of 1840 had fostered selective emancipation from the field toward the factory, and by 1860, out of a modest industrial labor force of 800,000, only about a third were serfs. By 1914 those who toiled in industry numbered approximately 3.5 million: a more than fourfold increase fostered by the state-driven industrialization that began in earnest in the 1880s.[2]

Were they, however, in a social-political sense, proletarians, "workers"? The question is important and multifaceted. Legally, according to the classifications of tsarist Russia's "estate system," very few were. The system did not recognize "workers" as an estate, and in 1900 about 90 percent of those who were, economically, urban workers were classified as peasants—a category the estate system did know as the successor to that of "serf." There was reluctance to give *legal* recognition to a new category.

Beyond this, the rapidity of industrial development in the extremely backward nineteenth-century Russia compressed phases of development that had assumed a more gradual character in the industrial revolution in the West. In the process of drawing on Russia's vast peasant mass for manpower, development had created a social mix not quite urban in the Western understanding. As Jerzy Gliksman put it in his classic essay, "Inevitably the peasant origin of the bulk of Russia's urban workers stamped them with certain rural characteristics. Not only did they master industrial skills more slowly than Western workers, who came largely from generations of artisans and craftsmen, but their enduring links with the countryside also delayed their transformation into a modern industrial labor class."[3] Managerial and engineering talent was relatively scarce, and this, plus the massive state organizational role and the heavy reliance on foreign capital, created a situation wherein workers in late nineteenth-century Russia were concentrated to a greater degree in large enterprises than in the earlier industrializing states of the West. This made for a confrontation between largeness of scale, the sophistication of imported machinery, and a nascent industrial labor force marked not only by rural heritage, but by the relative backwardness of Russian countryside life versus rural life in better-developed states.

Russian industry, however, could draw but a negligible number of recruits from the small group of urban artisans. Even the peasant *kustari* (cottage-industry workers), who were compelled to give up work in their homes under the pressure of competition from factory-produced goods, formed a relatively small element in the factory labor force compared with the great mass of plain land-tilling peasants who entered it.[4]

Beyond rural heritage, a more serious political and historical dimension of the question, "Were they 'workers,' rather than . . .?" involved the legal links of the majority of urban workers, through their membership in rural communes (*mir*, *obshchina*), to the land and its obligations, as well as the degree to which the urban workers factually retained family and work links to the countryside. For Marxists, a true "proletarian" could only be one without property, sundered from village life, living "from day to day" by the labor power that was his sole asset. Without a supply of such, where are proletarian revolutions to come from? As a recent historian of Moscow workers' political activity in 1917 puts it,

> Soviet historians, following Marx, insist that it is a hereditary urbanized proletariat that will provide the foot soldiers for radical political movements, and it has been the task of these historians to prove the existence in Russia of such a proletariat. Moscow workers, Bolshevik leaders feared in 1917, were still too closely tied to the land to be of much use in a revolutionary situation.[5]

The historical judgment, on the whole, expresses the mix of proletarian and "peasant" characteristics in the decades just prior to revolution. Legal ties to the rural commune (the right to participate in periodic land redistribution, the duty to pay taxes, and the obligation to renew one's passport, allowing one to work in the city) were real, though for many they may have had a proforma character. Stronger for others were social and economic ties—a wife and children in the village, a regular return home in the summer to do agricultural work, and the remittance home of wages earned in urban areas by those who, in massive numbers, lived there without family, crowded into slum barracks and associating with their *zemliaki*, that is, with other workers from the same region.

But even those with such roots were not newcomers to urban life and work. The number and share who were "hereditary" workers was large, whatever this implied about their attitudes and behavior. As Gliksman observed, "At the turn of the century between one third and two thirds of the industrial workers were what we may call 'hereditary proletarians,' that is, persons whose fathers had been factory workers."[6] Further data sharpen the picture somewhat. A study of Moscow textile mills in 1880 revealed that two-fifths of the total labor force had worker fathers; of weavers alone, more than two-thirds were hereditary workers.[7] At the large Tsindel' mill in Moscow nineteen years later (1899), 94 percent of the workers were legally registered as peasants, but 56 percent had worker fathers: "Many juridical 'peasants' in Moscow . . . had never seen the village of their parents."[8] Workers in metal fabrication had a more "proletarian" cast in this respect than textile workers—a 1908 study in Moscow showed that 54 percent of metalworkers were "hereditary" compared to 43 percent of the textile group.[9] But the disruptions of war, revolution, and the beginnings of the civil war were reflected in 1918 in statistics from Petrograd showing that by then, in that city of heavy industry, only 20 percent of the metalworkers and 24.8 percent of the textile workers were of worker parentage.[10]

First-generation versus hereditary-worker status did not necessarily signify the presence or absence of significant rural linkages. As Robert Johnson put it in a review of some turn-of-the-century studies, the majority of workers in the factories investigated "were male, and . . . most lived in barracks without their families. Their children were raised in the countryside by their mothers. . . . The existence of a second generation at the factory was no proof that its members had severed ties with the 'patriarchal' village."[11] Indeed, even many hereditary workers still retained their land allotments in the villages.[12]

Thus, *what* the Russian worker was, as the revolution came, remains an issue full of ambiguity. No snapshot in time will allow an easy characterization of workers in general, or even those in the large cities. Neither the sociological question of the predominance of trends backward toward the peasantry or forward toward pure urban proletarian identity, nor the political one of whether it was "uprooted peasant" qualities or those of the "hereditary urbanized proletariat" that provided more foot soldiers for revolution, find definite answer here.[13]

In the midst of this complexity, economic conditions and social consciousness were creating some workers in the model of the proletariat: ones who had no ties to the land, who looked upon those recently arrived from the countryside as hicks and bumpkins, who had learned, as their rural cousins had not, to "tuck their shirts in and leave their trousers out" (in reversal of the peasant dress of loose *rubashka* and pants tucked in boots).[14] Even some village-born workers reached a high degree of skill and fashioned ways of life "based on a distinctly urban model"; for such, and for many who may have looked up to them, a cultural hierarchy existed: "At one end of the scale, the proud, self-reliant *masterovoi* [highly skilled workers]; at the other, the unskilled, 'unenlightened' masses, still attached to what were seen as peasant ways."[15] Such trends had not gone far enough, by 1917, to resolve the ambiguity and complexity. For Gliksman, the "permanent cadres" of industrial workers generated by developments between the 1860s and the revolution of 1917 "tended to form a separate social unit with the characteristics of a modern urban working class"—but they were, relatively, "extremely small" in number, and the urban labor force was of quite "dual character, half-peasant and half-proletarian."[16] In the last decade, younger historians have made much the same point: "The hereditary workers . . . of the 1880s . . . were not skilled craftsmen and should not be equated with the relatively privileged and better paid artisans of western Europe,"[17] writes one, while another, examining the sociopolitical geography of Moscow in 1905, observes: "If few workers were fully separated from the land, it is clear enough that a permanent working class existed. What is less clear, and indeed doubtful, is whether more than a small number of workers represented the ideal type of the modern proletarian; bereft of all economic resources but his own labor and dependent on a social network fully integrated into urban life."[18] History yields a picture that is constantly being refined. Some Russian workers of the early twentieth century were surely "proletarian" in a full enough sense to satisfy any Western Marxist of the time; these in their vast majority would have been hereditary in their links to city and factory. Others were at various middling points, and the most recent additions to factory labor, in the industrial upsurge of 1910–14, were necessarily drawn from, and remained close to, the countryside. Militants in the strikes and protests and the various organizations of the 1905–14 period came from diverse segments of the workers' world. If the most proletarian sectors contributed their share, the same must be said of young workers recently recruited from the villages, in the years immediately before the war.[19] Not only those from whom Marxism "expected" protest manifested it. The urban labor force was growing rapidly under economic and political pressures and undergoing rapid, sometimes contradictory, changes. That its essence is difficult to capture is, then, no surprise.

Here we can leave the prerevolutionary phase. War and the fall of the tsarist government, the collapse of the February–October 1917 provisional government to Lenin and the Bolsheviks, set Russia on a course of political, economic, and social change which would render some old ambiguities and complexities irrelevant, and create new ones in abundance.

Disruption and Rebuilding: Civil War and NEP

In essence, the major developments of the 1918–28 period can be summarized simply. The urban labor force and its proletarian element shrank rapidly in the stress and disorder of the revolution and the "War Communism" period that encompasses the civil war and struggles against foreign intervention. It bottomed out in the early 1920s and began to grow—though moderately—during the later years of the New Economic Policy (NEP): Lenin's 1921 compromise with the market and with an exhausted society in the pursuit of economic restoration and growth.

The strains of the civil war, the vicissitudes of the War Communism that abolished the market in favor of politicized rationing, saw the collapse of the linkage between hitherto goods-producing cities and the grain-producing countryside, the depopulation of large cities like Petrograd, and, with it, the near collapse of much of the industrial economy. (By 1929 the urban share of the population would be no higher than it had been in 1913.)[20] Urbanites left idle factories and headed for the countryside and farm connections in search of the wherewithal to live.

St. Petersburg/Petrograd, soon to be Leningrad—the tsarist capital, one of the industrial centers of the empire—provides an example of the process of working-class/industrial retrenchment and recovery in these years.[21] A population of 242,000 "registered workers" on January 1, 1914, had swollen under the drive of wartime industry by 58.5 percent, to 384,000 on January 1, 1917: about 15–17 percent of permanent, or well-established, workers had been drafted into the military since 1914, but 150,000 new hands had entered by 1917—some from the peasantry, some from proletarian city elements—to more than replace them.

The October Revolution took Russia out of the war, an act formalized in 1918 by the Brest-Litovsk Treaty. The year 1918 saw massive "de-manning" as Petrograd industry fell to disruption and the demand for war-related production ended. Amplified by the drafting of workers into the new Red Army and of other core proletarians into party and economic posts, this meant that by April 1, 1918, only 41.9 percent of the January 1, 1917, worker total were still working in industry. By October 1, this figure had fallen to 30.3 percent; most of this number, however, consisted of long-experienced workers.

Civil war intensified, and recruitment of workers into the army reduced the 120,000 people who had been in Petrograd in summer 1918 to a mere 50,000 by war's end. They formed the majority of a postwar total of 90,000, which thus included 40,000 recruited after the war into industry from urban strata socially foreign to the working class. The decline continued after the civil war; from the start of 1921 to the middle of 1922, workers in registered industry in Petrograd fell from about 95,000 to 66,700.

Disorder and industrial collapse were imminent when Lenin announced the NEP in 1921—the "strategic retreat" that would leave agriculture in the hands of the peasantry, and small industry and trade in private hands. The turnaround in factory employment would follow, but at first many "nonproletarians" entered the plants, to Lenin's chagrin. When Shliapnikov, head of the Workers' Opposition faction in the party, twitted Lenin at the Eleventh Party Congress (March 1922) with the words "let me congratulate you on being the vanguard of a non-existent class," he was making a political point—but it had a demographic rationale as well.[22] As a sympathetic observer of revolutionary Russia put it years later, by the time the civil war period gave way to the NEP, "the few million workers who had manned the barricades in 1917 had become dispersed and, as a coherent social force, had ceased to exist."[23]

The crawl upward was painful. Petrograd was the microcosm of a country that had claimed about 2.6 million workers in large-scale industry in 1917, and had only 1.1 million by 1922.[24]

As NEP began to take hold, the situation changed. From mid-1922 to mid-1923, the number of Petrograd workers rose by 33 percent.[25] By the beginning of 1925, the city had 122,000 workers, and this population grew by almost half again, for a total of 196,500 by the end of the year.[26] On whose account was the working class rebuilding itself? Were "real workers" returning, adding again to the "class," or were new recruits from the nonproletarian, "backward" countryside diluting it? Clearly, when the worker population was smallest, those who remained were generally of the core proletarian sort. In 1923 only 11.2 percent of the male workers had land holdings, and fewer than 7 percent helped in active farm operations.[27] Then, as numbers began to grow, two streams of workers flowed into Petrograd's, and the whole country's, urban economy. The first stream, the experienced and hereditary workers, demobilized from the Red Army or from jobs in the *apparat* of party and state, resumed factory work as the hyperactivity of the War Communism period gave way to the moderation of NEP. (As a 1929 study showed, those who began work in Leningrad's metal and textile industries in 1922–25 were, respectively, 55.1 and 64.5 percent of worker origin.[28] The national picture seems to have been similar.)[29]

The second stream, important if not dominant in 1922–25, increased later and consisted of the peasantry and other nonproletarian elements. By summer 1924, the return flow of "cadre workers" into Leningrad was largely exhausted,[30] and other elements began to gain weight as the worker population expanded. A 1929 study in Leningrad revealed figures for the inflow, by social origin, into the city's metal and textile industries from 1905 to 1928. In metal industry, fully 52 percent of workers who had begun to work before 1905 were of

peasant origin; in textiles, 52.7 percent. After 1905, persons of working-class origin predominated among those entering these areas; by
1928, only 33.1 percent of those entering the metal industry and 18.5
percent of those entering the textile industry were of peasant origin.[31]
Peasant inflow, then, was low in the late NEP years in comparison
with the "dilution" of prerevolutionary times.[32] Though important,
the peasant contribution was not massive—there was no swamping of
new, young workers of worker origin and of older returnees, many of
whom were proletarian in both origin and previous work experience.

In the second half of the NEP, the peasantry made its contribution
nationwide as well, but it did not yet lead to peasantization of that
quasi proletariat of 1917. The boundary condition was that all this
growth was relative: the number of workers in large-scale industry,
2.6 million nationwide in 1917 and down to 1.1 million in 1922,
reached the 2.5 million mark again only in 1928, and exceeded it marginally in 1929,[33] as the country stood poised on the edge of the first
Five Year Plan (FYP) and Stalin's social and economic revolution.

The new Soviet Russia thus ended the postrevolutionary decade
with a working class not much larger than under tsarism. In 1929 over
half the workers in large-scale industry were ones who began that
work before 1917. The working class of that year was, to a substantial
degree, the direct descendant of its 1917 predecessor.[34]

But, in another way, things had changed profoundly. The years
that separated the October Revolution from the first FYP witnessed not
only the restoration of the factory work force, but also saw the effective destruction of any independent political-economic role of conse-
quence for trade unions and the effective binding of the workers—the
class "for whom" the revolution was made—in subjection to the Soviet state. Some Bolsheviks, as well as Mensheviks and the representatives of other leftist/socialist parties, attempted to establish a place
for labor unions independent of the party and state, as a distinct arm
of proletarian power. They were ultimately defeated. The story of the
demise of the trade unions has been told in detail elsewhere.[35] A few
relevant points here will meet our needs.

First, Lenin and his followers were ambiguous with respect to the
"consciousness" that workers could develop on their own. This ambiguity was expressed in the notion of the ideologically correct vanguard party that is more conscious of the long-term "objective" and of
"historical" interests of the workers than they could be themselves.
As Trotsky put it in 1921, the party was "more important than some
formalistic principle of workers' democracy"—it knew the fundamental interests of the working class "even during . . . a temporary waver-
ing of its mood."[36]

Second, historical circumstances interacted with the Bolsheviks' Marxian perceptions of necessity and peril. Lenin recognized the backwardness of Russia and that it might be premature to seize power in a country that was overwhelmingly peasant, in the name of an ideology that saw a large working class as its necessary mass vehicle. Radical and risk taker that he was, he proceeded nonetheless with some confidence that the developed proletariat of Germany and other Western states would follow along the same revolutionary path soon. But as Moshe Lewin put it, "Bolshevik power . . . was about to find itself all alone, in an underdeveloped country, left with no resources but its own to count on—and these seemed far too meager for the task at hand."[37] That isolation—internationally, among industrial states whose proletarians stubbornly refused to launch successful revolutions, and internally, with a still-small working class, low in consciousness, poor, uneducated, in a peasant society—produced a crisis mentality Lenin was to moderate only somewhat during the NEP. (Though what Lenin might have done had his health lasted past 1922 is a matter of debate.)[38] Whatever the might-have-beens, Lenin in action gave short shrift to the representatives of direct "workers' control," or various currents of syndicalism, in the cadres who had made the revolution. Aleksandra Kollontai, marked among Bolsheviks for her social radicalism, asked whether communism was to be realized "through workers or over their heads, by the hands of Soviet officials,"[39] but such protest fell on deaf ears. Revolution, and then reconstruction, always beckoned as more important.

Third, Lenin—decisive in action—was also in a real sense a simplifier in his view of what "socialism," working-class "power," and other ostensible objects of the revolution meant. When were these to be deemed achieved, at least in essence? Lenin's answer was a political one, on the macro level: he believed "that the transition to socialism was guaranteed, ultimately, not by the self-activity of workers, but by the 'proletarian' character of the state power."[40] Thus the seizing of state power in 1917, and its retention through the civil war, was the central fact. Within its context his belief that a socialist economy "could be built only in the basis of large-scale industry as developed by capitalism, with its specific types of productivity and social organization of labor"[41] left no real room for either self-management at the workplace nor a free association of self-regulating workers' "communes." (Far from being a syndicalist, Lenin was, if anything, a Taylorist with respect to his admiration for the promise of tight organization and minute subdivision of tasks in the workplace.)[42]

A different matter, but not unrelated to the priority of concentrating political and economic power in a strong central state, is that Lenin's

designs had no place for trade union independence in the representation of workers' claims to state management, however their work
might be organized. In the months after the revolution, the Bolshevik
trade union activist Lozovskii raised the issue of how workers could
be represented *to* a "workers' state" when the state was also the *employer*, arguing that union independence "is dictated not only by general theoretical considerations, but also by considerations which are
highly practical. The worker masses may present unfulfilled demands
to the state and in this case the trade unions cannot come forward as
representatives of the workers because [unions fused with the state]
will be that 'employer' to whom the demands are presented."[43] To
which a stock answer was given by many Bolsheviks, the following
one being Zinoviev's:

> I ask . . . from what and from whom is it necessary to be independent?
> From your own government, from your workers' and peasants' govern-
> ment, from the Soviet of Workers' and Soldiers' Deputies? Let it be under-
> stood, we are also for the independence of the trade union movement, but
> from the bourgeoisie. We overthrew the power of the bourgeoisie and at
> the very moment when the working class together with the poor peasants
> has achieved power for the working class, when your union is part of that
> power, what kind of real significance has independence? It has real signifi-
> cance among representatives of the right wing; independence from the So-
> viets of Workers' and Peasants' Deputies . . . means independence in order
> to support those who fight against the workers' and peasants' government
> so that in the name of the sacred right to strike, and in the name of the
> freedom of coalition they may support those who strike against the work-
> ing class.[44]

Ideological debate—to some degree a cloak for a raw power struggle, to some degree real enough in these early years, when the shape
the regime would assume under Stalin was not foreseen—played a
role in setting the terms of the struggle. In 1918 Lozovskii raised the
point of whose *class* organizations state organs and unions were, contrasting the role of the People's Commissariat of Labor (Narkomtrud)
to that of the unions. The former, a state organ, seemed likely to him
to wind up dominating the unions. But the state, avowedly, represented not only the workers, but the much larger mass of peasants
("petty bourgeois" in their ownership of land) as well. Could unions,
representing the workers alone, the "leading class," the revolutionary
core, be subordinated, in a Marxist state, to such bodies? Lozovskii's
answer, formulated in terms that should have carried some persua-
sive power, was a clear no: "As organs of state worker-peasant repre-

senting the interests of two classes, the proletariat and petty bourgeoisie, the Commissariats of Labor cannot also become organs attached to the trade unions."[45] Politics resolved the question—against union independence. But the Leninists were not without an ideological formulation of their own. The key here was the relationship between the party as the conscious, vanguard organization of the workers and the more inclusive unions. The former included the more "conscious" workers, the latter, effectively, all whose position in relation to the means of production made them workers. Given Lenin's consistent emphasis on the politically preemptive role of the vanguard and his enduring distrust for the "spontaneity" (the opposite of "consciousness") that was bound to be widespread at this time in any mass organization like the trade unions, there could be no question as to which must lead:

> The place the trade unions occupy in the system of the dictatorship of the proletariat is, if we may so express it, between the Party and the state power. In the transition to socialism, the dictatorship of the proletariat is inevitable, but this dictatorship is not achieved by the organizations which embrace all the workers without exception. . . . What happens is that the Party, so to speak, absorbs into itself the vanguard of the proletariat, and this vanguard carries out the dictatorship of the proletariat.[46]

One might go on, but only with similar observations. Lenin's own totalitarian/centralist tendencies, the internal and external crises that seemed never ending, and his inability to conceive of the party in anything but the leading role, as other than indispensable ("If the trade unions . . . appoint . . . the managers of industry, what is the use of the Party?")[47] determined the subordination of the unions. Thus the only organs that could conceive of workers' interests that might need defense against a workers' government and its ruling party—and those in that party who thought they should have that defense—lost the battle. The ascent of Stalin to power in the late 1920s marked the subordination of all mechanisms of party and state, of all organizations, to total domination from the center. At the Eighth Trade Union Congress in December 1928,[48] the party-dominated Central Council would endorse the massive investment and gargantuan growth targets proposed for the first FYP. It effectively said farewell to any role, not only in management, but even in the defense of "narrow" economic/social interests of the workers. The carrying out of the plan would drive the living standards of those then within the working class well below the 1928 standard, but no union worthy of the name would remain to utter protest.

Stalin's Social Revolution

With Stalin's defeat of elements in the party who presented a challenge to his leadership and who advocated more moderate policies of balanced economic growth—an extension of the "restorative" NEP—the first FYP, with its hugely ambitious economic goals, came into effect. The hunger for industrial workers it created would have enormous effects: the smallish working class of the end of the NEP would give way to one swollen by newcomers from the rural-peasant base of traditional Russian life.

The massive peasantization of the work force is reflected in figures that outline, on the whole, the economic revolution that took place between 1928 and the onset of World War II. A 1933 report estimated that the number of "workers and (white-collar) employees" grew by 12.5 million during the first FYP, and that 8.5 million of these were ex-peasants.[49]

The first FYP, in demographic terms, amounted to a social explosion. Workers in industry, numbering 3.1 million in 1928, were 6 million by 1932; in transport, their numbers rose from 894,000 to 1.47 million. The massive commitment of resources in these years to the construction of new plants is expressed in an almost fourfold growth in the number of construction workers: from 630,000 in 1928 to 2.48 million in 1932 (though, given the nature of the work, many of these were seasonal workers).[50] Indeed, even figures such as these understate the paroxysm of growth in 1930–31, which accounted for most of these numbers. At a time when the countryside was in bloody turmoil, as the collectivization campaign worked its own revolutionary logic, these two years accounted for fully 82 percent of total first FYP growth in workers in large-scale industry, and 68 percent of the near-quadrupling in the numbers of construction workers.[51]

Such growth was impossible, of course, without a massive drawing on the labor resources of the countryside, one which dwarfed the share occupied by rural inflow in the years from the mid-1920s to the first FYP. The working class, which had restored for the most part its hereditary majority as it rebuilt itself through the 1920s to near its old, prerevolutionary size, was about to be swamped by new recruits from the villages. Several statistical sources indicate the approximate dimensions of the change during the first FYP. A 1931 four-site survey of metalworkers in four areas showed the rise of the peasant-origin and the decline of the hereditary-workers' share, as NEP gave way to the FYP. In Leningrad engineering plants in 1926–27, only 34 percent of the workers were of peasant origin; by 1930, their share had grown to

48.5 percent, while the hereditary-worker share had fallen in the same years from 55.6 to 38.8 percent. In metal plants in the later-developed Urals, what had already been a farm-origin majority of 54.2 percent in 1926–27 became an overwhelming 69.9 percent by 1930.[52]

Some of the more useful data reflecting these changes derive from several "censuses" of trade union members, conducted during and immediately after the first FYP. (These figures probably understate the ex-peasant share, since those from socially "alien" classes, especially ex-*kulaks* ["rich" peasants] were barred from union membership, and because union coverage of all workers and employees was at this time only at the 85 percent mark.) In the second half of 1931, the origins of new trade union members in the three sectors of the economy where most workers were to be found revealed peasant predominance: in industry (56.7 percent), in construction (77.4), and in transport (55.5), recruits from peasant origin outnumbered those from worker backgrounds (34.7, 18.4, and 32.6 percent, respectively).[53] A trade union census of 1932–33 offered more data on social origins of members, by the period of entry. In the more skill-demanding metallurgy area, worker-origin hires predominated (67.6 percent) among those who had started work before 1917, declining then over the years to 50.4 percent among those who began work in 1928–29. After that, peasant-origin recruits were the majority (62.1 percent of those who started working in 1932). In construction and in the cement and ceramic industries, the doors had always been open wider to would-be entrants from the villages: before 1917, peasants made up 55.6 of those starting work in construction, and 47.1 percent of those entering the cement industry; by 1931–32, they made up over three-quarters of new recruits in construction, and over two-thirds of the new entrants to the cement/ceramic industry.[54]

Déclassé elements of neither peasant nor worker origin had made their own contribution to the growing working class at the beginning of the FYP. Political pressures, the greater preference for workers in rationing, and reductions in the number of routine office and other nonmanual jobs all played a role in encouraging some to seek worker status. After 1930, however, this downward mobility as a source of recruitment ceased to play any significant role. In 1929 only one industrial worker in thirty was of white-collar origin.[55] Beyond this, craftsmen and artisans, formerly independently employed or working in small-scale private industry (NEP allowed them these options), were in large measure squeezed out of their old contexts during the period after 1928. Small-scale industry employed over four million workers in 1929; by 1935 the number was down to a little less than half a million. Soviet statistics show no large inflow from these groups to the working class, where, by virtue of their skills, they would have been valuable. They may have entered as "peasants" (since most were from rural areas); many may have been absorbed into the work force of the collective farms; some continued in the producers' cooperatives the state allowed well into the FYP era.[56]

Reciting such dry figures can divert attention from the human drama of the years 1929–31—the sheer disorder, the convulsive character of the transformation in which millions found themselves engulfed. For a regime that would, ultimately, bureaucratize and control a great deal, Stalin's did—or could do—little to make the inflow into industry and the cities smooth or orderly.

The late NEP economy[57] experienced both a shortage of skilled labor and unemployment among those with fewer skills to offer employers. But the sheer demand generated by the FYP rapidly transformed the situation—planners had assumed labor surplus for the first FYP, but by October 1930, with 300,000 still registered as unemployed, Narkomtrud ended unemployment benefits. The "reserve" was quickly exhausted. Narkomtrud lacked any effective mechanism for planning hirings and the allocation of labor, and ministries and their subordinate plants thus were forced into an anarchic, competitive situation in the quest for workers.

Some examples of plant expansion beggar description. The Nevskii engineering works expanded its work force by 82.7 percent in 1930; employment on the construction site of the Kuznetsk iron and steel plant grew from 4,100 in September 1929 to 14,925 a year later. A Moscow auto factory with 3,500 workers in 1929 had 12,000 in 1931 and 14,000 by 1932.[58]

Turnover in jobs reached immense proportions. Even during the NEP, it had averaged 100 percent per year in the major industries, but this cloaked large differences among them and between more footloose younger, less-skilled workers and the older, more stable types. In coal mining, where turnover had already been a very high 192 percent in 1929, it reached an incredible 295.2 percent in 1930.[59] More and more plants and construction sites competed for scarce skilled labor, and failing to find it, substituted the quantity of new, unskilled labor for quality. The percentage of skilled workers among the employed dropped rapidly.

The economic forces propelling the disorder, and underlying the voracious hunger for labor that resulted, were too powerful to control. While the Supreme Council for the National Economy (VSNKh) might complain of the lack of planned allocation, Narkomtrud, despite periodic purges of its staff, lacked the teeth to affect the situation. Things remained this way until 1933, when Narkomtrud was abolished. No nationwide labor-allocation organ was established to replace it. Until

Khrushchev's time, ministries and large plants would confront the worker directly, doing the hiring and firing and backed in their exercise of power by various state measures to cut back turnover and otherwise, in a gradually stabilized situation, to facilitate the "extraction and exploitation of labor power."[60]

By the end of the first FYP, ex-peasants formed a majority in many branches of industry. The summary statistic of what percentage (of all workers? industrial workers?) was hereditary and what was of peasant origin is not one the Soviet data provide, nor one readily calculable. It is quite possible that, in large-scale industry, a peasant-origin majority existed by 1933.[61] If it did not, the second FYP (1933–37) surely produced this result. Data, unfortunately, are much poorer than for the previous period: a broad clampdown on social sciences, on empirical study, and even on statistical recording ended the activities that might have yielded broad data on social origins of new workers after the early 1930s.

What we do know indicates that the relative intake of peasant-origin recruits had to remain large. In the first FYP, the number of industrial workers almost doubled; in the second, it increased by less than a third,[62] but from the larger base of 1932, this still meant large absolute numbers. Still, the diminished total inflow could draw on elements of the urban population (especially women until now outside the regular labor force), and it is possible that the "push" factors of disorder, abysmally bad living conditions, and other forces accompanying collectivization had abated enough to increase the number of peasants willing to remain in the countryside. Against these must be balanced the fact that urban labor reserves as of the beginning of 1933 cannot have been abundant, so that any notion that the working class could have become largely self-reproducing in the second FYP is farfetched.[63] One Soviet historian, writing at the end of the 1950s, estimated that 54 percent of the additional workers entering during 1933–37 were of peasant origin, as were 40 percent of those coming to work during the third FYP, interrupted by the war.[64] In line with this, a Gosplan report of 1940 listed the sources of new workers, 1933–37, as follows: 1.4 million from factory schools; 1 million housewives, other urban reserves; "about" 2.5 million from the countryside.[65] "Factory schools" are not a social origin, and the rough and ready institutions included under this rubric trained many rural/peasant youth. To the estimated 2.5 million, some portion of the 1.4 million could thus be added, increasing the likelihood of a peasant majority among new entrants to the working class in 1933–37.

Whatever the details, the "demographically necessary" result surely obtained by the beginning of the war. The enormous expansion from 1929 to 1932, the more moderate but still large (more than 30 percent in five years) growth of the second FYP, and the shortened third FYP had created a working class—better, *mass*—wherein hereditary workers were a minority, and (given the size of other feeder groups) those of peasant origin, a majority. The first indirect snapshot Western observers acquired of this period came with the postwar refugee interviews of the Harvard Project on the Soviet Social System, which collected biographical and attitudinal data from over two thousand emigrés who remained in the West after World War II. Harvard Project data allow an estimate that only 46.1 percent of those men aged 21–40 who were workers in 1940, immediately before the war, were hereditary workers[66]—probably not too much off the mark from a national statistic we shall probably never know.

Numbers, however, do not account for everything that should be said about this period. In social, psychological, and organizational terms, the confrontation of a recently recruited peasant mass with modern machinery and tasks was dramatic. Some peasant entrants to the industrial labor force during the later years of the NEP tended to have skills relevant to the urban economy, acquired by way of seasonal or part-time work outside agriculture. But in the massive peasant inflow of the first FYP, most new arrivals had nothing but the experience and rhythms of agricultural work to bring to new jobs;[67] educational levels ranged between minimal schooling and illiteracy; machines were alien. The confrontation was, on the one hand, wasteful, and on the other, the beginning of a process of assimilating tens of millions to urban-industrial life, albeit under the special conditions of the Stalin era. Two Soviet authors express, in terse language, the first aspect: "At the beginning of industrialization rapid quantitative growth of the ranks of the working class ran ahead (and furthermore could not but run ahead) of the development of its skills, education, and work habits."[68] More lyrical and lengthy is this Soviet treatment of another aspect of the process, the psychological urbanization and political consciousness-raising of yesterday's peasants:

> The intensification of the flow of the rural population into industry had great significance also in that to an immense degree it promoted a rise in the consciousness, literacy, and cultural level, and a broadening of the outlook of the peasantry. Coming into permanent and temporary work in state enterprises from the distant corners, from isolated settlements and villages, collective farmers and individual peasants immediately came into the atmosphere of struggle and tireless labor of production.
>
> Thus, socialist industrialization . . . made possible the socialization of the toilers in the spirit of socialism, the development of new forms of life and culture, the intensification of the influence of industrial centers on the village, the strengthening of the union of working class and peasantry.[69]

John Scott, a young American who went to work in the 1930s in the construction project that produced the "steel city" of Magnitogorsk, strikes another note as he quotes the words of a new peasant recruit, whose concerns and reactions cannot have been atypical: "It took us two weeks to get here . . . walking over the steppe with our bags on back and driving that goddam cow—and now she's not giving any milk. . . . Here we came all the way to Magnitogorsk because there was bread and work on the new construction, and we find we can't even feed the cow, let alone ourselves."[70] Scott's observations on the generally rough-and-ready resolution of man versus machine issues in the first FYP are also illuminating: "Semi-trained workers were unable to operate the complicated machines which had been erected. Equipment was ruined, men were crushed, gassed, and poisoned, money was spent in astronomical quantities. The men were replaced by new ones from the villages, the money was made good by the State in government subsidies, and the materials and supplies were found somehow."[71]

Growth was financed by stringency and reflected in a massive fall in average living standards. The diversion of vast resources into investment cut current consumption drastically. The extraction of a "surplus" from agriculture via the imposed organizational apparatus of the collective farm became in fact (in the judgment of many economists) the extraction of essentials from a rural economy which produced less under collectivization than before. The massive flow of new hands into the cities for growing industry found no commensurate housing construction. The horrendous overcrowding of Soviet urban life, the "communal apartment" born of the continued subdivision of existing housing stock, was the result.[72] Economic pressures and privations at the grass-roots level were great, but Stalin was determined on "staying the course." A distinguished economist's words give a good précis of the times, and a crisp judgment on how Stalin dealt with the costs his program imposed:

Rationing of essential foodstuffs was introduced for urban consumers by the end of 1929, and life became exceedingly difficult. The great investment drive led to inflation. Goods, at fixed prices, disappeared. There developed a variety of "closed shops," available only to employees of priority sectors, or to those with rank and influence. "Commercial" stores were opened, to sell rationed goods at very high prices. Others sold scarce goods only for foreign currency or gold. A market for peasant surplus was tolerated, but in near-famine conditions of 1932–1933 prices were sky-high. Quality declined. Service worsened. "Take what you're given, don't argue and don't hold up the queue"; that is how a Soviet writer described the situation of the customer. Consumer goods production suffered from shortages of materials, which were diverted to priority industries, and also from the elimination of small private businesses and most craftsmen. Food supplies were adversely affected by the consequences of collectivization. Everything was affected by transport bottlenecks, which led to the railways being put virtually under martial law. . . .

Typical of Stalin was a speech he made when conditions of life had reached a very low point: "It is clear," he said, "that the workers' living standards are rising all the time. Anyone who denies this is an enemy of Soviet power." An excellent example, too, of how to stop empirical social research: who would dare inquire into cost-of-living indices and real wages? No wonder it was thought politic to stop publishing such statistics. Of course it is true that statesmen do not always speak the truth, but most others, Lenin included, would have talked about the necessity of sacrifices, rather than blandly denying that any sacrifices existed.[73]

The numbers indicate something of the pressures on a rapidly growing urban labor force. Official data, unlikely to be totally fanciful, indicate that during NEP real wages of industrial workers had been on the rise; by mid-1927, they were 11 percent over the 1913 level, while the length of the workday decreased from 10 to 7.5 hours. The share of a working-class family's wages going to food declined from 57 percent in 1913 to 42–46 percent by 1923–27. [74]

Pressures on living standards increased as grain-procurement became problematic from late 1927 on, and though Stalin and other leaders painted a rosy picture, the logic of the FYP drove the standards lower still. Nominal wages rose 126 percent for workers and white-collar employees over 1928–32, but prices in state and cooperative trade rose 155 percent, deflating real 1932 wages to 88.6 percent of what they had been in 1928; in Moscow, they fell to 53 percent of the 1928 level.[75] Prices rose precipitously in the free and black markets, while the variety and quality of services declined rapidly. A society on the move was confronting an economy of shortage.

Workers on the whole did not do as badly as they might have. Labor hunger meant that more members of worker households found employment, adding to the family budget even as real wages dropped. Workers were favored in the rationing process over other groups, and consumed more than their share of foodstuffs.[76] Still, there was much to complain about, especially among the skilled workers whose experience went back to the NEP period or beyond, and who thus had a context in which to place the deterioration of living standards.

Privations of this sort grew. At the same time, the period from the late NEP into the first FYP saw major shifts in wage policy, which cut in a number of directions. Tensions between socialist egalitarianism and the need to promote production by paying a premium to those with scarce skills had never really been resolved. Political fears of a dilution of the core working class by nonproletarian elements, peasant and other (who, as we have seen, joined throughout the NEP), and of workers' presumed support for the regime may have been a major factor in the policies that moderated wage differentiation between 1927 and 1930, making for more equality than in the earlier NEP.[77] To the fervent revolutionaries, egalitarianism made sense, unlike the market differentiation of the NEP. Whether it also made sense to the highly skilled workers—presumably seasoned proletarians supportive of the regime—was another question.

Beyond policy, other trends favored an egalitarian pattern. The rapid inflow of 1929–30 was mainly made up of new, unskilled workers; their numbers alone led to a leveling of average wages, pegged to skill levels (or the lack of skills, in this case). Within the working class, rationing was conducive to greater real egalitarianism. Even though wages depended on skill levels, "excess wages" of the best-paid workers did not go far in the purchase of nonrationed goods and foodstuffs. Although the lowest-paid workers might not have been able to afford everything that their ration status allowed them to purchase, the endemic shortages took away a good deal of the ruble's purchasing power in any case. Result: less differentiation.[78]

In the 1929–30 turmoil, many skilled workers, whose scarcity would have dictated more elevated rewards, moved frequently in search of a better deal. They resisted semispontaneous tendencies toward an equal sharing of "communal" wages in production brigades that combined the skilled and unskilled, though some saw this as the essence of socialism.[79] All in all, the costs of wage egalitarianism became more and more evident to Stalin and the leadership. The old workers' not totally unsuccessful defense of their interests, and the new workers' low levels of skill, commitment, and consciousness needed to be dealt with, however, before a shift to a new policy could be imposed. What was required was a greater breakthrough on the factory floor in the direction of maximizing production.

This was accomplished via the unleashing of a social and generational force that combined sincere revolutionary enthusiasm with a certain viciousness, as well as a hankering after the militancy of the War Communism period, which found little satisfaction under the NEP. The regime deployed its own rate busters. As Kuromiya describes them,

> They were mainly young urban males who had experienced the revolution and the civil war in their teens or younger, first entered industrial work shortly after the revolution, and therefore had had several years of work experience and some skills by the late 1920s. Predominantly party and

Komsomol members, they were thus in a position to be critical of both the work culture of older workers and the peasant culture of new arrivals from the countryside. They were new forces in the factories who, impatient with the given rate of industrialization, pressed for even higher tempos; who, free of the old "work culture," promoted industrial modernization; who, intolerant of managerial bureaucratism, pressed for one-man management; who, eager to find "class aliens" in the apparatus, actively sought to be promoted into positions of responsibility; and who, hopeful of tomorrow's gratification, endured today's difficulties.[80]

Ideological kin to the tough young urbanites who pushed collectivization in the countryside, they met resistance, sabotage, and other obstacles, but with the state behind them, the breakthrough was accomplished. While much of the struggle took place during a period of relatively egalitarian wage patterns, its success deprived both old and new workers of the capacity to resist. They fought, but then many joined.[81] By 1931 factory-floor resistance was effectively crushed, and Stalin turned toward the policy of skill- and branch-based differentiation ("we cannot tolerate [that] a rolling mill worker earns no more than a sweeper . . . a locomotive driver . . . as much as a copying clerk")[82] that was to be the hallmark of the Soviet economy for decades to come. The skilled workers who had resisted egalitarianism now found an opportunity to cash in their skills for higher wages. The rate-busting "shock workers" were in many cases slated for promotion into state and party *apparats* for other tasks. Stalin had thus given the green light to a degree of wage/salary differentiation that would ultimately reproduce, if not exceed, that of contemporary capitalism, and this in a much poorer country. Partially, the inequality was justified as a spur to the acquisition of education and skill by new workers, an incentive to "rise higher." As Scott put it, the "population, and particularly the peasants, had to be made to want to study. . . . If pay were the same for shepherd boy and engineer, most peasants would graze their flocks and never trouble Newton and Descartes."[83]

But the dynamics of inequality in this period must be understood from another angle as well. A massive reshaping of the population's occupational structure was under way. The ranks of workers grew, mainly from the addition of peasant-origin recruits. Driven by an expansion of the need for professional and bureaucratic manpower and by the development of a system of mass education (at the elementary level, at least), ex-workers, their children, and some peasants crossed the line into white-collar work in large numbers, and soon came to predominate in those ranks over hereditary nonmanuals. The social historian Moshe Lewin notes this fact, and poses the consequent problems of interpretation:

For millions there was upward mobility and social promotion in the midst of the whole upheaval. This statement needs to be qualified. Peasants going to factories could not see it then as promotion—for many, the factories meant a drop in their standard of living and self-respect. But it may have been different for the great number who became officials, however low the rank and however bad the pay. For those who went to universities and to responsible jobs, or acquired new skill, the social advance was undeniable, and the new possibilities were seized on eagerly.[84]

Lewin is clearly right about those who became officials, and about those who received educations. They had a stake in the system—at least to the degree (a very considerable one) that they felt such upward mobility would have been impossible for them under the ancien régime. This process of promotion, which sometimes led directly from the shop floor to an administrative-managerial job for proletarians (with the appropriate "styles" many newly recruited peasants probably sought to acquire), contributed to building regime support.

Certainly, the opinion that it was better to be a worker than a collectivized peasant came to be generally shared, even if at first, as Lewin observes, many saw it differently. Soviet emigrés in the Harvard Project study, when asked to assign rankings (converted into a 1–100 scale) to various occupations, rated collective farmer at the bottom (18 points), and a rank-and-file worker much higher (48 points).[85]

Thus, along with privation, there was social mobility on an unprecedented scale. If the worker's life seemed to many ex-peasants less affluent than the one prosperous peasants had enjoyed, the fact was that prosperous peasants no longer existed. And, as we have seen, the social drama of the first FYP was, for some, a "time for heroes"— the first such time since War Communism. Billed as a massive assault on nationwide backwardness and ignorance, in a Russia surrounded by a hostile capitalist world,[86] the FYP generated positive support. Coercion and violence dealt with the villains in the drama; these methods found some support as well. In the Soviet collective memory, this brutal transformation, and even the period of Stalin's great purges that followed strike a note of ambiguity, as strongly expressed in a controversial interview conducted by George Urban with the exiled Soviet dissident author Alexander Zinoviev in *Encounter* in 1984. Zinoviev looks at the fate of his peasant family from two angles—reaching the city and rising in the social structure:

Life in the big cities, however, offered irresistible temptations. Country life was primitive and boring. My family lived on the land. We had a large and comfortable house. In Moscow the ten of us had to make do with a single room of ten square metres—one square metre per head. Can you imagine?!

Yet, we *preferred* life in Moscow.[87] . . . [M]y own family . . . were peasants. As a result of the collectivization of agriculture my parents lost everything they had. But my elder brother eventually rose to be a factory manager; the next one to him in age made it to the rank of colonel; three of my
older brothers qualified as engineers; and I became a professor at Moscow
University. At the same time millions of Russian peasants were given a
formal education and some became professional men and women.[88]

"Stalin's was a time," Zinoviev said, "of idealism, dedication, and
even heroism."[89] This reflects, one presumes, the experience of many
at the time—and surely, many were dedicated workers in the building
of a new social order, one in which they believed. But a more summary judgment comes in Zinoviev's response to Urban's question
about the "tortured and dying, the hangings and shootings"[90] under
Lenin and Stalin.

> The things you describe were tragic but not criminal. The Revolution
> brought education, health, upward social mobility, and a new beginning.
> We have discussed all this before. Some people perished; others made
> good. If you made a count of the number of people for whom the Revolu-
> tion meant a great new opportunity and those for whom it involved a trag-
> edy, you'd be surprised to find by what a colossal margin the beneficiaries
> of the Revolution exceeded those who lost out by it.[91]

What is involved here seems to be a separation of *social* and *political*
spheres of judgment.[92] "Dynamism," the progress toward an urban-
industrial society, is seen as the main achievement, while "body
count" is seen as deplorable but not vitiating the accomplishments.
Some key to understanding such a perspective may lie in realizing
that the political expectations of Soviet people of the time were not,
and could not be, "Western." The tsarist heritage was not that of a
"civil society," the ancién regime had, in the mass, subjects, not citizens. If the direction of change had been toward weakening of the
state's grip on society, it had not gone far by 1914. The NEP had
yielded economic autonomy to many, but little political voice. Society
was weak, and mute. Nor did the humbly born experience the violence and terror of the Stalin years in the same manner as the bigger
fish. Ten million peasants died during collectivization, but many who
survived were able to come to the cities and become workers. The
Great Purge of the late 1930s[93] took people of all social classes but
overselected better-educated urbanites with responsible jobs and
higher status. In a sense, it is probable that many workers and peasants—first-generation literates, readers of the tendentious accounts of
perfidy, treason, and "wrecking" among their superiors that came to
dominate the Soviet press—believed in the guilt of the accused, expe-

rienced some rough satisfaction in seeing yesterday's bosses laid low, and, in any case, felt the force of Stalin's secret police much less directly than the better-placed. Some confirmation of this attitude comes from the responses of emigrés in the Harvard survey who, asked to name elements of the system that "must go" under any post-Soviet regime, spontaneously nominated "terror and injustice" in the following proportions: intelligentsia, 67 percent; white-collar employees, 52 percent; skilled workers, 33 percent; ordinary workers, 26 percent; and collective farmers, 27 percent.[94] Those who were workers and peasants in the purge period were much less likely, then, even among this predominantly anti-Soviet group, to specify political repression as a major point demanding redress than were white-collar people.

In raw numbers and in their percentage of the population, workers had, by the late 1930s, increased massively, in a Soviet Union far different than that of 1927–28. Stalin's "second revolution" had altered the economy and social structure, forging a degree of dominance of state over society, a simultaneous mobilization and containment of social forces, that neither tsarism nor the 1917–28 USSR had achieved. For our purposes here, we must distinguish between what "the workers" now were and what they had once been.

Workers: From Class to Mass

So far we have used the term "class" rather loosely. Now, without seeking a conceptual specificity beyond the reasonable, we must ask if workers actually constituted a class, and when.

Certainly, in the period up to 1914, the picture is mixed. Rapidly growing as a social category, industrial workers, as long as they were heavily of the first generation out of the village and retained their many links to it, would not automatically take on class characteristics as they grew in numbers. But as the evidence also indicates, a growing number were second- or third-generation workers and urbanites, some of whom had cut their ties to the village while others retained some. At least some of the social characteristics of a class were developing in Russia's industrial cities, which could form a base for *identity* and *opposition*.

But the tsarist state was neither politically nor conceptually (the "estate" system) comfortable with the notion of class. Becoming a class is a tall order if class is to be seen as a collectivity with a certain ability to regulate its membership; to generate a solid sense of shared identity among those members (and, perhaps, against other classes) on the basis of similar background, work situation, and relationship to authority; to influence its members' behavior, and to exercise a certain amount of clout in various ways, organized and unorganized, against other classes and/or the state. So is the attainment of all four of Mann's characteristics. Under tsarism, while many social characteristics of a proletariat were developing, the political system, until its fall, blocked many of the political manifestations. It did not block them all—strikes did occur, and workers' movements, including those of the socialist parties, developed—but in a context far from the "civil society" in which a workers' movement could lay a claim to legitimacy.

If we may call the proletarian-urbanite core of 1914 a nascent class, then—under the Soviet state, 1918–28—that core was first dispersed in the civil war/War Communism period, and then partially reconstituted during the NEP that followed. It shared factory space with new peasant recruits and with people from other social strata, but was not yet numerically overrun by them. With Stalin's industrial revolution and the FYP it *was* overrun. Many core workers were promoted upward,[95] and those who remained were numerically overwhelmed by a peasant draft. Identity, already weakened when it had existed, was dissolved.

These were not the appropriate conditions for class formation from a social standpoint. And, from a political standpoint, one can argue that the Stalinist system made the formation of any class impossible.[96] Such pervasive totalitarian rule was a maximal denial of society's autonomy from the state, and an unprecedented exaltation of state over society. It left no space for the formation or survival of classes, and, even less, organized representation of class interests: it was starkly "uncivil."

Despite the rhetoric that tied the regime to the making of a working class as a major political and economic objective, it is unlikely, to say the least, that Stalin—and probably Lenin—had any such objective in mind, when one considers what their political priorities were and what "class" means. Elements of internal cohesion, shared perspectives, the autonomy to organize, to pursue goals *collectively* might counterpose workers to a regime that ruled in their name, as the trade union controversies of the 1920s showed. This was not likely to be countenanced by a regime that sought to liberate itself from the restrictions of any class base so it could rule and transform society. Donald Filtzer, an analyst who has worked in the Marxist tradition, puts it this way:

No amount of theorizing within the Bolshevik Party about the party being the "representative" of the working class or the defender of its "interests" could alter the fact that the party, at least partially by force of necessity, had substituted itself for the proletariat which had made the original revolution. This relationship contained within it an incipient conflict between a nascent bureaucracy which now controlled the apparatus and the workers who were expected to produce the surplus product which this bureaucracy would control.[97]

Whether the proletariat "made" the revolution or not, there certainly was substitution and an ambiguity toward what regime leaders called the working class. Stalinists could comfortably counterpose the vanguard to "predominant moods among the workers," and assign the former the task of guarding the "general interests of the entire proletariat" against the "particularist, cliquish" interests that sometimes prevailed in those "moods."[98] This was, obviously, an elastic formula. Raw peasant recruits lacked the political consciousness to distinguish between old capitalist bosses and the new directors of socialist industry; this was to be expected. But old skilled workers, who were political supporters of the revolution but unconvinced that they had no need of trade unions, or resisted on the shop floor the invasion of shock workers and stimulators of socialist competition, could find themselves labeled "elements alien to the working class."[99] Any peasant who resisted collectivization could be labeled a *kulak*, even if not rich; any resisting worker became an "alien element."

If some Bolsheviks saw the development of a large working class as the guarantee of the regime's prospective stability, then others, more powerful, did not—or, confronted by evidence of worker spontaneity, changed their minds. What Stalin wanted was industrial workers, in the millions, to man a planned, state-dominated economy. The smallish proletariat of 1921 had elements of a class: a hereditary core, with a set of distinct traditions, a certain political tempering from tsarist times, revolution, and civil war. It had supported the infant regime through the years of NEP, though it was, increasingly, deprived of the ability to exercise any collective power.[100] Stalin could dispense with such support.

With the first FYP Stalin's commitment to totalization of power over a society he had set on the path of convulsive change signaled the impossibility of tolerating any class independence. In the words of Filtzer, the regime "had to defeat the working class, all the while hiding its attack behind the rhetoric of building socialism."[101] Stalin wanted more workers, but no working *class*.

Whether, and how long, the workers constituted even a remote potential threat to the Soviet regime, something that "had to" be defeated, remains a question. More certain is the fact that the regime did "win"—that, in Filtzer's words, "the old working class was ultimately eliminated and the new workforce that took its place encountered political, working, and living conditions that made it virtually impossible for it to reconstitute itself as a militant class able collectively to define, and fight for, its own radical needs."[102] Stalin's victory was accomplished through a variety of means. Coercion and repression in society as a whole were critical; workers felt them, as did others. The emasculation of trade unions helped set the stage for the economic policies of massive reinvestment, and eliminated the possibility of organized protest against declining living standards. The breakthrough on the factory floor, added to the economic pressures of survival, focused workers' attention on individual rather than collective concerns. Patterns of evasion would develop, but collective confrontation was ruled out.

These were purposeful outcomes. More automatic were the consequences of the massive inflow of peasants, "having no traditions of industrial life and therefore of industrial militancy and collective action,"[103] and lacking in skills and education. What there was of an old "class" was dissolved and submerged in this new mass of rural origin. Important as well was the co-optation of many workers into the new elite and bureaucracy. This was driven by the need of the regime for vastly expanded administrative manpower and supported by individual motivations ranging from greed, ambition, and survival to revolutionary impulses to play a role in "socialist construction," however heartless the process. The new political elite would appear, and be, proletarian in background. Russia's rulers would speak in the accents of workers, affect the tieless peasant shirt under the suit jacket, project the image of sons of the proletariat. But they would not be the agents of any working class.

In essence, Stalin finally resolved the dilemma Lenin and Trotsky found themselves facing in 1920–21, when, as one commentator put it, "the principal task of the dictatorship of the proletariat became, paradoxically, the creation of a proletariat *in the place and in the proportion* needed by the state, imbued with attitudes *favourable to the maximization of productivity and free from autonomous defensive organizations* that might have frustrated these goals" (emphasis added).[104] Lenin confronted the task, partially. The compromise that NEP represented with economic realities saw a tightening of political control over the small working class, a generally effective emasculation of the trade union organization that might have become its autonomous defensive organization. But in place and proportion, and in attitudes, much of that class was not what was required.

Workers might politically support the revolution; few, one may presume, looked back to tsarism with fond memories. But a sense of class *identity* and *opposition*, built up over the years of experience in the factories and to some degree sharpened by Bolshevik and Menshevik propagandizing, operated to impart a sense of worker interests as a critical agenda item: interests that should be served by the policies of the new state, interests whose violation was possible by "red directors" as well as capitalist bosses.

If a feeling of class totality has rarely been reached anywhere, Soviet Russia in the 1920s was not an exception. Not that the compensations, the distractions of nonwork life, and consumption in what were straitened times could have been great. The stubborn spontaneity of workers who were mainly interested in getting more pay for their work, as much from the socialist as from the tsarist state, suggests that many workers did, in a general way, define themselves critically as workers and subsumed their whole relationship with political authority in this fashion. But in times of revolutionary rhetoric, in the wake of a recent revolution with proletarian iconography, totality in the sense of active opposition to the "workers'" state, spurred by a consciousness of an alternative society, could hardly emerge. The partial alternatives articulated by some political figures (and, we may assume, by some more sophisticated workers) involved syndicalism versus managerialism, the independent versus the "transmission-belt" union, all within a broad acceptance of post-October socialism.

If NEP, under Lenin and later, saw an effective blocking of most of the political effects of class, it left class identity, and some potential for opposition, in place. Stalin's self-set task, one in which he engaged the energies of many radicals who hankered back to War Communism and despised NEP compromise, was to break through those as well. The massive peasant draft into industry assured at least that the identity of new workers would be fluid, ambiguous, confused—anything but a *class* identity. The final smashing of trade unionism, the increasingly terroristic police control, the realm of material necessity imposed by the strictures of the plan, all reduced to the zero point any possibility of class opposition by those who had been part of the old class. Material divisions within the workers' world and the promotion of so many of worker stock to administrative and political roles eroded any possibility that blue-collar solidarity could develop, that workers could have reached a feeling of class totality, even under a freer political system than that which came into being. The vast masses of marginally literate, parochial Russia, the peasants-become-workers among them, were finally subjected to a mass campaign for literacy and basic education, which fed them a political and economic line designed to eliminate any concept of an alternative society, and awareness of any but the most tendentious details of the world outside.

Stalin's success drew on the sheer scale of the transformation he sought to bring off and on the totalitarian power he brought to the task. One may still debate the nature of totalitarian power, the short-falls even of the USSR under Stalin from the model of totalitarianism, but as a matter of degree, Stalin's system sufficed. Its success was manifest in the result: "For the first time in history, . . . an industrial workforce made to the specification of the masters of the state ma-chine. It was a workforce that owed its existence, its expectations, its knowledge of the world, indeed its literacy, to that same state that controlled all its avenues of movement, promotion, or even physical survival."[105] "Nowhere," then, in the world of the 1930s was there, outside the USSR, "such a large industrial workforce so devoid of the characteristics that, according to Marx, defined the proletariat."[106]

How did the new workers adjust to factory and urban life? If tsarist authoritarian politics considered the workers a problem, an alien if necessary presence in the cities (like other authoritarian polities emerging from an overwhelmingly agrarian base), Stalinist totalitari-anism welcomed them and happily counted their growing numbers as a mark of its success. But this tells us little about the texture of every-day life, about the personal histories of urbanization, of becoming a "worker"—the record is clearer on the state acting upon the workers than on their own processes of acculturation. Full answers will have to await a richer and fuller social historiography. What we can probably say fairly confidently is that the 1930s mass movement to the city and the factory was felt to be permanent by its participants in a way that it had not been under tsarism. If the pull of cash wages and the push of rural poverty drove the process in 1880–1914, there was for many the possibility of return to the village, recurrently or permanently. But an exit from the village after 1929 was an exit from a countryside in turmoil, from a life no longer familiar; there was no going back. Hard work, terrible crowding—for families as well as the workers them-selves—may have been difficult to bear, but the lack of any alternative put a premium on a readiness to adjust to the new circumstances, to make the best of being the urban worker one had become so swiftly. However overblown, the official rhetoric gave the new worker an honored place as one of the millions building socialism as part of the working "class," something tsarism had neither the ideology nor the grammar to offer. To the degree that one took the welcome at face value, achieved literacy, or upgraded job skills, one might increase personal or familial benefits. Such accommodation worked—for the regime, for the worker. It carried, as yet, no danger of a developing *class* consciousness.

In 1937 the third FYP was launched, only to be interrupted by war. The USSR would survive it at great cost and emerge as a society with a large industrial sector but still predominantly peasant in makeup. Transitions less violent by far, but extending from Stalin's twilight into the Khrushchev and Brezhnev periods, would again change the characteristics of the growing mass of workers. Over the Khrushchev and earlier Brezhnev years, a proletariat did develop. This was not a class in the full sense, but certainly a proletariat of other than the type intended, with attitudes hardly favorable to maximizing productivity and one not bereft of autonomous defenses. The unanticipated consequences of development began to produce not the intended proletariat, but an "accidental" proletariat.

2

A New Working Class?
Hereditization and Education under
Khrushchev and Brezhnev

> Our working class today is two-thirds of the
> country's population. It is tens of millions of
> educated, technically literate, politically ma-
> ture people.
>   (*L. I. Brezhnev, 1977*)

FORTY-NINE YEARS separate Brezhnev's confident words from the
concerned ones of Manuilskii that introduced the previous chapter.
The first twenty-five were years of social revolution and war, massive
transformation, and massive destruction. The remaining twenty-four
were marked by more gradual, yet inexorable, social and demographic processes that were once again to change the society, both
exhausted and mobilized, that emerged from World War II.

War and Aftermath

The toll of the war was great. Physical destruction of the plants in
which ex-peasants were becoming workers, the deaths of millions—
hereditary workers, ex-peasants who had made the agricultural-
industrial transition during the first and second Five Year Plans (FYPS),
rural youth dead in uniform who would have become workers had it
not been for the war—all left their mark.

In some areas, the draw-down of experienced workers for military
service was necessarily immense. Though the experience of block-
aded Leningrad must be counted as extraordinary, one source reports
that, as of spring 1942, only 5.6 percent of prewar workers remained
in the ranks at the Kirov works—the industrial heart of the city.[1] In
this as in other plants, similarly affected, women workers drawn from
the local urban environment must have taken up a good deal of the
slack, but ex-peasants from a still-large labor pool supplied large numbers of new hands during the war.[2]

With war's end, a new phase began in reconstruction and in re-stocking the depleted ranks of workers. The village continued to provide the major additions to the cities' blue-collar work force. As one scholar put it, "The principal sources of recruitment into the working class during the first postwar years were men demobilized from the armed forces and people moving from the country to the city, plus youth graduated from the Labor Reserves Schools."[3] Large numbers of ex-peasant youth were, of course, to be counted among those demobilized soldiers and among the graduates of the Labor Reserve system. The pull of the city and the push of conditions in the countryside worked as they had earlier on. The same author notes that it was not only the needs of industry and the effects of agricultural mechanization (modest, one must think) but also errors in agriculture that drove the rural exodus of these years; the provision of "little personal material incentive" meant, essentially, the reimposition of the harsh, extractive regime in the collective farms, one that had been relaxed, to some degree, in the war.[4] Until "well after" the war, the peasantry remained a large source of working-class recruitment.[5] Studies on regions as diverse as the Lithuanian republic[6] and the Mari ASSR[7] cite the rural and farm population as the critical source of new hands for industry in the postwar years.

This pattern persisted into the early 1950s. From 1950 to 1954, some nine million people moved from rural to urban areas,[8] a good many obviously making the peasant-to-worker transition. From 1951 to 1953, according to another report, an average of 660,000 collective farmers became industrial workers annually.[9]

Retrospective data gathered by Soviet researchers in the 1960s and thereafter confirm high peasant input, or a high "nonhereditary" recruitment (which in the conditions of Soviet society in the 1940s and 1950s was a near equivalent). Reporting on a 1967–68 survey in "one of the large industrial centers of the Russian Federation" (almost certainly Taganrog), two authors note that among workers 26–39 years old during the study (who had thus begun working in the latter half of the 1940s and through the 1950s), about 30 percent were children of peasants, versus roughly 45–50 percent for workers age 40 and over who had typically started work in the 1920s, 1930s, and the war years.[10] Such proportions kept the peasant-origin figure high even in developed industrial areas, in the years of transition from late Stalinism to the Khrushchev period. Workers who entered the labor force in the 1945–50s period generally showed a moderate "hereditary" percentage. In the city of Sterlitamak in the late 1970s, of those aged 40–49, who probably came to work mainly in the first ten postwar years, only 41.7 percent were of worker origin themselves.[11] In the Kirov mine complex in the Kuzbass region, of workers aged 36–45 in a study done around 1970, and who thus probably began work in the late 1940s to mid-1950s, fully half were not offspring of workers.[12]

From Stalin to Khrushchev

The Khrushchev era brought massive change in many areas of Soviet life, a slackening of repression, and a growth in living standards. Less dramatic but more inexorable demographic trends, from 1953 through the mid-1960s and the years that followed, would cumulate in a broad structural redistribution of the labor force. Statistical and real effects of policies which changed the legal status of persons hitherto counted under a category other than "worker" would also play a role.

The major nonagricultural branches—industry, construction, and transport—continued to grow while agriculture declined in absolute and relative employment terms. This signaled both a working class with continued absorptive capacity and a long-term decline in the "pool" of the rural and peasant population. Changes in the significance of farm-to-factory mobility had to follow.

Varied and approximate statistics convey an outline of what was happening in the 1950s and 1960s. In 1952 the organized recruitment system (orgnabor), in which recruits were mobilized on behalf of enterprises in industry and construction, had found 60 percent of them in the villages and 40 percent in urban areas; but by 1958 urban sources were providing 66 percent of its industrial requirements.[13] The Khrushchev years combined the end of a period of rapid change and the onset of greater moderation in the occupational and territorial movement of the population. From 1939 to 1959, the urban population had grown by 40.4 million, or 67 percent. Eight million of this was "natural" growth—urban births added to the preexisting urban population—another eight million the result of redesignation of areas hitherto rural as urban. But fully 24–25 million were the product of migration from village to city, feeding many peasants into the ranks of urban workers.[14] From 1929 to 1940, agriculture's share of the labor force fell by a massive 26 percent; over the next quarter century (1940–65), the ranks of agriculture were depleted by a further 22 percent.[15] According to one calculation, on the average for 1951–65, the number of collective farmers fell annually by about 600,000, about 240,000 of whom went into industry and the rest continuing agricultural pursuits but now as state farmers (sovkhozniki), and thus added to the official "statistical" working class (see below).[16] But this fifteen-year period witnessed large variations over shorter periods in the numbers of collective-farm peasantry who left agriculture for industry (and, presumably, related branches). During 1951–53, this flow was large, but Khrushchev's attempts to provide more livable circumstances for collective farmers as producers and consumers stemmed the flow in the 1954–58 period. As one source puts it, "as a result of measures taken by the party for the strengthening of agricultural production," the collective farm outflow to industry fell in these years to about 140,000 per year.[17] In 1959, and for the next few years, the trend reversed itself. Incentives for retaining rural and agricultural manpower were "weakened anew," and rural-urban migration, amounting in 1953–58 to about 0.4 percent of the rural population annually, rose to 1 percent in 1959–64.[18] A reported 340,000–400,000[19] collective farmers left for industrial jobs annually in the period 1959–65, or over double the 1954–58 number. (A further half-million per year became state farmers.) The Brezhnev period saw in its early years a sharp moderation of this outflow process, as the collective farm and general rural populations declined. Between 1966 and 1970, 360,000 collective farmers became "workers and employees" annually, but only 220,000 of these were in industry, while the rest went to the state-farm sector.[20] In all, rural-urban movement as a factor in the "increase in labor resources," which contributed a 17 percent share in 1961–65, made up only 12 percent from 1967 to 1970, and fell to 9 percent in the 1970s.[21]

All this made for a pattern in which the younger workers and those more recently come to the factories showed more incidence of urban and worker heritage than did the older ones.[22] The blue-collar world was still growing, but now it was increasingly drawing on its own internal recruits in the process.

The ranks of workers also grew from other sources. Cuts in administrative and office personnel under Khrushchev had, by 1960, cut the numbers in the administrative apparatus by 586,000 from its 1950 total; some of these were retirements, surely, but others found their way, in uncertain numbers, to worker jobs.[23] Given that many were likely of working-class origin, this reverse mobility, statistically, returned hereditaries to the blue-collar world. Khrushchev also presided over the liquidation of most of the remaining cooperatives outside agriculture, whose craftsmen, earlier counted as a category separate from workers, now became workers in large numbers. One source cites 1.8 million "in the 1950s,"[24] another 1.2 million in 1960 alone.[25] Over the 1970s official statistical reclassification of certain service occupations—barbers, telephone operators, photographers, telegraphers, some salespersons, film projectionists—from the employee to the worker category added some numbers, equal perhaps to around 7 percent of the 1970 worker total.[26]

The post-Stalin years also saw the state's statistical worker total grow as collective farms became state farms, and their cultivators thus became "workers." Over 1951–65, around 5.4 million were "mobile" without really moving,[27] accounting for much of the growth from 1.6 million state-farm workers in 1940 to 7.7 million in 1965.[28] By 1980 there were over 11 million state-farm workers, and two-thirds of the 1960–80 growth in this category was accounted for by the reclassification of collective farmers:[29] not mobility into the nonagricultural working class by Western standards, but rather a complication in Soviet statistics where nonagricultural workers whose parents were state farmers are reported as being of worker origin.

All in all, as a recent author has calculated, the total effect of such transfers—cooperative artisans and collective farmers into the state sector, and statistical reclassifications—over the two decades since 1960 amounted to 10–11 million people, or about one-eighth of the working class of the late 1970s.[30] Subtracting the same author's estimate of 4.04–4.1 million collective-farm to state-farm transfers gives us about 6–7 million people added to the ranks of nonagricultural workers.

The 1960s to the 1980s

Soviet society of the 1960s and 1970s reflected the long distance traveled since Stalin launched his massive industrialization campaign at the end of the 1920s. No longer in a rapid process of transformation, the Soviet social structure was stabilized and now displayed properties that would further contribute to the shaping of a hereditized working class. A Soviet scholar could write in 1967 that the "working class, having become the largest class in society, began to replenish itself mainly on its own account."[31]

Basically all strata became more self-recruiting. The professional/intelligentsia strata continued to grow, but from a base increased by earlier development. Their children, by dint of their own developed skills plus parental resources, influence, and desires to secure status for those children, were rather successful at filling the places that opened up in the upper strata, thus reducing the chances of working youth without inherited advantages to move up. The peasant/farm sector remained, as in every society, essentially a self-reproducing one but one that declined in relative and absolute size. These were marks of a certain "hardening" of class lines, a slowing of mobility in the mature, and inegalitarian, Soviet society. The broadest dimensions of process and outcome in this area are part of the overall "quiet revolution"—we will touch upon some of them later in this chapter. They have been, in any case, the subject of a good deal of writing.[32]

The large worker share in society also showed the combined effects of ideology, policy, and inertial force that had long favored "material production" in the USSR and assigned less priority to activities broadly characterized as the service sector.[33] The USSR manifested little tendency toward becoming a "service economy" or "postindustrial society." As a Soviet author put it as late as 1983, "about 76 percent of all workers are in material production and in the future no essential changes are foreseen."[34] The rather satisfied tone in which Brezhnev-period reality was described—standing in sharp contrast to Gorbachev's later interpretation of growth of numbers in "material production"—reflected a situation in which a high degree of self-recruitment to the workers' world was unavoidable. So it was with recruits of the 1970s, as data for various surveys indicate. In Sterlitamak in the late 1970s, the hereditary component among workers age 21–25, who thus came on the job in that decade, reached 63 percent (versus 52.3 percent for the next older—26–30—cohort). Among workers age 20 and under, 71.3 percent were hereditary.[35] Workers aged 18–25 around 1970 at the Kirov mine, most of whom started work after the Brezhnev succession in 1964, were 80 percent workers' sons—about an 8 percent advance in hereditization over the 26–35 group.[36]

Other studies that include some sort of age breakdown present a similar picture. Studies of personnel in a Sverdlovsk wood industry plant[37] and a tractor factory in Cheliabinsk[38]—the first in the late 1960s and the second in the early 1970s—showed hereditary components in the youngest cohorts (under 20) as 69.7 and 58.1 percent, respectively, contrasted to the oldest defined cohorts' (46 and older, 50 and older) 36.5 percent in both cases. In Taganrog, the Russian industrial city that has to some degree come to play the role of Muncie (Indiana's Soviet equivalent as a "Middletown"), a near-national-average urban site for social research,[39] studies a decade apart show a similar trend. In 1967–68, workers under age 25 were about 66 percent of worker origin, and 20 percent of farm (collective-farm peasant plus state-farm "worker").[40] In 1978 workers under 30 were 69 percent of worker origin, 17 percent of farm.[41]

Had the 1978 study's cut been made at age 25, like the 1967–68 version, the differences would have been larger. (In the 1978 study, the workers age 50 and older numbered in their ranks fully 40 percent farm origin versus 50 percent hereditary workers.) A report of a long-

TABLE 2.1
Indices of Hereditization, Various Soviet Studies (in percentages)

	Hereditary Workers	In Oldest Group	In Youngest Group	Farm Origin	Nonmanual Origin
I. 1960s					
Taganrog		45.0–50.0	66.0		
Sverdlovsk	54.4	47.6	69.7	36.5	9.5
Kazan	49.0			31.9	
Leningrad	57.0			21.9	
Lithuania (1)				56.9	
Lithuania (2)				53.6	
II. Late 1960s/early 1970s					
Cheliabinsk		36.5	58.1		
Kirov/Kuzbass		25.0	80.0		
Bashkir ASSR			58.1	36.4	5.1
Moscow *oblast'*			55.8	15.2	25.0
Sverdlovsk area			56.2	18.7	24.5
Galich	52.0			36.0	12.0
Nerekht	47.0			43.0	10.0
III. Mid-late 1970s					
Sterlitamak	51.8	27.8	71.3		
Nab. Chelny	69.1				
Magnitogorsk	70.3				
Elista	69.4			26.2	
Taganrog	58.0	50.0	69.0	28.0	13.0
IV. Outflow: percentage of all worker-origin who became workers					
Ufa (1970)	55.8	—	—	—	—
Magnitogorsk (1976)	72.7	—	—	—	—
Kazan (1974)	75.3	—	—	—	—

Sources: Panel I—Taganrog: L. Gordon and E. Klopov, *Sotsial'noe razvitie rabochego klassa* (Moscow, 1974), p. 12, cited in David Lane and Felicity O'Dell, *The Soviet Industrial Worker* (New York: St. Martin's Press, 1978), pp. 111–12; Sverdlovsk (wood-product plant): M. N. Rutkevich and F. R. Filippov, *Sotsial'nye peremeshcheniia* (Moscow: Mysl', 1970), p. 89; Kazan: Murray Yanowitch, *Social and Economic Inequality in the Soviet Union* (White Plains, N.Y.: M. E. Sharpe, 1977), p. 109, based on figures in O. I. Shkaratan, *Problemy sotsial'noi struktury rabochego klassa SSSR* (Moscow: Mysl', 1970), p. 433; Leningrad (machine-building workers): L. S. Bliakhman, et al., *Podbor i rasstanovka kadrov na predpriatii* (Moscow, 1968), p. 153, cited in Lane and O'Dell, *The Soviet Industrial Worker*, p. 125; Lithuania (1) Zhalgiris factory, and (2) Kaunas turbine plant, both 1960: N. A. Aitov, "Nekotorye obsobennosti izmeneniia klassovoi struktury v SSSR," *Voprosy filosofii*, no. 3, 1965, p. 8, citing data from K. G. Surblis, in *Razvitie rabochego klassa v natsional'nykh respublikakh SSSR* (Moscow, 1962), pp. 111–12.

term (1965–79) study of workers born after 1950 and covering enterprises in the Russian Republic, Ukraine, Belorussia, Moldavia, Latvia, Tadzhikistan, and Georgia further specified the decline of the peasant contribution to the working class: in older industrial cities, the farm-origin share was no more than 15 percent and never quite reached 40 percent even in new cities. Over one-half the workers responding were "second or third generation" workers.[42]

Were this an ideal world, we could now add to these comments summary statistics on the composition by social origin of the working class in different times and places. But, as in so many areas of social research involving the USSR, it is not ideal. The foregoing discussion has not exhausted the available data, but what remains is hardly systematic. Table 2.1 lays out a fair amount of the available Soviet data on the Brezhnev-era composition (inflow shares) of the working class. It adds as well some data on the reciprocal aspect of mobility: the outflow of workers' offspring into both the hereditary worker category and other (farm, nonmanual) destination categories.

We have here what amounts to an informative if also bewildering array of data—a spotty mosaic. Panel I consists of studies done in the 1960s; II, those done, as far as we can determine, in the late 1960s–early 1970s (Soviet sources are often unclear as to precisely when a study was conducted); and III, in the 1970s. As many data as possible have been included on each study: the average hereditization of the

Table 2.1 Sources, cont.
Panel II—Cheliabinsk (tractor plant): F. R. Filippov, "Sotsial'nye peremeshcheniia v sovetskom obshchestve," Sotsiologicheskie issledovaniia, no. 4 (1975), p. 16, cited in Lane and O'Dell, The Soviet Industrial Worker, p. 112; Kirov mine, Kuzbass: A. A. Khaliulina, "Istochniki i formy popolneniia rabochikh kadrov v tiazheloi promyshlennosti kuzbassa," in AN SSSR, Sibirskoe otdelenie, Chislennost' i sostav rabochikh Sibirii v usloviiakh razvitogo sotsializma 1959–1975 (Novosibirsk: Nauka, 1977), p. 113; Bashkir ASSR, Moscow oblast', Sverdlovsk area: G. A. Slesarev, Demograficheskie protsessy i sotsial'naia struktura sotsialisticheskogo obshchestva (Moscow: Nauka, 1978), p. 116; Galich, Nerekht: E. V. Klopov, Rabochii klass SSSR (tendentsii razvitiia v 60–70-e gody) (Moscow: Mysl', 1985), p. 137.
Panel III—Sterlitamak, Naberezhnye Chelny, and Magnitogorsk: N. A. Aitov, Sovetskii rabochii (Moscow: Izdatel'stvo politicheskoi literatury, 1981), p. 25; Elista: Slesarev, Demograficheskie protsessy, p. 211, table 39 (sum of all origin families classified by father's occupation); Taganrog: Klopov, Rabochii klass, p. 136.
Panel IV—Ufa: N. A. Aitov, "Sotsial'nye peremeshcheniia v SSSR," in W. Wesolowski and M. N. Rutkevich, eds., Problemy razvitiia sotsial'noi struktury obshchestva v Sovetskom Soiuze i Pol'she (Moscow: Nauka, 1976), pp. 222–23; Magnitogorsk: Aitov, "Dinamika sotsial'nykh peremeshchenii v SSSR," in AN SSSR, Institut sotsiologicheskikh issledovanii, Sovetskaia sotsiologiia, v. 2 (Moscow: Nauka, 1982), pp. 197–210 (trans. in Soviet Sociology 24, 1–3 (Summer-Fall-Winter, 1985–86), pp. 254–70); Kazan: E. K. Vasil'eva, Sotsial'no-ekonomicheskaia struktura naseleniia SSSR (Moscow: Statistika, 1978), p. 93.

whole worker sample; the figures for the oldest and youngest age groups, where these were reported; and again by availability, the percentages of the worker sample of other social origins.

The research sites are diverse enough in scale to confuse matters as well—the Sverdlovsk study in panel I was done in one large plant, that in II apparently in a number of them—a key to understanding the lower rate of hereditization among young workers in the latter than in the former (studies limited to "young workers" are reported in the "youngest group" column). Large gaps persist in the percentage of hereditary workers between oldest and youngest groups, as noted earlier. Long-developed industrial areas, like Leningrad and Sverdlovsk, show solid hereditary majorities even in studies conducted in the 1960s, while as late as the late 1970s, a relatively new industrial area like Sterlitamak, or the smaller cities of Galich and Nerekht in Kostroma *oblast'*, show a near-even balance of hereditary and "mobile" elements. Among the newer studies, the heavy hereditary majorities in Magnitogorsk and Naberezhnye Chelny are what might be expected of settled industrial areas of the RSFSR. The 61.4 percent figure for Elista, capital of the Kalmyk ASSR, seems high; lacking data to further characterize the context of this reported figure, we can speculate that we may have here a case of a small, self-reproducing working-class population in a region not noted for a long history of massive industrial development.

Downward mobility, on these figures, hardly seems a major factor moderating hereditization. Most of the figures for persons of nonmanual origin as a percentage of current workers are in the 5–15 percent range. The higher figures for Moscow and the Sverdlovsk area in panel II may reflect peculiarities of the sample or, in the case of Moscow, an area with a larger population of routine, as well as professional, nonmanuals. (Very few sons of the elite, indeed, descend to worker status: the 9.5 percent in the panel I study in a Sverdlovsk plant included a 7.4 percent component for children of routine white-collar workers, and only 2.1 percent from "specialist" families.)[43] The relative shares of routine and specialist nonmanual-origin workers in the Moscow *oblast'* and Sverdlovsk studies in panel II were 19.6:5.4 and 16.2:8.3, respectively.[44]

Panel IV presents data from three studies on another facet of the process: the tendency of sons of workers to become workers—to reproduce their father's status rather than move to another, in the outflow from origin—a process distinct from the inflow measure, which focuses on the tendency of current workers to be worker-origin. In a time of rapid working-class growth, workers' sons may become workers in the vast majority of cases, thus scoring high in the outflow figures, yet still constitute a minority among all workers, demographically overwhelmed by the peasant inflow. Today, levels of worker-to-worker outflow guarantee that the inflow figures will remain at a high level; the younger, more hereditary cohorts enter the factory, and older cohorts with larger shares of peasant-origin leave. As a Soviet writer put it, on the basis of a fourteen-region study conducted between 1982 and 1985, the major social groupings were now largely self-reproducing, to a level of about 75 percent.[45]

More than enough data, surely, to make the point. If some gigantic Soviet computer had kept a daily tally of the social origins of the country's work force—of each new addition, of each retirement—then on one day, sometime in the Brezhnev years, more than half the male workers in industry, construction, transport, and communications, plus worker elements in other branches, would have registered as "of worker origin"—when the day before they had not. That number would continue to grow, reflecting not just a bare statistical fact, but the basis for a modernization of outlook in the blue-collar component of what was less and less an ex-peasant society and more and more one in which the workers reflected tastes, expectations, and demands shaped by city and factory as a natural environment, rather than as the end point of a stormy and disorienting passage.

Gorbachev would thus inherit a different social reality than had Khrushchev or Brezhnev. Hereditization and self-recruitment were important: so would be the results of years of rising educational levels among the workers.

Education: The Rising Curve

In the late 1970s, research revealed an impressive set of statistics on the educational levels of machine-building workers in Leningrad, a group often studied as a microcosm of the core Soviet industrial working class. From a woeful 2.1 years of schooling in 1918, attainments had grown impressively to 4.5 years in 1929. Over the next thirty-five years—throughout industrialization and collectivization, the purges of the 1930s and the trials of war, the late Stalin years and Khrushchev's time in power—they climbed to an average of 8.2 years (1965), moving then slowly upward to 8.4 years in 1970 and 8.9 in 1976–77.[46]

Growth had not been linear. The major post-1929 advances in the educational levels of Soviet workers had come mainly after 1953, in the post-Stalin era. Other Leningrad data from a survey of "production personnel" in a metalworking plant compared figures for 1948

TABLE 2.2
Educational Levels, Sverdlovsk Plants, 1950–51, 1959 (in percentages)

	1950–51		1959		1959
Educational	Labor	New	Labor	New	All Workers
Level	Force	Hires	Force	Hires	under 25
Less than 7 years	74.5	71.5	46.6	39.2	31.4
7–9 years	23.0	26.5	39.7	43.7	41.8
10 years or more	2.5	2.0	13.9	22.1	26.2

Source: Adapted from M. I. Iovchuk, "Sotsial'noe znachenie pod'ema kul'turno-technicheskogo urovnia rabochikh," Sotsiologiia v SSSR, vol. 2 (Moscow: Mysl', 1966), pp. 36–39 (trans. in Soviet Sociology 6, 1–2 (Summer–Fall, 1967), pp. 15–16.

and 1958. In 1948 over three-quarters of them had had fewer than seven years of schooling; by 1958, the fraction went down to a bit less than half. The number with seven to nine years of education had nearly doubled, while those with a complete secondary education had grown from 1.8 percent of all personnel to 15 percent.[47]

More data (from factories in Sverdlovsk, for roughly the same periods), presented in table 2.2, tell us something of the process of educational change, as reflected in the school attainments of new hires versus the existing labor force. In 1950–51 existing worker cadres of low educational attainment experienced little change by the addition of new personnel. The newly hired differ little from those they join: the educational distribution is reproducing itself. Changes are clearly in evidence by 1959. By then there are fewer in the existing labor force who still lack the seven-year incomplete secondary education, but the number with a ten-year (complete secondary) education is still low.

More revealing is the fourth column. The "new hires" of 1959 are markedly better educated compared with the whole labor force than was the case in 1951. These new hires represent a mix: some young workers, just out of a school in which they spent more years than their forebears, other older job changers with lower levels of education. This is clear from the fact that column 5 shows all workers under 25 years of age with an average educational profile more "upscale," especially in terms of completion of secondary education, than the new hires of that year. The overall 1959 figures in the Sverdlovsk study, in essence, are quite similar to the Leningrad metalworkers' 1958 figures cited earlier and somewhat more advanced than the figures for urban workers in the USSR as a whole in 1959. Nationwide, only 9.9 percent had a complete secondary, or higher, education in that year, while

56.8 percent had only primary (four-year) education or less.[48] (The profiles of individual plants may vary widely; even in Moscow's Zil auto plant [see table 2.3] educational levels in 1959 were below these.)

Work, Education, Policy: The Khrushchev Reform

The educational attainment figures for the late 1950s showed progress but were controversial as well. They set Khrushchev on the course of an attempted "school reform" that had much to do with calculations about what kind of a labor force the USSR needed.[49] As a policy response, it is of more than historical interest. Some of the problems Khrushchev "diagnosed" in the late 1950s at one level of development were again to be faced in the early 1980s at quite another level, during the transition between the Brezhnev and Gorbachev eras.

Khrushchev—or, more properly, those who placed education on his agenda—perceived a complicated situation. First, student numbers in the eighth to tenth grades of academic schools had grown greatly between 1948 and 1956, and enrollments had increased fivefold.[50] These grades, which at the time were the "complete secondary" component of a general academic education, aimed mainly at preparation for higher education. Yet by 1957 the tenth-grade output represented an excess of 800,000 over the combined full-time enrollment capacity of higher educational institutions, or vuz (vysshie uchebnye zavedeniia), and the "secondary specialized" *tekhnikums* for people who had already finished an academic secondary education.[51] No plan existed to expand space in these institutions in lock-step with the growth in secondary graduations. The problem was one of overproduction of academic high school graduates.

Second, these grades of the secondary school were seen—not inaccurately—as the place where many youth developed a certain contempt for manual labor, and as the seedbed of aspirations to higher education for a much larger share of the 18-year-old Soviet population than the system could, or expected to, satisfy.

A third problem was the social class imbalance in the upper grades of Soviet academic secondary schools. Their larger student bodies of the late 1950s were still upscale, heavily weighted toward children of educated professionals. Worker and peasant youth, though their numbers (especially working-class youth) in the eighth through tenth grades had been increasing, wound up after seventh grade, in large numbers, in the trade schools of the State Labor Reserves system. In Khrushchev's view, in line with a sort of "visceral populism" he manifested against the notion of a self-perpetuating social-professional elite, this made for a very uneven race between even talented working-class youth and those whose family resources virtually guaranteed their attendance in the eighth to tenth grades, the sine qua non for competing for admission to higher education.

These three problems emerged against the background of a fourth: an impending shortage of new hands entering the labor force. The economy was beginning to feel the demographic echo of the war—the smallish numbers of people reaching the ages of 15–16, at which decisions were typically made about further education. In 1957 the number of 18-year-olds began to decline, with an expected deep trough by 1962–63.[52] Khrushchev's launching of an ambitious Seven Year Plan, however, put a premium on new additions to the labor force, just as the tendency of Soviet youth to remain longer in full-time education was manifesting itself.

Khrushchev's response, revealed in September 1958, was a striking departure from previous patterns. It called for

1. Work, combined with part-time schooling, for all, once they had completed the eighth grade of the general academic school (now defined as "incomplete" secondary); in effect, *abolishing* full-time ninth- to tenth-grade education;

2. A period of full-time work after completing the tenth grade as a requirement before one could apply for higher education;

3. Part-time study in higher educational institutions for the first two years, while one continued to work.

According to the reform's logic, more of those in their mid and late teens than before would enter the labor force. For workers' children, this would be no great change. For the children of white-collar professionals, it would be new indeed; the prospective abolition of the schools in which they predominated threatened to put them, willy-nilly, into the world of work. The required work before and after tenth-grade graduation would make more hands available and bring an end to the privileged direct passage into full-time higher education. Many would, over the time spent at work, lose their unrealistic desires for higher education and not apply. Many who did apply would not qualify. Among them, presumably to Khrushchev's satisfaction, would be the pampered, less resolute, and less talented children of the intelligentsia, who would join the working class. On this "level playing field" talented and energetic sons of workers might win a merited place in higher education, later to join a more truly meritocratic and "toiling" intelligentsia.

This, roughly, is how Khrushchev must have seen it; he was not fated to gain it all. The Central Committee resolution and the decrees of November 1958 watered down his program considerably. It preserved the ninth to tenth-grade full-time school, adding an eleventh year. "Labor training" was introduced into this three-year program. Whether the extra year was added to accommodate this new training—ostensibly the rationale—while preserving the content of the old two-year academic program in toto (against Khrushchev's thrust) or to deter selection of the full-time track (partially accommodating his priorities) is a matter of debate.[53] This left in place the social gap between the full-time schools that had been the preserve of the privileged, and the evening-school alternative for those already employed, to which many worker youth went. (And, incidentally, continued to go. A study in Leningrad day schools in the mid-1960s found white-collar employees', workers', and peasants' children in the proportions 57.9, 35.9, and 6.2 percent, respectively, while in evening schools the respective figures were 19.2, 74.5, and 6.2 percent.[54]) The requirements that one must work full time before application to higher education and that the early years of higher education be combined with work were softened and made a matter of discretion for the institutions themselves.

It was not a total gutting of the reform. Pressures did direct more eighth-grade graduates to work, cutting back for the earlier part of the 1960s the number of people who proceeded to tenth-grade graduation at the ages of 17–18. (Their number—1.07 million in 1955—fell to 709,000 in 1960 and rose to 913,000 by 1965.)[55] After secondary graduation, many did seek work experience of some sort before applying to higher educational institutions. But even before Khrushchev's ouster, a new decree of the Central Committee and the Council of Ministers in August 1964 restored, as of 1966, the eight-year/two-year pattern of incomplete/complete secondary education, reduced the vocational training component, and put new emphasis on full-time attendance in higher educational institutions.

The most plausible explanation of the outcome is bureaucratic and group resistance, exploited perhaps by other political leaders, who could make Khrushchev, in the collective leadership of the time, settle for less than all his desiderata.[56] Teachers and administrators in the academic secondary schools wanted to maintain enrollments, and thus their jobs, and had a pedagogical prejudice in favor of academic education, as did the upper bureaucracy of the education ministry. Scientists saw the "work before and during higher education" requirement as posing risks of the decay of prior education and loss of young, creative years for those whose education would thus be delayed. Factory managers showed no great enthusiasm for young, unwilling workers who had to be trained as they worked, under regulations that specified shorter hours at normal (if low) skill-related pay rates. Parents were reluctant to see children sidetracked from full-time school at a tender age into the factories that many, if not most, wanted them to escape.

Thus a program combining a quick fix for a threatened labor shortage, an attempt to strike a blow at the capacity of the professional strata to use the educational system to pass advantages on to their offspring,[57] and a reduction of a growing population of high school graduates whose higher-education aspirations the state would not satisfy came to naught. The underlying problems, including the distaste for factory work that Soviet academic secondary schooling seemed to breed, would remain. The compromise reform had put the academic secondary school in a difficult situation, requiring that it provide vocational training without much specificity on which vocations were to be emphasized, while avoiding the matter of whether even ten years of school were functional, given the rather modest intellectual demands of most of the jobs available and for which schools could provide training.[58] In the industrial city of Nizhnyi Tagil, only 22.6 percent of tenth-grade graduates had gone directly to work in 1954. This had risen to 42 percent in 1958 on the verge of the reform, and to 62 percent by 1962.[59] Their number would continue to rise, driven on the one hand by the aspirations that prompted people to complete their secondary educations, and on the other by the countervailing demographic logic that dictated that so many of these would have to take workers' jobs rather than find the desired place in a vuz. The picture would grow more complex in the later 1960s and 1970s.

To School Again: Brezhnev and Beyond

The near-term consequences of the Khrushchev reform emerge, in our statistics, in the comparatively slow pace at which educational attainments of all workers, including the young, increased in the later years (1959–64) of his power. Data from the Zil automotive plant in Moscow (table 2.3) are indicative. As compared to the Sverdlovsk data shown in table 2.2, attainment of a complete secondary education is even less common in this plant. While improvement from 1959 to 1965 is significant and quite marked in the "under 30" group, the growth between 1965 and 1970, and between 1970 and 1975, is more striking: there are larger age cohorts in the secondary-school years, but also an

TABLE 2.3
Percentage of Workers with
Complete Secondary Education,
Moscow Zil Plant, 1959–1979

Year	All Workers	Workers under 30
1959	8.4	11.3
1965	12.0	18.9
1970	23.1	38.7
1975	37.0	62.0
1979	50.7	77.8

Source: Adapted from T. A. Babushkina, V. S. Dunin, and E. A. Zenkevich, "Sotsial'nye problemy formirovaniia novykh popolnenii rabochego klassa," *Rabochii klass i sovremennyi mir*, no. 3 (1981), p. 47.

increasingly typical locus of 15–17-year-olds in school rather than in the factory. The average age at which the youngest entrants arrived at the factory gates had risen markedly, from 15.5–16 years old in the 1920s and 1930s to 18.5–19 years old by the beginning of the 1980s;[60] many of those arrivals of the 1920s and 1930s, it should be noted, had not been in school to ages 15–16, but were engaged in farm or other labor for some time, after a minimal education.

The trends toward a more educated working class picked up speed and continued into the late 1970s and 1980s. In the Zil plant in Moscow, 50.7 percent of all workers had a secondary education by 1979, up from 12 percent in 1965. A survey of enterprises in the industrial area of Gorky showed more modest progress: 29.3 percent had secondary credentials in 1979, up from 10.7 in 1964–65, but in each case workers under age 30 in 1979 had contributed greatly to this result. In the Zil plant 77.8 percent and in Gorky 80 percent had a secondary education, whether academic or specialized.[61]

The picture was not totally uniform nationwide. Around 1985, 17.5 percent of the workers in a large study of fourteen regions still lacked incomplete secondary (7–8 year) education (while 30.5 percent of collective farmers were similarly situated).[62] Many of these were older workers who would leave the scene in the not-too-distant future. But among those lacking complete secondary education, some were surely recruits of the late 1950s to mid-1960s who had never been effectively motivated to finish their schooling but still had before them half their working lives.

Economic returns on added education were not an incentive for the young worker. A 1966 study of workers already 3–5 years on the job found that 33 percent of those who lacked even an incomplete secondary education earned over 100 rubles per month, while only 28.5 percent of those with complete secondary earned that much. Into the 60-rubles-and-under category fell 12.5 percent of the high-school graduates and only 8.3 percent of those with less than 7–8 years of education.[63] Seniority, skill (although 3–5 years were surely long enough for skill acquisition by the younger, better-educated workers), and settlement in a "good" job with an easy production target and a good piece-rate counted for more than education, and reduced the motivation to acquire a diploma in evening school.

By the 1980s then, the academic secondary school, or rather its last two grades, had become the wellspring of a large number of young workers. The specialized secondary schools and *tekhnikums*, which awarded the academic diploma after a longer para-professional training, took some 10–15 percent of eighth-grade graduates. A third alternative, the secondary vocational-technical school, or SPTU, growing in numbers since 1969, offered training in a labor specialty along with high-school certification on the basis of grafting an academic curriculum onto the old PTU, the short-term vocational-technical school that was the lineal descendant of the old Labor Reserve Schools of the Stalin era. All of these contributed to the statistics on the share of workers with complete secondary education—but the academic school most of all. Critics had long noted that its final grades logically prepared people only for higher education. As long as it remained the preserve of only that minority of students who would indeed go on to higher education, the problem was minor. However, with the demographic growth that swelled their numbers, unbalanced by commensurate increase in places in full-time higher education, it was inevitable that high school graduates would be found in growing numbers somewhere other than in university lecture halls. Rutkevich's estimated ratios for the number of academic secondary-school graduations in a given year, versus admissions to full-time higher education later in the same year, make the point: from 2.4:1 in 1965, they rose to 3.9 in 1970, 4.6 in 1975, and fell only moderately to 4.2:1 in 1980.[64] Fewer than one in four graduates were entering full-time higher education. In the early 1950s, more than one in two had, from the more restricted school population.[65]

Such figures provoked discussions in Soviet journals and among Western observers. The relative advantage of white-collar and professional children over their worker schoolmates in the competition for admission to higher education was one theme: access was not evenly distributed. Another was the destination of those secondary-school graduates who fell on the wrong side of the ratios. For the majority of them it was the working class.

Economy and Social Structure

The stabilization of the Soviet working class on the base of a hereditary majority was part of a general maturation of Soviet society. Changes in the size and share of major occupational groups—white-collar, workers, farmers—in the population were now gradual and incremental. This was a far cry from the transformations of the 1930s, and it was natural. Cataclysmic change, by definition, could not be a constant process. With a slowing of change in labor-force distribution came a slowing of mobility, both within the span of a career and between the parent and child generations—a reduction of the career contingencies individuals faced, on the whole, in contemporary Soviet society. What had been called an economy at "middle age"[66] restricted the opportunities for workers' children, and workers themselves, to move upward into professional/specialist positions. While the occupational structure on the whole had grown much more complex than in the past—giving rise to a social diversity that was to prove more and more difficult for the regime to map and regulate—that same complexity made long-range mobility between classes all the more difficult.

A 1982–85 study found a striking difference in career mobility (intragenerational, or that which occurs between the beginning of one's working career and the time of the study) among different age cohorts. While in general about one-third of respondents had been mobile between classes (i.e., beginning in the farm sector and ending in nonfarm work, or going from a start as a worker to a nonmanual job, etc.), and over half mobile within a class (from lesser to greater skill, income, etc.), those who entered work in the 1970s and 1980s had been markedly less mobile than those who started work in the 1950s and 1960s.[67]

The broad picture of mobility experience by period of beginning work, based on the 1982–85 study of 55,000 biographies, presents the following picture of percentages of workers who were mobile between classes up to the time of the survey: began work before the 1950s, 61.7 percent; began work in 1950s, 61.3 percent; in 1960s, 57.4 percent; in 1970s, 41.9 percent; in 1980s, 20 percent. [68] It is not completely clear if these figures reflect only career mobility and do not contain the intergenerational component as well (i.e., peasant sons who began their careers as workers). But for our purposes this is not terribly important. The picture of what the Soviet investigators call the "increasing stabilization of the social structure (*sostav*)"[69] limits both varities of mobility. Between the oldest and the youngest entry cohorts, hereditary transmission of status among workers (offspring of workers becoming workers) rose 1.4 times, among white-collar personnel, "specialist," and routine clerical by 1.7 times; while the incidence of peasant intergenerational mobility to worker status declined by 2.0 times.[70]

The moderated movement of persons who began work in the 1980s is not simply an artifact of an exposure of only a few years' duration to the contingencies of mobility. If they come, such changes come most often at or shortly after the commencement of work.[71] More recent entry cohorts also began work at an older age, by which they had presumably already achieved most of their education. (More than half of those who began to work in the 1950s did so before 18 years of age; 80 percent of those who started in the 1980s did so at or after that age.)[72]

A late 1970s study of working youth (aged 16–30) in four socialist countries, which included as its Soviet component a sample of one-quarter of this group in the "typical" city of Kostroma, yielded some interesting figures. Overwhelmingly, those who reported worker fathers had first jobs as workers, with little difference by the skill level of their fathers: over 86 percent of children of unskilled workers began their careers as workers, and over 82 percent of children of skilled workers did the same. Of the latter category, however, 7.44 percent were advantaged in that they began work as intelligentsia with higher education, versus only 2.89 percent of the children of the unskilled—overall, testimony to the modest numbers from the worker milieu who enter and complete higher education.[73]

Initial mobility does see some resorting of worker-origin youth within worker-skill categories. Almost half of those from unskilled backgrounds begin work as semiskilled; almost a quarter start as skilled workers. The majority of the children of semiskilled workers begin work in that category (about 63 percent), while the children of the skilled more typically begin one level lower than their fathers (37 percent semiskilled and 33 percent skilled).[74] None of this really alters the larger picture, nor the tendency of the worker category to maintain its predominance in the occupational structure of Kostroma. In the sample, 86.9 percent of the whole group had started their first job as workers, in the proportions 37, 35.5, 14.4 percent for unskilled, semiskilled, and skilled categories, respectively. At the time of the survey, an only marginally reduced 82.2 percent of the sample were workers, but with a career upgrading reflected in new respective percentages of 10.8, 46.9, and 24.5 across the skill categories.[75] These overall figures are produced by an upgrading of unskilled starters to semiskilled (48.8 percent) and skilled (17.9); by many more semi-skilled starters rising to skilled (16.6) than falling to unskilled (3.1); and by those who begin skilled and remain skilled. Fragmentary data indicate relatively few who are career-mobile into any level of white-collar occupation, whether or not it requires much education.[76]

A 1980–82 study of Soviet urban social structure that cast a net much broader than Kostroma underlines several points. While independent of age cohort, more unskilled workers came from collective and state farm origins than from worker origins (45 versus 39 percent); farm-origin workers were already a minority: among unskilled workers aged 15–29 (essentially the same "youth" as in the Kostroma study), fully 45 percent were of worker origin and only 30 percent of farm origin. Among the skilled, overall origins were 42 percent farm, 46 percent worker; those of ages 15–29 were 50 percent worker.[77]

"Youth" in general showed career histories that tended to lock those of worker origin into working-class destinations. In the smaller cities of the sample, 49 percent of those of unskilled worker origin remained there and 19 percent rose to the skilled level; of the offspring of the skilled, 56 percent in smaller cities inherited the parental level, while 28 percent became unskilled workers. In cities with populations over one million, the tendencies to inherit working-class status were even stronger for the children of the unskilled and about the same for the children of the skilled.[78]

These are male-plus-female figures. There are no detailed breakdowns by gender, but other figures from the study indicate the very different dispersion patterns of males and females in general—strong male predominance among skilled workers; a near even distribution or female predominance among the unskilled; and strong female predominance in routine white-collar office work, in paraprofessional categories (those requiring specialized secondary education), and, though to a lesser degree, among those with higher education. All in all, this means—as other evidence over a long period indicates—that females born into the urban blue-collar milieu follow lives that take them out more often than do males. Sons inherit worker status rather predictably in the USSR, as it has taken shape since Stalin's time, and daughters less so. Female marital destinations may, however, often be in the class of origin. The male component of the working class, less concerned with housework, more centered on the world of work,

TABLE 2.4
Sectoral Distribution of Labor Force, by Birth Cohort and Career Phase,
1959–79

Type of Work	Born 1910–19	Born in 1930s			Born in 1950s
	In Their 40s (1959)	In Their 20s (1959)	In Their 30s (1970)	In Their 40s (1979)	In Their 20s (1979)
Industry	38	49	47	48	53
Agriculture	40	32	23	22	13
Information	7	7	10	9	13
Services	9	10	13	13	16
Organizational	6	2	7	8	5

Source: Adapted from L. A. Gordon and V. V. Komarovskii, "Dinamike sotsial'no-professional'nogo sostava pokolenii," Sotsiologicheskie issledovaniia, no. 3 (1986), pp. 100, 106.

more critical of working conditions, is the component most heredi-tized and the one that dominates in so many critical branches of in-dustry, especially at the skilled level.[79]

The slowing of change in the occupational structure is also evident in the relative growth of different occupational sectors in the 1960s compared with the 1970s. In the 1960s the total number employed in "industrial occupations" rose 109 percent, but also an impressive 64 percent in "education and services" and 58 percent in "information-related occupations" ranging from computer operators to design engi-neers. While in the 1970s fewer new hands were entering the work force, and growth slowed in "industrial occupations" (to only 23 per-cent), the growth rates of other sectors, where shifts away from the lagging, heavy-industry economy might have been expected, also fell significantly to 30 percent for information-related occupations and 18 percent (less than the industry rate) for education and services.[80] Through the end of the 1970s, industry persisted in claiming a good deal of new additions to the labor force. Data drawn from the 1959, 1970, and 1979 censuses further illuminate industrial employment sta-bility, the gradual decline of agriculture, and the growth—large in percentage terms, less so in absolute—of other sectors. As table 2.4 indicates, agriculture continues to lose its share of the employed. The oldest group contributed four of every ten of its members to agricul-ture (1959); we can assume that few of these now-retired people ever left it. The cohort born in the 1930s, which we can trace through three census periods (1959, 1970, 1979) as it ages from its twenties to forties, contributed a smaller share to agriculture when it was young, reduced even this by almost one-third ten years later, and then another per-

TABLE 2.5
Labor Force by Sector, 1959, 1970, 1975

Type of Work	1959	1970	1979
Industry	42	48	51
Agriculture	38	23	18
Information	7	10	12
Services	9	14	14
Organizational	4	5	5

Source: See table 2.4 above.

cent by 1979. Very few of those born in the 1950s went into agriculture at all. The industry picture is quite different; effectively, the share of those born in the 1930s holds across the twenty years, at about half of their number, and industry absorbs more than half of all those in their twenties in 1979. That youngest cohort is also better represented in the other sectors in 1979 than are the people in their forties (born in the 1930s). But in fact their presence in these sectors is not much above that of the total employed population in 1979—and their 53 percent representation in industry is also a bit above the 51 percent of the total population found in industry in 1979. The data in table 2.5 indicate the distributions of the total employed population, independent of age cohort, in the three census periods.

These figures show the progress over twenty years in reducing shares in agriculture more than they show growth of the nonindustry sectors likely to represent developmental progress by world standards. Examining 1979 through the two tables gives one a strong impression of a stabilized social structure in the Brezhnevian twilight. It is not a surprise that those then in their forties have a profile a bit more agricultural, a bit less industrial than the general population. The tendency of the economy to replicate itself is manifest in the small 1970–79 changes among the total employed. Working-class youth, if they aspired in large numbers to leave that class, found the economics of the 1970s of little help—a reason to anticipate some discontent.

Those young workers are, after all, more likely than the older ones to have developed, in the ninth and tenth grades, the desire for upward mobility and less likely by far to have been upwardly mobile into the working class from farm origin. They have spent a greater proportion of their lives in a period when living standards failed to improve significantly, as compared to their elders who remember the Stalin years and saw the great improvements implemented in Khrushchev's and Brezhnev's times. Those elders weathered the stagnation of the 1970s; the improvements of 1953–70 had probably been well beyond their expectations. But the young workers lack this context, and indeed probably underestimate the degree to which policy and drift, in the Khrushchev and Brezhnev eras, fostered a creeping egalitarianism raising many workers' material rewards to and above those of educated specialists and professionals. (Evidence here comes from the Soviet Interview Project of the early 1980s, tapping the experience of Soviet emigrés. Asked in which era—Stalin's, Khrushchev's, Brezhnev's—they saw the greatest inequality and the power of "privilege" in Soviet life, the youngest respondents [born 1941–60] chose the Brezhnev era more often than any of the other age groups.[81] By no measure is this true, at least with regard to economic inequality, but beliefs have consequences independent of their factual base. A large share of younger, better-educated Soviet workers who were born from 1950 to 1965 lack the career-mobility experience and temporal frame of reference that could produce positive evaluations of trends in the Brezhnev period, or much of what followed.)

Toward the Possibilities of Class

From the FYP-driven social transformations of 1928–40 through the crucible of war and on to the renewal/replacement of worker cadres through largely peasant postwar "drafts," the Stalin era had been inimical to processes through which class characteristics might develop spontaneously among workers or other groups. Society remained rather simple in its group structure and enjoyed minimal autonomy.

The years since 1953 have seen an increase in society's relative autonomy, following a slackening of political pressure. Growth also slackened after a time and slowed the rate of social mobility, fostering greater self-reproduction among workers and other social categories even as the society grew more complex in its group structure. The likelihood grew that workers' sons would go to the factory rather than on to other destinations, as did the probability that once there, they would meet other workers' sons rather than those of peasants.

Classically, such processes of hereditization and homogenization of social origin have been seen as class-forming. Similarly, high rates of society-reshaping mobility have broken old class or other group boundaries and "dissolved" classes. Class identity, in the sense we have used it here, is a subjective category—to exist, it must be felt. But to be felt, it must draw on real similarities among people. Over the course of the Khrushchev-Brezhnev years, similarities of origin/inheritance/environment were restored to a blue-collar work force whose number, and percentage of the whole society, had grown enormous by the standards of 1928; with them came a base for enhanced feelings of class identity.

This is not to claim class uniformity. There is much diversity in wages, skill levels, and so on among Soviet workers; differentiation per se within a working class, however, need not mean it cannot be a class—its impact can be overemphasized.[82] Working-class origins resemble each other more than they resemble the typical origins in intelligentsia or farm families. The organizations and authority structures under which workers operate in industry, construction, or transport may be diverse, but resemble each other more than they resemble the work environments of office or farm. The social/educational selection processes whereby worker-origin youth are channeled toward worker destinations (see chapter 3) provide similar experiences as well. Much, then, favors the development of workers' class identity.

The data and observations discussed here do not speak directly to questions of class opposition and totality, but they are not totally irrelevant. Rising educational levels may in themselves gratify workers and make the acquisition of skills easier. But they may in fact promote tastes, aspirations, and expectations that conflict with the authority structure and the intrinsic content of the jobs on offer in the Soviet economy. What we know about increased general educational levels (the result of a combination of state policy that saw more education, up to a point, as "better" and the spontaneously pursued desires of many for more education) makes it doubtful that blue-collar work performance or satisfaction should necessarily increase with years of education.[83] The better-educated work force of today need not be better adjusted, and may well be maladjusted, to the work, the structure of authority, the plant. From such tensions oppositional attitudes toward the bosses may develop, and more education could be conducive to a readier perception of shared (class) identity with those similarly situated.

Elements of identity, opposition, and totality may come together with potentially critical impact among younger, male workers, mainly Russian or East Slavic, who most bear the marks of hereditary status and heightened education. For these, there has been none of the economic "leap forward" that older workers experienced under Khrushchev and the earlier Brezhnev period; they have had no reason to feel that Brezhnevian policy particularly favored the worker—at least not until Gorbachev-era reform plans and economic woes put that policy in a different light. But the general drift of late-Brezhnev life, marked by shortages and corruption, was likely to make the segment of the work force with the most potential for class identity feel more opposition, both to factory life and to the lackluster economic performance delivered by those in command. This opposition, if not felt purely as a worker affair, may well have been part of a sharpening "we-they" divide, wherein workers saw themselves as a major component of the "we." A "we-they" consciousness, given the enhanced literacy and education of younger workers and a greater ability to conceptualize than their fathers had, could move in the direction of totality—a feeling that authority structure and economic circumstance constrain workers such that their status as workers is the most important, almost total determinant of their lives. Whether this is true or not, a feeling of totality is probably possible only on the basis of a sort of reflection on one's condition that was beyond the capacities of earlier, peasant-origin Soviet workers.

3

Forming Workers:
Choice, Selection, and Tracking

> State TV and radio, the republic's Ministry of
> Education and Committee on Vocational-
> Technical Education present, according to a
> special plan, a cycle of broadcasts for school-
> children and those in vocational-technical in-
> stitutions, and their parents (among them
> "Stories About Jobs," "A Job One's Whole
> Life," "The Whole Class—to the Collective
> Farm, to the Factory," "Today a Model Stu-
> dent—Tomorrow a Leader of Production,"
> . . . "Worker Dynasties". . .).
> (A. Barkar, 1983)

FOR A LONG time, the pretensions, if not the reality, of the Soviet
planned economy included fitting together, with minimal friction,
those entering the labor force and the available jobs, while tolerating neither the unemployment nor the "anarchy" that market systems
were deemed to foster. For the majority, this involved being slotted
into workers' occupations. Generating enthusiasm about entering
rank-and-file jobs is a difficult matter, and one may wonder how effective tub-thumping measures such as those quoted above were, and
are.

Some people are ready to become workers: their occupational aspirations have neither a higher nor, most often, a sharp focus. Others
are not ready at all yet will find their way into the working class. The
fit is not always good. In this chapter we will examine some aspects of
social and self-selection into the working class or away from it. We
will also address some problems of the available job structure and the
changing and constant aspects of the general and vocational-educa-
tion channels by which the USSR has attempted to "produce the producers"—the working class.

Choice and Drift

Educational aspirations—and thus, indirectly, career aspirations—differ according to the social origins of those who express them. This uncontroversial generalization found confirmation, in the Soviet context, in social research that began in the 1960s. (The data it produced were very rich considering the times, are generally well known, and can be found in the Western literature.) When educational levels on the whole were still rather low, working-class youth expressed a lesser desire to continue from eighth grade into the "academic" ninth grade than did intelligentsia youth, and exhibited a greater readiness to combine work with part-time evening study: the respective ninth-grade aspirations were, for example, 30.3 versus 58.4 percent in a study in Sverdlovsk in 1965, while working-class youth were three times more ready (17.9 versus 5.4 percent) to combine work and study.[1] At the tenth-grade level, research into the plans of youth to attend or forgo higher education showed answers consistent with these. In one study 47 percent of intelligentsia children indicated the desire to go to a higher educational institution (vuz); only 16 percent of worker children did so.[2]

We are dealing with tender ages here: eighth graders, in a system where seven year olds enter first grade, were generally 15 years old when surveyed. If the aspirations of 1960s Sverdlovsk teenagers seem modest, we must remember that they were formed in a context where, despite their modesty, they would be hard to achieve. Soviet estimates indicate that in 1965 only 40 percent continued on to ninth grade, while 42.5 percent went directly to work, with the rest heading for *tekhnikum* or PTU.[3] In those late Khrushchev/early Brezhnev years, many went to work at a tender age—many more than wished to, even among working-class youth who were readier to do so than children of other classes.

Significant numbers of worker youth dropped out before eighth or tenth grade. In the 1960s research showed a falling share of working-class youth as one ascended the grades in the academic school track (years 1–11 to reach a "complete secondary" level in the Khrushchev period). In the six largest schools in the industrial city of Nizhni Tagil, studied in 1961–65, working youths' share fell from 72 percent in first grade to 60 percent in eighth grade, to 55 percent in ninth grade, and to 44.2 percent in eleventh grade.[4] Leningrad figures from 1968 showed, in the eighth-to-ninth-grade transition, a 46 percent increase in the share of intelligentsia children, but a fall of 10 percent among skilled and 54 percent among semi- and unskilled workers' children.[5]

Throughout the 1960s, eight years of full-time education in the general school was probably more than sufficient intellectual training for most Soviet jobs. Those who, at this point, opted neither for ninth grade nor *tekhnikum* but for work and part-time study or for the blue-collar "trade school" PTU, were, we may generally assume, aiming at or settling for a worker's career. They were mainly children of workers and peasants, with some admixture of people of lower white-collar origin, but very few from intelligentsia families.

For those working class youth who did find themselves in the final year of academic secondary school, however, aspirations toward other than a blue-collar job were clear. Research in 1965 in two districts in Sverdlovsk showed moderate differences between the VUZ aspirations of intelligentsia (90.9 percent) and worker (70.9 percent) children in a mainly working-class district, and virtually none (91.6 versus 89.1) in a mainly white-collar district. Independent of origin, 78.1 percent in the first and 90.3 percent in the second district aimed at higher education, while only 14.2 and 2.8 percent, respectively, were ready to go to work after the end of secondary schooling. A re-survey in the fall after graduation showed respective shares of 39.2 and 32.2 percent working. Entry into a VUZ was becoming more competitive for a more socially mixed group of secondary-school graduates than it had been earlier: the supply of spaces was below demand, while demand in the blue-collar sectors of the labor force had grown.[6]

Beyond this, however, class-origin differences played their own role in deciding who went on from secondary school to full-time higher education: the "demographics" did not affect all teenagers equally. Shubkin's pioneering studies in Novosibirsk in the early to mid-1960s used six origin categories, ranging from urban nonmanual to agricultural worker, and indicated much greater divergence in outcomes than in aspirations. Of urban nonmanual children, 93 percent wanted to continue in full-time schooling (VUZ and, presumably, some in postsecondary *tekhnikum*). Eighty-three percent of the children of industrial and construction workers, and 76 percent (the lowest) of agricultural workers' children wanted the same; however, the fulfillment rates were, respectively, 82, 61, and 10 percent. Workers' children were not nearly so disadvantaged as farm children but lagged well behind the children of the nonmanuals. (Of the latter, although only 2 percent had wanted to go to work full time, 15 percent actually did. Of workers' children, the 11 percent willing to work full time grew to 36 percent who actually worked, rather than went to school, in the fall.)[7]

Though Soviet teenagers in the 1960s were overfulfilling their own work-force aspirations, this was not the stuff of any demographic crisis. The economy readily absorbed manpower. If larger numbers than ever before stayed in school through the tenth and eleventh grades, many were leaving after the eighth year for the worker careers that awaited them. The numbers in the secondary-school graduating classes were too large to be accommodated in the vuzy. Aspirations were thus bound to remain unfulfilled. But this was, at the time, another matter. The main concern, judging by the focus of research and the tone of commentary, was more long term: the implications of a growing disinclination to settle for a working-class career in what seemed destined to be an overwhelmingly blue-collar economy for the foreseeable future. Not only children's aspirations but parental desires were playing a role in this. As the data on parents' hopes for their children, gathered in a survey of the Uralmash complex in Sverdlovsk in 1965, indicated, workers were hardly enthusiastic about passing on their vocations to their offspring: fully 64.9 percent aspired to see their children become specialists with higher education, and only 10.4 percent were willing to see them in a worker's career (intelligentsia parents expressed comparable aspirations, respectively, of 89 and 0.2 percent).[8]

Any large mobility out of the working class via higher education would have worked against hereditization. But statistical evidence of the 1960s shows that barriers stood in the way of working-class graduates of secondary academic schools in the vuz competition. Among intelligentsia children, better preparation, "test-wiseness," and other attributes made for better performance in entrance examinations. Already statistically overrepresented among those who took the entrance examinations, they increased their overrepresentation further in the composition of first-year vuz classes. For working-class applicants, the share of vuz entrants was smaller proportionally than their share of examination takers.[9] In addition, Soviet higher education divided into full-time day programs and evening and correspondence tracks. Working-class children were better represented in the latter two categories than in the first—but the rate of dropout in these two was much higher. Nor was it surprising that those predominantly worker and peasant youth who had completed *secondary* education on an evening basis, and then managed to enroll in higher education, were heavily in evening and correspondence studies rather than in the day divisions of vuzy.[10]

In the 1960s, then, plenty of working-class youth entered the world of their fathers. Dropouts after eighth grade (or before it) could hardly go elsewhere. But, despite some of the ideological claims of the time, the data suggest that, even then, few youth actively aspired to enter the world of the worker—save for peasant youth for whom, in the

1960s as earlier, it was actually the next step up. Much hereditization was involuntary. Nor had children of professional, white-collar background any desire to move downward. Significant numbers of worker youth entertained higher educational and occupational aspirations. Some, surely, made it: they were underrepresented, but not absent, from university and institute lecture halls. Many, however, fell short.

How intense were their aspirations? How did young people who, despite their ambitions, became workers in the 1960s—and later— deal with this sacrifice? These are important questions, though answers cannot be exact. Youth with only average grades must have had some awareness that they were not in a very competitive position for places in day vuzy and to expect admission was unrealistic. They had the alternative of attending the evening and correspondence classes. But finishing these programs with a degree was a harder, longer process, and many students left along the way. Did they feel cheated, alienated? Or did they see it as a confirmation that, as individuals, they did not quite cut it in a necessarily competitive system?[11] Or was it simply a matter of giving up an objective that was once attractive but probably unrealistic to begin with?

Again, the answer is probably mixed. Many, no doubt, felt frustration, but others probably did not see it as unjust that they became workers. They had plenty of company, and it is in this company that they would spend most of their working and socializing time. Soviet literature is replete with portrayals of the settling-in of young workers who had higher aspirations, their adjustment after a while to somewhat curtailed part-time educational plans, and finally the finding of their "place," along with a measure of satisfaction, in the life of factory and household.[12] But new issues would arise when, as workers, the recruits of the 1960s would confront problems in the 1980s.

The Brezhnev Era

As the 1960s gave way to the 1970s, patterns of education in the USSR changed radically. Some of the problems of educational aspiration, of supply and demand, that had marked the Khrushchev period surfaced again in a more complicated form. Table 3.1 offers an informed Soviet estimate of the pattern of dispersion of eighth-grade and tenth-grade graduates, respectively, in 1965, 1975, and 1980.

Several points are striking. Eighth-grade graduates (panel I) ended their educations in large numbers (42.5 percent) in 1965 and went to work, perhaps with an attempt to finish a ten- or eleven-year education on a part-time basis. Marginally fewer continued into the ninth

TABLE 3.1
Destinations of Eighth- and Tenth/Eleventh-Grade Graduates,
1965–80 (in percentages)

I. Eighth grade to:

	9th Grade	Tekhnikum	PTU	SPTU	Work
1965	40.0	5.2	12.3	—	42.3
1975	60.9	5.2	21.4	10.2	2.3
1980	60.2	6.2	13.8	19.3	0.5

II. Tenth/Eleventh grade to:

	Higher Education	Tekhnikum	TU	Work
1965	41.4	42.4	—	16.2
1975	15.8	16.0	12.9	55.3
1980	16.3	15.6	26.9	41.2

Source: Adapted from M. N. Rutkevich, "Reforma obrazovaniia, potrebnosti obshchestva, molodezh'," *Sotsiologicheskie issledovaniia*, no. 4 (1984), p. 24.

grade, while 12.3 percent pursued a trade school route that would not yield a high school diploma. By 1975 virtually none went to work, a solid majority entered ninth grade, and almost a third chose either the PTU trade school or the rapidly developing secondary PTU that offered, in a typically three-year course, vocational training and the high school diploma. The latter category grew markedly, to 19.3 percent, by 1980, while other categories were relatively stable.

Panel II tracks the high school graduates of the same years. Changes were remarkable. There was a threefold rise in those who went directly from academic pursuits to work between 1965 and 1975, then a drop in this figure as the "TU"—the program in the PTU/SPTU that offers to high school graduates a shorter vocational training—picked up increasing numbers. While more than two in five high school graduates entered full-time higher education in 1965, less than one in five followed the same route by 1975.

By all indications, the eighth-graders who went to work or PTU in 1965 were heavily of worker (and peasant) background—net contributors to the developing hereditization of the working class. Ten years later, many of them stayed in school to complete a full ten years. All that we know about the varying access to higher education by social origin suggests that solid majorities of the 55 percent in 1965 and the

41 percent in 1980 who went to work were of worker origin and thus made their "hereditary" contribution.

From the viewpoint of planners, how must the 1975 and 1980 figures have appeared? Six of every ten Soviet youths who finished eighth grade in the 1970s went on to a ten-year schooling system still structured to provide an essentially college-preparatory program. None had received anything like effective vocational training, yet over half went directly to work in 1975, and over 40 percent in 1980. Furthermore, 18.9 percent in the former and 42.5 percent in the latter year started learning a specialty in the same sort of institution they might have entered two years earlier. Such "waste" of a two-year exposure to a strictly academic and perhaps psychologically unfitting prelude to work must have seemed expensive in an economy that anticipated a labor shortage in 1975, and experienced it by 1980.

Were the high school graduates entering the labor force in the late 1970s willing entrants, or had they once nurtured hopes for higher education? Here, Soviet writers of the late Brezhnev era had a good deal to ponder, and the question provided grounds for debate and disagreement.

The data of the 1960s had shown that a large share of all tenth graders aimed at higher education. These data were taken as indicative of the national situation for a long time, and their implications seemed clear: more were oriented toward intelligentsia occupations by far— worker offspring among them—than the economy could accommodate. If Soviet educational policy had actually dictated expansion of places in the vuzy at a rate sufficient to accommodate a high percentage of the tenth-grade graduates that wanted them, the strain would have grown immense as completing ten years of schooling became much more normal for 17–18-year-olds.

This, of course, did not happen. Yanowitch's estimates (lower than Rutkevich's in the previous chapter) for annual full-time vuz admissions compared to the size of secondary-school graduations over three periods are eloquent in their testimony. From 1950 to 1953, about 65 percent of graduates went on to vuzy; during 1960–63, this number fell to 33 percent, and in the years 1970–73 to only 19 percent of graduates.[13] Thus, as the structure of secondary-school populations grew more representative of the society as a whole, the payoff from the investment of time declined in terms of higher education.

But did this mean a massive increase in frustrated aspirations? Such numbers tell us nothing about motivations of tenth-graders, or about possible changes between the 1960s and the world of the 1970s and 1980s. The numbers cited by most Soviet writers indicated a moderation of the desire to continue with higher education after the tenth grade. F. R. Filippov, in a 1977 article, noted that in the 1960s, 80–90 percent of tenth-grade graduates intended a direct transit to a vuz, but that the level of such aspirations had fallen, nationwide, to 46 percent in the 1970s.[14]

Slesarev cited a 70–90 percent level of vuz aspiration for the 1960s, and, in contrast, five 1973 city-based samples of tenth-graders that showed moderated aspirations for immediate continuation in full-time higher education, with Moscow the highest at 58.2 percent and Sverdlovsk/Nizhnyi Tagil the lowest at 47.8 percent.[15]

In a 1982 article, Bolotin and Chizhov cite an 80–90 percent aspiration figure for the 1960s, and a figure of almost 50 percent, on the basis of regional research, for the 1970s. The same article also claims that the ratio of applications to slots fell from 2.9:1 in 1966 to 2.3:1 in 1976, even though the number of ten-year-school graduates had grown.[16]

Other data that support a moderation of aspirations came from a 1977–79 study in "large industrial centers," including 3,177 "upper-classmen"—(ninth- and (?) tenth-graders). "vuz" and "prepare for vuz" added up to 45.5 percent, with another 14.9 percent favoring the tekhnikum and 12.9 percent the trade school (PTU/TU).[17]

If we assume that these figures are broadly an accurate reflection of expressed aspirations, what accounts for the fall-off from the 1960s? Slesarev argues that the addition to the upper secondary school grades of substantial working-class and peasant components reduced the percentage that had a strong orientation toward pursuing higher education, thus producing "a shift in the [proportional] relationship between groups with a maximal and minimal intensity of orientation toward higher education."[18]

But other writers doubt that an "aspiration decline" has really eased the problems of the large population of tenth-graders on the edge of what seems forced entry into the labor force. In 1983 a writer in *Sotsia-listicheskii trud* asserted that "it is known that today three-quarters of school graduates tie their life plans to a continuation of study in higher or specialized secondary institutions and only one-quarter to the acquisition of a worker's profession."[19] Posing the question as one not only of vuz aspirations but also of the *tekhnikum* focuses attention more effectively on the total dimensions of implied avoidance of a worker career over the short and long term. Research in the Lithuanian SSR in 1976 indicated more vuz aspirations among intelligentsia children than among those of workers, and less desire to enter the *tekhnikum*. Among worker youth, while more wanted to enter vuzy than *tekhnikums*, they were more ready for the latter than were intelligentsia children. Overall, rather similar numbers wished to extend their studies; few in either category looked toward near-future entry into full-time work.[20]

More pointed still was the 1983 argument of V. N. Turchenko, in the serious and widely read Novosibirsk journal *EKO*. Challenging the assertion that the decline in vuz orientation in the 1960s and 1970s was one from "80–90 percent" in the 1960s to "45 percent" in the mid-1970s, Turchenko raised the point of the *absolute numbers*, related to the labor force's needs and the size of the age group. He argued that in 1965, 913,000 people graduated from day secondary school; the sizable remainder of this age group was already working or receiving some vocational training in other institutions or settings. In 1975, 2.7 million day students graduated, nearly tripling the size of this population in a decade.[21] Allowing for some of the estimates of the percentage fall in vuz aspirations, he continued that "consequently, the orientation of this age group of youth toward vuzy, has, as a whole, not lessened but grown, and toward worker vocations, on the other hand, lessened. Research carried out in various regions of the country shows that the share of tenth-graders, oriented toward the vuz, was in the mid-1970s not 46 percent, but significantly higher—65–88 percent."[22] Turchenko added that including those aspiring to specialized secondary (*tekhnikum*) education would raise the number of those aiming at nonmanual work to 80–96 percent. Leaving the mid-1970s comparison point, he referred to the results of "representative" researches, in 1977 and 1980, which showed no large change in the tendencies he cited. "In particular, if, in 1977, 85 percent of tenth-graders planned to enter day vuzy or *tekhnikums*, and 14 percent to trade schools or work, then in 1980, respectively, [the figures were] 94 and 6 percent."[23]

No firm conclusion is really possible here. Regional variations in aspirations and performance are large, and some of the figures cited without further comment seem impossible compared to other figures. In 1981 tenth-graders in one Moscow *raion* were vuz-oriented to the level of 81.3 percent—quite believable; but the same study cited a 14.6 percent aspiration level for the country as a whole—*very* low indeed.[24]

There was no great goodness of "fit" between the aspirations of youth and the needs of the economy. The "readiness" of youth who originated "above" the working class to join it—stressed by some writers because some did descend—did not justify assertions that the workers' world was becoming more attractive. The paths elected by many youth of worker origin indicate that many of them had no great desire to follow their fathers, even if they were on the whole readier to settle for the blue-collar world than were children of the intelligentsia—not exactly a striking index of the success of Soviet vocational guidance and education. These had to contend with changing tastes and aspirations, hard to alter—and to work within the constraints imposed by the sorts of jobs available to workers. There were, and are, limits on the degree to which those jobs could exercise real attraction.

Jobs and Takers

As N. A. Aitov put it in 1966, only 12 percent of the Soviet working population was engaged in the sort of "mental work" for which ten-year schooling was a reasonable preparation. Through the 1970s, this share was scarcely able to rise above 30 percent[25]—hardly enough to satisfy the aspirations developing among teenagers increasingly likely to complete ten years of school.

The economy was heavy in blue-collar jobs, and the gradual reduction of the farm population was likely to increase their weight. Within the range of worker occupations, the upgrading and automation that might reduce the share of unskilled, arduous jobs proceeded slowly; one evidence was a rise of 150 percent in the number of "warehousemen, weighers, and packers" in Russian Republic industry between 1959 and 1969.[26] This growth continued in the 1970s. Of manual workers, 36.5 percent were in "heavy physical labor." Fully 7 million workers (outside the collective farms) were in loading and unloading, hoisting and freight handling in 1975—almost a million more than in 1965. In industry alone, 49 of 100 workers were "auxiliaries" in 1975—up from 46 in 1965.[27] For the economy as a whole the ratio of auxiliaries to "basic" workers was around 85:100 in the mid-1970s;[28] this compared to a 38:100 figure for the United States. While productivity of basic workers in the Soviet economy was (too optimistically) estimated at 70–75 percent of their American counterparts, that of auxiliaries was only 20–25 percent.[29] Such inefficiency imposed a heavy "tax" on the expensive Western technology the USSR imported in the 1970s. A 1980 report on utilization of imported chemical plants estimated that the USSR operated them with 1.5 times the number of basic workers required in their countries of origin, and with eight times the number of auxiliaries.[30]

Definitions and statistics in this area were sometimes confusing. A 1980 article, referring to the late 1970s, put the share of manual labor in industry at 41.9 percent; one in 1984 cited only 32.8 percent[31] of workers in industry in 1979 as doing "hand (*ruchnyi*) labor,"[32] but this was perhaps a more exclusive category of totally unmechanized physical labor. The figures in these ranges all indicated a persistence of job categories unattractive to a changing, better-educated labor force.

As an alternative locus of employment, the service sector presented problems as well. While seen by some as a key to upgrading the overall profile of jobs, it was growing slowly. As the economist V. Kostakov put it in mid-1974, the growth in numbers of "workers and employees" had been above plan in 1971–73, and the excess had all been in material production. Almost half of such growth for the whole of the ninth Five Year Plan (1971–75) was slated to occur in the service sector. Yet at the end of 1973, it had accounted for only a little over one third.[33] Whether growth in the service sector would signal any kind of upscaling was questioned in 1979. Noting that from 1965 to 1976 the share of workers producing "tangibles" had fallen only from 79.6 to 76.1 percent, N. A. Aitov asserted, on the basis of a ten-city survey, that workers in the slow-growing service sector were inferior by skill—60 percent unskilled in services, versus only 15–20 percent unskilled in industry.[34] All this stood in sharp contrast to a tone struck in the 1960s, which had hailed the effects of the coming "scientific-technical revolution," and had seemed to promise a rapid transformation of the classic poster-art proletarian, posed before smokestack and blast furnace, into a lab-coated pusher of buttons on automated control panels. In 1975, exploring the causes of low labor discipline among younger workers, Iu. P. Sosin estimated that "industry is able to provide only 30 to 35 percent of young workers with work on a par with their knowledge."[35] *Pravda*, in 1983, expressed reservations about excesses in touting the impact of technical progress. "The result of our sometimes dithyrambic extolling of future automation is that young people's reluctance to work with their hands is growing at a rate far greater (15 to 20 times as great, according to the most conservative estimates) than the rate at which modern technological marvels are being introduced."[36]

One could see the problem as (1) a failure of development in the occupational structure, and in the intrinsic "content" of jobs to keep pace with rises in educational levels; (2) an overinvestment in general academic education, out of line with the spectrum of jobs available; or (3) primarily as an attitude problem—the tendency of young people with a high school diploma to consider any working-class job "beneath" them. All of this made sense, all reflected the fact that average levels of education and average levels of jobs available, especially for young and entering workers and for worker-origin youth as well as those born into white-collar strata, were not very happily matched.

Overeducated as they might be, young people were also in the vast majority undertrained and unskilled. Graduates of the ten-year academic secondary school were going to work in large numbers—there was no other place for them. Of these, the vast majority lacked any relevant vocational training, any skill. As a writer in *EKO* put it in 1977, "educated youth are more demanding with regard to the nature of their jobs, the working conditions and the pay they receive. But 80 percent of them have had no vocational training, and they are often used in unskilled jobs or those calling for heavy labor."[37] Nor were they doing very well at them. A 1978 study found that the youngest workers (under age 22) in a range of plants lagged on nearly all indicators: fulfilling quantity and quality output targets, participating in socialist competition, observing labor discipline, relating well with their work collectives, and so on.[38]

The "overeducated-undertrained" syndrome had a long history. Khrushchev's abortive reform of 1958 had attempted to ensure that work training had a priority place for eighth-grade graduates. But neither the "polytechnicization" of complete secondary schools, nor the poorly equipped trade schools (PTU) really made an impact. Large numbers of 15-year-olds entered the labor force, to be sure, but generally to learn skills on the job.[39]

As the 1960s became the 1970s, and the numbers in ninth and tenth grade grew, the problem of providing vocational training and a familiarization with workers' habits shifted to the upper grades. In January 1977 the USSR minister of education, M. Prokofiev, projected that about 14 million people would complete secondary education in the 1976–80 period. Of these, 6.5 million would continue their education either in higher education, in the specialized secondary track (*tekhnikum*), or in a trade school for ten-year graduates—the TU (*tekhuchilishche*). But 7.5 million would go to work.[40] Later, in June of the same year, Prokofiev's deputy for labor training and vocational guidance wrote optimistically about the Interschool Production-training Combines (Mezhshkol'nye uchebno-proizvodstyennye kombinaty, or MUPK), organizations that serviced academic secondary schools with vocational training. These had grown from 250 nationwide in 1975 to about 500 by 1976–77, each serving an average of ten schools. Summer work training was growing as well: in 1974, about 7 million ninth- and tenth-graders had participated; in 1976, 10 million.[41]

The optimism was misplaced. A study reported in 1981 found vocational training in secondary schools (presumably of the MUPK variety) generally useless. Over three thousand students questioned reported that "work" was on the order of classroom cleaning and light repairs to school equipment (81.7 percent), picking up scrap metal (65.0 percent) and the like. Only 27 percent had had work training in the summer.[42]

Tenth-graders in Moscow secondary schools, surveyed on their career plans in 1981 and recontacted in 1982, supported this grim appraisal. The certificates of training issued by the MUPK's "had no force"; factories and plants generally found it necessary to retrain the newly hired in the same specialties ostensibly acquired in schools. When questioned if they wanted to work in or further study the vocation they were learning via the MUPK, only 14.2 percent answered yes, 50.9 percent no, and 34.9 percent had no response. In the 1982 assessment of actual outcomes (presumably among the percentage of all graduates who had entered the labor force), 23.9 percent were working in the area of their training, 13.1 percent partly so, and 63 percent reported there was no relation between their jobs and their MUPK training.[43]

Nor did they stay on the job for long. A 1975–76 study of 23,000 workers in the Russian republic found that 34 percent of all new workers who had graduated from tenth grade left the job within one year, joined by another 16 percent in the second and 7 percent in the third year.[44] In 1983 young workers were still exhibiting itchy feet—some in finding a new job, some in the hope that a second chance would allow them to depart for a higher educational institution (vuz) or tekhnikum.[45]

In all, through the early 1980s, there were few signs of impending change, in reality or policy, in the "material production" emphasis in the economy. Unskilled handwork might gradually decline, but the future seemed to hold the prospect that assembly-line jobs would grow, offering little by way of enhanced work content. Blue-collar labor productivity remained low. It seemed likely that it would continue to require a large number of workers to produce what the Soviet economy produced.

With the advent of Gorbachev, the tone changed, reflecting many concerns expressed by economists in specialized journals in the later Brezhnev years. The service sector's perennial weaknesses were now authoritatively linked with the economy's lackluster performance as a whole—it was slated for growth and upgrading. "Material production"—talisman of the prereform economy—came to be seen as an expensive, inefficient absorber of manpower. The economist Kostakov projected that under reform, 13–19 million jobs would be cut from material production by the year 2000;[46] he then had to assure a public, still capable of shock in 1986, that this would not mean unemployment.[47] Other economists by and large held to this scale in projecting reallocation of labor by the end of the century.[48] The service sector, and the most efficient and high-tech areas of material production, were slated to grow. Soviet workers would, evidently, bear many of the overhead costs of reallocation. All this was controversial. Even with employment guarantees, as Kostakov put it, men would have to look for jobs rather than expect jobs to look for them. Whether the remainder of jobs in material production and in new service-sector jobs would better match the desires and expectations of Soviet workers was—and remains—a question.

Part of the answer depends on the kinds of workers the system produced—on how well the system of vocational training, outside the lackluster elements offered in academic school, works.

The Vocational Track

The development of a vocational school track[49] began, effectively, with Stalin's establishment of the State Labor Reserves (SLR) system in 1940, whereby 800,000 to one million youth aged 14–17 were mobilized annually for training and work. The need was clear—the labor-draft program (Orgnabor) had typically sent untrained peasant hands into industry; academic schools offered neither more nor better vocational training than they would later.

Under the SLR system, the FZU (uchilishche) offered two-year courses, generally to those who had completed the seven years of schooling which then counted as "incomplete secondary" education. The more modest FZO provided courses of less than one year's duration and catered to people who were headed for the least skilled jobs. Degrees of compulsion in recruitment varied. In the FZU, half the intake of 1946 was "mobilized"; conscription for these was ended by 1951. The less attractive FZO, however, drafted 70 percent of its intake in 1946, and was still compelled to draft nearly one-third of its students into the mid-1950s.

The SLR system focused primarily on youth from worker and peasant strata. While at the time no large share of Soviet 14-year-olds was going on to the eighth to tenth grades or to the tekhnikums, Stalin's resolve further intensified social selection after the seventh grade. In 1940 tuition fees were imposed both for higher education and for the eighth to tenth grades of academic schools and tekhnikums. The charges involved were not large for the better-fixed bureaucrats who would continue to send children to school, but they were large enough to make further academic education impossible for those whose families would already have faced hardships without having the potential income of a young worker. As a Western expert writes, "the balance of social priorities so revealed requires no comment."[50]

The SLR intake reflected its social aims. Rural youth made up 51.4 percent of recruits in 1946, 67.2 percent in 1947, and was still as high as 49.3 percent in 1954, according to data from Sverdlovsk. In that city, the makeup by social origin of students (shares of nonmanual/worker/collective farmer) were 7.1/52.1/40.7 percent in the 1947–48 school year and 3.1/68.1/18.2 percent in 1957–58 (the missing 10.6 percent is not explained).[51]

Khrushchev abolished the State Labor Reserves system in 1959, replacing it with the USSR State Committee on Vocational and Technical Education (Gosprofobra).[52] The old SLR schools were merged into a new institution on the FZU model: the vocational-technical school (*professional'no-tekhnicheskoe uchilishche*), or PTU. It provided a vocational education for those who had completed "incomplete secondary" education, now eight years; it did not issue a secondary diploma. The period of training varied; two years was typical. Like the FZU, the PTU was often attached to a sponsoring factory or plant and still tended to draw from worker (and peasant) youth. In the 1962–63 school year in Sverdlovsk, the nonmanual/worker/collective farmer origin ratio was 12.9/74.4/9.7.[53]

The PTU had reputation problems. Its students came to be thought of as delinquents, "rubes," and low-lifes by the increasingly bourgeoisified upper strata. PTU attractiveness was low, complicating the Gosprofobra plan. Targets for admittance to the PTUs were still underfulfilled in 1972 by 26 percent, in 1974 by 19 percent. Academic school administration and staff salaries depended in some measure on the numbers enrolled; there was thus a reluctance to send orderly, "good" eighth-graders into the PTU.[54] Complaints that academic secondary schools competed with PTUs and indeed were encouraged to do so by the academic-financial logic that defied pro-PTU policy pronouncements continued through the 1970s. The PTUs in the RSFSR and the Ukraine were undersubscribed in the early 1970s.[55] An *EKO* article in 1977 despaired of academic secondary schools directing sufficient numbers into the PTUs since they faced "high plan targets for admissions to ninth grade"[56] themselves.

Socially and academically, and in career orientation, a large gulf divided the experience of students in academic secondary schools and those in the PTU. Experiments in bridging the gap by combining the two into an all-purpose institution dated back to the 1950s. One report cites 1956 as the year in which the PTU (FZU) program was first merged with a full secondary education (over a 3–4-year period) in Leningrad, Sverdlovsk, Riga, and "other cities."[57] A 1978 source identifies a PTU in Krasnogorsk (Moscow *oblast'*) as one of the "very first": operating since 1956;[58] another claims that the "first SPTU [for *srednee*, or secondary PTU] in the USSR" was opened at the end of the 1950s: PTU no. 68

in Leningrad, under the Kozitskii Production Association.[59] (Wherever the "patent rights" lay, Leningrad did take the lead later in developments that would see, for a time, major SPTU changes.)

Though not without shortcomings, the combined schools did tend to receive more bouquets than brickbats. From 1966 on, the USSR State Committee on Vocational and Technical Education grew in resources and clout, and the SPTU was pushed as a solution both to the overload of combining PTU and evening academic education, and to the disinclination of students toward work thought to develop in the purely academic ninth and tenth grades. It was also seen as a way of providing usable skills along with an educational foundation that would permit further skill development and mastery of new specialties on the job.[60]

The end of the 1960s saw moves toward an expansion of the SPTU as a mass alternative to the academic school. On April 18, 1968, *Pravda* reported that the party's Central Committee and the Council of Ministers considered necessary the transformation of current PTUs into institutions with a three- to four-year program that combined training in "the most complex professions" with a full secondary education. There should "already" have been 50,000 students in such institutions, and by 1975 the number of first-year students was projected to reach 300,000.[61]

A joint party-state decree of April 2, 1969,[62] put the force of law behind the program to convert existing PTUs into SPTUs. Model curricula for three- and four-year programs for various occupational specialties were published,[63] and the number of reorganized schools began to grow rapidly. A. Bulgakov, then chairman of the USSR State Committee on Vocational and Technical Education, reported in 1971 that 5,350 PTUs contained 2.4 million students, and 660 SPTUs held about 200,000[64]—a major increase over 1969. In 1976 the SPTUs graduated 205,000, and in 1978 a vastly increased 447,000.[65] By the 1979–80 academic year, large numbers of eighth-grade graduates were entering SPTUs, some of whom previously would have been in PTUs.

But were there significant numbers entering SPTUs who would otherwise have stayed in the straight academic track? While some Western observers suggested that this was the case,[66] it seems dubious. According to one Soviet estimate, only about 28 percent of 1982 eighth-graders moved on to the SPTU, versus 61.5 percent who entered ninth grade.[67] In its earlier years, certainly, there had been a lack of enthusiasm for the SPTU. For many, not drawn to the "complete secondary" academic school, the PTU, with a shorter course, seemed preferable to the SPTU. In a 1973–74 study (when SPTUs were newer and fewer) of about 11,000 eighth-graders, social differences affected their intention to go on to ninth grade, but enthusiasm was moderate for the SPTU, even among workers' children. Only a third of these aimed at ninth grade (versus 60 percent of white-collar children), but 23.9 percent were ready for a PTU, work, or evening school, while only 13.6 percent elected the SPTU.[68] Independent of social origin, those who intended to become skilled workers opted marginally in favor of ninth grade in an academic school over an SPTU (28.5 versus 27.1 percent).[69]

As the 1970s proceeded and PTUs became SPTUs, low aspirations probably came to have a less selective effect. Willy-nilly, many youth were placed in programs that promised a diploma as well as a skill. One observer noted that the SPTU, with respect especially to the academic part of its program, had peculiarities that might affect those who were initially more motivated:

> It might indeed be claimed that Soviet boys have been "cooled out" to excess. Once they have taken up PTU or *tekhnikum* courses they seem to abandon higher educational ambitions, even though the new general-education component of the curricula supposedly keeps open the chance of eventual VUZ entry. Perhaps this is not so surprising, as several Soviet commentators have pointed out, when skilled manual workers are as much in demand as graduate engineers and can command wages as high as, or even higher, than the latter. Moreover, the standard of teaching and attainment in the general-education part of PTU programmes is acknowledged to be much inferior to that in regular secondary schools and hardly constitutes an adequate preparation for entry to higher education. Because of these considerations, not to mention the obligation on PTU and *tekhnikum* graduates to complete a compulsory work assignment after training or to be subject to military call-up, the vocational track effectively rules out or considerably reduces the chances of acquiring higher education after it.[70]

But it seems clear that it was precisely a reduction of orientations toward higher education that was a target of SPTU development. The notion to equip job-bound 18-year-olds with job skills is sensible; just as "sensible" was an attempt to get ideas of higher education out of their heads. "Much inferior" academic training means that the SPTU gives a diploma, but not an education. It is not a better-organized equivalent of a ten-year academic secondary school with more serious vocational training than the earlier-mentioned *kombinaty* provided for academic students. It is not, and cannot be, all things to all. The SPTU began with a questionable pedigree. But the statistical impact of the changes after 1969 was great. In the words of one Western expert, the "level of general secondary education in the vocational-technical schools has always been shockingly low, but the number of people officially credited with possessing a full secondary education grew enormously as a result of" the addition of the academic program to the PTU.[71]

What motivated those who chose to go to an SPTU in the 1970s? It is hard to assume that it involved a change of heart, an increasing appreciation of workers' professions, even of the fact that young skilled workers can outearn young degree holders: this, after all, had been the case for some time. Some, surely, entered the SPTU because they found a trade-school-with-diploma more attractive than a trade school without one. Few can realistically have seen them as alternative paths to a VUZ.

But even with respect to their vocational objectives, the trade schools suffered from underinvestment and what critics called "poor vocational guidance": in the city of Ashkhabad in 1977, the city was supposed to direct more than two thousand eighth-grade graduates into the trade schools, versus three thousand to ninth grade. Although the academic schools made their quota, only six hundred pupils actually reported to the trade schools.[72] Low grades through the eighth year and a general weakness in basic educational preparation were noted as impediments to trade school students' mastery of "highly skilled" specialties in a 1977–79 study.[73] A 1982 study in a metallurgical plant in Krivoi Rog, and of its attached PTUs, showed that only 20 percent of graduates who came to work in the plant were still there after six years. While they were in trade school, 46 percent of them had not been pleased with the specialty they were learning, and on-the-job evaluators concluded that 44 percent of the PTU graduates had not received training adequate for their work. The graduates were themselves less than enthusiastic about their jobs: 40 percent reported themselves as "unsatisfied," and an additional 15 percent were "very unsatisfied," with their work in the plant.[74]

By the late 1970s the economy's flagging growth, the looming manpower shortage, and the lack of skills among 17–18-year-olds entering the work force spurred policy discussions about reshaping the educational system. Two emergent viewpoints were clear by the early 1980s. According to one side,

> The considerable reduction in the size of the able-bodied population in the next 10–15 years will necessitate a sharp increase in the admission of eighth-grade graduates of general education school to secondary vocational-technical schools, coupled with a corresponding reduction in admissions to the ninth grade and to secondary specialized educational institutions. The distribution of graduates of the eighth grade of general educational schools among various levels of education in Leningrad is taken as the model of differentiation of secondary education in the year 1990. According to this

variant of distribution, half of the eighth-grade graduates continue their studies in secondary vocational-technical schools while the other half attend the ninth grade of general education school.[75]

In essence, such a projection promised—given the nationwide figures—something on the order of a reduction from 60-plus percent continuing on to ninth grade to 50 percent—not a radical change.

> There is also another point of view. Its proponents propose that the percentage of admissions of eighth-grade graduates to the ninth grade of secondary school remain virtually stable in the next 10–15 years (at the 60 percent level). This view assumes a moderate increase in admissions to secondary vocational-technical schools chiefly as a result of the gradual reduction of the admission of eighth-graders to secondary specialized educational institutions and the conversion of admissions to the latter to include the tenth grade. In the training of worker cadres for the immediate future, the basic emphasis is placed on accelerating the development of technical schools with an abbreviated course of study and on admitting tenth-grade graduates to these schools.[76]

In this alternative, post-tenth-grade vocational training was emphasized. First, it would increase the share of admissions to the specialized secondary *tekhnikums* after tenth grade. Such admissions were about 1.5 times those from eighth grade in 1977,[77] and youth who chose the *tekhnikums* after tenth-grade were obviously less likely to aim at higher education down the road than eighth-grade graduates who chose to get their secondary diploma through this route.[78] Second, admissions to the TU (*tekhuchilishche*) would also rise. The latter were, typically, one-year programs offering accelerated PTU-type vocational training to youth who had academic diplomas and the inclination to train for skilled-worker jobs.

The pros and cons of each approach were evident. The first variant might focus the attention of youth on a job, a specific job, and help "overcome the one-sided orientation of youth, parents, and the [academic] school toward higher education";[79] industrial regions especially sensitive to the labor supply issue would favor an emphasis on the SPTU. However, major expenses were to be anticipated in developing these SPTUs if a "lowering of the general educational levels of young people"[80] was to be averted. "Sociological resistance" from parents who could support their children, did not need their work contributions, and favored the academic school could also be anticipated.

The second alternative's strengths lay in preservation of educational quality through preeminence of the ten-year school and its consequent provision for more tailored vocational programs thereafter. It also demanded less new expenditures from the state. But, as the same source put it, it did not really respond to the hard problems that had generated the discussion to begin with.

> Nonetheless, under the second variant it is far more difficult to resolve the worker-cadre problem than under the first, since the "sociological aversion" of young people with secondary education to mass occupations involving primarily physical labor is significantly stronger than among graduates of incomplete secondary schools. The successful realization of this variant requires a large complex of social and economic measures to implant in the social consciousness the social equality of various types of labor. This requires the appropriate material prerequisites: the implementation of a broad program of comprehensive mechanization and automation of production making it possible to eliminate heavy physical labor and all manner of unskilled labor and to secure radical improvement in the organization of labor-training and vocational guidance. But it is impossible to do this in a short period of time.[81]

By the early 1980s, high-level work was under way toward a major reform of the USSR's educational system. The "school versus SPTU" issue was not the only reform issue to be addressed. But the reform, when it emerged in 1984, would speak eloquently to the education-versus-training issue.

The 1984 School Reform

In the four months of January to April 1984, the draft of a comprehensive school reform was published,[82] subjected to "mass public discussion" in the Soviet manner, and, in a flurry of publicity surrounding the Central Committee plenum on April 10 and the session of the Supreme Soviet on April 12, was finally adopted in a series of party-state decrees.[83]

The prospect of a reform package emerged clearly at the June 1983 Central Committee plenum, when General Secretary Iurii Andropov called for "serious thought" on school reform, including the vocational and technical sector.[84] A commission to draft reform proposals, chaired by Chernenko (who then occupied the "second secretary" slot in the Politburo), was formed thereafter.

As adopted in April 1984, the final version promised to have a remarkable impact on the paths to be followed by those leaving the ninth grade. The reform decreed the reorganization of the various vocational institutions into a single type: essentially, the SPTU, with two-year programs (a tenth and new eleventh grade, following upon *nine* years of academic schooling as the new "incomplete secondary" norm) encompassing vocational training and a complete secondary education. The radical point was the specification of a target number of those who could attend: "The number and proportion of ninth-grade graduates entering secondary PTUs will in the future approximately double. In this matter the specifics of different regions, of urban and rural areas, should be taken into account."[85] If the proportion going to the SPTU were to double, the implication was that the number and share of youth continuing their academic secondary education in the tenth and eleventh grades would fall. Anticipated and perceived sensitivity to this drop among Soviet parents, students, and the teaching staff of academic schools—and consequent lobbying—probably accounts for part of the difference between the draft document and the final version. In the draft, the basic decisions determining who and how many would go where were to be made in connection with the "national economy's requirements, and with consideration for the pupils' desires, inclinations and abilities."[86] This stark assertion of state interest, weakly modified by the "with consideration" qualifier, was softened by further text specifying that "the parents' wishes and the recommendations of the teachers' councils of schools"[87] would also be taken into account.

This provision was a tough version of the first "variant" in educational thought discussed earlier, and it seemed to promise major change. If we take the figures on the dispersion of eighth-grade graduates in 1980 provided by Rutkevich (see table 3.1), eliminate as marginal the 0.5 percent who went to work directly, and if we assume that they are likely SPTU candidates and that the share of eighth-grade graduates going to the secondary specialized *tekhnikum* remains about the same, at 6.2 percent, we get the figures in table 3.2. Alternative estimates from several Soviet sources for the 1979–80 school year have slightly larger shares of eighth-graders moving into *tekhnikums* and the PTU, and smaller shares into ninth grade. If one combines PTU and SPTU entrance for reform and school consolidation purposes the results are essentially similar.[88]

The reform was designed to ensure that all Soviet youth continue on to obtain a high school diploma, via the academic secondary school, the new SPTU, or the *tekhnikum*. The upbeat connotations were stressed in a discussion that focused on the earlier problems of students in the trade school system:

Almost four-fifths of the pupils in secondary vocational-technical training schools receive, as a rule, grades that are not higher than "3" [indicating

TABLE 3.2
Destinations of Eighth-Grade
Graduates in 1980, and Potential
Destinations under 1984 Reform
(in percentages)

Destination	1980	Reform
9th grade	60.2	27.1
SPTU	19.3	66.7 (SPTU)
PTU	13.8	
Tekhnikum	6.2	6.2
Total	99.5	100.0

Note: See text for discussion.

"satisfactory" performance] for the general education subjects, and some-times this mark even overstates their actual level of knowledge. Some young people who complete the old kind of vocational-technical training school, which does not offer a secondary education, are even less knowl-edgeable. The reform envisages that "the diverse types of vocational and technical educational institutions that presently exist are to be reorganized into a single type of educational institution—the secondary vocational-technical training school." In this way, the entire younger generation of the working class will be lined up evenly at "the societal starting line."[89]

But lined up evenly with whom? Those who would still attend the academic secondary school? It was clear what the reform had to do with recruitment to the working class. The SPTU was not meant to multiply the career options of adolescents by providing a secondary academic diploma to those who would not otherwise earn one, but to direct them earlier toward the working class. Who would "escape"? Presumably, those whose academic qualifications, tutoring, and so on would allow them to pass through the narrow gate into the academic track for the final two years of secondary education. These were likely to be disproportionately those favored by social origin: by the educa-tional and occupational levels of their parents, the per capita income of the household, the readiness to spend money on supplementary training, by encouragement of academic effort—even the use of influ-ence to affect the "teachers' council" recommendations. In this com-petitive context, the children of workers would be disadvantaged. This would remain especially true of sons, who were in general more likely than daughters to opt for the PTU/SPTU route.

If the SPTU was seen as a way of producing youth suitable for the labor force and happy, or at least willing, to stay in their work, this perception was not necessarily without some warrant. A study in three factories in Nizhnyi Tagil in the mid-1970s concluded that SPTU graduates made a better adjustment to factory life than ten-year academic graduates or the products of the "regular" PTU. The SPTU graduates were more satisfied with being workers (57 percent) than were their academic peers (38 percent). The desire to change one's status via part-time study reflected this satisfaction: of the academic graduates, 18.2 percent were studying part-time or by correspondence in vuzy, compared to only 5.6 percent of the SPTU products (22.9 percent of the latter were studying part-time in secondary specialized institutions while working, but only 19.17 percent of the former).[90]

Did SPTUS represent a social milieu conducive to conceiving of oneself as a future worker? Research in Leningrad on the friendship patterns of youth in various educational tracks stressed the diversity of social contacts of SPTU students: 35.2 percent reported friendships with SPTU peers, 19.3 percent with children in other secondary schools; their contacts with young workers were cited as twice as great as with secondary-school students (presumably 38.6 percent). If this is accurate, the sum of contacts with workers and the SPTU peers adds to 73.8 percent—an indication, if anything, of the degree of closure rather than diversity in the social world of the SPTU trainees.[91]

Despite the rhetoric about even lineups at the societal starting line, such closure was no drawback for those who prevailed in the design of the 1984 reform. They had not hesitated to deny that the increasing self-reproduction of classes meant a hardening of the social structure. As one wrote in 1984, this did not mean "stablization" of social structure, but simply reflected "a conscious resolution of youth to choose the same area of activity as that of their parents."[92] The same author noted that in some circumstances parents' aspirations were less realistic than either the children's desires or the economy's needs: in one study reported in 1979, while 5.4 percent of a group of tenth-graders were willing to become workers, only 2.9 percent of their parents approved; 41.3 percent of the same group aimed at a vuz, while 59.4 percent of parents desired this.[93] All in all, what was most impressive was the tiny number showing any desire to become workers.

"Selling" the Reform

In 1984 Soviet politics was still "Soviet politics" rather than the disorderly and contentious free-for-all it later became. Party-state approval of the reform thus obviated the need for any plebiscite, any attempt to convince the public. (The realization that there was now a real "public," indeed *many* publics, at least potentially, as a product of the slow but sure development of a more complex society with variegated aspirations and senses of just expectations, had not yet become a premise of policy, however much it already figured in the thoughts of sociologists and economists.) Still, the fate of Khrushchev's reform and the lack of clear result in other social policy initiatives of the Brezhnev era suggested the utility of assuring society that the reform was sensible and fair. The selling process focused on a denial that administrative selection onto the SPTU track was, really, forced or carried negative social connotations. In a speech to the Supreme Soviet session of April 13, 1984, Deputy Prime Minister Aliev noted that the Politburo's reform commission had found "impracticable" suggestions that after ninth grade (which would be the last year of incomplete secondary schooling under the reform), admission to academic secondary schools be made "competitive."

> Apparently, the correct premise to adopt here is that all ninth-grade graduates should be given an equal chance to complete their secondary education. They can continue their studies in the tenth grade [of a general education school], enter a vocational-technical training school or a secondary specialized educational institution—but let him choose for himself, giving due consideration to both his own inclinations and capabilities and to society's requirements, though parents and educational collectives are expected to help him make the correct choice.[94]

Of course, given the language of the reform, it was hard to see how the process of moving on from ninth grade would be anything *but* "competitive." Central Committee secretary Mikhail Zimianin contributed some triumphal rhetoric, and a backhanded acknowledgment of some of the problems of presenting the SPTU to the public: the trade schools, "with their monumental and glorious history, provide an excellent schooling for young people going into the world of work." Still, it was also "necessary to contend with the inertia that has been generated by some persistent misconceptions about the vocational-technical education system's role and place in our society and about the vocational-technical training school's putatively 'second rate' standing among educational institutions."[95] These were, after all, "equal," since "vocational-technical training school alumni wishing to enroll in higher educational institutions will be put at no disadvantage in comparison with secondary [general education] school pupils."[96] Indeed, this theme was offered as a major point that party propaganda lecturers could stress. As their "guidance" magazine *Politicheskoe samoobrazovanie* put it,

The vocational-training education system, in addition to training skilled worker cadres, fills another, no less important, role. As the reform progresses, the societal base of higher education intake will be significantly broadened by graduates from the vocational-technical education system, which means that more of the young men and women accepted into higher educational institutions will already have made a responsible and aware choice of occupation [by the time of admission].[97]

In the typical "readers' letters" press discussions of the draft reform principles, some had considered tracking into the SPTU as necessary and rational. Others had been opposed, on grounds ranging from broad social-educational concerns to the narrower ones of worry about their own children's path. The first deputy minister of education in the Belorussian republic argued the instrumental view: schools should "issue recommendations to [ninth-year] graduates for a certain type of educational institution and occupation . . . but in such a way that these recommendations have binding force."[98] In clear disagreement, an engineer argued that the 15-year-old boys who made up the vast majority of the 40 percent who now went to the PTU after eighth grade were not ready to be serious about learning a skill. If the decision on "direction" to an SPTU were to be made on academic performance alone, the fact that so many adolescent boys were not yet serious about academic work would guarantee that *all* tracked out of the academic school would be boys; he advocated the degree of free-choice "voluntarism" provided in the prereform system.[99] But another engineer applauded the "early start" on a career the reform would give, and he asserted—against the evidence—that it was "high time to abandon, once and for all, the view of the vocational-technical school as a second-rate educational institution where the [general-education] schools send their below-average pupils."[100]

In somewhat similar fashion, the vice chairman of the Belorussian SSR's State Committee for Vocational-Technical Education attacked the presumption against trade schools, argued the anti-elitist point that graduates of the SPTU should be given preference in admission to vuzy, and complained that, instead, "we divide the pupils beforehand into those who will be connected mainly with the working class and those who are headed for the ranks of the intelligentsia."[101] The establishment of that working-class connection through the PTU involved, for many parents, fears of their children associating with what *Literaturnaia gazeta* admitted were "incorrigibles" in the public mind: PTU students "openly smoke, use foul language, and skip classes."[102] Those who toiled in the groves of academic education had themselves been propagators of the image.[103]

TABLE 3.3

Student Opinion on Increase in Intake at sptus
(in percentages)

	Academic School Students	Special School Students	Construction sptu Students	Trade sptu Students
Agree	4	14	70	52
Disagree	28	55	13	15
Hard to say	48	31	17	33

Source: See note 105.

More systematic evidence of a generally cool reception came from public opinion studies. In a survey of about sixteen hundred people in various Russian republic cities and regions, three-quarters of the respondents approved the reform directive on doubling the number of students in the sptu, "in principle."

> However, when the question is transferred from the plane of abstract propositions into the sphere of personal interests, many expressed more reserved estimates of the ptu. Obviously, here the low prestige of these educational institutions, which has developed in mass consciousness, is having an influence, even though in recent years the material base of ptus, as well as pupils' attitudes toward them, has improved.[104]

Another, smaller survey of parents, students, and teachers in one regular academic secondary school, another that taught in a foreign language (a *spetshkola*, for academically advanced and typically privileged teenagers), and two sptus, all in Moscow, showed much more reserve on the part of students in academic schools than in sptus about the increase in intake of the sptus.[105] (See table 3.3.) Parents in the same study were rather noncommittal, and even working-class parents were far from a ringing endorsement of the planned increase in sptu enrollment (see table 3.4).

How rapidly the full force of the reform would be felt in the redirection of 15-year-olds was a matter of some confusion. Zimianin had "envisaged . . . in the immediate future" the doubling of sptu intake.[106] This projection was improbable and inaccurate. The fall 1985 target figures indicated that 57.6 percent of graduates of eighth grade were to enter general academic ninth grades—hardly a major cut from the years of the recent past.[107] The conversion of ptus to sptus was to proceed rapidly, but with "quality considerations" paramount. Still, in 1986, articles in the main organ of trade school education focused

TABLE 3.4
Parental Opinion on Increase in SPTU Intake
(in percentages)

Opinion	Worker	Lower White-Collar	Specialist
Agree with increased intake	36	50	28
Disagree	12	24	25
Hard to say	52	26	47

Source: See table 3.3.

on the lack of preparation, the unfitness of some current PTUs for SPTU conversion.[108] This, surely, was to be expected, given the long-derided status of PTUs and the gulf that existed between the preferences of the people and the decision makers and advisers whose dedication, as Jerry Hough had eloquently put it earlier, "to vocational education for all teenagers is tempered by the fact that few want their own children and grandchildren to have to spend much time on that type of education."[109] The whole project would not work.

The End of Reform

By 1988 the reform, insofar as it dictated the forced march into the SPTU, was dead. Its gradual demise had taken place in public. There was no surprise when decision makers admitted early on that problems existed in converting PTUs into SPTUs, but complaints and objections had marked the reform from the outset. Schools were still gladly sending their lackluster students to the SPTU, as one writer noted in late 1986.[110] A. P. Dumachev, who had been appointed the new chairman of the USSR State Committee on Vocational-Technical Education in early 1986, was, by late 1987, also attacking central aspects of the reform. In one interview he asked where the idea of doubling SPTU enrollments had come from and complained that students were being forced into the SPTU.[111] Later he called the certification of high school completion a "sham diploma" and observed that the linking of academic and vocational education was a failure.[112] In this he joined the head of the Russian Republic Gosprofobra, who had earlier admitted that the SPTU did not really offer academic secondary education.[113] Finally, then CPSU second secretary Egor Ligachev, in a February 1988 speech to a Central Committee plenum, complained that the

SPTU push had led to an arbitrary fall in the numbers going into ninth grade. Vocational training should be, he noted, organized on the base of academic training, but that it should follow rather than be combined with it.[114]

The reform's windup was hardly, of course, a major theme in the politics of 1986–88; it was a very minor chord in the new composition of glasnost', perestroika, and the excitement, confusion, and alarm of the Gorbachev era. It was a time when, clearly, the relevance of a more complex, less malleable society, of group interests and the resources to defend those interests, was recognized by a leadership that realized, at least to some degree, how little it knew about the society it was trying to lead into new territory. (It was also still a time when surgery on organizational structures was a major emphasis: on March 8, 1988, Gosprofobra, as well as the Ministries of Education and of Higher and Specialized Secondary Education were abolished and replaced by a new USSR State Committee on Public Education.[115]) But the rejection of the forced march to the SPTU was not openly based on any grounds of equity per se, on any sensitivity to its likely forcing of workers' children into an essentially vocational track. More in the forefront was criticism of the low quality of vocational training and the dilution of academic content in the SPTU. "Self-selection"—and social processes—would again operate "spontaneously." Was this a sort of "benign neglect"? As discussions of the reform had grown more critical in 1987, suggestions were made that compulsory academic schooling might best be limited to nine years[116] (the new "incomplete secondary" point): those who went only that far would, of course, have no diploma. The new head of the merged State Committee on Public Education made this point more clearly in an interview shortly after taking the job, announcing plans to "abandon the drive toward a compulsory secondary education for all. If a young man or girl wants to learn certain skills and become a high-class worker, it's only to be welcomed."[117] Thirty years on, there is perhaps more than a bit of Khrushchevian thinking here: a readiness to assume that those who will opt for less schooling in connection with career plans that do not require more are to be encouraged. But Khrushchev, however crudely, stood as a populist in his attempts to reduce the dominance of privileged children in higher education; there is nothing of this in the reversal of the 1984 reform. It no doubt relieved the fears of middle-class parents that offspring might be forced into the SPTU, but it left undisturbed the combination of social class-selection and self-selection that reduces the number of worker offspring who complete secondary education; among these, those who apply to higher educational institutions; among these, those who get admitted. Thus, by itself the fall of the reform leaves, as before, the dynamics of privilege and liability that have already contributed to the hereditization of both the working class and the intelligentsia.

At the same time, however, it looms as a potential part of what may later come to be seen as a "de-credentializing" of access to economic opportunity in the USSR. As the years 1988–90 have shown, the real money is not to be made on a professional's salary or on a worker's wages (even high wages) but as an entrepreneur—in the new individual and cooperative sectors. Opportunity in these sectors comes to those with degrees as well as to those without; entrepreneurial skills, and luck, have a good deal to do with success. It is still a bit early to tell, however, whether, a social origin that leads to higher education also leads to the private sector and large rewards more often than does worker origin. As we shall see later, what is clear is that "cooperators" have generated a great degree of egalitarian public resentment, in which a large segment of the working class shares.

Education, Training, and Class

Despite the lengthy treatment we have accorded them, education and the associated issues dealt with here have not been major agenda items for Gorbachev and other Soviet leaders, who have had many more pressing matters to concern them.

Still, the sorting processes discussed here *are* important. They make, in clear ways, distinctions between those headed for workers' careers and others—before those careers have begun. Systematic and unsystematic evidence of patterns of deployment of eighth-grade graduates, of friendship patterns, of the durable negative public image of vocational schools indicates social processes that convince a substantial number of male youth that they are future workers even before they go to work. Some, we may assume, follow this path readily. Others may hanker after educations and careers that are finally denied them. In both cases, such selection produces elements of class identity; one "knows" that one is, or will be, a worker.

That so much evidence speaks to greater aspirations of worker youth and their parents may also signify potential for class opposition, born not only of the experience of the adult worker versus authority on the shop floor, but of the consciousness that the game rules of educational selection were set against the higher aspirations of blue-collar youth. A large "they"—bureaucrats, perhaps "intelligentsia"—set these rules: "we" cannot affect them, "we" fall short of the competitive standards "they" have concocted. Oppositional attitudes may also find fertile soil in the confrontation of young men who have eight or ten years of schooling, with or without PTU training, and a work experience that yields so little by way of intrinsic satisfaction with the job.

Class totality, on the other hand, is not an element likely to emerge in the early years of a work career. The mobility of young workers, the typical series of job changes before settling down, means that they often exercise an "exit" option available to the young and unattached.[118] A young worker may connect negative experience with a particular job, supervisor, or plant: he can change these, and so long as he can, he is unlikely to come to view his relationship with the plant and its authority structure as the total of his existence. The abundant leisure and lack of obligations of the young further reduce the power of the job to dominate life.

Still, what young workers experience overall in the preparation/selection phase and in the breaking in to factory life is quite plausibly linked to a developing sense of class identity and opposition. What we have seen gives little reason to argue that the education that produces workers, and the early years of work, are diversifying, enriching experiences. The population of young workers shows reservations about its collective fate that are rather different from its predecessors: at entry, less satisfaction than the upwardly mobile peasant youth of the past; and at work, expectations, bred of longer schooling, that exceed what the jobs can offer combined with a lack of skills that jobs demand. All in all, not an uncomplicated mix, compared to the previous experience of the Soviet regime and society. The reform and the SPTU were in effect ways of fitting the "new" working class into the old occupational structure; they were unlikely to be successful, representing as they did a kind of management that failed to confront new elements of occupational specialization, dissatisfaction, and inequality. The reversal of reform may have been a recognition of the limits of social policy, along with a judgment that the objectives were mistaken. It was certainly added evidence that the state that would, by 1989, confront unprecedented worker militancy was far from infallible.

4

Work, Wages, and Welfare

> In the 1960s and 1970s, the idea that striving
> for high wages in no way belonged to the
> sum of values deserving social approval grew
> stronger in the public consciousness. . . .
>   In reality . . . the role of wages as a motive
> for labor activity, as a stimulus to its activiza-
> tion, is very great. . . . Wages exert a much
> greater force in people's real behavior than
> [people] say and (often quite honestly) think.
> *(E. V. Klopov, 1985)*

THE WORDS quoted above, by a distinguished Soviet sociologist and
student of the working class, offer a commentary on a proverb long
common to the USSR and the East European states—"we pretend to
work, and they pretend to pay us." The proverb makes several points.
It admits that few work hard. It implies the reason—low wages, or the
difficulty of assuring an expected living standard on the basis of what
those wages can actually buy. It expresses, from a grass-roots perspective ("we"), the social dichotomy that makes a distinct "they" of
state authorities, as bosses, paymasters, and welfare provisioners. In
a sense it implies that "they" have forgotten, or failed to understand,
that work is motivated by a just level of reward.

Klopov, certainly, is convinced that rewards count. So, indeed, was
Stalin, who denounced wage egalitarianism in 1931 and presided over
an economic regime of enormous wage-salary differentiation—one
that underwent very significant change in the post-Stalin years. This
chapter tracks some of those changes, via a general review and survey
of the "wages and welfare" of Soviet workers. The patterns that will
emerge will tell us much about a worker's life and how it is perceived.
They should also reveal the outcome of the regime's attempts to motivate work that is of acceptable quality and quantity with the finite
resources it commits to consumption, while also undergirding social
peace by running a welfare system in what remains a relatively poor
society.

The Working Class and Relative Rewards

How then have workers, members of the "leading class" in the first society to take Marxism as its lodestar, fared in their pay? A combination of ideology—an economics that regarded the "creation of material values" as the center of productive activity—and relative scarcities of various manual and mental skills—produced the long-term realities reflected in the indices of relative pay levels for workers, lower white-collar personnel ("employees"), and specialists (intelligentsia) in industry over the near fifty-year span from Stalin's plan era to the twilight of Brezhnev's, as shown in table 4.1.[1] Although data on pay levels leave out much—for example, the effects of bonuses and supplements, of piece-rate norms that are easy or difficult to fulfill, of various open or secret supplements for managers, and so on—the direction of these figures is clear. Workers gained against the other groups, and markedly so, over a long period. This gain partly stems from the rises in the minimum wage that tended to benefit workers in low-paid industrial branches in a general sense (as it did workers in some other sectors). Also, these figures are for industry—they tell us nothing of the fate of industrial workers compared to those in agriculture, transport, construction, and other areas. This requires some comment.

On the one hand, lower white-collar personnel maintained a comparative advantage so long as the cash value of literacy and numeracy,

TABLE 4.1
Indices of Relative Pay Levels,
1932–78 (Workers = 100)

Year	Worker	Employee	Specialist
1932	100	152	272
1940	100	111	215
1945	100	101	230
1950	100	93	176
1955	100	89	166
1960	100	82	148
1965	100	83	142
1970	100	85	136
1975	100	82	124
1976	100	83	122
1978	100	81	118

Source: See note 1.

even at an elementary level, was maintained by scarcity.[2] This period, effectively, came to an end in the immediate postwar years, and the trends in the worker's favor have intensified since. It is doubtless true, as a Soviet author argues, that the justification for workers' upward movement compared to routine "employees" depends on skills and education being equalized, and office working conditions being less strenuous.[3] But one must also take into account that the "employee" category is overwhelmingly female—much more so than the ranks of industrial workers. Feminized sectors of the labor force, including some branches of industry, the "helping" professions such as medicine and teaching, and office personnel have been paid less than skill differentials and job content would seem to warrant, both in the USSR and in a number of other socialist countries.[4] It is likely that wage planners calculate females as secondary earners in households, despite their high degree of labor force participation, and thus justify the moderate wages. Evidence further indicates that Soviet poverty, as measured by the structure of households with very low per capita incomes, is rather feminized.[5]

Workers' relative economic progress compared with that of managerial and specialist personnel is another matter. The workers' wages grow closer to those of the higher echelons. But many managerial and engineering personnel—unlike routine office employees—do have access to more perquisites of a bureaucratic sort. These can be material rewards in the form of special salary supplements, or in kind, and give many of them a greater advantage over workers than the modest index numbers of the 1970s indicate. But for some—the younger diplomaed engineers and other specialists beginning or near the beginning of their careers—their specialized skills have brought no real economic advantage over workers. In the 1970s the small overall difference in wages between the two became a target of some economists and sociologists who argued that it devalued education, making people more reluctant to upgrade their credentials and seek the specialized learning that could lead to a career transition from worker to specialist.[6] Later it would also come to be seen, by reform economists, as unfair and socially corrosive. Workers would not necessarily agree.

One Class or Many? Blue-Collar Differentiation

Differences in pay rates and in average pay between different branches in industry as well as between industrial workers and those in other sectors have made for a diversity of rewards within the work-

TABLE 4.2
Rank of Selected Industrial Branches by Average Wage,
Various Years

Industry	1924	1928	1935	1950	1956
Coal	10	14	4	1	1
Iron ore	15	12	6	2	2
Iron and steel	13	9	5	3	3
Petroleum	11	8	1	4	4
Printing	1	2	8	9	13
Footwear	2	4	9	15	14
Leather/fur	3	5	10	12	10
Machinery/metal processing	4	1	3	5	6

Source: See note 7.

ing class. The interbranch differentials are products of complex inter-
actions between the policy and arithmetic of differential-setting (see
below), which are then reflected in the composition of the labor force
of a particular industry. But another source of the differences lies in a
history of political judgments about what has been important (heavy
industry) and unimportant (light and consumer industries). These
judgments, not the ones the market would necessarily make, first
took effect with the onset of Stalin's five-year plans. The data in table
4.2 on the rank of selected branches (from a seventeen-branch total)
by average wage show a decisive alteration—and a generally lasting
one—between the NEP year of 1924 and the year 1956 (since then, the
pattern has seen little change).[7] We choose extremes here, tracing the
top four branches in 1924 versus those in 1956.

Extractive and heavy "base" industries escalated sharply in rewards, from medium to low rank in 1924 to the top; three industries
with "consumer" linkages occupied top slots in 1924, but then were
demoted to low rank. (Two other industrial branches with obvious
consumerist profiles—food processing and clothing—ranked sixth
and eighth, respectively, in 1924. Ten years later they were very near
bottom, and by 1950 had assumed the lowest—sixteenth and seven-
teenth—slots.)[8] Office as well as blue-collar personnel were affected
by this system of priorities, despite the near-identical nature of certain
work. As Abram Bergson has reported, in 1956 a cashier in the nonfer-
rous metals industry earned 718 (old) rubles per month, while a similar functionary in the low-priority meat-processing sector received
only 379.[9]

This is, surely, a large differential; viewed in the concrete, it suggests something about inequalities early in the post-Stalin era, many of them persistent. It is time, then, to look more concretely at some of the sources, and outcomes, in the area of wage-salary inequality, both within the working class and between workers and other groups. This is an area of great intricacy and uncertainty, with a mass of confusing detail—one not even exhausted by detailed book-length studies by economists.[10] We cannot recapitulate all the details here, but we can examine, in turn, (1) the bases on which intraworking-class differentials are calculated, (2) the outcomes in terms of inequalities within and between branches, and (3) the trends in these inequalities over the post-1953 period.

The ostensible root of differentiation has been, since the 1920s, "skill differentials"[11]—the complexity and demands of jobs, the presumed time and effort necessary to learn how to perform them. In principle, the diversity of jobs performed in a given branch or branches is studied and analyzed, then ranked on a basic, abstract wage scale (*tarifnaia setka*): the least-skilled jobs are rated at 1.0, then in ascending order through the more skilled jobs, ranked by ratios to the 1.0 level. Theoretically, the number of categories can be large or small, depending on how great the job-skill differentiation is in a given branch between top and bottom, and how many complex gradations the rate setters wish to recognize. A given *tarifnaia setka* can thus be steeply or less steeply differentiated, and it can be relatively simple or complex in the number of levels it contains. The *setka* in place, it takes only one sum in rubles—that which gives meaning to the "1.0" bottom rung, the *stavka* or "base rate"—to tell us the wage structure. What determines the *stavka*? To some degree, it is recognition of the higher or lower levels of skill required up and down the *setka*, but another major consideration is the economic significance of a given branch in the national economy. Thus coalminers earn more than shoemakers, steelworkers earn more than food processors. The gaps can be very large. How demonstrable the principles of skill differential and economic significance are is questionable; as Alastair McAuley put it, one "suspects that [different base rates] reflect custom, tradition, and the prejudices of Soviet leaders."[12]

Beyond this, there are two other sources of differentials. First, branches where workers operate under a piece-rate system rather than a time-rate and where some do "heavy" work or work in "hot and unhealthy" conditions are provided with "working-condition" differentials.[13] The piece-rate supplement has ranged between 5 and 15 percent on the normal scale. "Economic significance" plays a role here; higher supplements have been connected with piece work in heavy industry. This has also been the case with supplements for work that is "hot," "heavy," or "hard"; percentage additions at each level of the *setka* vary. In the early 1960s, some branches of heavy industry paid a 17 percent supplement, while arduous or unhealthy jobs in the clothing industry were given only an 8 percent addition.

Second, there are "regional" differentials (percentage supplements to rates in the relevant *setka*) to compensate those who work in extreme geographical or climatic conditions. In some industries the size of the supplement varies with the extremity of condition, escalated cost-of-living and provisioning, and so forth.[14] They have ranged from the modest (15–20 percent in certain areas in the Urals, Siberia, and Central Asia) to monumental (a whopping 100 percent supplement for certain Far North areas). Conditions in these latter areas, of course, approximate or exceed in severity even the conditions encountered in the construction of the Alaska pipeline; some areas are simply beyond normal human habitation. The percentage of the work force in these areas has been small. Around 1.5 percent of the work force could be found in the Far North in the 1960s, and only about 10 percent of the total work force was located in any area authorized for supplements. Indeed, not all those who worked in these areas were entitled to supplements, at least until the mid-1970s. Agriculture, light industry, food processing, and service-sector workers received no supplements at all until 1968, and the practice evidently became universal (and consistent with the harsh-local-conditions/higher-cost-of-living logic) only by 1974.

These, then, are the bare bones of a system whose elements have been expressed in Soviet wage policy for some time. The system need not be overly complex if (1) there are relatively few different *setki*; (2) these contain a moderate number of steps, and for the most part the same number; (3) there are relatively few different *stavki* to put actual "meat" on the bones; and (4) work conditions and regional differentials are reasonably simple and consistent.

At the end of the Stalin era, these criteria could not have been further from realization. As Alec Nove put it, at the time of Stalin's death and until the establishment of the State Committee on Labor and Wages in 1955 began the process of "bringing order" (*uporiadochenie*), the

wages structure was in a tangle. There had been no systematic overhaul of wages since long before the war. The prevalence of piece-rates and bonus schemes enabled some enterprises and some ministries to increase pay, while others, especially those on time-rates and fixed salaries, had been less lucky. Different ministries adopted different wage-zones. Pay of persons of similar skills and even identical occupations, in different ministries, varied without reason. Norms were overfulfilled on average by 60 percent to 70 percent. The unskilled grades in many industries were virtually unstaffed; the least qualified workers were graded as semi-skilled, so as to pay them something nearer to a living wage. "Progressive" piece-rates led to many abuses. Reform was essential, but was also exceedingly difficult.[15]

Thus, far from the image of an iron order imposed from the top, the Stalin-era Soviet economy produced a mélange of scales, stavki, supplements, and practices that made it difficult to understand what was happening, what the total wage bill might be, how much buying power different workers possessed, and so on. As an official Soviet summary put it, the 1953–55 pattern involved[16]

- "around 1,900" setki,
- ranging from 5 to 15 grades,
- with the ratio of pay for top grade to bottom grade from 1.25:1 to 4.1:1,
- calculated from "several thousand" base rates (stavki),
- with 90 regional coefficients.

This was anything but central planning or control. The history of the post-Stalin era saw a simplification, a "bringing of order." In broad outline, by the mid-late 1970s, setki had been reduced to three, ranging from six grades to eight; the several thousand stavki were reduced to seventeen, the regional coefficients to ten.[17]

Beyond this, what turns out to be an "equalizing" intrabranch trend was reflected in a range of ratios from 1.58:1 to 2.1:1 among the three setki. An examination of the extremes in three industries indicates some of what happened between the "bringing of order" in the mid to late 1950s and the mid-1970s.[18] In underground coal mining, an eight-grade scale in effect from 1958 to 1968 set the top at a 3.75:1 ratio to the bottom; after 1972, a six-grade scale set the relative rewards of the top at 1.86 times the bottom. In machine building, a 1959–68 scale (six grades) with a 2:1 extreme fell, after 1972, to 1.71:1. Light industry's 1.8:1 in 1959–68 moderated its six-grade spread to 1.58:1 by 1972.

This was a far cry from the elevated peaks of Stalin-era setki. The Stalin era, however, had an extremely low state-guaranteed minimum wage. A great deal of the "equalization" in the post-Stalin period derives from increases in that minimum. Table 4.3 addresses several industries over a thirteen-year period and attaches ruble values to the scale extremes.[19]

TABLE 4.3
Extremes and Ratios of Pay Levels in Selected Branches of Industry,
1962 and 1975

	1962				1975			
Industry	High (Rubles)	Low (Rubles)	High: Low	Grades	High (Rubles)	Low (Rubles)	High: Low	Grades
Low-paid								
Food processing	81	45	1.8	6	111	70	1.58	6
Light industry	81	45	1.8	6	111	70	1.58	6
Leather	81	45	1.8	6	—	—	1.71	6
High-paid								
Underground coal	230	61.4	3.75	8	230	124	1.86	6
Ferrous metal-								
lurgy	164	51.2	3.2	10	202	96.4	2.1	8

Source: Janet C. Chapman, "Recent Trends in the Soviet Industrial Wage Structure,"
in A. Kahan and B. Ruble, eds., *Industrial Labor in the USSR* (New York: Pergamon
Press, 1979), p. 155.

In all cases, the *setki* grew more egalitarian over the period; still,
high-paid branches retained a very considerable advantage over the
low-paid, whether comparing the tops or bottoms of the scales. The
1962 picture shows the food processing and light-industry branches
beginning their scale at the minimum wage established in 1959—45
rubles per month. This is a small sum; by the standards of later Soviet
discussions, per capita income of under 50 rubles per month left a
family in dire straits. Still, this represents a significant advance over
the Stalinist past. Until 1956 the minimum wage had been about 22
rubles per month, raised to a range of 27–35 rubles in September of
that year, and to 45 rubles three years later. Even at 45 rubles, this
amounted to a minimum "substantially below the poverty level."[20]
Indeed in 1956 the ratio between average wage and minimum wage in
an anything-but-affluent Soviet economy was 3.4:1.[21]

A 1968 increase in the minimum wage to 60 rubles substantially
compressed the scales in many low-paid branches and sectors. No
major adjustments were made in wages that were already above the
minimum; especially in the more modestly paid branches of industry,
the distance between bottom and top of scale grew minimally;[22] for
the whole economy, the ratio of average to minimum wage fell to
1.8:1[23]—a clear pattern of leveling up.

The 1975 figures represent yet another phase. In the early 1970s, the
minimum was raised to 70 rubles per month, and this is, again, the
bottom rung of the less-paid branches. But those at the modest tops of

these have also, on the average, benefited. In fact, their increment of 30 rubles (81 to 111 rubles) exceeds the minimum-wage-driven rise of the bottom rung (25 rubles). Raising the top levels in both low- and high-paid branches may to some degree have been a matter of retaining some proportionality between these top blue-collar rates and some increases for managerial engineering and technical personnel, or the "intelligentsia" of industry, in 1972–76.[24] In any event, by 1976, the ratio of average to minimum wage had moved upward to approximately 1.5:1.[25]

But branch differentials are large. Senior coal miners vastly outearned senior food processors in 1975, as in 1962, even though the gap had closed by 30 rubles; at the bottom of the wage scale, novice coal miners increased their advantage to outearn even the senior workers in the lower-paid branches. Highly skilled workers in ferrous metallurgy have also increased their advantage.

Workers: Priority or Neglect?

The regime's Marxian bias may have favored the producers of *things* and the elevation of workers above the stratum of routine white-collar functionaries who historically outearned them, but the results have been mixed. Wages (or wage rates) are most directly under central control; here, nationwide statistics indicate a clear advantage of workers as a group over nonspecialist employees. Yet, at least through the mid-1970s, in some areas the pay of these lower white-collar personnel exceeded the pay of unskilled and semiskilled blue-collar workers if only a little. Data from three cities in the Tatar ASSR (selected because of the closeness of its economic composition and developmental level to the USSR average) indicate a mixed pattern, with lower white-collar people enjoying a pay advantage ranging from 6 to 19 percent over unskilled and semiskilled workers in 1975, while skilled workers outearned them, enjoying a 46 to 70 percent advantage over the unskilled.[26] Since the mid-1970s, many low-skill jobs have been paid better, probably further reducing the gap. It is not a matter of a rise in the absolute skill content of jobs still regarded as relatively low-skill, as much (in the view of many Soviet economists) as one of balancing the better-educated, more demanding labor force with the numerous unattractive jobs that must be filled, and paying a premium to accomplish this result.[27]

The worker-nonspecialist employee hierarchy changes somewhat when we look at per capita income in households belonging to one or the other group. Earlier data from the USSR and Eastern Europe

TABLE 4.4
Aspects of Monthly Family Income, Workers and
Employees, in Rubles per Month (Emigré Sample,
1972–74)

	Production Workers	Office Employees
Family disposable income	342.8	362.4
Total wages	320.9	332.1
Main earner	175.1	157.3
Second worker	105.3	114.3
Other workers	8.8	16.4
Additional jobs	31.7	44.1
Nonwage income (total)	21.9	30.3
Social consumption fund	7.8	17.4
Other sources	9.9	9.8
Help from relatives	4.2	3.2
Income per family member	100.9	104.3
Income per member of standard family	83.5	86.5
Income per worker	164.5	169.1
Persons per family	3.397	3.476
Workers per family	2.084	2.143
Families in group	285	21

Source: Adapted from Aaron Vinokur and Gur Ofer, "Family
Income Levels for Soviet Industrial Workers, 1965–1975," in
A. Kahan and B. Ruble, eds., *Industrial Labor in the USSR* (New
York: Pergamon Press, 1979), p. 203.

showed a tendency for average per capita income in lower white-
collar families to exceed that of worker families (defined by the major
breadwinner, generally the "male head of household").[28] (While the
lower white-collar category as a whole was overwhelmingly female,
the male minority in this category—those who head households designated as lower white-collar—enjoyed earnings well above the
average for the stratum, and some exceeded worker wages. Research
on Soviet emigrés of the earlier 1970s added detail to the picture.) A
careful survey of family income gave the results in table 4.4 when
the families of "production workers" and "office employees" were
compared.

The families of the office employees show a modest income advantage over the production workers—in sum, a quite different picture
from the one between nonspecialist employees and workers. The
employee families have higher incomes; though their main-earner

TABLE 4.5
Social Composition of the Three Household Types (in percentages)

Predominant Household Type	Employees and Engineering-Technical Personnel	Education/ Health Personnel	Skilled Workers	Unskilled Workers	Retirees and Dependents
Unskilled (U)	2.7	0.9	14.4	40.1	41.9
Skilled (S)	3.3	1.6	40.6	13.6	40.9
Nonspecialist (E)	15.2	4.1	20.1	14.9	45.7

Source: See note 29.

wages are lower, "second worker" and "third worker" wages virtually cancel this disadvantage out, especially since there is a greater tendency of employee families to have additional jobs. An almost 10-ruble monthly advantage of employees over production workers in the "take" from the social consumption fund may be explained by a greater ability of such families to work the system, or simply by the somewhat greater propensity of such families to send their young members on to higher education, thus claiming the stipends for living expenses that are received by students.

Research within the USSR, evidently conducted at the end of the 1970s or beginning of the 1980s, amplifies these impressions. In what seems to be a national survey,[29] families were classified into types by predominant social position: the three types in table 4.5 were characterized as "predominantly" unskilled worker (U), skilled worker (S), and nonspecialist employee (E). The merging of "employee" and "engineering-technical personnel" is troubling, but it is true that households are often, to a degree, socially mixed. The percentage of dependents/retirees does not vary by much across these types, though the disadvantage would seem to be with the "E" types. (Still, one need recall that additional children are typically not so costly as the first child added to an earning couple that was previously without dependents,[30] so that the disadvantage may be illusory.) E-type families contain, effectively, no more unskilled workers than do the "skilled" (S) families; they contain a higher percentage of skilled workers than the U families. E families have major advantages in educational attainment of their members, and in the share of members who had supervisory functions in their jobs.[31] The final accounting emerges in data on per capita income, property, and living space (see table 4.6).[32] Here, the unskilled (U) families and the skilled (S) are equal in raw per capita terms: the result of a smaller "load" of dependents to workers, but also due to the higher wages for the unskilled/

TABLE 4.6

Income, Property, and Living Space of Households, by Household Type

Household Type	Per Capita Income (rubles)	% with over 90 r. per Capita	Sq. Meters per Capita	Property (thous. rubles)	Ratio: All Members to Working Members
Unskilled (U)	65.5	12.3	7.9	3.6	1.17:1
Skilled (S)	65.2	12.5	8.3	4.6	1.86:1
Nonspecialist (E)	74.3	26.3	8.4	5.2	1.28:1

Source: See table 4.5.

unattractive jobs the USSR still offers, in excessive numbers, to a better-educated work force. Housing differs little across the three groups, but the accumulated property reflects the relative time since the family was formed (U, 13.5 years; S, 15.5; and E, 16.9) and thus time to amass goods.[33] More striking are the per capita income figures: E families have a solid advantage here over both types of worker families. Fully 26 percent of them have at least achieved security—but not affluence—in that 90-ruble per month per member, more than double the percentage in either type of worker family. It is sobering to recall that, on the assumption of a standard family of working father and mother and two children, Soviet statisticians calculated a "normative minimum" of 51.4 rubles per capita for 1965–70, and projected a 66.5-ruble figure for 1971–75.[34] At the end of the 1976–80 period, these worker families had apparently not quite achieved even this.

Other Soviet data offer a picture that is similar overall: "class" differences that are not, on the whole, large, but that tend to show more worker disadvantage than advantage, within a broad situation of significant interclass overlap on various indicators of material welfare. A detailed study of workers and engineering/technical personnel (*inzhenerno-tekhnicheskie rabotniki*, ITR) in Taganrog in 1978 (table 4.7) showed moderate wage/salary differentiation but a virtual equality of per capita incomes.[35]

We encounter here evidence of a pattern often cited as characteristic of "late Brezhnev"—that skilled workers evidently outearn "leaders" in pay, on the average. (Inter alia, this is a product of a long—perhaps twenty-five-year[36]—period wherein directors, supervisory personnel, and related plant professionals received few or no real raises, while workers were bumped up year by year.)[37] The authors attribute per capita equalization to variations in the number of children and in the age structure of households, and consequent leveling. (For example, while 39 percent of skilled-worker households contained minor chil-

TABLE 4.7
Wages and Family Income, Per Capita,
of Workers and ITR, in Taganrog,
1978 (in rubles)

	Wage	Income per Capita
Workers		
Unskilled	107.3	103
Semiskilled	145.8	106
Skilled	170.0	107
ITR		
Leaders	151.3	107
Specialists	129.1	107
Engineers	145.4	106

Source: See note 35.

dren, only 19 percent of unskilled workers' families did; only 4 percent of skilled workers, but 12 percent of unskilled, were in single-member households.[38]

Differences in Taganrog were much more marked in housing. Here, "engineering-technical" people enjoyed a systematic advantage over workers; even the lowest paid of them lived more often in individual, and less often in communal, apartments than the best-paid (skilled) workers. More workers than ITR lived in detached houses; but in the USSR this is no advantage, given that one bears more of the costs oneself, and that such homes often lack running water, central heating, and other amenities.[39] ITR also enjoyed a small advantage in the possession of various household appliances. Enough goods are subject to various forms of bureaucratic distribution in the USSR to distort any evident effect of wage/salary differences: sometimes, they may work to moderate these, at other times to intensify them. If the leaders in Taganrog earned less but were better-housed than the skilled workers, surely in some areas bosses enjoyed both better housing and higher wages.

Even in the limited context of wages, post-Stalin policies look less *ouvrièriste* when examined in a broader spectrum, including trends in the pay of state and collective farmers, as well as workers outside the "core" industrial sector (in construction, transport, communications, etc.).[40] No doubt workers benefited; but others, relatively, may have benefited more, indicating that workers' wages and welfare were not the most critical issue for the policymakers. This is true, especially in view of what has happened to the rural "floor" of Soviet society: the workers of the *sovkhoz*, the collectivized peasants of the *kolkhoz*. Minimum-wage policies that affected those at the bottom could not but move the agricultural sector up relative to other workers. From 1957 to 1973, the average wage of "all workers and employees" rose by 83 percent, the minimum wage by over 200 percent.[41] This meant that state-farm workers' wages went from 58 percent of industrial workers' wages in 1960 to 79 percent in 1971, and collective farmers' wages from only 32 percent of workers' wages in 1960 to 58 percent in 1971. Income levels, including nonwage items, showed an even closer approximation by the end of the 1960s. Industrial workers/state farmers/collective farmers were "scaled" 100/93.6/75, respectively.[42] The bringing of *kolkhozniki* into minimum-wage and social welfare coverage in the 1960s had a great deal to do with this.

By 1978 the ratio of workers' wages in industry to those in agriculture (*sovkhozniki*) was 1.24:1,[43] while a 1982 report indicated 1980 average monthly wages of 185.5 rubles for industrial workers, 149 rubles for those in agriculture—in ratio terms, essentially the same.[44] All in all, one economist calculated that, from 1961 to 1975, the average wage in the whole national economy had risen by 81 percent, that of state farmers by 240 percent, and of *kolkhozniki* by 320 percent.[45]

In a detailed study of Soviet economic inequality, Alastair McAuley calculated yet a broader measure than that employed here—the per capita disposable income in industrial-worker and other households. This allows the inclusion of some calculations regarding family size, the burden of dependents, the income elements beyond the basic wage rates, and the earnings of wives of those men whose employment defines a household as "working class." The findings, ranging from 1960 to 1974, are summarized in table 4.8.

TABLE 4.8
Index Figures, Per Capita Disposable Personal Income,
Various Groups (total population = 100)

	1960	1965	1970	1974
Total population	100.0	100.0	100.0	100.0
All state workers and employees	108.4	103.6	102.9	102.3
Industrial workers	130.7	119.7	101.5	104.5
Collective farmers	81.9	88.9	87.1	89.0

Source: Adapted from Alastair McAuley, *Economic Welfare in the Soviet Union: Poverty, Living Standards, and Inequality* (Madison: University of Wisconsin Press, 1979), p. 42.

What has happened? First, a "total population" that contained a much larger share of collective farmers in 1960 than in 1974 has gone upscale. This eroded the moderate advantage of "all state employees" (all workers, nonagricultural and agricultural, plus the professional and lower white-collar strata)—that is, the majority—over the remainder. The approximately 30 percent advantage of industrial workers erodes as well, in the face of *sovkhoz* and *kolkhoz* advances, especially those made between 1960 and 1965 (when *kolkhozniks'* income growth per annum was in the 6 percent range, industrial workers' only about 3 percent).[46] As McAuley summarizes the 1960–74 period, "Industrial workers and their dependents made substantial gains in absolute living standards; on the average, they moved from a position barely above the poverty level to one in which they could afford a rational pattern of consumption. At the same time, they have seen their relative affluence eroded; their standard of living is now little better than that of other state employees."[47]

Wages and Welfare: Appearance and Reality

Wages are important. They *have* risen and Soviet material life *has* improved greatly since 1953. But neither wages nor the measure of their improvement constitutes the whole story, given other persistent characteristics of the Soviet economy. Some policymakers at least, as well as workers, economists, and the bureaucrats of trade unions and the State Committee on Labor and Social Problems, share another concern: shortages of goods and services, and what these do to create a gap between increases in wages and increases in "real" income as measured by what one can acquire with added rubles. Connected as it must be with this shortfall between supply and demand, there emerges the problem of suppressed inflation. According to government claims through the Brezhnev era, workers as well as other citizens were insulated against this possibility; under Gorbachev, as we shall see, a different reality was recognized.

The impressive increases in wages recorded since 1953 have been part of an increase in real incomes. In a very poor, goods-starved society, the Khrushchev program of increasing both wages and the production of consumer goods made the matching of extra rubles with goods easy enough. (In the late Stalin years, price cuts on various basic items were seen as the main mode of increasing "real income,"[48] even though the prices so lowered had been very high relative to wages.) As long as wages in general remained low (even allowing for increases from the nadir of the Stalin years), increments were still useful in the acquisition of more and better food, clothing, footwear, or other durables. The modesty of all this still bespoke Soviet poverty in an international context, but it was progress over the Soviet past.

Wages continued to increase for some time, so the mid-Brezhnev years, compared with 1953, showed great advances for workers and other Soviet citizens. Yet by that point bare figures on wage increases more and more overstated the story of real improvements. Wages were rising faster than supplies became available. Failure of consumer industry to respond to the more sophisticated demand made for shortages of desirable goods and rising inventories of unsold and unsalable products. As an economist and distinguished specialist in wage and labor issues was to ask, rather rhetorically, in Brezhnev's last year, "What is the object of distribution according to labor—monetary income or actual consumer goods that satisfy personal needs of socialist production workers and members of their families?[49] The Novosibirsk economics journal *EKO* had, in fact, already answered the question in 1981 as it related to the effect of incremental rubles on workers' work and budgets, in an editorial following the Twenty-sixth Party Congress. "Money that has not found goods and services lies idle," it observed, and called for a realization "that the imbalance of supply and demand objectively devaluates the ruble and undermines the material incentive of the working people to increase labor productivity."[50]

Rubles—workers' rubles large among them—were indeed lying idle, in low-interest state-bank savings accounts, as well as in other repositories. This was the case well before the 1980s. According to one report,[51] workers' and employees' annual average earnings had risen by 191 rubles between 1961 and 1965. Over the same period, the average increment in savings accounts was 117 rubles—a healthy addition in a society where people do not save for rainy days and in a period wherein targeted long-term savings for the acquisition of big-ticket items, such as automobiles, were probably still quite rare.

Between 1971 and 1974, as a 1975 source[52] tells us, workers' savings accounts grew more rapidly than those of white-collar personnel, partly because of "more significant" raises, partly because their share of the total population increased. The general picture was an interesting one. Average monthly wages of workers and employees had risen 15 percent for the period and retail trade had increased 27 percent in volume, while the number of deposits in the state savings system had increased 69 percent and the average size of a deposit by over one-third: from 581 to 789 rubles. The 1976–80 period, that of Brezhnev's gathering twilight, saw an average rise of 90 kopeks per savings account for every additional ruble in average earnings.[53] By 1980 total savings equaled seven months of national retail (state and cooperative) trade turnover, and, as an authoritative source put it, was hypothetically enough for all people employed in the national economy to take 209 days of unpaid leave, and survive![54] (From 1966 to 1980, the wage fund rose 160 percent; retail turnover, 150 percent; and savings, 740 percent.)[55]

Neither in the realm of goods nor in service areas—where time wasted waiting for repairmen to arrive, lack of replacement parts, inconvenient hours, and so on all tended to restrict the demand on the state sector[56]—were rubles worth what they could have been.

Soviet society was not yet "affluent." Indeed, many were—and still are—poor, even by minimal Soviet standards.[57] Still, inflation of various sorts faced the Soviet consumer, if moderated by the physical unavailability of many items on which savings might gladly have been spent. Meat prices—to choose a sensitive indicator—were held stable in the state retail network from 1962 on. Supply was rarely up to demand—this in a society where the shortage of durables increases the propensity to spend one's meager rubles on dietary improvements. Thus workers, among others, have had occasion to turn to the "free," collective-farm market, where prices floated to reflect demand. Here the gap between the fixed prices of the state and those of the markets, where meat *was* available, widened: free-market meat prices exceeded state prices by 32 percent in 1965, by 76 percent in 1975, and by 109 percent in 1980.[58] Records are not available for the actual cost of various services supposedly rendered at state-fixed prices, that is, for the actual bribe-cum-price paid to acquire certain goods in state stores and, in general, for the cost of doing business in the real Soviet world. Even bulging savings accounts do not contraindicate a substantially higher real cost for many goods and services than state figures indicate.

Beyond this—and most importantly—one must remember the bureaucratic, nonretail-market distribution of so many scarce goods in the Soviet economy. A real differentiation in Soviet "real incomes"— one that cannot be traced in income and wage statistics—emerges from one's rank, from bureaucratically regulated access to "special stores," "closed distributors," and other sources of luxury foods, clothing, and durables at low prices. These are goods that money cannot buy—at least not money expressed in the figures on wage increases for workers. As Arcadius Kahan put it, there were different levels in the consumption hierarchy, and the "transition from one level to another depends not only upon the relative increase in money wages, but also upon the movement from one recognized level in the social hierarchy to another. It is more often the latter that determines the former than the other way around."[59] Neither collective and state farmers, rank-and-file lower white-collar personnel, nor most workers figure in this hierarchy in any important way.

In other ways, however, bureaucratic arrangements may, for some, cushion the effects of being outside the ranks of the distinctly privileged. One index item may be meat—the center of Soviet diets, in a land as yet little troubled by fears of health effects of its overconsumption. Gorbachev-era glasnost' provoked by early 1988 an admission that, effectively, meat was not really available in state retail outlets at subsidized state prices, except in Moscow, Leningrad, and in the fourteen republican capitals (and to those who work in state retail meat stores!).[60] (By the end of 1990, rationing was near universal in a much more alarming situation.) Yet recent emigré survey data indicate that large numbers of urbanites eat meat daily; a majority eat it several times a week.[61] Not all are getting it on the black market; not all are paying the high prices of the free *kolkhoz* market. For some workers, in-plant distribution of meat and other food goods is the major source of access, and evidently at state prices.[62] It seems more than probable that large plants, in priority sectors, are the ones where such arrangements are most likely. They are also the ones where average wages are apt to be highest.

Still, this speaks to relative matters. Knowing such things does not yet tell us how they appear to workers and how they are experienced by them. Rare, after all, is the citizen under any economic system who has a developed, nuanced idea of "how it all works." Savings may make for feelings of added security or affluence among some. Price stability over decades may appear "populist" and good; shortages may not be linked, in the consumer's mind, to such pricing policies. None of the numbers tell us how satisfied or disgruntled the worker may be with his economic lot, or how that lot corresponds to individual or classbound notions of social justice. These are issues to which we will turn later in this chapter.

Workers' Life . . .

The contrast between the last NEP year of 1928, the poverty of the Stalin era, and the early years of the climb out of this nadir, through 1958, provides a good starting point. Janet Chapman's extraordinarily informative 1963 calculations[63] led her to conclude that "the Soviet consumer enjoys a real *per capita* consumption perhaps a tenth higher than that of the 1890 American and only one-third of that of the Amer-

TABLE 4.9
Measures of Per Capita Real Consumption:
USSR (1958) and USA (1890, 1958)

	USSR, 1958	USA, 1890	USA, 1958
Food (per capita)			
Potatoes (kilos.p.a.)	150	85	48
Meat/poultry/lard (kilos.p.a.)	38	89	91
Urban housing (per capita)			
Sq. meters	5.5	—	15–32
Rooms	0.3	1.0	1.2
Other (per 1,000 pop.)			
Telephones	11.5	3.7	379
Radios	177	—	734
Televisions	12	—	254
Washing machines	5	—	259

Source: Adapted from Janet Chapman, "Consumption," in Abram Bergson and Simon Kuznets, eds., *Economic Trends in the Soviet Union* (Cambridge, Mass.: Harvard University Press, 1965), pp. 252–53.

ican of today [1958]."[64] Figures like those in table 4.9 led Chapman to this rather stark conclusion. These figures, derived from a much longer list,[65] are not for the working class alone, but for the total USSR population. Allowing for the still very depressed living standards of the large farm population in 1958, workers on the whole should have done better on many of these indicators. Yet the picture is still one of a very goods-poor, crowded society in 1958. Potato consumption is the only category in which the Soviets lead, and it reflects the core of an adequate (calorically) but low-quality diet. Meat is the indicator of an improving diet, and the Soviets in 1958 produced less than half the per capita amount of the United States in 1890 and 1958. The following series for kilos of "meat, poultry and lard" per person in various years is from Chapman's other calculations:[66]

1928	1932	1937	1940	1950	1955	1958
32	17	18	24	27	32	38

The massive fall in meat output during the early Plan Era marks the effects of collectivization; the figures for the immediate pre- and post-war years are still well below those of 1928, whose level is only reachieved in 1955. For Soviet citizens with thirty-year memories, 1958, however it looked in absolute terms, was the best year that *they* had seen in a long time.

A similar if less extreme pattern is apparent when the 1958 urban housing supply of 5.5 square meters per person—itself well below the official Soviet "sanitary norm"—is put into historical perspective.[67]

1928	1932	1937	1940	1950	1955	1958
5.8	4.9	4.6	4.5	5.0	5.1	5.5

The housing shortfall of the 1930s may not have been as precipitous as in the area of meat, but housing had not even recovered its 1928 level thirty years later.

Such figures do not measure the semi-invisibles—health care, education, and other services whose contribution to per capita consumption can be measured. When these are taken into account, the figures benefit from the fact that the production of such services expanded rapidly in the Soviet period. When they are not taken into account, Chapman's 1958 calculations show that the average real wage of 1928 had not yet been reachieved in 1958. Taking the average annual wage for "workers and employees" outside of agriculture in 1937 as 100, a series similar to those cited above assumes the following character:[68]

1928	1932	1937	1940	1950	1955	1958
175	—	100	94	101	141	164

These figures are compatible with some rise in certain aspects of material welfare both for workers and for other essentially urban groups. Adding the value of educational and health services to the calculations of per capita material consumption changes the picture, as the shortened series in table 4.10 indicate.[69]

The contradiction in the figures is illusory rather than real. Over the period, vast numbers of peasants became workers, earning regular "real wages" for the first time, and joining the networks of educational and health-service consumption that developed far faster in city than countryside. Economic pressures after 1928 also brought many urban women, previously not employed outside the home, into paid employment. The agrarian society of 1928 had changed; 9 million non-

TABLE 4.10
Trends in Real Wages and Consumption, 1928–58 (1937 = 100)

	1928	1937	1950	1955	1958
Real wages	175	100	101	141	164
Consumption	103	100	114	159	191
Consumption, including communal services	91	100	116	157	185

Source: See note 69.

agricultural workers and employees in 1928 grew to over 48 million by 1958, and as Chapman put it, by the latter year a large share of the population was working in "nonagricultural occupations at wages which, although not at the 1928 level, were considerably above earnings in agriculture in 1928."[70]

Few, obviously, were the workers who by 1958 could remember, or sense, that their real wages on average were not quite what they had been thirty years earlier—the 1958 "statistical worker" was, after all, still an ex-peasant for whom the prevailing wage levels represented a living standard superior to that of his rural origins. The USSR, in its urban component at least, was a society of the upwardly mobile with a mass of nonhereditary workers who were not yet a class.[71] Soviet workers lived in more space, probably, than urban American workers of 1890, though not by much. The urban American workers of the old-law tenements may have shared bathrooms with other households, but they typically had private kitchens; in 1958, Soviet workers still lived in communal apartments where neither facility was usually limited to use by one family.[72] Soviet workers enjoyed employment security, unlike the varying degrees of unemployment risks encountered by their American counterparts. All this was experienced in the context of a society where the GNP, in general and per capita, was much lower than that of the United States, and one in which the share of the GNP going to consumption was also smaller: about 60 percent in the 1950s in the USSR, compared to 70–75 percent in the United States,[73] according to one estimate. (Such estimates, however, may turn out to be much too high in the light of Gorbachev-era revisions.)

A later range of data takes us forward nearly twenty years, into the mid-Brezhnev era, and a time when Soviet living standards had advanced considerably, though not enough to close East-West gaps outside those areas where saturation is possible. Overall, Soviet families were living better: in 1975,[74] 61 percent had refrigerators, compared to only 11 percent in 1965. Washing machines were in 65 percent of family households in 1975, versus 21 percent in 1965. (Assuming families of four people, this itself was an advance over 1958, when by our earlier "per 1,000" data, only 2 percent had them!) Television had come as well: one-quarter of all families had a set in 1965, three-quarters in 1975[75]—while the rate must have been lower than 5 percent in 1958. Workers benefited from all this, no doubt less than the better-fixed members of the professional classes, but more than the peasantry. As a predominantly urban class, they probably exceeded a number of these nationwide averages, whereas rural dwellers, on the whole, fell well behind.

TABLE 4.11
Per Capita Annual Consumption of Potatoes and Meat
(in kilos)

	1958	1965	1975	Workers 1971
Potatoes	150.0	142.0	120.0	115.7
Meat	38.0	41.0	57.0	81.4

Source: See note 76.

Workers, too, were relatively advantaged in the quality of their diet, which also showed great improvement in the Brezhnev era. Restating the 1958 calculations on per capita annual consumption of the ("low quality") potato and the ("high quality") meat/meat products line (see table 4.11), we can compare them with similar nationwide figures for 1965 and 1975, and with data for the families of industrial workers in seven regions in the European USSR in 1971.[76] As the figures show, by 1971, industrial workers were well above the national average in meat consumption—essentially double the national average of only six years before. Their potato consumption was also lower than that of the national average of four years later. While a nationwide sample of industrial workers might have moderated these figures, the European regions involved were the locus of much large-scale industry, and thus of a very significant share of the whole country's industrial work force.

Still, these were not the marks of an affluent class. Workers, like many others, lived in crowded communal apartments in many cases, though the move to separate apartments continued under the construction programs of the Khrushchev-Brezhnev years.[77] As a deficit item, housing was in many senses a rationed good, and although a strong tendency toward uniformity in design and small size made for a rather egalitarian-appearing modern housing sector in the cities, workers were typically absent from official enumeration of categories of people "entitled" to an allocation of space above the norm.[78] Small indeed was the size of a dwelling: urban per capita dwelling space rose roughly from 7 to 8.3 square meters in 1965–75, still below the "sanitary norm" of 9. Even this average could conceal some extraordinarily substandard conditions; as one student put it, even the achievement of the 9-square-meter norm as an average "must still mean slum housing for many."[79]

Well into the 1970s, the structure of Soviet workers' budgets, and other aspects of their material life, bore the marks of relative poverty—the legacy of underdevelopment, the preference for investment over consumption, the lingering effects of World War II. Family budgets of Soviet workers were still heavily committed to food—according to one report, 44 percent in 1965, and a probably underestimated 38.2 percent in 1975. In the United States in 1934–36, food accounted for 33.5 percent of budgets. This share fell markedly as society grew more affluent and the smaller budget share bought more and better food. In the America of the mid-1930s, annual per capita consumption of meat was 50.1 kilograms; in the USSR, it reached 55 kilograms in 1976, though this number included fats excluded from the US figure. In 1976 the USSR remained well ahead of the United States in the consumption of starches in basic forms (grain products were 142.6 kilograms per capita in the USSR versus 99.3 in 1934–36 America; potatoes, 119 versus 65.6).[80] Outlays for housing were much lower: 17.1 percent in 1934–36 America, 2.9 percent in the 1975 USSR;[81] Soviet housing remained well behind the people's physical needs, as well as the effective economic "demand" (at those low rents) for more and better space.

The tired reader may find useful yet another approach to fleshing out our appreciation of what labor can "earn" for Soviet workers. Thus we may take a comparative look at the cost of goods and services, stated in terms of the hours/minutes of work at the average job required to meet costs, in the USSR (Moscow) and four Western cities (New York/Washington, London, Paris, Munich). Calculations such as these, done periodically by the research division of Radio Liberty in Munich, may be inexact, and they certainly solve far from all problems of comparison—but they are based on palpable realities, *things* whose cost gives concrete meaning to the effort expended at work.[82] Relating prices to work time—paid at an average for workers in manufacturing in each of the national environments—gets us around the thankless task of converting the (nonconvertible) ruble into dollars or other Western "hard" currencies at the administratively set Soviet exchange rate, and avoids the technical problems of otherwise constructing a more realistic rate. Observations for 1971, 1976, 1982, and 1986 give us a perspective on changes over relatively recent times. Tables 4.12 through 4.15 provide a selection of the rather large (about 160) number of separate items covered in the original studies.

There is much to compare and contrast in these figures, so let us look at a few items of interest. Bread represents a critical component of the diet, especially in relatively low-quality diets. White or rye, it has remained a relative asset in Soviet society, and it was cheap and plentiful until the recent economic crisis. Over the years it grew moderately cheaper, from 15 to 11 minutes of work to pay for the more common rye loaf. Potatoes, the other main Soviet source of starch,

TABLE 4.12
Retail Prices, in Minutes/(Hours) Worked, Various Cities, November 1971

	Moscow	New York	Munich	London	Paris
Foods (kilo)					
Bread (white)	23	8	27	25	24
Bread (rye)	15	15	17	27	39
Beef (roasting)	168	52	121	115	206
Pork (loin)	172	24	93	79	179
Chicken (frozen)	144	15	45	53	43
Salmon (creamed)	164	35	232	117	174
Potatoes	8	3	4	7	3
Butter	295	39	89	79	133
Milk (liter)	25	7	10	17	11
Eggs (doz., large)	128	12	32	31	55
Tea (100 grams)	85	8	18	10	23
Coffee (100 grams)	369	35	195	147	90
Durables					
Refrigerator (large)	(460)	(43)	(75)	(144)	(119)
Washing machine	(178)	(62)	(92)	(114)	(194)
Television (color)	(1,169)	(165)	(261)	(498)	(552)
Fiat 124 (months worked for)	43.3	4.4	7.6	10.6	11.7
Rent	(8)	(55)	(53)	(67)	(102)
Clothing					
Nylon stockings	82	14	36	25	15
Men's shirt	607	80	221	305	309
Men's suit	(151)	(13)	(32)	(56)	(55)
Miscellaneous					
12 red roses	492	60	81	143	489
Light bulb (100 W)	25	6	20	10	25
Bus fare (3 km)	4	6	8	6	26
Subway fare (3 km)	4	6	8	6	13

Source: Adapted from Keith Bush, "Retail Prices in Moscow and in Four Western Cities in November 1971," *Radio Liberty Research Paper*, no. 49 (1972).

also remained cheap through 1982, then became costlier in the 1982–86 period.

The cost of beef and pork declined as well over the period, reflecting a rise in pay rates versus relative stability of state retail tariffs. But with regard to meat (a component of higher-quality diets), relative costs to Soviet workers were astronomical compared to their American counterparts, and still high compared to European workers. Be-

TABLE 4.13
Retail Prices, in Minutes/(Hours) Worked, Various Cities, May 1976

	Moscow	Wash-ington	Munich	London	Paris
Foods (kilo)					
Bread (white)	20	21	22	10	18
Bread (rye)	13	22	16	11	45
Beef (roasting)	144	66	115	147	166
Pork (loin)	137	50	91	107	120
Chicken (frozen)	216	26	37	56	48
Salmon (canned)	na	82	na	128	110
Potatoes	7	8	8	23	13
Butter	260	46	61	57	78
Milk (liter)	21	7	9	11	8
Eggs (doz., large)	97	10	22	13	27
Tea (100 grams)	75	9	29	6	18
Coffee (100 grams)	325	63	149	137	86
Durables					
Refrigerator (large)	(501)	(81)	(76)	(110)	(88)
Washing machine	(432)	(52)	(79)	(116)	(112)
Television (color)	(780)	(86)	(191)	(220)	(327)
Fiat 131 (months worked for)	37.5	6.9	7.7	11.1	10.6
Rent	(10)	(46)	(32)	(48)	(36)
Clothing					
Nylon stockings	144	16	18	16	14
Men's shirt	534	176	204	238	286
Men's suit	(106)	(25)	(36)	(40)	(36)
Miscellaneous					
12 red roses	606	159	74	137	281
Light bulb (100 W)	30	8	12	8	10
Bus fare (3 km)	4	6	6	8	4
Subway fare (3 km)	4	6	6	12	4

Source: Adapted from Keith Bush, "Retail Prices in Moscow and in Four Western Cities in May 1976," *Radio Liberty Research Supplement*, June 16, 1976.

yond this, it is well to note that availability has typically been much lower in the USSR (and Moscow is the best-supplied city by far); that quality, though hard to measure, is typically lower; and that these are, after all, state retail-store prices. Those seeking reasonable-quality pork or beef in Moscow may well have recourse to the *kolkhoz* market, with demand-set prices which, as we saw earlier, were by 1980 twice the state prices. The Soviet price of tea—the "popular" drink—while

TABLE 4.14
Retail Prices, in Minutes/(Hours) Worked, Various Cities, March 1982

	Moscow	Wash-ington	Munich	London	Paris
Foods (kilo)					
Bread (white)	17	16	27	25	18
Bread (rye)	11	21	18	21	37
Beef (roasting)	123	69	150	115	119
Pork (loin)	117	16	24	31	28
Chicken (frozen)	185	16	24	31	28
Salmon (canned)	251	57	138	65	73
Potatoes	7	7	4	3	4
Butter	222	55	52	50	47
Milk (liter)	22	6	7	9	8
Eggs (10, large)	80	9	18	22	18
Tea (100 grams)	53	10	10	5	17
Coffee (100 grams)	1,231	62	85	114	48
Durables					
Refrigerator (large)	355	61	54	75	69
Washing machine	165	47	96	81	56
Television (color)	701	65	143	132	106
Ford Escort or Zhi-guli 2106 (months worked for)	53	5	6	11	8
Rent	(12)	(51)	(24)	(28)	(39)
Clothing					
Nylon stockings	366	18	18	18	17
Men's shirt	615	137	289	237	208
Men's suit	(109)	(25)	(15)	(22)	(13)
Miscellaneous					
Light bulb (100 W)	25	4	6	9	10
Bus fare (3 km)	3	7	8	11	9
Subway fare (3 km)	3	7	8	13	4

Source: Adapted from Keith Bush, "Retail Prices in Moscow and in Four Western Cities in March 1982," Radio Liberty Research Supplement, June 4, 1982.

falling, remains relatively high; that of coffee, treated by state pricing authorities as a luxury item, is very high, reaching the astronomical in 1982 and falling to what was still an absurdly high level in 1986.

Durable goods also show a distinct Soviet disadvantage. Prices have tended to decline, but they have risen in certain circumstances—for example, when more automated washing machines came on the mid-1970s market. The Soviet worker's time required to gain these items is

TABLE 4.15
Retail Prices, in Minutes/(Hours) Worked, Various Cities, October 1986

	Moscow	Wash-ington	Munich	London	Paris
Foods (kilo)					
Bread (white)	17	6	25	11	20
Bread (rye)	11	18	19	10	34
Beef (roasting)	111	46	140	75	120
Pork (loin)	106	42	60	37	86
Chicken (frozen)	189	18	17	20	31
Salmon (canned)	228	47	—	47	91
Potatoes	11	9	5	3	9
Butter	195	40	37	38	63
Milk (liter)	20	4	6	6	8
Eggs (10, large)	75	5	16	13	17
Tea (100 grams)	42	12	19	6	20
Coffee (100 grams)	1,115	67	112	179	121
Durables					
Refrigerator (large)	(274)	(72)	(75)	(52)	(61)
Washing machine	(177)	(46)	(49)	(52)	(61)
Television (color)	(669)	(30)	(54)	(75)	(106)
Ford Escort 1.1 or Zhiguli-VAZ 2108 (months worked for)	45	5	7	8	8
Rent	(11)	(55)	(24)	(26)	(15)
Clothing					
Nylon stockings	279	16	16	14	17
Men's shirt	892	129	276	173	276
Men's suit	(118)	(18)	(33)	(16)	(34)
Miscellaneous					
Light bulb (100 W)	25	7	5	7	8
Bus fare (3 km)	3	7	7	9	5
Subway fare (3 km)	3	7	7	9	5

Source: Adapted from Keith Bush, "Retail Prices in Moscow and in Four Western Cities in March 1982," *Radio Liberty Research Supplement*, January 21, 1987.

much larger than that of his or her foreign counterparts. Clothing is relatively expensive as well. For example, as the quality of old-fashioned nylons rose in 1971–76, so did their price: the 1982 and 1986 versions are pantyhose, more than twice as costly in time worked as items of similar function in 1976. Six hours of work was the cost of one pair; in 1986 it was still nearly five hours. In 1982 a Soviet worker had to work over two and a half weeks to buy a suit, and even then it was of typically much lower quality and cut than that of his Western counterparts.

Housing costs, however, are another matter. Comparability is very difficult to achieve with respect to the nature and amenities of the apartment. For 1976 the comparison was made between Soviet apartments and small Western apartments (about 50 square meters, or close to the Moscow average) under subsidy or rent control. For 1982 the comparison was the same, with the added proviso, in the Western cities, of being "in one of the least expensive suburbs." Soviet rents are by any standard quite low: two days' work, versus over a week in the West, will rent an apartment for a month. There are few Western cities without a shortage in subsidized rental housing, so one cannot say that such accommodations have always been offered at those rates. But the Soviet housing shortage remains so acute that housing at these "social" prices remains an item rationed by years-long waiting lists, and compromised as well in quality, amenities, durability, and other attributes; considering these, one must be careful not to overstate how much of a deal the Soviet worker-renter is getting for his near-nominal payments.

All in all, from a Western viewpoint this is grim picture. Whether one looks at the simple per capita or the per one hundred-households calculations on the possession of various items, at broader comparisons that show striking parallels between the USSR in the late 1950s and the United States in 1890, or at other indicators such as the cost-per-hour figures just discussed, Soviet poverty is clear. This should not be surprising. Figures from 1971 to 1982 by themselves illuminate very little of the comparative affluence of Soviet life in the 1970s and 1980s, when compared with the 1950s and early 1960s. The journey from dire penury to even a threadbare consumer life has been a long one, and it does impress those Soviet citizens who have experienced both the beginning and the end points. Those who were, say, 15 years of age in 1953 and thus still have some memory of the living standards under "high Stalinism" are now around 50—and within ten years of retirement. The considerable share of the work force that is younger and has little recollection of the Khrushchev years (or none at all), has no context from which to evaluate living standards that involve two hours' labor for a kilo of beef, two weeks for a suit. Human nature being what it is, we may suspect that Soviet citizens "at home" do not necessarily look with gratitude toward the state for cheap housing: minimal rent (after the long wait for an apartment) is part of their life, an entitlement, and the contrasting high costs to renters in the West are not a "reality." In those circumstances wherein the Soviet worker invests more hourly effort per consumer item than his Western counterpart, citizens have had a shortage economy to thank—one that had grown, by 1990, much more acute and provoked unrest.

To readers anxious for a "real" comparison of what Soviet earners make relative to their American or West European counterparts ("What's that in dollars?"), I would say that such numbers will not really clarify matters. The ruble is not convertible—it is a "soft" currency and has no value outside the USSR. Inside, the Soviets set exchange rates, and they have typically set them high. The 1986 study that brought us table 4.15 calculated the take-home pay of an American industrial worker at $1,196.85 per month and, converted at Soviet exchange rates, the Soviet worker's monthly 211.70 rubles to $279.23 in dollar equivalent.[83] A calculation made on December 1981 data, using an independent estimate of "consumption purchasing power parities," credits the American worker with $983.98 monthly and deflates the Soviet counterpart's 177.30 rubles monthly to a $171.05 equivalent. (This, however, involves projecting a ruble-parity figure calculated in 1972 across a decade wherein the "cost-of-living index" in the USSR is assumed to have risen by 2 percent per year—a figure that, in the light of acknowledgments under glasnost', seems quite low.)[84]

What those rubles will buy was reflected in some measure in our earlier time-expenditure data. But recall that Moscow—the site of all the research—has been generally better-provisioned than other cities. Availability of goods/services falls off steeply as one moves from "the center"; what one can consume depends on what is available. The East-West disparities are significant indeed, and not so readily subject to quantification. It is one thing to read numbers, another to have some familiarity with the "feel" of Soviet life, with the stores, with the interior size and amenities of "average" apartments, to compare these with life in New York, or Washington, or elsewhere, and then try to make sense of a "how much" question.

One of the most impressive efforts to calculate real per capita consumption in the USSR relative to American levels (not the same as take-home pay, but closer to the focus of the "living standard" question so frequently asked) arrived at an estimate that, in 1976, the USSR figure was 34.4 percent that of America's.[85] Gertrude Schroeder's calculations were methodologically sound and difficult to fault. Yet, at a level perhaps more metaphysical than methodological, they failed to satisfy another experienced observer of Soviet and Russian reality, whose extended reaction is worth quoting at length:

In the West, some fantastic statistics circulate about the Soviet standard of living. A contributor to a recent Congressional study, for example, claims that *per capita* consumption by the Soviet population in the late 1970s was one third that of the United States and less than one half that of West Germany and France. Such conclusions undoubtedly rest on very professional analysis of official Soviet statistics, but they fly in the face of common sense as well as data obtained from other sources, especially those that have the benefit of personal contact with Soviet reality. One good indicator of living standard is the proportion of income spent on food—the higher a country's living standard, the smaller the share of the family budget that is devoted to food purchases. In the United States, this figure stands at 23 percent for a family with an intermediate income; a high proportion of that money goes for proteins, vegetables and fruits. In the USSR, according to recent figures, 54.4 percent of the average family's income is spent on food (much of it starches), which represents a higher proportion than is devoted to this purpose in Greece and Portugal, and even slightly exceeds that which a Russian family had spent on feeding itself in 1900.

The sheer difficulty of obtaining food in the Soviet Union, which is, after all, the most basic indicator of living standard, makes mockery of comparisons with the United States or Western Europe.[86]

Let me allow that both Schroeder and her critic, Richard Pipes, are "correct." Let it be understood that the gaps at the absolute level were huge between Soviet workers and the average for Western workers. For the Soviet worker, this was not, for a long time, necessarily critical. Compared to other population groups, Soviet statistics have shown "workers" doing not badly; the same statistics, at a greater level of detail, show some workers (in well-established large plants in priority industry) doing well indeed compared to other citizens, but those in small, light-industry plants were among the relatively disadvantaged. We must look at subjective perceptions of these matters in Brezhnev-era data—aware that in recent times of growing economic disorder, no one is really satisfied with what their rubles will buy.

. . . and How Workers View It

What do we know about how workers feel about the wages and welfare they derive from their work? Evidence that young workers, especially, have found little that is interesting or inherently rewarding in many of the jobs they perform is not surprising. But they may have no complaints about the pay; the core of the problem may be the expectation of younger people, who have not known the material want their elders knew, that work *should* be interesting and offer intrinsic satisfaction. Older workers will have more modest expectations about work itself: satisfaction with pay, hours, and travel time may equal "work satisfaction," period.

But satisfaction with a "just reward" probably will not depend solely on some personal equation of pay versus job. It may also involve comparisons with others, perceptions of their work and what *they* make. Satisfaction may also turn on definitions of aspirations toward a "reasonable" or "comfortable" standard of living, and an assessment of how closely one's earnings approximate those needed to achieve such a standard.

Research by Aaron Vinokur in various Siberian plants in the late 1960s provided a picture of workers who in large measure were dissatisfied with incomes below what they considered necessary to lead a "normal" life.[87] Partial results of his study (table 4.16) indicate a good deal of dissatisfaction with the failure of per capita family income and family needs to balance and thus produce a "normal" living standard, no matter *what* the level of pay. The table shows only some of the income levels in the lowest and highest ranges, plus a "middling" category—61–70 rubles per capita monthly—whose bottom end equals the minimum wage set in 1968, which had a strongly equalizing effect for a time. That large majorities found 21–40 rubles per month "much below needs" is hardly surprising; but solid majorities in three of four samples at the 61–70-ruble level felt the same. Only a minority of those with high per capita incomes (91 rubles and up) find even this level "satisfactory" to their households' needs.

Needs, of course, are subjective; but this is precisely the point. Even workers whose family per capita income was *well* above the average of the late 1960s felt a significant shortfall between that level and their own ideas about what material resources were required for a "normal" life; on the whole, the shortfall was about one-third, as table 4.17 indicates. When they were asked to estimate their "needed" per capita level, workers in each of the groups (I–IV) in table 4.16 specified the "needed" amounts (column 2) versus their current average per capita household income (column 1),[88] in rubles per month. Columns 3–6 express the actual reported income as percentages of "needed" income (column 3); of the minimum norm (51.5 rubles) established for the European USSR (column 4); of the official estimate of per capita income in the "average family" in 1967 (59.0 rubles) (column 5); and, finally, of the "rational level of consumption"—a comfortable living standard—calculated by Soviet economists at 153.3 rubles per capita monthly (column 6).[89]

TABLE 4.16

Evaluations of Incomes, Siberian Workers, Late 1960s (percent)

	21–30	31–40	61–70	91–100	100 +
I. Metallurgical plant, Novosibirsk, 1967					
Satisfactory	—	—	8.0	66.7	40.5
Slightly below needs	—	2.3	23.9	10.0	21.7
Much below needs	100.0	97.7	67.0	23.3	37.8
Hard to say	—	—	1.1	—	—
II. Steel workers, Kuznetsk, 1968					
Satisfactory	—	—	3.1	33.3	35.8
Slightly below needs	—	12.5	21.9	11.1	12.5
Much below needs	100.0	83.3	75.0	55.6	52.5
Hard to say	—	4.2	—	—	—
III. Blaster/roller workers, Kuznetsk, 1968					
Satisfactory	—	—	12.5	29.4	32.3
Slightly below needs	—	19.0	15.0	5.9	16.1
Much below needs	100.0	66.7	60.0	52.8	45.2
Hard to say	—	14.3	12.5	5.9	6.4
IV. Electric machine plant, Novosibirsk, 1968					
Satisfactory	*	2.0	16.2	(51.1)**	*
Slightly below needs	16.7	15.6	36.5	(20.6)**	*
Much below needs	33.3	82.4	47.3	(21.8)**	*
Hard to say	—	—	—	(6.5)**	—

Source: Adapted from A. Vinokur, *Material'naia zainteresovannost' rabochikh sotsialisti-cheskoi promyshlennosti v trude i ego rezultatakh* (Novosibirsk, 1970), pp. 108–109, as cited in Aaron Vinokur and Gur Ofer, "Family Income Levels for Soviet Industrial Workers, 1965–1975," in A. Kahan and B. Ruble, eds., *Industrial Labor in the USSR* (New York: Pergamon Press, 1979), p. 195.

* Missing data.

** Per capita income 90 rubles and above.

Findings such as these are given additional context in the large-scale research on some 2,900 Soviet emigrés of the late 1970s conducted under the Soviet Interview Project.[90] Perceptions drawn from the Soviet experience of the late 1970s show workers at 57.5 percent only slightly behind the sample average of all occupational groups (61.4 percent) in being convinced that living standards had declined "over the previous five years."[91] Strong evidence emerges as well from the emigré survey that workers as well as others perceive a lack of mate-

TABLE 4.17
Real Per Capita Income, and Estimates of Adequacy, Siberian Workers,
Late 1960s

Category	Actual Rubles Per Capita (1)	Per Capita Rubles "Needed" (2)	(3)	(4)	(5)	(6)
I	57.3	86.4	66	111	97	56
II	55.4	84.6	65	108	94	55
III	53.2	75.8	70	103	90	49
IV	50.3	72.7	69	98	85	47

Source: See table 4.16.
Note: See table 4.16 for categories I–IV, and see text for columns (3)–(6).

rial incentives as a critical factor in declining labor productivity—the
latter diagnosis shared by a majority of the total sample.[92] Tendencies
to blame either bad management, or the economic system as a whole,
were much less pronounced. Asked to rate sources of job satisfaction,
blue-collar respondents in the emigré sample mentioned their income
in only 0.5 percent of cases (lower white-collar personnel hardly
more, at 1 percent), while professionals mentioned this in 27.3 percent of their responses.[93]

These emigré survey results square, roughly, with nationwide Soviet research of 1980–81, not reported until 1986 (table 4.18) on peo-

TABLE 4.18
Estimates of Material Situations, Various Social Groups, 1980–81
(in percentages)

Situation	Worker	Collective Farmer	Lower Nonmanual	Specialist
1. Live day to day; no savings possible	11.1	10.9	12.8	9.0
2. Day to day sufficiency; save for clothing, etc.	21.9	19.1	25.1	17.7
3. Some savings, but not enough for large durables	42.6	36.2	38.9	40.8
4. Sufficient to buy durables, but not for car	16.6	21.8	13.7	23.8
5. "We deny ourselves nothing"	7.8	12.0	9.5	8.7

Source: V. D. Sitnikova and A. A. Michurin, "Sub'ektivno-otsenochnoe vospriiatie
obraza zhizni," Sotsiologicheskie issledovaniia, no. 4 (1986), p. 90.

ple's characterization of their own material situations, by socio-occupational group, according to how satisfied they were that their wants were met.[94] Allowing that the collective farmers' rather high estimates of their situations may depend on a set of assumptions and expectations about consumption that is lower than that of the other, predominantly urban groups, it is striking that workers were not much more dissatisfied than other groups. There is no evidence that they saw themselves as being advantaged, but a comparison of worker with specialist responses does not show workers massively *less* satisfied with the adequacy of their lot compared to their better-certified white-collar colleagues.

But they were not, in an absolute sense, very satisfied, either. There are ample reasons for workers to feel dissatisfied with their levels of material reward. We need not assume that the blue-collar rank and file have kept tabs on the minimum wage-driven rise of agricultural workers and its diminution of old worker advantages, nor that it is aware of the dynamics of marriage choice and fertility, which allow many routine white-collar families to do as well or better on a per capita basis. Not all standards can be comparative in this sense. For many workers, the basis for dissatisfaction will be a discrepancy between one's income and perceived effort: even high earners, in arduous heavy work, might regard their wages as inadequate compensation for the burdens of the job, especially when those wages do not command desired goods and services and when the real benefits lag behind the additional rubles in the pay packet. (The July 1989 outbreak of strikes among Soviet coal miners was a notable example of this kind of collective judgment.) It is also noteworthy here that subsidies—nominal rent in state apartments, essentially free utilities, stable prices for many basic goods—have not been felt to compensate for inadequate wages. Acceptance, and assumption, of these benefits seems by now built into Soviet mass (including working-class) psychology and it is unlikely that many Soviet citizens would have been willing to give them up. Habits run deep. At the end of the Brezhnev era, few people perceived a trade-off between endemic shortages and subsidized low prices. Workers must have shared the predominant attitude reported of the late-1970s emigrés of the Soviet Interview Project, who "saw little relationship between the low price of subsidized meat in state stores and supply shortages," wanting both the below-cost prices "and a perfectly elastic supply at those prices."[95]

The Soviet worker, by the end of the Brezhnev era, was the long-term product of a system that had, at first, materially favored educated professionals over workers and, just as clearly, workers over peasants. A political-economic state preference for heavy industry over consumption had further led to a sector and branch bias in favor of workers who extracted the wherewithal, and built the products, of the "metal-eating" and related industries, and against light/consumer industry.

Over more recent times, since the passing of power from Khrushchev to Brezhnev, workers had benefited more than professional white-collar groups from the diminished scarcity value of the professionals and from the persistent labor-hunger, for skilled or unskilled workers alike, of an essentially coal-and-steel industrial economy. Worker wages increased, drifting markedly upward relative to those of bosses, engineers, and other upper-strata production personnel. But long-overdue attention to the least advantaged in Soviet society also saw a rise in farmers' wage and income levels closer to the workers' average. Successive increases in the minimum wage lifted bottom-range pay in many sectors and branches. Within many historically "priority" branches, the skill-based wage spread on the *tarifnaia setka* narrowed, as unskilled jobs came to command a premium because of their unattractive aspects.

Far from a tightly managed bureaucratic machine, the mechanism of pay allocation for the workers as a whole included many variant, situational, near-spontaneous elements. Though simplified from the near chaos of the late Stalin era, the wage system was still subject to various adjustments on the factory floor: conceptions of what a worker "needed," of what the factory needed to pay to keep a worker in a necessary but low-rank job, often led to adjustments upward in the scheduled wage and in the pursuit of good industrial relations and a generalized sense of justice. On the whole, the effect of these adjustments was a leveling one.

All this took place in an economy poor by West European and North American standards—poor in Stalin's time, poor in the late 1970s, though in its own historic terms at a much higher level in the 1980s than in the 1950s. The effects of this poverty were, however, less than dramatic. Until glasnost' brought them the bad news in the late 1980s, Soviet workers remained largely isolated from international standards of comparison. Older workers with any memory of Stalin-era privations saw much progress in the two decades after 1953; they were less likely to feel poor by their own chronological calculus. Younger workers, more demanding of their jobs, have seen less progress by far in their material status, since they started from a higher level. But workers on the whole exhibited a dissatisfaction with their wages (and what they buy in living-standard terms) not very much greater than other occupational groups. Large numbers were dissatisfied in the blue-collar ranks, but this was true of the professional strata as well, in what are now seen as the early phases of the economy's accelerating collapse.

To any dramatic expression of such dissatisfaction, the Soviet state before Gorbachev was generally and effectively hostile. But it seems likely that the dissatisfactions themselves were cushioned, to a degree, by other aspects of life. The relative egalitarianism was one element—workers could not "see," in this goods-poor society, others doing visibly much better. Prices on the daily necessities were subsidized, and low. Even if many of these were often unavailable, the worker was not insulted by price tags beyond his ability to pay if the goods were there. On the factory floor, the nexus between excess effort and excess earnings, and on the street between excess earnings and excess consumption, was weak—more shortage-based "egalitarianism," and a reason for the relatively low effort of many workers.

From all of this emerge some of the contradictory elements in the picture provided by both Soviet and emigré research. A fair degree of dissatisfaction has been evident. On the other hand, the Soviet Interview Project revealed that, among the emigré respondents, majorities rated themselves very satisfied or "somewhat satisfied" with their Soviet living standard, with their housing, and almost 80 percent with their jobs; only on the availability of goods were the vast majority dissatisfied.[96] The respondents were not just workers; they were more urban than the Soviet average; but they were not necessarily an extraordinarily privileged group. This does not amount to an insoluble puzzle. Satisfaction with a Soviet apartment may be high, either because acquiring it has been so long a process, or because rent is minimal or because one anticipates large profit from its sale if one owns it. Job satisfaction in general may rank high if the job is secure, involves little effort, and allows one to be part of a familiar social circle. Expressions of discontent over pay per se—over what is available in the stores versus what one's rubles would buy if supplies were adequate—amount to looking at a glass half-empty. Expression of retrospective content with a familiar job or getting a cheap apartment one had waited long to acquire are ways of seeing that same glass as half-full.

However conducive all of this once was to social stability in the context of slowing growth, growing distortions, and inefficiency as the Soviet economy moved through the lackluster years of the 1970s, it came more and more under attack by economists who regarded the result as the long-term costs of egalitarianism and security at low effort. While they had long offered quiet cautionary comments about wage trends and egalitarian "drift" on the pages of academic journals—with little effect—from the mid-1970s on, their tone grew more urgent. They claimed that equalization of wages between blue-collar skill levels and the narrowing of the gap between workers and professional and technical personnel in and outside material production had gone too far, sapping motivation and efficiency and bringing matters to a dangerous impasse.

In 1978 two distinguished economists, while endorsing in general terms diminished income differentiation, argued that it could only be justified by reductions in the "qualitative heterogeneity" of labor: the upscaling of the occupational structure that should come with mechanization, skill-upgrading, and elimination of low-content jobs.[97] Meanwhile, in their view, *greater* wage differentiation was essential.[98] The reduction in differentiation, via the bidding up of the price for work in low-skilled, unattractive jobs, was an expensive, inefficient leveling, greatly accelerated by labor shortages: "The higher demand for personnel in various occupations (especially at the low and middle skill level) reduces the differentiation of wages even when it is due to shortcomings in the organization of production and planning."[99]

Striking a similar note, another economist in 1980 implied that social considerations were fostering egalitarian trends not economically justifiable (reductions in differentiation were "conditioned not only by economic, but also by social factors, and above all by the social policy of the state").[100] Looking backward, he cautioned against the 1960s trends which saw a reduction in the average-minimum wage ratio from 3.47:1 in 1964 to 1.81:1 in 1968. These had not answered economic-development needs,[101] and—by implication—a drift along the same path in the later 1970s augured poorly for meeting those needs in the future.

Specialist consensus seemed to build as the Brezhnev era neared its end. In the wake of Twenty-sixth Party Congress decisions, a 1981 article in *Voprosy ekonomiki* cited the need for an increase in pay for engineering and technical professionals, to produce a "better correlation" with workers' pay, as an "urgent problem."[102] Seventeen years of leveling had done its work: the wage advantages of engineers and technicians over workers in industry had been 45.9 percent in 1965, 36.3 percent in 1970, and by 1979 it had fallen to 15.9 percent.[103] Four years later the labor economist E. L. Manevich struck the same note, finding "serious shortcomings" in a system of reward wherein the span of differentiation across engineering and technical personnel, skilled and unskilled blue-collar workers had been so greatly reduced.[104]

Labor "shortages" (the interactive result of smaller cohorts entering the work force, excess openings of new plants, and continuing low per capita productivity) and the persistence of bad habits among managers who had stronger incentives for volume production than for efficiency had played a major role in the leveling, which many now saw as sapping motivation. Seniority, and the acquisition of higher skill levels that normally accompany it, should have had more effect than was evident to two students of work life, writing in *Sotsiologicheskie issledovaniia* in 1984:

> We can hardly consider it proper . . . that the average wage of respondents who have worked in the same occupation and at the same job for over 10 years is lower than for those with seniority of 7 to 10 years and approximately the same as for those who have worked at the same job for 4 to 6 years (respectively, 233, 239, 221 rubles). The obviously inflated wages of those who have insufficient experience in their occupations are the results of recent labor shortages and efforts on the part of enterprises to fill positions at any cost.[105]

The skill rationale for increase in wage level had also worked at cross-purposes to the extra compensation—whether built into the system of differentials we saw earlier, or "fiddled" in the individual plant—that was paid for arduous, heavy work. In the wood/cellulose industry, as the two authors noted, "the physical demands of a job are often in inverse proportion to the skills it requires."[106]

Finally, they tied together elements of the labor shortage, of reduced differentiation between the engineering-technical professionals and manual workers, and of the concept of social justice and the minimum a worker was seen to "need," in characterizing how the real patterns of compensation had departed from the "system":

> The wage differential system has taken into account only a limited number of primarily geographical, technical, and economic factors, such as which branch an enterprise belongs to, its location, a worker's occupation and wage category, his position, etc., but has not taken into consideration any social factors. Social aspects such as the content of labor, its attractiveness, and differences in working conditions at various places within the same occupation have not been considered. . . .
>
> The result of all this is that actual wage differentials deviate significantly from established norms. Wage levels are often determined not by established norms and wage categories but by unwritten rules about the standard of living a worker should enjoy which have developed locally, essentially without regard to the actual skills or demands of the job. Administrators in the various branches of industry, especially those in factories with small-scale production and in construction organizations, have only fitted norms, orders, and regulations on awarding prizes to this standard, overstating the amount of work actually done and permitting other

inflationary practices. Wages for workers in occupations in short supply are increasing uncontrollably rather than according to any plan. As far as control over wages is concerned, here we often find not administrative decisions which take account of objective shifts in the quantity, quality, and effectiveness of job performance but rather belated reaction to increases in labor turnover. Under such circumstances, wages for work of greater complexity but in less demand, especially in engineering, have inevitably lagged behind those for other jobs.[107]

Sentiments and analyses such as these seemed to predominate in the late 1970s, at least in the major economic journals. Yet they were not unanimous, and the economists who expressed them had not been guiding policy. It was the outcome of policy, or, better, an absence of policy that had allowed "drift," that these economists were attacking. An opposite view is expressed by the economist V. Maier in his 1977 article in *Voprosy ekonomiki*.[108] Maier struck a relatively noncontroversial note, crediting the directives laid down by the Twenty-fifth Party Congress to raise wages and salaries in the nonproductive sector with anticipated cuts in interbranch differentials, and called for further "comparability" adjustments toward "full equalization" of wages and salaries for jobs of equal complexity and arduousness independent of branch (hardly something for which the Soviet economy had been notable).[109]

But beyond this, Maier—and others like him—called for a fine-tuning in various areas of wage setting which, while all aiming at consistency with the principle of "distribution according to the quality and quantity of labor" and with the need for incentives, could produce "a stable ratio of the existing differentiation of wages."[110] Far from a puritanical egalitarian, Maier also argued for policies to raise levels of real consumption and standards of living for the whole population—a necessary element in reducing group and individual inequality. But his remarks on the price mechanism at a time when subsidies in the state retail networks were already coming into open questioning seemed off the track: "In order to satisfy the population's demand, prices must be maneuvered on the basis of *a stable or—still better—a declining level of state retail prices*. In such a case it is naturally necessary to divert some of the resources that promote a direct increase in money incomes *to lower the average price level*" (emphasis added).[111] While Maier may have had in mind a supply-driven lowering of prices on durables which, according to his views, should be produced in much greater numbers (thus, perhaps, to soak up some of the latent demand reflected in growing savings deposits), his price-reduction proposals seemed generally to run counter to a line many would soon advocate:

a cutting of state price subsidies, especially on food, and a distribution of some of the funds thus saved in wage-packet compensation, to balance ensuing price increases. Maier was writing during a period of transition, with little hint yet of the massive problems to come. His comments on "equal pay for equal work" were fairly standard positions, however far the Soviet economy's bias toward heavy and against light industry may have been from such equality. Raising living standards was hardly controversial, though advocacy of price cutting was. Such measures were redolent of the more utopian elements evoked in Khrushchev's 1961 party program that emphasized the meeting of people's "needs," independent of the kind of work they did, as one of communism's promises. Increasingly predominant in economic discussions was an emphasis on the fact that the USSR was still in a socialist phase, wherein people's work, rather than their needs, must determine most of their material outcomes—and wherein subsidies, rather than prices, would be candidates for cutting.

All in all, the selection of policy alternatives in these areas was not subject to a great deal of public ventilation in the pre-Gorbachev USSR. After broad plan parameters for output, assortment, the input of labor, and the total wage bill were determined in an interaction between Gosplan and the ministries, which worked from Politburo-approved guidelines somewhat affected by these bodies, via their expertise and agenda definition. The parties that had some role in fleshing out the details affecting wage rates and differentiation were the State Committee on Labor and Social Problems (Goskomtrud)—a ministerial-level body—and the All-Union Central Council of Trade Unions (AUCCTU). The difficulties of obtaining the details of this sort of politicking are great. On the whole, it seems that Goskomtrud—and its staff economists in their public statements—tended to be the party of "efficiency" and differentiation, while the AUCCTU, though hardly a combative actor on behalf of working-class interests, took a more egalitarian, "welfarist" view, likely to argue against the sort of incentive and "stimulation" programs that encompassed sticks as well as carrots at the plant level.[112] One analyst attributed "clout" to the Brezhnev-era union, based on the fact that, on the organizational chart of the Soviet system, the AUCCTU, as opposed to Goskomtrud, was not a ministerial body but outside the government, only responsible (as was the government) to the party.[113] But this likely overstated both the independence and bureaucratic impact of the AUCCTU in affecting matters. What is clear is that policy had favored rough egalitarianism, within broad branches and sectors, for the Soviet masses, notably the workers. At the rarefied heights of the Politburo, its diverse members can scarcely have entertained precise notions of "correct" wage differentiation. But their general perceptions may well have reflected convictions that "welfare" at the bottom remained important for stability and worker motivation, as was the tendency to favor upgrading minimum wages thus stressing equality and to maintain price subsidies and social consumption benefits. Given the strength of the state and the political quiescence of Soviet workers, political leaders were not likely to fear a revolt; nonetheless, they must have felt that to err on the side of those "unwritten rules about the standard of living a worker should enjoy"[114] was only prudent, and that there was as much risk as promise in an alternative anti-egalitarian path to greater efficiency and productivity. It was a consensus that would not long survive the new economics of perestroika, nor the clouds that gathered over the Soviet economy.

Gorbachev's Perestroika: Effort and Merit

With the accession of Gorbachev, the premises of economic policy and the stability that had seemed to guarantee blue-collar Soviet society a quiet and familiar life began to shift radically. Gorbachev's calls for radical reform, for acceleration (*uskorenie*) and restructuring (*perestroika*) were based on a deeply negative appraisal of the Soviet economy's performance and prospects. Growth had slowed to near-nil. The economy squandered increasingly expensive inputs while producing outputs below world standards that were unsalable abroad and increasingly unacceptable to the home market. The technological gap with the West continued to widen. Top to bottom, people "worked poorly." Skilled and unskilled, drunk and sober, swift and slow, all received too-similar rewards. Those rewards bought little beyond that stable minimum to which the mass had grown accustomed; now, even that minimum was threatened. An economy so misdirected, with so little effective effort invested, could scarcely be a cornucopia of desired goods, no matter how rich its resource base. Central in the calls for reform was the notion that nothing could be done unless attention were paid to the human factor.

One core concern was motivating, and effectively rewarding, work: complex work "deserved" more compensation than simple work (in an economy overstocked with arduous, unskilled jobs, in any case), good work more than bad. From the beginning it was clear that Gorbachev and his supporters and advisers had in mind broad changes in wage and salary policy, ones that would depart from any long-term solicitude for blue-collar workers. As the economist Oleg Bogomolov put it in a United Nations report in late 1985, "Fundamental changes may be expected in systems of wage rates and in the differentials between pay of particular categories of workers. For example, the Soviet Union . . . intend[s] to raise the salaries of engineers and technicians, scientists, designers, teachers, and medical staff."[115] The categories he named were, of course, those jobs either in material production ("engineers and technicians") or in the broad service sector, where pay had not risen much during the Brezhnev years, ones seemingly perennially underpaid relative to the upward-moving wage rates of blue-collar workers in industry. These early signals were more than borne out as the trend of wage policy became clearer in 1986 and 1987. The Gorbachev program, echoing the calls of so many economists for less egalitarianism in reward between different levels of skill in the working class, and in the relationship of workers' and college-educated professionals' pay, bade farewell to the policies of the Brezhnev era. As one Western student put it, Gorbachev was risking conflict, via a policy of "squeezing the traditional working class,"[116] in pursuit of a social policy which implied "a markedly different set of prospective winners and losers than obtained under the rule of his predecessors."[117] The reformist sociologist Tatiana Zaslavskaia, in an interview with the Hungarian daily *Nepszabadsag*, was hardly less pointed: "If we want . . . radical changes . . . there will be a relative change in the situation of classes, groups and strata of society, with advantage for some . . . disadvantage for others.'"[118]

More joined the chorus of voices, attacking as muddled the thinking that, over the years, identified "social justice" with equality of distribution, with "leveling," with padding the pay of those with low wage rates to bring them up to some satisfactory level. November 1986 saw the publication of strongly differentiated guidelines for pay increases: 20–25 percent, on the average, for workers in production; 30–35 percent for the various categories of (white-collar) engineering and technical personnel (ITR); and 40–45 percent for "leading categories of specialists, such as designers, technologists and foremen."[119] Underpaid professionals in education, medicine, and other non-goods-producing services were to receive raises of about 30 percent,[120] some of it meant to correct the contrast so typical of the Soviet system, say between skilled steelworker and rank-and-file physician, wherein *he* earned much more than *she*. Commitment to greater differentiation of reward within blue-collar ranks was furthered by a proviso that, on the typical six-grade *tarifnaia setka* for a given industry or branch, workers at level III and above—but not the less-skilled lower levels— would be eligible for 12–14 percent bonuses for high-quality output.[121]

But such raises, for workers at least, were not to be automatic, and not to be financed, as hitherto, from the state budget. They were tied to plant output and "profits" and conditional on material and labor saving. "More and better" output could finance raises, as could savings that could result from laying off unneeded workers (a possibility which, as we shall see, was very controversial) and taking advantage of wage-fund recapture. Less specific than announcements of increases tied to result was the logical corollary—that if a more demanding measure of "results" by way of fulfilling the production plan were imposed, wage decreases might be in the offing through the loss of bonuses for plan fulfillment that had come to be regarded effectively by workers as part of their base wage.

How many workers benefited, and how much, from the raises authorized in 1987 and early 1988 is not really clear. Some plants were likely to do better than others in meeting performance targets that would allow the funding of raises which the new policies had authorized. But a significant number, in a confrontation with the new methods of measuring their "results" as suggested above, lost ground, leaving their workers in a fundamentally new situation.

For years, Soviet workers had experienced the protective effects of a weak link between the quality of their finished products and their acceptability. No "market" disciplined the line worker. The designated consumers of the substandard products could not easily reject them, and the producers had already been paid. Within the factory, inspection tended to laxness: inspectors, after all, worked for the same factory management as the workers. Workers and bosses had a stake, in wage/bonus terms, in assuring that the volume plan was fulfilled; inspectors were unlikely to quibble with output and jeopardize their quotas. Such expectations were built into the "social relations of production": part of the predictable rhythm of the workplace, and the psychological security of the anticipated wage-plus-bonus.

Though poor-quality output had been a perennial complaint in the economic press (we speak here of decades, not mere years), the very persistence of such patterns had given workers little reason to anticipate change. But, as the rhetoric of perestroika grew louder in Gorbachev's second year, a party-state resolution in July 1986[122] authorized a new form of quality control, via the "state acceptance commission" (gospriemka), which would place a new kind of inspector in factories—one unbeholden to factory management and working under the aegis of the State Committee on Standards (Gosstandart). Introduced on January 1, 1987, these measures at least promised a new departure.

At a Central Committee conference on November 14, Gorbachev delivered a pep talk on gospriemka, asserting that its emphasis on quality of output was quite compatible with the acceleration (*uskorenie*) he had been calling for.[123] A few days later, I. I. Isaev, the deputy chairman of *Gosstandart*, reviewed some of what was to be expected, in a speech on Moscow television.[124] In all, 1,500 industrial enterprises would come under *gospriemka* in 1987. A selection of inspectors was under way, often from the factories over whose product quality they were to mount guard; however, the nominations of factory directors were frequently ignored in favor of those higher-up in party organizations.

An experiment with *gospriemka*-type practice had already shown that worker reactions were likely to be anything but positive. A strike arose in the giant KamAZ truck plant—a showpiece of imported industrial technology of the 1970s—when disgruntled workers found that tougher, independent quality control had cut into expected bonuses via lowered plan-fulfillment figures.[125] Late in December 1986, the chairman of Gosstandart had good warrant in expressing the belief that the new system would cause financial problems in some factories.[126]

The year 1987 opened the era of *gospriemka* as policy and practice, and the shakedown cruise was anything but smooth. Two weeks into the year, the daily *Sovetskaia Rossiia* reported that *gospriemka* was bringing wage cuts in some plants.[127] At a large farm machinery plant in Tiumen' *oblast'*, average pay suffered a 33 percent cut in January as inspectors found output quality wanting.[128] Reportedly, fully 60 percent of the 1,500 plants under the new system failed to meet the January plan targets because tougher inspectors rejected their output.[129] Generally, reports indicated shop-floor tension, with workers angered over the unfamiliar discipline.[130] In January 1987, enterprises under *gospriemka* saw 83.9 percent of their output passed by the inspectors[131]—numbers, though not striking in themselves, had a wage impact that was much magnified in the effect on bonuses for plan fulfillment.

The new system put both workers and managers in an unfamiliar situation. A major difficulty was to convince both parties that, after many years of second-level priority, output quality was now a major concern. Not only workers and managers, but also the local party officials who bore final responsibility for the performance of enterprises in their areas were reluctant to "get aboard." With six months of experience, the first deputy chairman of Gosstandart reported resistance on the part of party officials in three *oblast'*s in the trade-union daily *Trud*.[132] Tension between old notions of plan fulfillment—that the plan was fulfilled when it was said to be fulfilled—versus the new inspection-based system was evident in the reported accusation aimed by the *obkom* secretary in Karaganda at the head of the *gospriemka* operation in a local machinery plant—that he was "not concerned with plan fulfillment."[133]

Patterns of evasion had been common in managerial behavior since Stalin's time. Over the Brezhnev years, managers had had time to further hone some of their techniques to an edge sufficiently sharp to counteract new forces. For example, a needle-fabricating complex in the Moscow area, faced with the new inspection system, managed to get its technical product specifications lowered to a level it could meet, making an "end run" around *gospriemka*. The same organization, faced with the inability of one of its plants to come even close to standards, hived it off into independence and thus out of the orbit of the 1,500 enterprises where the *gospriemka* ran![134]

For workers, there was much evidence that the combination of minimal effort that had worked in the past, and the worker-management collusion that had guaranteed the expected *vyvodilovka*—the adequate, justified wage no matter what the real output—no longer met the purpose. One reader of *Trud* complained that *gospriemka* created extra work—should it not, then, mean raises in pay? The answer was, predictably, negative.[135] The experience of wage cuts exacerbated factory conflicts. In a ceramic-fixtures plant, a worker characterized the *gospriemka* inspectors as "parasites" and "useless people"—even those who had been employed at the plant before the new system.[136]

Worker feelings that they, particularly, were targeted by the new system—that their "social right" not to work hard, rather than directors' rights to collect high salaries, was the specific object of the January 1987 changes—were pronounced. Even before its introduction, other "pay-by-result" schemes, linking wage-plus-bonus totals to accepted or marketable output generated complaint: in one of Gorbachev's walk-arounds during a visit to Vladivostok in July, a worker complained to him that while he and his fellow workers were on "pay by result," the management was not. The General Secretary responded that all, including management, would be.[137] Over a year later, on a television call-in show, Ivan Gladkii, chairman of Goskomtrud, answered a complaint from a worker: in his plant, blue-collar pay cuts averaged 50–80 rubles per month under the new conditions, but management seemed to be getting bonuses! Gladkii replied that this contravened the whole rationale of the system, that managerial bonuses, just as workers', were tied to production, and he invited the worker to call again with the name of the enterprise involved.[138] (Other commentary and wage/salary guidance materials made clear that managerial and professional bonuses—up to a generous 75 percent of base salary under the new system—were themselves to be linked to "results";[139] but there was much evidence that workers still found themselves in situations where, while they might face effective pay cuts or get minimal raises, management increments seemed much higher, independent of results.)[140]

On the level of broad policy and its implementation, the changes and tensions that workers and managers felt were all part of a grand design. They were part of a "reform" of wage and salary scales that, with the onset of 1987, was meant to cover blue-collar and white-collar personnel in the material production branches of the economy: 75 million workers and employees, or about two-thirds of the labor force in the state and collective economy.[141] Policy guidance came in a flood of articles in the economic press as well as in specialized journals.[142] It required a forty-page article in Goskomtrud's monthly journal to lay out the detailed mechanics of the new wage/salary/bonus-setting procedures.[143] Just as *gospriemka* was a last-ditch example of trying to get results by "command-administrative" methods rather than by economic levers, so the bureaucracy still assumed, in the area of wages and bonuses, an immense burden of detailed regulation in the absence of market-determined wages.

Major and consistent themes involved the linking of pay to "results." In terms of the base pay, authorized raises all around were to be conditional on the plant's fulfillment of its delivery plan and hence its earnings. Bonuses, again, were to remain just that. The last recalculation of wage and salary levels in the production sectors of the economy had taken place in 1972–75, and by late 1986 average earnings had risen 1.5 times, though base wage and salary levels were the same. Bonuses, then, for many amounted to almost half of their pay.[144] New output norms were meant to cut back on this result of drift, and managers and engineering-technical personnel, for whom handsome bonus levels were authorized as an additional recognition of their "underpayment" in recent years, would find these dependent on plan fulfillment[145] as much as line workers.

Obviously, moving all the enterprises in industry, construction, transport, communications, and state agriculture onto a new system was problematic. Early reviews of experience in introducing the pay reform showed a fair diversity,[146] and various problems emerged—or persisted—as the banner year of 1987 wore on. Some plant administrations probably sought savings by using their new "self-financing" right (and obligation) to release workers without following all the guidelines for consultation, retraining, and the like: they were warned that "spontaneity" in this regard was not permitted.[147] Other administrations made the bonus process overly complicated, adding on their own all sorts of conditions to the awarding of bonuses that were evidently not related to the economic results,[148] while *vyvodilovka* reasserted itself in smoothing out distinctions in performance between individuals and groups. In one factory, two shops increased their output to a level 111–117 percent of the target, four others only a bit above the 100 percent base—but all involved in all six shops received essentially the same 10 percent bonus.[149] All in all, 1987 was a year of tension and confusion, with little indication of any uniform movement along the lines laid out. One year-end review noted that nothing was working mechanically, and that the diversity of pay practices nationwide was still huge: hardly a surprise, since, as the author revealed, there were factories that in 1987 had still not shifted their activity onto the principles that applied to them from what remained of the 1965 reform![150]

Reactions to the new pay practices were, predictably, tepid. A 1987 poll, repeated in 1988, encompassing some 11,000 workers and employees in 130 enterprises, asked respondents whether the new policies had been effective in improving their remuneration and in increasing their interest in the results of their work. In 1987 only 9.8 percent rated them very effective, as did 15 percent in 1988; 61.1 percent saw no change in 1987, and 31.5 percent felt this way in 1988. Worse, however, was the fact that those who saw the effects as only negligible went from 17.2 percent in 1987 to 29.6 percent in 1988, and those who saw change for the worse increased from 2.5 percent to 13.9 percent across the two years. Workers made up 40 percent of the sample, and there is little reason to think that, separately, they would have proven more positive than other groups.[151]

For all the confusion, the new pressures on the worker were clear; the reformers showed little reticence in justifying it on meritocratic and efficiency principles, in asserting that more differentiation and more inequality were dictated by "social justice" as well as economic need. Notions that the wage should serve a nonwork, "social compensation" function were dismissed as leading to a "leveling" of rewards, which was undesirable.[152] As the head of the wages section of the Goskomtrud put it, the old system had seen instances where "a lathe operator earned more than a qualified engineer. The new system has eradicated this injustice."[153]

Many workers may have perceived the old situation as unjust, but many others must have been disturbed by another change. More rational utilization of labor "in place" was a major objective of the new economics. This dictated that many factories operating on a single shift be transferred to a two- or three-shift system, essentially by cutting the manning of the first shift and redistributing many of the freed workers over one or two additional shifts. The new guidelines authorized 20 and 40 percent wage supplements, respectively, for the inconvenience of swing and night shifts: but, as one top official made clear, the factory itself would have to finance these supplements, as it would the base wage increases. They would not be automatic; they would not come from the state budget.[154] In some cases, then, they would not be paid.

Would workers who had long been beneficiaries of the state's preference for material production, for the "basic" over the "optional," the heavy industry over the light, find their advantages under assault under the new dispensation? Matters were not clear here. There were implications, in the recognition that the service sector was radically underdeveloped and that many heavy and extractive industry enterprises were losers, that shifts in the allocation of the labor force might occur. But what of wages themselves, of the sectoral and interbranch differentials? Some criticized these in no uncertain terms. The labor sociologist L. A. Gordon,[155] attacking the long-accepted rationale, argued that wage policy still reflected a "status" rather than a "results" system, where certain sectors/branches/jobs were paid more because of a priori notions about their significance for the economy: notions not, in fact, defensible, at least once the economy had gone beyond the base building of the 1930s. If rewards in agriculture had risen by so much since the 1960s, asked Gordon, why should pay in retail trade, health care, and so on remain so far behind industry? Retaining the old status-based differentials neither corresponded to the demands of contemporary economic development nor to an "elementary sense of social justice," when essentially the same job might be paid 1.5 to 2 times higher in one sector than another. To all this, Gordon added the meritocratic view that intrabranch differentials were too low.[156] Others, however, remained ready to defend interbranch differentials.[157] Anticipations of rapid and dramatic shifts in the old hierarchy of wages probably exaggerated the real possibilities. But the long-standing preference for the heavy industry had finally been challenged as a matter of economic logic, policy, and justice. Potentially, some winners might indeed become losers.

Thus emerged the early signs of the displacement of the worker in Soviet social policy. A wage policy that so clearly reckoned less generously than hitherto with blue-collar Soviet society suggested the view that workers themselves were a major problem in the economy, and that they might be dealt with in a manner both economically more harsh and socially and politically less "sensitive" than in the past. At the core was a denial that wages were "welfare"—support society "owed" its members by virtue of their existence. Principle and pragmatism were united here, with the clear implication that the state could not afford, nor would the citizen benefit from, the added "paper" rubles of old-style wage increases in the absence of more useful output.

Thus those professionals and managers with skills, responsibility, and training greater than those of workers deserved more, and would get it. Workers with skills deserved a greater edge over those without, and would get it if they earned it. Leaner manning policies would put more workers on less-desirable shifts: they deserved compensation for the inconvenience, but again it would be paid out only if earned. The assumption that one's factory would go on forever, independent of its balance sheet, and that one's job tenure was thus secure was put into question: a factory that could not "cut it" would need to release workers, and might close. This, at least, was the long-term prospect, however much time—and courage—it might take to implement such policies.

These new policies were likely all the more controversial as a much greater information flow within the USSR focused attention on general material inadequacies in Soviet life, both confirming suspicions that there were many "poor" and confounding those who had asserted that things were, if not perfect, in good order.

Rendering a precise picture of the finances of working-class families in the late Brezhnev to early perestroika years must await more, and more precise, data than have been readily available. Ratios of young and old dependents to active earners, if these vary by class, will affect any picture considerably, as will the very broad dispersion of "chances" to consume around the availability of basic goods at state prices. But the general picture that is being clarified more and more with data published under the new dispensation of glasnost is a grim one.

Near the end of 1987, angry readers' letters to *Izvestiia* attacked statistics published in October, pegging the average monthly wage at around 200 rubles, and the share of the family budget going for food at 28 percent.[158] A mid-1988 report cited an average (mean) household per capita income of 125 rubles—with, predictably, more than half the households below this level; and fully 20 percent of the population living on about 70 rubles monthly—the minimum wage level, and, by 1988 prices, real poverty.[159] While a minimum provisioning level of 205.6 rubles for an urban family of four was established in the 1960s, clearly any calculations pegged to this sum were far out of line by the 1980s[160]—but one Soviet source made the point that the various average and minimum family budgets worked out over the years by scientific research institutes had never really been used in planning, in any case.[161] Indeed, a researcher in the Academy of Sciences backed the irate *Izvestiia* readers on the "poverty" nature of the average Soviet family budget, calculating that 59 percent, not 28, went to food.[162]

Poverty is not simply a "worker's" problem in the USSR—elements of all strata, to one degree or another, will fall into the trap of "under-provisioning" (*maloobespechennost'*)—a polite word typically used until recently. Indeed, many white-collar engineering-technical personnel "feel" poor and do not have the wherewithal to achieve the living standard that their diploma and position lead them to expect.[163] Given the rough nationwide picture, many working-class families necessarily fell below even a modest living standard.[164]

The period from the mid-late 1970s through the early Gorbachev years was also one in which first Western analysts, then Soviet critics themselves, came to recognize and detail symptoms of a social decay—a collapse in the nonwage elements of "welfare"—of major proportions. These were years of rising infant mortality, of declining male life expectancy and rising mortality among males of diverse age groups, and of precipitous rises in alcohol consumption and its associated acute and long-term health problems. They were years of a culmination of ecological-environmental abuses perpetrated by a planned economy that would render areas, from "smokestack" cities in the European USSR to played-out and poisoned cotton areas in Central Asia, essentially unfit for human habitation. Wage rises, bonuses, work in "preferred" industries—often the most unhealthful—could not compensate for this abuse of the USSR's human resources. It was not the working class alone that suffered from such conditions—but it was in areas where such conditions were most pronounced that a wave of strikes and labor militancy were to emerge, as we shall later see, to threaten the system's foundations.

Class and Economic Reward

The new financial measures—and others to be discussed in the next chapter—amounted to a revision of the old social contract that, in some measure, bound workers to the system and sought to preempt worker discontent, in whatever form it might appear. What impact were they and the policies that had preceded them likely to have had on workers' tendencies toward class identity, opposition, totality?

On the basis of the Khrushchev-Brezhnev era trends—that is, more equality within the factory due to a compression of the *tarifnaia setka* differentials; somewhat less differentiation across branches and sectors as the minimum wage was raised (though this of course raised farmers' incomes relatively more than workers'); and more equality between worker and manager/intelligentsia pay scales—one can argue several points. First, if the Stalin-era inequality of pay within the blue-collar ranks weakened any potential worker solidarity, later trends reversed this considerably. Second, to the degree that these later policies favored workers, they may well have promoted a certain class identity, but hardly opposition, as long as the broader economy "worked." The male skilled workers in industry may indeed have taken pride that on the average their pay packets were high compared to those of many white-collar functionaries, and they may have been proud of being workers. This too is "identity," but not one that breeds opposition. Wage policy in the Brezhnev years was not designed to test whether workers were, consciously, a class. Third, the relatively greater benefit of rising minimum wages on farmers and on female workers in light industry was unlikely to be perceived very clearly by male industrial workers as slighting *their* interests. If anything, the point at which workers might experience a certain identity and opposition against farmers on economic grounds would be in the *kolkhoz* markets, where they pay high prices for food that state outlets could not provide. But workers would, in fact, share whatever chagrin they felt against "rich farmers" with other urban groups who needed to trade in the same markets.

The general poverty of living conditions perceived by observers with a Western perspective might have had a class-forming impact to the degree that the burdens of poverty were seen to be unequally imposed, to the workers' specific detriment. What we have seen in this chapter suggests that older workers, given their life histories, educational levels, and, perhaps, lesser tendency to analyze situations, were least likely to view things this way. Younger workers, however, have seen less general material improvement over the span of their lives, and are likely to be better informed and more likely to reflect on, or perceive, "privilege" and the specific reward/consumption advantages of a favored few—as in the evidence that younger emigrés ranked the Brezhnev era, the only one they "knew," highest on inequality and privilege. Still, on the whole, privileged consumption in the USSR was, in the pre-Gorbachev years, more private than conspicuous, much removed from mass witness, and this will have moderated its effect.

With Gorbachev and perestroika, however, new forces and conditions with a different potential impact on class identity and opposition emerged. Real and symbolic threats to the proletarian who had for so long had pride of place in Soviet poster art came with reform. Even if workers were not a specific target, wage and salary guidelines did not favor them. *Gospriemka*'s most direct impact was felt by the workers who manufactured the items subject to tougher inspection; workers could well feel that the threat of inconvenient shifts, of manpower cuts and enterprise closings, affected them more, and more of them, than the bosses and "their" auxiliaries. All our indications, general as they may be through the first three or four Gorbachev years, are that worker reactions to economic reform plans ran from hostile to confused and noncommittal. Some workers may have been more receptive to the long-run prospect of a more affluent society and better living standards, but more, we can reasonably suspect, felt that while glasnost' was fine for the intelligentsia, perestroika over the initial run was front-loaded with negative consequences for themselves. To that degree, class identity and opposition, if we had a way to measure them over 1985–88, would probably have shown an increase. And, to the degree that these years brought so much new and unfamiliar to a "class" that many analysts saw as one identified with the system, as conservative, there were some who necessarily felt that the whole way of life they had assumed to be permanent was under assault. For these besieged workers, there may have emerged something close to a feeling of totality—that the central dilemma Soviet society faced came down, economically and politically, to the real and symbolic displacement of the working class in the system that relied upon it as its social base.

Perestroika, thus, had the potential of making the latent class characteristics of the workers more manifest. Beyond this, the egalitarian drift in Brezhnev-era wage policies (balanced by both "legitimate" and corrupt distribution of de-equalizing privilege) and the choices among groups all of which could not be satisfied, as is evident in Gorbachev's policy reversals, revealed the general difficulties posed to the Soviet state by the more complex society that had slowly assumed certain characteristic forms. A belief that coal and steel mattered most might drive wage and investment policy but could no longer guarantee quality work in return for those wages. Relatively low pay in education, health, and in the retail trade might save money but would generate costs in the poor quality of services available to the blue-collar workers of favored sectors, plus foster corruption and a redistribution of rubles toward low-paid teachers, doctors, and retail clerks who have control over scarce services and goods. Too many groups and too many interests had emerged for the available policy instruments, even under the most inclusive interpretations of the social contract.

5

Labor, Authority, Autonomy

Let Lenin do the work; he's immortal.
(*Soviet proverb*)

THE HALF-CENTURY that separated the Stalinist industrialization from the Brezhnev-to-Gorbachev transition saw massive changes in many contexts of Soviet life, among them the factory floor. This chapter deals with post-Stalin changes in the world of work, the continuities that developed in Khrushchev's and Brezhnev's times, and some of Gorbachev's early responses to that legacy.

Stalinism and After

Workers had been driven harder and harder in the 1930s plan era for the sake of production. With the 1938–40 period,[1] this drive was capped with a set of new laws and regulations deservedly labeled "draconian" by Western commentators. December 1938 brought an intensification of administrative penalties for lateness to work, in addition to those for absenteeism. The fines, cuts in benefits, eviction from factory housing, and other punitive measures did not yet amount to criminal penalties. These came in a set of 1940 decrees that criminalized

1. Absenteeism: one offense required a sentence to "compulsory work" at one's plant, with a deduction of up to 25 percent of wages.
2. Lateness: twenty minutes late was considered a full day of absenteeism; two offenses required a mandatory jail sentence.

Other provisions tied workers to their jobs. Quitting without permission became a criminal offense. New laws lengthened the work day from seven hours to eight, and the work week to six days out of seven instead of five days out of six. (The USSR had not organized its work weeks with a "fixed" day—Saturday, Sunday—off.) Living standards began to stagnate from 1938 on and the decrees added to the harshness in regime-worker relations. At the outset, workers were not even protected from the more bizarre possibilities inherent in the application of such laws. The evidence of court-*prokuratura* practice is, in Alec Nove's words, "almost beyond belief":

> Thus, one woman teacher was prosecuted while she was actually in a maternity home; a woman with a sick breast-fed baby at home, and five months pregnant was sentenced to four months' imprisonment for leaving work, and this sentence was actually confirmed by the republican supreme court; another woman with two young children whose baby-minder left was sentenced to two months'; still another one was given three months' imprisonment for being absent, after producing a medical certificate proving an attack of malaria, and so on, and so forth. By the end of the year, in cases like these, the chief prokuror in Moscow was intervening to set aside unjustified sentences. To explain such outrages one must remember that the great purge, with its excesses of terror, was fresh in everyone's mind.[2]

These were, surely, extremes—but the times themselves were extreme, and the strident demands for discipline and effort, the threat of disproportionate penalties, were not so much "linked with the danger of war," as "presented as logical and right" in themselves.[3] The laws and decrees of the late 1930s represent the peak of the Stalin style in labor legislation, just as 1936–38 marked the peak of domestic terror in the Great Purges. Continuity in war-sharpened harshness of administration and the economic pressures of a poor, devastated economy offered no substantial relief in the late 1940s. The criminal sanctions for absenteeism and lateness were, in fact, lifted in 1951—but (an interesting comment on Soviet practice in the Stalin era) the decree was not made public.[4] With Stalin's death, the floodgates opened slowly but decisively in many areas of Soviet life, mitigating some of the most abusive policies. Maternity leave, cut to 70 days in 1938, was restored to its original 112; reduction in the length of work days and overtime followed, and disability and pension benefits were now linked in a more rational manner to real earnings, while their link to employment over the long term in the *same* plant was loosened.[5] By 1956–58 the workers' links to their jobs had more to do with choice and the labor market, and less with military-type discipline and compulsion. Still, the "labor book" each worker had to keep in addition to an internal passport remained a legacy of 1938, providing a record of work, rewards, and penalties. Many benefits continued to be linked to length of service.[6] As one observer put it, these Khrushchev-era policies, both in the area of labor and in general social welfare, were better than "late Stalin" but really no more than equal to "middle Stalin" (up to mid-1930s) policies.[7]

Further evidence of a new work atmosphere came with new attention given to the trade unions. Their "failure to represent and defend the workers" came up for party criticism in 1957[8] (of course, one can only wonder what might have happened to union leaders who *had* tried to "represent and defend"), and their oversight prerogatives in certain areas of managerial decision making were expanded. After a long interruption, an All-Union Trade Union Congress was finally held in 1959. There was reality as well as rhetoric in this area, so it was no surprise that, as social policy moved generally in a more humane direction, trade unions were accorded more welfare functions. Yet, as even a rather sympathetic Western observer noted, "this awakening of union activity did not arise independently from workers and their demands, but came only when the Communist Party opened the door to greater union effectiveness by its 1957 decision."[9]

The Khrushchev years peaked in the utopian Program of the CPSU in 1961, with its promises of the material and spiritual benefits of "full Communism" by 1980—to workers as well as all others in Soviet society. The reality was to be less impressive, but the Brezhnev period that began in 1964 saw (along with an edging away from Khrushchevian flights of futurism) continued growth in living standards and the emergence of relatively stable patterns of work life. These reflected both change, in the enhanced official and unofficial autonomy that blue-collar Soviet citizens could exercise, and continuity, in elements of their work organization. All this came in an atmosphere of openness which, if qualified by many restrictions, represented a break with Stalinist secrecy and revealed more information about the world of Soviet blue-collar work than had been available since the 1920s.

Work: Content and Discontent

The Western literature on Soviet work life is of considerable volume and informative on many points.[10] We need not recapitulate or summarize it here but rather search the sources to get some grasp on what Soviet workers expect or "value" from work: which aspects are most important, most central to them? From this, there follows an inquiry into how satisfied Soviet workers are with what their working life yields. As we have already seen, dissatisfaction with the prospect of life as a worker is widespread. Similar dissatisfaction with the adequacy of material reward is a fact—how significant a fact of course depends on how central material expectations are to one's evaluation of one's work. Here, we address the range of expectations of those who *are* workers.

A whole range of Soviet studies, beginning with a 1962–64 survey of young workers in Leningrad (which, published in 1967 as *Man and His*

TABLE 5.1
Ratings of Work Satisfaction Factors by Young Leningrad
Workers, 1962–64

	Satisfied	Unsatisfied	Range
Job does-does not require			
thought	.40	−.32	.72
Pay is good/bad	.31	−.30	.61
Opportunity to raise skills			
present/absent	.25	−.33	.58
Work has variety/monotony	.33	−.15	.48

Source: See note 13.

Work [Chelovek i ego rabota], was perhaps the first serious factory-based survey-research to emerge from the USSR and come to Western notice),[11] have rather consistently shown that four elements rank at the top.[12] These are wages, work "content" (evidently the level of mental effort required), the opportunity to increase one's skills, and variety in work (perhaps difficult to distinguish from "content"). These categories reflect the pattern produced by workers' responses to questionnaires, which may actually stimulate more categorical thinking on the nature of one's work week than would otherwise be "normal."

This information is in itself not critically important. It is of more value to know what matters more, the extrinsic wage or the intrinsic elements of the work itself? Has the relative importance changed over time? If so, under what influences?

The picture is not altogether clear, but the basic trend seems to have been in favor of a moderate-to-middling rise in the significance of wages over other bases for satisfaction in the 1960s–70s. The young (under age 30) Leningrad workers of 1962–64, rating what emerged as the four most salient elements of the work situation on a scale from −1.0 (low) to +1.0 (high), produced the pattern in table 5.1.[13] "Content," then, ranked first, and pay second; but pay was a strong second. The 1962–64 Leningrad findings occasioned some self-congratulatory rhetoric on their evidence of growing "Communist [i.e., nonmaterialistic] attitudes toward labor." But this seemed misplaced, as other studies attested to the continuing salience of wages, both among young workers whose burdens might not be so great and among their older confreres. Indeed, 1976 replication of the 1962–64 study indicated that while concerns with work content remained strong for the young workers of the mid-1970s, the salience of wages had increased by about 25 percent.[14]

TABLE 5.2
Factors Determining a "Good Job" in Three Soviet
Cities (in percentages)

	Leningrad (1962–64)	Tallinn (1965)	Kishinev (1972)
Pay only	15.0	11.2	32.9
Pay primarily	30.7	38.8	19.3
Content primarily	31.1	31.7	16.7
Content only	23.2	15.2	24.4

Source: See note 16.

Other studies, among a diversity of worker populations, provided a mixed picture and perhaps some indication of the importance of *how* questions were asked, as well as differing proclivities to give "socially approved" responses. Studies in the Volga auto plant (1972) and in an Odessa ship repair enterprise (1970–74) showed work content rated first (as in Leningrad, 1962–64) among elements of job satisfaction, and satisfactory wages ranked lower (sixth at the Volga plant, fourth in Odessa).[15] But studies in Tallinn (1965) and in the Kishinev tractor plant (1972), which replicated the Leningrad study's survey of responses on the definition of a "good job," with four possible responses, provided a picture that was more wage-centered. The percentages choosing various ways of defining a "good job" are shown in table 5.2.[16]

Summing of the first two categories provides a more mercenary picture in Tallinn and Kishinev than in Leningrad. Other studies have suggested that higher wages and rewards may help in evoking positive responses about the job itself, about "content." A survey in various plants in Ufa in 1970–72 found different categories of workers agreeing, to varying degrees, with a statement to the effect that "work is my biggest satisfaction"; for highly skilled workers, 61.6 percent; for skilled, semiskilled, and unskilled, 43.0, 44.7, and 37.4 percent, respectively.[17] Even though the correlation of wage levels with skill ratings is hardly perfect in the Soviet economy, these figures give reason to believe that higher wages are indeed a big element in increasing job satisfaction. A 1981 study in a Novgorod electronic plant found that "material interest" was the most frequent (40 percent) response to the question, "What motivates you to do high quality work?"[18] When one adds to these indications the results cited in the last chapter from the emigré-based Soviet Interview Project, which strongly indicated that deficient material incentives are important in explaining various Soviet economic shortcomings, we have substantive evidence that "money talks" and makes itself heard, however many other elements may contribute to the "noise" in Soviet factories.

No detailed nationwide studies exist that render a general picture of the "statistical Soviet" and how that person views his or her work. But a myriad of localized studies yield a picture of comparatively high levels of dissatisfaction and job indifference. Murray Yanowitch's array of summary data from a large number of Soviet studies[19] affords a base for some general observations. Of fourteen studies of manual workers, the unweighted average who identify themselves as "satisfied" or better with their work was 56.4 percent, with a range from 40.2 percent (the 1976 replication of the 1962–64 Leningrad study of workers under age 30) to 76.8 percent for a 1974 study. Expressed dissatisfaction with one's job averaged 18.9 percent across the fourteen studies.

Such figures, deriving from research spanning the period 1962–64 to 1979, show that workers express less satisfaction than engineering-technical personnel: five of the studies (between 1965 and 1979) yield an average of 70.1 percent satisfied and only 16.6 percent dissatisfied. In Yanowitch's words, they also "seem somewhat more restrained in expressing satisfaction with work and at least as willing to report job dissatisfaction as their American counterparts"; in U.S. studies, rates of expressed dissatisfaction rarely go above 15 percent.[20] Soviet studies, as the figures averaged above imply, generate a largish share of "other" answers, and in those that have included an "indifferent" alternative, many have selected this response (seven such studies averaged 16.7 percent for dissatisfied, and 18.4 percent for "indifferent": taken together, no evidence of great enthusiasm). (On the other hand, research on Soviet emigrés in the Soviet Interview Project found virtually no difference between the recollected job satisfaction of blue-collars, white-collars, and professionals.)[21]

Whether such responses—prompted, after all, by the intrusion of researchers into the plant—overstate (do workers without the survey stimulus *think* much about the job?) or understate dissatisfaction (fears of nonanonymity, habituation to "positive" responses) is a complicated question. All in all, evidence would seem to suggest dissatisfaction may be even greater than these survey figures indicate. Expressed reluctance (parents' as well as children's) to choose a worker's career, evidence of difficulty in recruiting candidates into training channels that guide them into the working class, run in this direction. Parents working in two Estonian plants, when asked if they would "choose" their present jobs, given the opportunity to do so, rejected them on the order of 38–41 percent; but when asked if they would want their children in the same jobs, three-quarters said no.[22] To the degree that asking directly about job satisfaction may evoke psychological defense mechanisms (a "dissatisfied" response reflecting, to the respondent, a summary judgment on whether his life has been a "success" or not), it may be that questions about the next generation evoke a more truthful response about matters affecting the respondent as well.

In the Gorbachev period, though the focus of much factory research shifted to what workers and employees expected from perestroika and how they were reacting to it, evidence indicates that responses to questions on work satisfaction followed similar, or deteriorating, patterns. A study of 18,000 workers and employees in 374 enterprises spread over four republics and five industrial sectors, as reported in *Izvestiia*, found 35 percent expressing satisfaction with work. In addition, 54 percent said they were "not fully satisfied," 8 percent expressed dissatisfaction, and 3 percent found it "hard to say."[23] Dissatisfaction with wages was most frequently cited by those who found fault with their jobs.

For most blue-collar Soviet citizens, it seems that intrinsic aspects of their work are not particularly satisfying. Dissatisfaction tends to be more marked among younger, better-educated workers slotted into an occupational spectrum that has not changed as rapidly as has the scale of aspirations. But it is not absent among older workers, for whom, as time passes, wages and working conditions[24] independent of job "content" seem to increase in relative importance, providing more fodder for discontent. Relative dissatisfaction seems lower among women workers and in the industrial branches where they prevail; as noted elsewhere, this may have to do with women's lower expectations of their jobs. In the Gorbachev-period study cited a bit earlier, satisfaction with work in the textile (37 percent) and food (40 percent) industries—traditionally feminized—was higher than in the more male-profile automobile (28 percent), machine/instrument-building (32 percent), and ferrous-metallurgy industries (32 percent).[25]

Wages, by themselves, are seen as deficient more often than not. Dissatisfaction with them, and with work as measured by them, may have grown over the years. Brezhnev-era economic policies emphasized private/family/household consumption (durables, automobiles, cooperative apartments), more than Khrushchev's collectivism. By the mid-1970s there was more of a premium on money income than there had been in the rather goods-starved Soviet economy at the time of the first (1962–64) Leningrad study. But the failure of the economy to provide the quality and assortment of goods that would give real meaning to wage raises that intensified in the later Brezhnev period might have exerted force in the opposite direction, reducing the significance workers might attach to wages per se: this, certainly, has been the conclusion of Gorbachev-era commentators. Still, if shortages mean that real, "under-the-counter" prices are higher, the salience of wages, as well as connections, should increase. The linkages are complex, to be sure; some studies show a very low job satisfaction among precisely those (male) skilled workers in heavy industry whose pay in the early 1980s was around 300 rubles per month, exceeding by half the national average.[26] Decoupling wages from goods and from "job satisfaction" in general is difficult. Some examination of the social structure of production, the way work is organized, may help in getting at some of the *non*material dimensions.

The Workplace: Authority and Labor

What is it like on the factory floor? What is the texture of work life for those millions of blue-collar citizens who, as we have seen, regard it with less than enthusiasm? One observer offers a Brezhnev-era characterization stressing politics and paternalism, wherein the

> worker is surrounded by a climate of permanent mobilization or politicization. Banners and posters proclaim his solidarity with this or that people in its heroic struggle for independence; slogans urge him to exceed the plan. These campaigns, whose impact on the individual varies considerably judging by repeated criticisms of the "formal" character of socialist emulation, serve as occasions for ceremonies in which telegrams are sent or read out, resolutions passed, red flags and medals distributed, in order to maintain social pressure and the authority of those whose job it is to distribute rebukes and rewards.[27]

But there is much to suggest that a great deal of this political-ideological "wallpaper" meant less and less and was little noticed—save to their annoyance—by workers accustomed to it as the Brezhnev period moved along. There may be an element of demographic insulation here. Workers experience primarily a "workers' world"—on the average, the blue-collar share of a factory work force is around 84 percent, with perhaps 12 percent being managers at one level or another, and a residual 4 percent are clerical staff of nonmanagerial status.[28] Psychological penetration of this workers' world was hardly assured by the traditional propaganda techniques.

All workers, however, confront essentially the same kind of authority system, the immediate and visible component of which is the foreman, or *master*. Situated between the shop chief (*nachal'nik tsekha*) above him, and the *brigadiry* below (the blue-collar leaders of primary labor collectives typically called "brigades"), he is the link between workers and an authority system which, by design at least, is highly centralized, according to "Leninist principles."[29] These principles involve a unity of political and economic leadership, evident most at the top, where the party Politburo long set economic policy, but reflected at the bottom in the campaigns and posters that bedeck the workplace; in "one-man" management (*edinonachalie*), it is manifest in the concentration of responsibility and authority, at each level of management, in a single individual (in contrast to the "syndicalist" alternative of consensual/committee-style administration). Leninism "balances" these principles with those of "democratic centralism," or the taking into account of initiatives and input from below when making binding decisions above; and "collegiality," which dictates that managers should consult with party, Komsomol, and trade union organizations before taking any action. They certainly could not escape the party, but democratic and collegial principles have played a very modest role in constraining managers.

On the floor, the dynamic *is* different. The *master's* exercise of authority is limited by what he can offer and what he must avoid. Within limits, he can set various work assignments, which determine whether or not a worker, at a given level on the skill chart and thus with a certain base wage rate, is given a job with an "easy" output norm that can readily be exceeded and therefore leads to bigger bonuses and more pay. He determines time off, vacation scheduling, and a number of nonwork elements that affect the shop atmosphere. These are, in the small world of the shop *kollektiv* of perhaps twenty to twenty-five people, no small matters. There is a general interest in avoiding situations wherein workers clash with a harsh foreman or are contemptuous of the ineffective organizational skills of a weak foreman when dealing with the chronic supply problems within Soviet factories—in the hunt for materials that keep the workers working and increase their output and bonuses.

Some of the problems, old and new, are reflected in a growing Soviet management and industrial-sociology literature. In an earlier time, workers and *master* typically shared a similarly modest level of education, and the latter's authority thus derived from "office" and the skills and seniority that helped him achieve it. But in recent years that authority has been compromised in some measure by the fact that young workers may average more education than their *master*.[30] It is not feasible to replace all foremen recruited "from the ranks" with certified, diplomaed specialists, suggesting that some training in management techniques to cope with the younger, better-educated worker is in order.

On the other hand, higher education does not guarantee good management skills.[31] While these educated foremen may be technically competent, their skills in human relations may fall quite short. The *master* is, in fact, different from the "foreman" of the West. As one Soviet author puts it, "himself belonging to the intelligentsia, the *master* leads another social category—workers."[32] "Intelligentsia" here is used in the administrative sense, referring to positions that "require" higher (or specialized secondary) education and wherein incumbents without these qualifications are regarded as *praktiki*—people who got the job without the "requisite" education. (Through most of Soviet history, of course, the *master* could scarcely have been well educated, and the notion that his job "requires" such education is a product of higher general-education levels.) But the idea is to achieve authority and subordination. The *master*, to judge by illustrations in management journals,[33] is a man, wears a suit, if not necessarily a tie; workers do not. The *master* may address his workers with the familiar, singular "you" (*ty*); workers, however, should use the formal plural (*vy*) when talking to him. (An exemplary story, in an economics journal, of a *master* who invited one of his workers for weekend fishing makes the point. On the river bank, they were "*ty*"; at work on Monday, the worker turned to the *master* with some problem, still addressing him as *ty*. The latter reacted negatively. The narrator saw the reaction as justified, without making too much of it. Leisure was one thing, work another.)[34]

What do workers expect foremen to be? What do foremen think their job requires of them? Evidence points to divergent expectations and attitudes. For workers, a reasonable informality across the authority divide (there is nothing *wrong* with weekend fishing), combined with the *master*'s effectiveness in taking care of "his" people while meeting management's demands, an understanding attitude toward the need for time off and so on, are probably the main considerations. For women workers, the human-relations aspect seems particularly important. A study in several plants in the European USSR in 1979–80 found women rating a *master*'s "occupational competence" and "personality" equally important. Asked which qualities, the "practical" or the "personal," the foreman needed to develop, foremen and workers produced quite divergent pictures: foremen chose practical qualities in 65.3 percent of the cases, and workers chose personal qualities in an almost identical 64.8 percent.[35]

(The focus on the "personal" reflects some long-acknowledged specifics of the woman worker's situation. Even though, in many if not most cases, the jobs women occupy have even less "content" than men's, women's job dissatisfaction has been no more than men's, and often less.[36] Less "content-centered," women's chief job-related concerns—in addition to supplementing family income—are the proximity of the workplace to their homes, the availability of child-care facilities, and the opportunity to work convenient shifts.[37] The unequal sharing of household burdens between husband and wife (or their sole assumption by women in frequent cases of divorce), the excess effort required for housework in a society still short of labor-saving machinery and a rational organization of shopping, and the channeling of women into occupations, sectors, and branches that generally make them "secondary earners" to their husbands all account for concerns not being entirely related to job "content."[38] Therefore it is natural for women to prefer foremen who are attuned to the "human/personal" dimensions. From the viewpoint of foremen and higher-level managers and planners, however, the indications from surveys since the late 1970s are less comfortable: women workers seem to be increasing their expectations with respect to intrinsic work content and are thus closing the gap with men in the area of potential dissatisfaction.[39]

Whether or not the *master* is sensitive, forthcoming, and "finely tuned," he cannot avoid a different set of expectations from above. Work- and output-related skills are (as we already saw) likely to loom larger in his list of desiderata than human relations. Given the opportunity to express a preferred management style, managers tend toward the "harder" side. In a 1976 study managers were asked to choose between three styles—liberal, democratic, or authoritarian; the second variant was clearly supposed to be the desirable one, wherein the manager is aware of responsibilities "upward" but conscious of a need to listen "downward," and the authoritarian one implied a tendency to sometimes "fly off the handle" in addition to being energetic and decisive. Nevertheless, two-thirds of managers chose the "authoritarian" mode.[40] The *masters'* lot is not necessarily a happy one. Despite their authority, or because so much authority is lodged above them, many may feel that they can do little to make things better for their workers; many move on. Though Soviet thinking seems to see this as a rather permanent slot, a study in Leningrad that tracked 262 *masters* from a first interview in 1967–68 to their destination ten years later found only 17 percent still in the same jobs.[41] As the Brezhnev era waned and the transition to Gorbachev took place, things did not improve. A study of *masters* conducted between 1978 and 1986[42] revealed a complicated picture of authority that was gradually eroding as new administrative angles were developed, such as the "brigade method" of organizing work discussed below. There was a deficit of "human relations" skills which even the *master* acknowledged were necessary, and a growing reluctance of vuz and *tekhnikum* graduates to become *masters*. In fact, they tended to avoid any job involving the "leading" of people.[43] How much "leading," however, did workers want or need?

Continuing low labor productivity and consequent slow growth, as well as problems of absenteeism and turnover (see below), gave rise by the 1970s to discussions about the workers' passivity and ways to increase the "consciousness," which they, as "collective owners" of the means of production in a socialist economy, were supposed to feel. As Yanowitch has observed, there is a mix of myth and reality in Soviet discussions of this type, when various proposals to increase worker participation are "typically presented as improvements in a system which is already highly participatory—when it obviously is not."[44]

Obvious, certainly, to workers. Even allowing for a bias toward a "positive" response, the rank and file generally signal a feeling that they are objects, rather than subjects, of authority, an attitude that persisted from the years of Brezhnevian "stagnation" into the Gorbachev period. When workers at five enterprises in Murmansk were asked in 1977 if they "personally participated" in managing the enterprise, only 12.2 percent responded "yes," 65.7 percent "no," and 22.1 percent "hard to answer." In Gorky in 1980, only 16.4 percent felt they could "affect decisions on matters concerning the development of their own collectives."[45]

Workers have a somewhat better grip on matters close to home, but there is little evidence of any feeling of "proprietorship." At a Cheliabinsk tractor works in 1974, workers were asked first if shop, then factory, managers considered worker suggestions (as all should under the dictates of democratic centralism). They answered "yes" in 45 and 28.2 percent of the cases, respectively, gave a flat "no" in 11.3 and 23.1 percent, and the remainder felt that suggestions were given insufficient consideration.[46] Lack of information given to workers underlies some of these results. For instance, workers at a chemical plant and an oil refinery in Ufa in the early 1980s were asked if they knew how the output plan was being fulfilled at three different levels: their own section, at the (larger) "shop," and in the plant as a whole. They replied "yes" in the proportions 70, 52, and only 17 percent, respectively, in the chemical plant; and 62, 41, and 17 percent in the oil refinery.[47] Low levels of information prevailed despite various "participatory" mechanisms that have long characterized Soviet plants and have obviously been more decorative than substantive. Even with the advent of

Gorbachev and new decrees empowering plant "councils of labor collectives" with expanded functions,[48] linking worker to enterprise by more active involvement proved elusive. Rather than exercising any managerial role, the new councils were greeted with a good deal of worker skepticism[49] and were often preoccupied with auxiliary or "busy work" that properly belongs with the plant's trade union or other organizations.[50] In early 1988 a letter to *Izvestiia* cited another problem—that of packing the councils with managerial personnel, who are not, in fact, barred from the councils. In the writer's Odessa plant, twenty-six of the thirty council members were leaders or administrators.[51] All this augured poorly for any rapid change on the factory floor, for a greater feeling of proprietorship—and would become an explosive issue in the coal strikes of 1989. As A. K. Nazimova, a student of worker problems observed, it was the most highly skilled, high-tech workers who were most oriented toward participating in management, but they actually showed very little effective managerial participation and had low feelings of proprietorship.[52] It was now the better-educated (if not always high-skilled) young workers who, in the main, confronted this ensemble of unattractive jobs and an authority structure that hung posters ballyhooing fake worker activism and involvement.

Many young workers see themselves as only temporarily at the plant—anticipating, presumably, a move to better work or a return to school. (In a recent survey, 77.1 percent of young Soviet workers said their educational level achieved thus far was lower than their original intent.)[53] The increased education they bring to the job, compared to older workers, is hard to convert either into benefit to the plant or to the profit of the workers themselves. A 1966 study had found no real "return" in the skills area to education beyond seven years;[54] a later survey of emigrés reporting wage rates and educational attainment found, for manual workers, no "systematic" wage returns on more than six years of education, whether received at a PTU or on the complete or incomplete ten-year academic track.[55] And a 1986 Soviet study showed an average monthly pay spread of only 12 rubles among seven thousand respondents, white and blue collar, whose educations ranged from elementary to incomplete higher education (158 to 170 rubles per month).[56]

The casting off of schooled-but-reluctant and generally unskilled young factory recruits into auxiliary, unmechanized, and unattractive work exacerbates the problem further. Two Soviet authors write of "units of the economy where pre-industrial and early industrial production are especially widespread" offering only "simple work that for the most part does not require any up-to-the-minute occupational training."[57] Nor does the nature of such units change with the entry of new workers. "Even an influx of well-educated young people has relatively little effect upon the structure of requirements among workers engaged in pre-industrial labor."[58] Tension results: young "violators of labor discipline" are drawn heavily from those in unmechanized work, rather than from those given some responsibility for machinery.[59]

Thus there are ample grounds for alienation. Dirty jobs, hard jobs, boring jobs—a vertical structure of authority, not necessarily always harshly exercised, that leaves workers with the feeling that neither their autonomy nor their effective input is great. Certainly, there has been a discussion of the matter, one in which many ideas have been broached both with respect to work itself (automation, job enrichment, job rotation) and the social organization of labor (various "experiments" involving autonomy for work teams, new modes of dividing production responsibilities, even the election of managerial personnel at various levels). It is this last area, suggesting the possibility of some moderation of top-down control, that has been most sensitive. Controversy over the election of supervisors, seen from the perspective of the rank and file and of those who currently supervise, yields some insight into attitudes toward the hierarchy of production that have developed over many years.

In terms of political context, it must be understood that the "Kosygin reform" of 1965 promised more autonomy to managers—and thus to enterprises—and that the election of managers and other supervising personnel by their subordinates found its place, logically, as an "issue" within this aspect of the reform. Moderated by Soviet political reality, the election discussion nonetheless reflected to some degree the sort of problem Anthony Giddens has described as likely to be generic in Soviet-type systems that attempt decentralization:

> The introduction of greater managerial independence, as justified in 'technocratic' terms, and involving an orientation to profits, is everywhere likely to meet strong resistance from the general body of workers in the enterprise. This is so precisely because there is no possibility of an orientation towards economism on the part of manual or lower non-manual workers in the state socialist societies. There is probably only one form of justification of independence of managerial control which is likely to be acceptable to the workers within the organisation: that is, *if this is linked to some form of workers' self-management.*[60]

The academic discussions were interesting,[61] but research data on attitudes were sparse. The major exception is Ia. S. Kapeliush's study published in 1969[62] (and conducted before it became clear that the 1965 reform would die of bureaucratic strangulation, never yielding even to managers the autonomy it had promised), which showed great dissensus on the issue of elections. Even in response to a question on the advisability of filling "certain managerial positions" (obviously, interpretable as *any* rather than *all*) by elections, workers and managers diverged markedly: 89 percent of workers approved, compared to 88.2 percent of engineers and technicians, and only 66.3 percent of lower and 52.4 percent of upper-level managers.[63] Those who exercise authority, then, seemed jealous of it "in principle"—an "upper level" manager, answering yes, need not have expressed a desire to see his own job made subject to election. The study indicated anything but a flood of participatory-democratic sentiment. No group, polled on the desirability of electing upper-level managers (enterprise or large-section level), showed more than 20 percent in favor. Pro-electoral sentiment focused mostly on those with whom the rank and file were likely to have most contact—the *master*, and those just superior to him.[64]

There is little evidence that managerial coolness toward elections altered greatly over the two decades that have separated Kapeliush's research from Gorbachev's time. Though a number of legislative and policy moves would back the election of managers and other forms of worker participation after 1985 (see below, this chapter), this aspect of perestroika, like others, would find resistance among economic bureaucrats and officials who generally oppose the reform of which it is a part, as well as managers who, even if they welcome more autonomy for their plants, are not logically bound to see the diminution of their power as appropriate.[65] Over the years managers had been subjected to many cross-pressures; the 1983 Andropov drive for greater discipline—anything but encouraging to permissive manager-worker relations or to worker participation—was hardly a prelude to Gorbachev's rhetoric of democracy. And to predictably cautious managerial attitudes, a certain measure of confusion was added. Mixed signals emerged: for example, in a 1987 piece, *Pravda* mocked current experiments with the election of plant managers as being against long-established "order and rules."[66] Other specialists offered guarded assessments of "what kind" of manager workers would be likely to elect.[67]

While late-1960s managerial reform was thus stillborn, discussions of how to enhance "involvement," "participation," and other types of activism among workers had surfaced again in the late 1970s and early 1980s. They were, perhaps, most significant because they signaled a recognition that a "new worker" existed in the USSR, different from the confused, ill-educated "peasant of yesterday" of whom the original Soviet industrial work force was forged. That new worker was, of course, better educated by far, likely to be "hereditary"[68] and "sophisticated" in an understanding of the written and unwritten rules and practices of Soviet work and life. These "positive" qualities, these new resources at the workers' disposal, allowed many writers to make the point that, in the face of the new workers, authority relations needed modification. The old rules, laid down long ago, would no longer work on the new human material.

In 1977 Kapeliush, the avowed partisan of managerial elections, tied the prospect for elections to the fruits of long-term development; a greater supply of trained, and fit-for-management, specialists (allowing choice *between* management candidates in a category no longer marked by scarcity); and a supply of educated, "conscious" workers sufficient to *make* choices.[69] Some authors counterposed the centralist, "command" principle of one-person management to the equally "Leninist" collegiality. They argued that while in the past one-person control over "backward" workers was justified because of the level of development, as that level was raised, collegiality could, and must, assume dominance.[70] Slowly but persistently, other commentators developed a coherent position advocating change on the same basis. The "new type" of educated workers, and their potential, were viewed in 1981 as the keys to productivity, if the workers were handled well: "Experience shows that where initiative from below finds no outlet and the creative potential of workers, employees, collective farmers is not used in full measure, there can and often do arise various disproportions and distortions. . . . Naturally, in such a situation society does not receive the expected economic benefit from workers possessing a rather high cultural level."[71] In an earlier time, talk of "initiative," of "high cultural level" would have been out of place for many reasons—Stalinism was surely "counterinitiative" writ large; a "high cultural level" was something possessed by very few. In 1983 Gordon and Nazimova expressed their assessment in terms of the antinomies in the term "democratic centralism." Although in the 1930s "plan era" centralized-command methods had "given a powerful impetus to development," their very effectiveness had "led to the formation of an economic mindset that could well be dubbed 'administrative-centralist' and whose inherent inertia is still felt to this day." This inertia/force ran against an "optimization of social and economic relations" that was now mandated by "the cultural development of the majority of working people"; this new level of development, and generally the "conditions of scientific-industrial production," required, finally, "thoroughgoing changes in the long-standing relationship between centralism and the democratic principle."[72]

Thus the pro-change, pro-elections position emerged with fair clarity and consistency. Workers were more educated, urban, "urbane," while managerial philosophy (if not, fully, practice) was still designed around the assumption of less sophisticated blue-collar material. This philosophy had worked on the material of the 1930s and 1940s, even perhaps the 1950s, and this, in addition to a political inertia that was to remain uncriticized until Gorbachev, explained its persistence into a period it did not fit. But the position remained that of commentators and theorists, since the Brezhnev era saw no practical advance in the electoral direction.

If old managerial philosophies did not work, this implied something further: that workers were *escaping* control, and that, at the factory level, managers might actually be modifying the old philosophy. The "new workers" were not so vulnerable to the "old style" as their predecessors had been; they demonstrated, on a day-to-day basis, the limits of their own subjection.

Negative Control: Rank-and-File Resources

Various forces and processes, which operated weakly under Stalin if at all but grew under Khrushchev and further intensified in the late Brezhnev years, facilitated informal blue-collar control over a number of aspects of Soviet work life.

The state's continuing commitment to full employment throughout the Khrushchev-Brezhnev years limited the degree to which violations of labor discipline—absenteeism, loafing on the job, drunkenness—could be punished by dismissal. It also underlay relatively cost-free job-changing by individuals in large numbers—the turnover, or *tekuchest'*, which was the object of so much hand-wringing in the press and economic journals. Full employment as social policy was backed by the labor-hunger of factory managers anxious to maintain a "reserve" of manpower against the exigencies of end-of-month (-quarter, -year) storming to fulfill production quotas. Beyond this, the vagaries of planning meant that, as a later commentator put it, the economy readily created new jobs when it was quite clear there were not enough prospective entrants to the labor force to fill them.[73] By the mid-1970s, the declining size of age cohorts entering their working years, retirements of older workers in great numbers, and the inefficiencies built into the system further exacerbated the "labor shortage" that put the economic future into question and increased the "clout" workers enjoyed as a scarce commodity.

Workers, indeed, *might* be fired, or, with a long record of drunkenness and other violations, quit just ahead of the pink slip. But in a large industrial city, as one writer put it in 1975, they simply moved into another slot in another plant looking for hands: "Enterprises, in essence, exchange violators of labor discipline."[74] In the early 1980s, M. Sonin of the Academy of Sciences' Institute of Economics and the senior Soviet specialist on labor problems reported on the degree to which management had found it necessary to reach compromise with a troublesome work force:

> I had occasion to talk with managerial personnel at the largest Leningrad enterprises and certain Estonian enterprises, and they told me: "In the past (before the manpower shortage became acute), we would not have permitted many of those working (this word frequently has to be put in quotation marks) today within cannon range of the enterprise's gates, but today we are even forced to recruit them."
>
> At the entrance to one enterprise I was once shown over a dozen bottles of vodka that those who like to drink on the job had tried to smuggle in. I asked: "What do you do with these potions?" and was told: "At the end of the working day, we give the owner another talking to and then return his bottle. We have to do so because it's his personal property."[75]

This was no new theme for Sonin, nor could it be. The labor-hunger was chronic. Of course, since the 1960s, the "Shchekino system," named after the chemical complex where it started, offered managers some incentives to cut work forces of unneeded personnel while retaining some of the original wage fund to provide enlarged bonuses for the remaining workers, who would combine functions and cover the work of those released. But in its Brezhnev-era version, Shchekino's "logic" was not that of the larger system. As Sonin put it, managers at every level—plant, section, even shop—were motivated to maintain a manpower reserve "that can be used for more intensive work in peak situations, that can be sent to perform harvest work in agriculture."[76] The old bad habits made themselves felt even at Shchekino. When the complex installed a new Dutch and Italian technology package designed to be run by 178 workers on its Western home turf, the new package provided employment for 806 Soviet workers: extreme, to be sure, but an example nonetheless of the "levels of overmanning and the degree of negative control exercised by the Soviet working class even *after* the implementation of an experiment designed to reduce such control"—the conclusion of a British student of Soviet workers.[77]

Absenteeism—the "recapture," or theft, of time from the employer—was epidemic in Soviet work life. It was imposed by the exigencies of a service sector whose hours were inconvenient for the employed adult majority and abetted by managers who, in any case, were not notably strict in the area of "unenforceable" rules and could

afford absenteeism when production slackened or halted due to absence of needed materials (just as they would require overtime in a
"storming" period after those materials were delivered).

The legendary lack of enthusiasm with which Soviet retail clerks
and service personnel address their duties generated, in the words of
one analyst, a chain reaction among factory workers, evidenced in
absenteeism, early departures, and late arrivals. Second-shift workers
leave "a little earlier," since public transport works spottily in the evening; line up for factory meals early, since the waiters are slow; come
late to work, because "they had to wait for the plumber" or the TV
repairman.[78] The losses of work time were large, on a national scale:
in a 1982 estimate, for every hundred workers, thirty instances of absenteeism occurred daily, for an average of 1.6 hours per instance.[79]
In Moscow, a study of factories and offices in the same year found no
more than 10 percent of workers in place during the final hour of
work.[80] All in all, it was hard to disagree with the veteran observer
Sonin's overall appraisal:

> The most common violation of labor discipline that depends on the workers
> themselves is tardiness and leaving work early. But the basic problem is not
> only to eliminate formal violations (even if we are talking about conscien-
> tious, skilled workers) so much as the urgent needs of the worker and his
> family. In order to bring about a fundamental solution to the problem, it is
> essential to eliminate the causes of such violations. The service and health
> care spheres, for example, exert a daily direct or indirect influence on the
> ability to work, on the use of working time, and on labor productivity. But
> many decisions to transfer their efforts to nonworking time have not been
> carried out. In most cases the schedules adopted are those convenient for
> the services or health care personnel but not for the people they serve.
> Therefore, even when management strictly prohibits absences and moni-
> tors the observance of this ban, the worker has no choice but to escape this
> monitoring or to use every means to obtain permission to be absent.[81]

Much of the "lost" time was thus built into the system and occurred
with the permission of factory administration, which was aware that
dry cleaners, food stores, repair shops, and others kept the same
hours as factories and hence closed as patrons ended their own work
day in factories and plants. The "Operation Trawl" crackdown at the
beginning of 1983, when the new Andropov administration scoured
the streets of major cities demanding that (presumably "working")
standers in lines and shoppers account for themselves was a serious,
if short-term, punitive response to absenteeism—but it *was* accompanied by some recognition that service enterprises needed more rational "open" hours.[82] Where decrees directing such changes had

been observed in the past, positive change did occur: studies in Krasnoiarsk *krai* attributed to better arrangements in the service and retail sector a 47.1 percent reduction in absences with management permission between 1971 and 1981, and by 1984 a further 25.7 percent reduction, presumably in contrast to 1981.[83] Still, absenteeism persisted as a major problem, indicating the "weakness" of the worker's hour-to-hour tie with his workplace, the situational factors that made a combination of the producer and consumer roles difficult, and the joint recognition of these facts by workers and management.

The various behaviors (drunkenness, loafing, other disorders) that are grouped under the "violations of labor discipline" heading—the topic of much Soviet commentary over many dreary years—are impressive not only for their ubiquity and persistence, but for the weakness of managerial reactions throughout the post-Stalin era. One looks in vain for evidence of a major sustained crackdown: rhetoric aplenty, but little else. The "problem" worker tended to be younger, with no more than two to four years at the current plant, likely having less than a complete secondary education and medium-level skills, and a drinker. But, after all, this was the sort of person who, in general, had been entering the industrial labor force for some time— young males out of the *profetkhuchilishche*, with some indifferent skills gained there, and a preliminary habituation (one recalls the public view of the vocational schools) to "swearing, smoking, drinking." At the factory level, many Soviet managers saw such workers as a burden, but one imposed by the natural environment—hardly a problem to be "solved" except through attrition. Revealing in this respect was a 1978 study in some Kharkov enterprises, which addressed the contents of the "plans for social development" filed by production units for the tenth (1976–80) Five Year Plan.[84] These development plans, new at the time, represented a state attempt to mobilize the shop-floor level for a number of economic and social objectives, and were a logical form in which to take note of continuing problems of labor discipline and to establish measures to combat them. In fact, only 65 of the 178 plans (36.5 percent) made any concrete reference to discipline. Of these, only 43.1 percent specified schedules or deadlines to accomplish whatever targets were specified, and only 21.5 percent made any reference to financial provisions for carrying out the targets.[85]

Thus the constantly running drama of violation versus discipline, evasion versus enforcement, in the Soviet factory held little real dramatic content in the Brezhnev years; it had become "conventionalized." The rough-and-ready adjustments made on the plant floor have little reflection in much of the "outside" commentary on labor discipline. A study of three Leningrad newspapers' coverage of labor discipline problems[86] between May 1982 and October 1983 (including, thus, the early Andropov disciplinary crackdown) found the papers' major themes to be persuasion and jawboning of workers (*vospitatel'naia rabota*) to improve behavior, and tougher punishments for violators, with only secondary concern for better work organization or more worker participation in management. Workers ranked the priorities very differently, with much greater emphasis on economic factors.[87] From what the data indicate, it was unlikely that management had much faith in, or reliance on, jawboning or crackdowns, either, as universal "policy."

But it would be inaccurate to see the Brezhnev-era Soviet workplace as any marvel of informal human relations, despite evidence of "permissiveness." Times may be slack early in the month, absences may be tolerated, the foreman and the manager may be in a laid-back mode; but in the last ten days, the same foreman may be a hard taskmaster indeed, driving, cursing, harrying, and hardly likely to excuse any absence. The reservations that Soviet workers have about their work, its lack of interest, its routine qualities, the segmentation of tasks and lack of autonomy in carrying them out, the general lack of material incentives to work hard, testify to a less than ideal world.

But there have been tolerance and collusion at the factory level. In many factories they have linked manager and worker in the maintenance of tolerable work rhythms and rewards. State policies have aimed at minimum material sustenance for all, but it was factory-level practice as much as higher policy that allowed output norms to be matched to planned "necessary" wage levels, rather than the reverse: "The foreman, in order to live more or less in peace, jots down in his notebook: so and so needs to get 200 rubles by any means, or else he will leave!"[88] Certain things in this centralized economy are settled at the local level, this among them. ("Humanization" of the threat of a low-skill/low-wage/high-norm combination defining a job's parameters even found a place in the Stalin years. The massive norm increases that affected Soviet industry in the general tightening of 1940, piled on top of an already inegalitarian wage scale within the factory, were met by managers, even in those harsh times, with a combination of simulation and manipulation, cushioning hardships that otherwise might have left coercion as the sole motivation for workers to labor.)[89]

However far a rough-and-ready humanization of the workplace proceeds, not all will be satisfied. Many will quit. This too is "control," an assertion of the autonomy of the individual in the labor force. Exercise of an "exit" option was made possible by the mid-1950s repeal of Stalin-era laws that locked the worker to the job. Western commentary on the "turnover" problem has been extensive,[90] and one need not attempt to be encyclopedic here—but the major aspects deserve notice.

Official estimates typically cite a 20 percent per annum job-changing rate among workers and employees outside of the collective-farm sector.[91] Some of this is attributable to management-initiated transfers, retirements, call-ups into the armed forces, and extended maternity leave; these "respectable" reasons account for perhaps 7 percent of the flow. The remaining 14 percent reflects voluntary leavings, and some firings—depending on the viewpoint, workers exercising "control," or displaying self-indulgent, inefficient, economically damaging "drift." Workers have asserted this control within a set of constraints that have gradually tightened in theory if not in practice: until 1981, two weeks' written notice to management sufficed; until 1983, one month was enough; and thereafter Andropov's "crackdown" imposed a two-month requirement. Until 1983, workers departing a job of their own volition had a month to find another and still retain the uninterrupted work record on which pension and other social benefits were calculated—a period shortened to three weeks at that point.

These changes reflected both the growing acuteness of labor shortage that marked the end of the Brezhnev era and a new emphasis on "discipline," a disdain for "drifters." The average job changers spent, according to one source,[92] twenty-four days between jobs, and, typically, their output tended to drop in the old job just prior to leaving and to remain below average in the new one for about three months.

On the other hand, the job changing itself was hardly an "odd" phenomenon. Negative incentives against switching were weak, positive incentives were varied and many. Many Soviet studies have pointed up their diversity, and table 5.3, drawn from a range of studies conducted in 1978–81 in the lower Kama industrial complex, provides an example of the range of motivations that respondents listed as reasons for changing their jobs, as well as the varying salience of different factors for different age groups. (Respondents were allowed to list several reasons and, evidently, not asked to rank-order them.)

Among workers under age 30, the feeling of a "dead-end" job (not affording the chance to learn a trade), uninteresting work per se, and low pay score high as reasons for moving. (The latter factor, however, is just as frequently cited by workers over 30, who presumably are more likely to bear family responsibilities, and heavier ones.) Health reasons, expectably, play a role only for older workers—many, we may assume, leaving heavy or hot work they handled without difficulty in younger years.

Older and more experienced workers cite overtime work as a major motivator for departure—it is they who presumably bear the major

TABLE 5.3
Motives for Leaving a Job, Lower Kama Production Complex, 1978–81

	Age Groups						
	16–18	19–20	21–25	26–30	31–35	36–40	Over 40
Not learning a trade	53.2	48.1	28.7	19.5	—	—	—
Low pay	31.9	24.0	36.8	29.3	37.5	31.5	36.0
Uninteresting work	24.4	23.3	9.2	—	—	—	—
Lack of housing	7.3	9.2	27.8	6.8	—	—	—
Entering an educational institution	6.4	—	—	—	—	—	—
Lack of kindergarten space	1.1	2.0	15.8	14.7	—	—	—
Bad relations with administration	0.1	0.4	5.8	7.4	—	—	—
Move to another city	—	25.8	—	—	—	—	—
Dissatisfaction with work in the present shop	—	9.3	—	—	16.6	16.6	—
Overtime work	—	9.3	25.4	48.8	50.0	25.8	36.0
Poor organization of work	—	9.2	18.4	24.3	—	12.9	—
Poor state of health	—	—	—	14.6	37.5	48.2	62.0

Source: Adapted from A. I. Rybakov and A. I. Siniuk, "Vozrastnye razlichiia v teku-chesti rabochikh kadrov," *Sotsiologicheskie issledovaniia*, no. 4 (1983), p.107.

burden of the end-of-month "rush" to meet targets—and also cite, more than others, a dissatisfaction with work in their own shop (though neither the 31–35 nor 36–40 age groups complain that the work is uninteresting). It may be that, as one reaches an age where "settling in" is normal, expectations of a quiet life, rather than interesting work, become more important. Disruptions by way of excessive hours or poor human relations in one's own section of the plant would thus appear as more of a "violation" than they would to younger workers.

It is among these younger workers—especially in the 21–25 age group, where one can expect a high degree of family formation and childbearing—that the Soviet housing shortage makes itself manifest. "Absence of housing" is a common condition for young workers, and the provision of nothing better than rooms in "workers' dormitories" by factory management has been cited as a major problem in retaining them.[93] Older workers do not refer to this—evidence that many have finally come to the top of a municipal or enterprise list and gotten an apartment, or settled for whatever accommodations they had. (Older workers, of course, are more likely to have children, which, added to seniority, makes for a stronger claim for adequate housing.) Overall, housing has been perceived as important; a 1979 decree bravely specified that factory housing "should" be guaranteed to workers of five years' tenure or more, and to young workers on the job for two years or more.[94] Decrees, however, do not translate automatically into brick and mortar. No overnight transformations on the housing front were forthcoming, and the situation at the end of the 1980s still remained deplorable.

There are, of course, dimensions beyond these. Very well-paid workers, especially those in less attractive areas of the USSR, may focus more readily on "noneconomic" aspects of a job or living situation. Confident that their skills and experience can be cashed in for somewhat lower wages, but better supplies, in a more attractive area, they may leave despite being at the top of the pay scale.[95] Young workers, less tied to job specialty, factory, area, or family responsibilities, are more likely to have itchy feet than others. As the number of young workers with a complete secondary education has risen, so have their tastes and the demands that entry-level jobs are unlikely to meet. Studies in the early 1970s in the Russian and Belorussian republics, focusing on the experience of twenty-eight large factories with young workers from secondary school, found that even the "best" factories were able to retain these workers for three years in only 43 percent of cases. On the average, over half left during this period: 34 percent of the new workers in the first year, 16 percent in the second, and 7 percent in the third.[96]

Heavy-industry employers with clout have also benefited from labor-force mobility; in the Brezhnev years, their more attractive offers were able to generate above-plan levels of employment, while smaller, light-industry factories with lower wages and fewer benefits were often stuck with labor deficits. These situations probably helped cause the failure of several Brezhnev-era experiments in organizing compulsory job exchanges in various cities, limiting the right of managers to "free hiring."[97]

Workers like these, as well as the well-educated but low-skilled younger workers who had higher aspirations and more sophisticated demands, belong in the category of the "new worker" described by Tatiana Zaslavskaia in her "Novosibirsk report."[98] That new worker, who "accurately recognizes [his or her] own interests and can defend them if necessary," a product of time, education, development, and "substantial changes in the socio-economic conditions of the people's sphere of activities"[99]—those producing both a more complex society, and one where social strata began to acquire *class* characteristics—

stood in striking contrast to the "old" worker of the 1930s, around whom (as had been suggested by partisans of the election of managers, as noted above) the mechanisms of authoritarian control had been constructed. Zaslavskaia characterized some of the contrasts.

> An overwhelming number of workers in industry had only recently left their villages and had a weakly developed sense of their rights. . . . Being relatively undeveloped, they were a convenient object of management. . . .
>
> Although formally speaking there was no unemployment in the country, in many areas and branches there were hidden structural labour surpluses. Fear of losing his job and difficulties in finding a domicile hampered the worker's mobility, and firmly bound him to the enterprise.[100]

With the Stalin period of generalized deprivation now history, the new worker emerged to present a "problem" different from that of the past. For the worker-beneficiary of post-Stalin policies and developments, it was in the labor market that a fair share of autonomy could be exercised. Those foreign observers who expected long habituation to the Soviet political system and the lack of independent labor unions to yield a disciplined, timorous, lock-stepping labor force found that matters were not so simple. Those inside the USSR who expected the new workers to be free of the old problems and of any new ones—that is, disciplined products of the system, "choosing" to channel their autonomy in directions the planners approved—had equal reason to be confounded. In response, they sought organizational remedies that might enhance discipline and productivity while leaving a still-unelected management in place. They found the "brigade method."

The "Brigade Method": Autonomy or Control?

Problems of work organization, product, and payment have long interacted in Soviet plants and produced results that satisfied neither political leaders nor ministerial bureaucrats. The system, for all its collectivism, typically left each worker as a single producing "unit" with a quota to fulfill and a wage to earn via base (piecework) rate plus bonus. Workers are as much at the mercy of other actors inside and outside the factory as they are "independent." Anomalies abound. In the absence of "technically based (output) norms," some workers have job assignments that are easy to accomplish; their guaranteed norm overfulfillment generates high total pay by way of bonuses. Others are not so fortunate. "Who is who" is a matter, to some degree, of the varying degrees of clout individual workers can exercise on the shop floor. By and large, mechanisms to block overproduction of some "profitable" item by pieceworkers, even if it uses up resources needed for other items, have not worked well. A shop, section, or whole plant may fall short of its output goals, while individual workers still earn bonuses. Some way of relating individual efforts and rewards to the collective result, to the goal of "real" plan fulfillment, was elusive—but attractive. In the late 1970s, discussion focused on the brigade method of organizing work as a way of solving a number of the problems.[101]

"Brigade" is a familiar word in Soviet terminology. It signifies a range of realities, from a group of individuals each doing a particular job with a particular quota, under one leader, to groups that are more interdependent, sharing responsibility, and charged as a group with greater degrees of autonomy. After 1979, policy favored the latter sort of brigade, whose organizational design was seen as promoting several intermediate goals on the way to enhanced efficiency and productivity.[102]

More cooperation in attaining goals among workers in "new" brigades was to flow from the "single order" (*edinyi nariad*)—an output task assigned to the brigade as a whole, not subdivided by management among the individual workers. Pay and bonuses would be earned by the brigade as a whole, promising advantage, rather than loss, to experienced workers who helped new ones, to those who, their task already done, lent their efforts to helping others complete theirs.

With wages and bonuses dependent on collective results, interest in maintaining discipline—in keeping slackers and drunkards on the straight and narrow—would also shift to the brigade, to those face-to-face situations where there had been less cost in tolerating violations in the past. (A harsher variant would involve collective responsibility—via financial penalties, etc.—for members' behavior,[103] independent of work results.)

At the brigade level, management of the division of tasks and responsibilities is assumed by the brigade leader (or in large brigades, a council), in consultation with members who, presumably, know each other: the promise is to have "deconcentrated," more efficient shop-floor management, rational decisions arrived at by those most affected. If the atmosphere in basic labor collectives determines the whole society's socio-economic climate, as one 1987 editorial put it,[104] such participatory methods should work better than the transmission or modification of orders sent from management, via *master*, to workers.

A promised reward of the flexibility of the brigade is enhanced job satisfaction. To the degree that monotony and the inability to develop new skills are factors in dissatisfaction, the possibilities of job switching, of combining functions, and so forth, within the autonomy of internal brigade organization may counteract them. Cooperation, better discipline, and greater work satisfaction have thus been seen as keys to better economic results—that is, to efficiency of production, quality of output. (This, however, as we shall see, is not the only rationale for the most enthusiastic proponents of the brigade method.) The early 1980s saw growth of what were called "brigades," but in many of these, none of the real marks of a "new" brigade were evident: compliance with the 1979 resolution pressing brigade formation was formal, rather than substantive, in many cases.[105] The range of types of brigade organization ran all the way from workers outside any brigade organization, including the merely formal, through four levels, as specified by three experienced Soviet students of work organization:[106]

I. Formal brigades, with work and pay on an individual basis;

II. Brigades on a "single order," where pay is divided among individuals on the basis of skill level (*tarifnaia setka*) and hours worked;

III. "Single order" brigades where a "coefficient of labor participation" (*koeffitsient trudovogo uchastiia*, or KTU) is calculated to apportion premiums and bonuses;

IV. At the most highly developed level, brigades that combine the characteristics of levels II and III with "self-financing" (*khozraschet*) status; allocated a set amount of resources and a "plan" for medium/long term, with the opportunity to increase bonuses and earnings by output increases, and by efficiency/savings in the management of inputs.

The same authors calculated that as of 1984, organization of brigades had not moved so far along as the policy lines of 1979 might have suggested. Their estimates of the percentages of workers in various types showed modest results: no brigade, 39 percent; level I, 11 percent; level II, 14 percent; level III, 19 percent; level IV, 17 percent.[107] (Such figures and definitions, in fact, convey a notion of clear divisions between various levels of brigade organization that are not really so evident in a complex reality. Soviet discussions of some of the attributes of, and distinctions among, higher-level brigades often seem to reflect a confused situation and what must necessarily be very incomplete information about work organization nationwide.)[108]

If brigade-type ideas preceded Gorbachev, the thrust of those ideas fit well with the general line of perestroika (at least until a more general economic crisis loomed from 1989 on). The post-1985 period has seen much positive emphasis on the further diffusion and development of brigade forms. But it was not only economic efficiency that attracts the brigade method's partisans. "Meritocratic" justice—the linking of pay to one's real contribution to a "real" economic result—is one attraction in the area of the "human factor." The economist/sociologist Tatiana Zaslavskaia saw brigade organization as thus providing an incentive to work hard, an incentive lacking when so many who do not work hard earn as much as those who do.[109] Likewise, Gordon and Klopov viewed brigades, especially those with single-order plus self-financing features, as combatting both the "leveling" tendencies and the derivation of unearned income in the state sector, by way of waste and the production of unneeded and unusable goods.[110]

Beyond this, some advocates of higher levels of brigade organization saw it squarely as a self-management form, a necessary component of democratization of industrial administration in the conditions of reform. As three such advocates put it, perestroika's emphasis on decentralized management, and the use of "economic indicators" to guide more autonomous managers at plant level, could not work without its extension to the brigade level. Just as real operation of the brigade method is impossible without real enterprise independence,[111] this was a very important issue to the reform-oriented.[112]

The position of such reformers is complicated, however. Obviously, many managers fear a loss of power and control to more autonomous brigades,[113] just as they resist managerial elections. While serious, this is an opposition that could be identified, and fought, by a committed central leadership. Grass-roots worker opposition to brigades and their presumed rationale present a potentially more serious problem. The resistance is not massive: many workers favor brigades, and there are divisions of opinion on a number of the characteristics of brigades. But there is resistance to the meritocratic, differentiating, "de-leveling" rationale of brigade organization. Just as earlier brigade-type forms of collective pay led, in Stalin's time,[114] and later under Khrushchev's "brigades of Communist labor,"[115] to decisions to share pay more or less equally, so have many 1980s brigades moved in the same direction. And just as such "spontaneity" was denounced in the past, so it has been now.[116]

Convinced egalitarianism is part of the reason—but surely not all workers are principled egalitarians. There is a rough sense of "social justice" in those Central Asian brigades that take a worker's number of children into account in dividing earnings, or in topping up the pay of workmates near retirement to increase their pension base.[117] But it is also true that guidelines for calculating the participation "coefficient" (KTU) are vague and loose.[118] Once a brigade leader or council is forced to calculate it, they may find that egalitarian or "welfare" principles are less likely to generate the sense of unfairness, of claims to "social justice" violated, than a coefficient that cannot satisfy all. The human consequences may be less disruptive overall, even if—as reform economists would predict—many hard workers will leave egalitarian brigades to seek better pay outside.[119] There are writers in the economic press who have thus defended "equal shares" brigades as more humane than those that put pressure on lagging workers (often older or inexperienced younger ones), for purely economic ends.[120]

In more general terms, workers' reactions make clear that brigades are no panacea. One study found that conflicts occur most frequently over pay and the division of tasks in the simpler brigades, while broader, less self-regarding problems of group work organization and the brigade's relations to other units predominate in those using the KTU.[121] But other data suggest that, as noted above, the use of the KTU to make distinctions among workers satisfies relatively few, and it can worsen relations among brigade members.[122] All in all, reactions in worker surveys to many aspects of brigade organization have been tepid,[123] with responses of "hard to say," and "don't like working under the brigade system" nearly as frequent as endorsements.

A brigade's organizational environment can also make for frustration, even when members are content with its internal workings. Efficient cost cutting and increased output versus the plan targets are punished rather than rewarded when ministerial or management directives violate plan stability by raising those targets, thus threatening future pay and bonuses—an old "habit" that contravenes a critical element of perestroika thinking.[124] A brigade on self-financing, with full material responsibility, suffers when its inputs are not delivered; such brigades depend on an environment largely made up of *non*self-financing units.[125] Under these circumstances, it is no surprise that brigades, like individual workers, compete, on the basis of group interest, to get "easy" assignments and "easy" norms to guarantee higher pay for their members.[126]

It remains unclear that productivity benefits have indeed emanated from application of the brigade method, whatever its balance of social consequences.[127] Separating the tangled web of general working conditions from differing levels of brigade organization and from the specific conditions of different factories and branches would be a daunting task, in any case. The absence of clear and consistent gains surely argues that the brigade method brought no revolution to the factory floor or to the economics of production, even in the times prior to the economic crisis of the end of the 1980s.

Such may be the natural fate of innovations aimed at conflicting objectives. Autonomy or control? For some advocates, the main attraction of the brigade was the autonomy, the organized, rational clout it promised workers. With self-interest, positive economic results should flow from it. For others, whose prime concern was quantity and quality of output, attractions like those brigades possessed turned on the promise that peer pressure could be mobilized to better control workers' behavior: collective material interest in raising wages (and avoiding sanctions) would lead to a discipline that manager and *master* had found difficult to impose in the past. There was a world of difference between the two rationales, and workers proved to be difficult material to mold. Neither conflicts over the differentiating KTU nor the rough solidarity manifest in those brigades that tended toward equal shares were what those who advocated the brigade method wanted. It was yet another instance of the degree to which workers were able, in various ways, to use the resources they possessed in defense of collective (and individual) interests, among them the preservation of aspects of work life with which they had grown familiar. As we will see later in this chapter, the brigade would not be the only innovation to which workers would react with concern and alarm as the Gorbachev era brought change to the factory.

Pressures, Safety Valves, and the Second Economy

An exogenous element of potential adjustment between worker and regime that takes us outside the factory requires some attention. The USSR, as is well known, has a large second economy, a quasi-legal to illegal but tolerated realm wherein goods and services are produced, exchanged, and consumed beyond the designs of the planners. It represents alternative sources of income for producers of goods and services, alternative sources of those things for consumers.

Worker involvement in the second economy is thus of interest. If workers are, on the average, more involved than other groups as producers, that involvement may generate extra rewards and provide an outlet for skills, entrepreneurship, and the simple desire to get out from under the world of the shop and the plant. If successful as producers, workers may well also figure as major consumers in the second economy, partly closing the gap between aspirations and reality left by state wages and the state retail system. If they are not heavily involved as producers, the same workers may find that the cost of second-economy goods and services is additional evidence that the cost of the life to which they feel entitled is even greater than what their wages, and the imbalance of state prices and state goods shortages, would indicate.

Evidence is not rich, but it is to the point. Vinokur and Ofer's survey of family budgets for 1,016 urban Jewish families who emigrated from

TABLE 5.4
Workers and Employers Involved in Private Work, Emigré Sample, 1970s

	% in Private Work	Monthly Private Wages (rubles)	Monthly State Wage (rubles)	Hours per Week, Private	Ratio, Hourly Wage, Private/State
Worker	14.3	19.7	162.5	1.70	4.5:1
Employee	8.8	10.3	196.7	0.72	4.1:1

Source: See note 128.

the USSR in the early 1970s yields a record of 2,146 working adults' earnings and work histories.[128] On the whole, blue-collar workers were more involved in extra, private work than white-collar employees. The difference was due almost entirely to male workers. While 4.6 percent of blue-collar women did extra work, and 5.1 percent of white-collar women, the respective figures for males are 14.3 and 8.8 percent (see table 5.4). Their involvement, in terms of hours invested and average number of rubles per hour earned relative to state-sector rewards, affects the average picture clearly, if modestly.[129] What these figures signify is that 14.3 percent of blue-collar workers who did private work, averaged with the 85.7 percent who did not, still added 19.7 rubles per month, on the average, to worker earnings for the whole sample. Their efforts amounted to 1.7 hours extra private work per week over the whole sample, and those hours were paid at a rate four and a half times the state-sector hourly rate. The employee figures run in the same direction, though more moderately.

By implication, then, the effects of supplementary private work for the people so involved are anything but marginal. Combining male workers and employees of all categories, who actually did private work, we find that

1. They averaged 10.7 hours private work weekly.
2. They earned an average of 127.6 rubles monthly from this work.
3. In addition, they earned an average of 165.6 rubles monthly from their state-sector jobs.
4. Thus they derived about 44 percent of their total earnings from private work.

Different worker and employee groups, however, fared differently. As the data on some selected groups within the sample (table 5.5) indicate, these males diverge greatly in their participation—or opportunity to participate—in private work, their consequent earnings, and their relative results. These figures, again, are averages across the

TABLE 5.5
Private and State-Sector Work and Wages, 1970s, Emigré Sample, 1970s

	% in Private Work	Monthly Private Wages (rubles)	Monthly State Wage (rubles)	Hours per Week, Private	Ratio, Hourly Wage, Private/State
Workers					
Heavy/machine bldg.	8.1	7.7	166.5	0.60	4.0:1
Light industry	21.4	36.1	159.2	1.20	3.0:1
Construction	51.9	73.7	188.4	6.90	3.1:1
Employees					
Engineers	7.7	5.3	208.5	0.51	2.9:1
Education	12.1	11.3	217.4	0.94	3.1:1
Dentists	53.9	147.7	123.5	7.77	7.6:1

Source: Adapted from Gur Ofer and Aaron Vinokur, *Private Sources of Income in the Soviet Urban Household* (Report R-2359-NA, August 1980) (Santa Monica, Calif.: Rand, 1980).

whole job category, combining private workers and those who do not "moonlight" alike. Thus male workers in light industries (wood, textile, clothing, and footwear) are nearly three times as likely to work privately as are the workers in core heavy industry, and the involvement of slightly over one-fifth of them in such work adds about 36 rubles to the approximately 160-ruble monthly income of the whole category. Lower participation of heavy-industry workers adds much less—8 percent do private work and add only 7.7 rubles on the average to the 166-ruble average pay of the whole category. Construction workers do best of all. Engineers—in the sample, mainly ones employed in heavy industry—do little outside work and consequently add little to their group's average returns by their involvement in private work, while educators, via tutoring, for example, do rather more. Dentists represent the extreme category, as the numbers indicate. A bit over half of all male dentists do private work, at more than seven times the hourly rate for state work, and work more extra hours than other groups—more even than construction workers. This level of involvement more than doubles the average monthly wages for all dentists.

Allowing for all the problems of representativeness of this urban Jewish sample, the general picture suggests no radical revision of what has been said in this chapter and in the preceding one. The second economy is large, but any idea of a society where "virtually all" citizens work on the side and earn significant unrecorded rubles is false. Private work is not a major safety valve for the frustrations of workers, with perhaps the exception of construction workers. Otherwise, only a minority of workers in each of the original survey categories does private work at all. In this sample, workers in the classic priority heavy industry/machine-building branches participated little in private work compared to those in the light/consumer industries whose skills, and access to materials, give them a better market position in the second economy.

Nor, for those who are involved in it, does private work necessarily redound to the regime's advantage by way of the worker's satisfaction with extra earnings. Some of the work done may be very onerous; the rubles may look too good to be rejected, but the balance of satisfaction may not be positive. Soviet Interview Project data indicate that, on the whole, people who earned private-sector income are less materially satisfied than those who did not, even controlling for differences in state-sector wages.[130] It may be that those who are already quite dissatisfied are the ones who moonlight—if so, the moonlighting does not improve their view of material life. For both categories, what was to come after 1985 was, on the whole, unlikely to lift blue-collar spirits.

Perestroika, the Plant, and the Worker

Innovations in wage policy and the effects of *gospriemka*-type discipline discussed in chapter 4 were likely to make workers feel they are special targets of Gorbachev's policy changes. The same may be said of some changes in the conditions of work and factory life that came, or were proposed, with perestroika.

The negative effects of Soviet-type employment security—what one Western student has called the "job rights/overfull employment" syndrome[131]—had been understood by some Soviet economists for a long time.[132] But ideas about tampering with that security were few, and muted in expression. However the trade-off between the efficiency of a lean labor force and the stability and security of guaranteed, if inefficient, employment was calculated, it seemed likely to remain a central and undisturbed part of the social contract.

But Gorbachev's diagnosis of the depth of the economy's ills altered this. Portents of change came on the heels of Gorbachev's accession. In early 1986 the economist Vladimir Kostakov had raised a furor with his projections that 13–19 million jobs in manufacturing would disappear by the year 2000, if productivity and growth targets were met.[133] In a streamlined economy, "one" would "do the work of seven,"

and more efficiently. Retirements and smaller labor-force entry cohorts and the expansion of service-sector jobs would moderate the
pains of the process, it was argued, allowing Kostakov to deny that
unemployment was stalking Soviet society.[134] Reform economists
continued to make the point that the iron job security of old was in-
supportable. Zaslavskaia connected the abolition of unnecessary jobs
with "laying people off,"[135] and Leonid Abalkin, then director of the
Academy of Sciences' economics institute, quoted a 20 million figure,
in a context similar to Kostakov's in mid-1987[136]—all this before the
downward slide of the economy at the end of the decade.

Of course, this drive for greater efficiency was not aimed at blue-
collar workers per se. The first major publicity went to the discharge
of about 3,200 bureaucrats and office workers in late 1985–early 1986
as six ministries and a state committee were merged into the new
Gosagroprom (State Agro-Industrial Committee), an "economy" that
allowed the state to reduce its apparatus by a reported 47 percent.[137]
Press coverage made much of the redundancy of many deskbound
functionaries, and there was little reason to doubt that reducing inefficient white-collar employment was a real policy target.[138] But both
impressionistic evidence and the results of emigré research suggest
that blue-collar workers rated job security higher among sources of
job satisfaction than did professional-level or even routine white-collar employees.[139]

In concrete terms, what would a weakening of job security mean? A
range of possibilities was implied, from the relatively minor to the
more radical. Intraplant reassignment of workers to other jobs as
theirs became redundant—a "Shchekino"-type change—was perhaps
least disruptive. Plants moving from a single to a two- or three-shift
system could redeploy some workers to less desirable shifts. Such disruptions are not small ones for workers long used to a predictable life.
Fewer workers would be expected to produce more on "their" shift
than a larger number did on a single-shift system, and without an
automatic guarantee of premium pay for night or swing shifts. Some
factories, evidently, had funds to pay the authorized 20 and 40 percent supplements for the second and third shifts, some could only do
half as well (10–20 percent);[140] some were able to top up the shifts with
30 and 50 percent;[141] others had no extra funds to provide. In any
case, as one authority on labor questions put it, the "right to work"
guaranteed to the Soviet citizen was not a guarantee of a right to a
particular *place* of work.[142] Some jobs disappeared. Many more jobs, if
perestroika meant anything, would have to disappear, a presumably
sizable number being abolished as retirements occurred.

Other job cuts promised to be more painful. Some economists
called for the closing down of enterprises whose output was un-

needed, unsalable at the standard price, inherently a loser. Such a policy was likely to put at special risk enterprises in classic heavy industry and extraction, whose workers had been favored in wage terms. Abel Aganbegian noted that thirty coal mines in the Donets basin consumed big money and manpower but yielded little coal: closing them would free up the resources that would allow the extraction of three times as much coal as they produced from other mines.[143] Could the miners who were let go hope to find other work in mining, or other jobs with equally high pay? It seemed unlikely: in 1987, one official source projected a 23 percent reduction in the work force in coal mining by 1990.[144] Where, then, would they go—to what sort of work and at what pay?

In 1986–87 the successful redeployment of large numbers of workers who were found redundant in their old jobs was emphasized. These included the well-publicized laying-off of 12,000 workers on the Belorussian SSR railways;[145] the cutting of industrial workers by 9 percent, construction workers by 15 percent in Zaporozh'e *oblast'* over three years; the closing of a Leningrad construction trust[146] that had 2,000 workers, and other instances.[147] But one could ask how cost-effective those new job placements really were: old habits die hard, and the "pull" to moderate the consequences of dismissal was, at this stage, fairly obvious. Goskomtrud chairman Gladkii cited in early 1988 a survey indicating that more than 60 percent of those made redundant in their old jobs found new ones in the same plant.[148] This squares roughly with a summary report on the Estonian experience, wherein about 9,200 people needed to be transferred (the total across a number of enterprises and organizations): 5,100 found work in new subdivisions with their old employers in second or third shifts or in jobs previously vacant, while of the remaining 4,100 fully 2,800 went on pensions. Only 100, evidently, were sent to find work in branches other than the ones they had worked in, and 1,200 were sent to local Goskomtrud organs to find jobs.[149] The Belorussian railway case seems less clear, and perhaps less on the "general" pattern. According to one report, "over 10 percent"[150] of those let go by late 1986 went to other branches; but another report indicates that over 5,000 of the 13,200 transferred by November 1986 went to other branches, or around 40 percent. The rest did not stay. Another 5,000 were pensioned off, leaving only a small number, it would seem, with railroad jobs.[151] It is likely that some fudging of numbers took place.

The logic of perestroika, while the economic situation seemed still under control, dictated that most new jobs should be in the service sector, broadly defined. Its buildup and improvement were seen as important for the overall economy, after decades of starvation in manpower and resources. But what, in concrete terms, did this mean?

Shifting high-paid production workers to service jobs for which they are not trained (or, perhaps, trainable), at the current low pay rates for those jobs? Turning coal miners into clerks? Or, as an interviewer for *Izvestiia* questioning L. A. Kostin, the economist who serves as first deputy chairman of Goskomtrud, put it,[152] moving lathe operators into barbershops? Kostin denied that this was the point, citing instead the need to reduce the inflow into industry and reorient training toward preparing people for work in nonmaterial production spheres. Fair enough, but this was no more than a restatement of broad policy; it did not specify how persons currently in one economic sector might be transferred to another, if this was the intent. Such dislocations loomed large among the contingencies that many blue-collar workers, long secure in plant and job, were likely to face. (Prime Minister Ryzhkov's speech to the Twenty-seventh Party Congress in 1986, projecting that *all* the net increase in the labor force would be added to services in the twelfth Five Year Plan, compared to the 50–50 industry-service "split" in 1981–85, was not reassuring.)[153]

Beyond the various adjustment pains of large-scale redeployment lay the matter of unemployment itself. This was an explosive issue long before any real policy changes came, and before the leadership admitted the depth of economic crisis in 1989–90. Early in 1986 Kostakov was controversial even in suggesting that, in the future unlike in the past, people might have to "look for jobs"[154] rather than vice versa—and he did not suggest that the looking would be too hard. The controversial economist and essayist Nikolai Shmelev, in a *Novyi mir* article in 1987,[155] condemned "overemployment," cited the "parasitical" aspect of the certainty of employment, and calculated that in reality labor turnover, plus some uncounted "tramps," made for a 3 percent Soviet unemployment rate at any given time. He argued that a relatively small "reserve" unemployed work force—supported by some state benefits—might serve as a guard against "laziness, drunkenness, and lack of responsibility." Losing a job, and going on a temporary benefit or to a job chosen for one, would be cheaper than stockpiling the destructive loafers at the workplace. He was not advocating a reserve army of jobless "losers," left to their own resources. The general tone of his article guaranteed controversy, but it was his view of losing a job, of paid (and, evidently, disreputable) unemployment that seemed to attract the most attention. Gorbachev, sensitive to the issue, expressed his disagreement with Shmelev's ideas on employment in a "meeting with voters," and distanced himself from unemployment-as-tactic, without reading Shmelev out of the multifaceted discussion of the economics of perestroika.[156]

Other reform economists dealt with the issue in a gingerly way. Gennadi Lisichkin, a pro-market economist frequently engaged in controversies in the press, argued that one of perestroika's tasks was the prevention of unemployment.[157] Gladkii, chairman of the State Committee on Labor and Social Problems, rejected the idea of unemployment as a "spur,"[158] although he did project a 10–15 million cut (smaller than Kostakov's projection eighteen months earlier) in production employment. He stressed that in certain branches of the economy, 10–15 percent reductions had already been achieved, with no problems in job placement of those released.[159]

In 1986–87, there was a balancing of tough talk with policy reassurance. Minister of Finance Gostev cited 13 percent of all state enterprises as unprofitable, and suggested they might be closed.[160] Aganbegian, in an interview with *Newsweek* in August 1987, spoke of cutting the prices on unneeded goods by 30 percent, to stop factories from producing more of them—a prelude, given some of his earlier statements, to the closure of such factories.[161] But recognizing that such action makes for unemployment came much harder. Even Abalkin, who was ready in 1986 to project the disappearance of 20 million jobs by the end of the century, in mid-1987 edged away from any notion of "tolerable" unemployment in an interview in *Sovetskaia Rossiia*;[162] and Aganbegian did not suggest that the state's responsibilities did not encompass providing other work for those released from jobs that were abolished.[163]

Such reassurance would not necessarily quiet workers' fears. The new mobility, the new insecurity, the new critical attitude taken toward the economic consequences of running large-scale, material-intensive extractive and "metal-eating" industries with large and relatively well-paid labor forces, all amounted to a major shift in the policy climate and the psychological climate in which workers operate. A caller to a Moscow television show featuring the chairman of Goskomtrud and the head of the nationwide trade-union organization complained of reductions in staff as "senseless" and "inhumane," despite assurances from the union head that people's "right to work" was protected.[164] Kostakov, in a survey of readers' letters in response to an article of his in *Kommunist*, quoted the words of one who obviously saw problems in the call to efficiency, which, once achieved, would make it easier to dismiss workers who had contributed to its achievement. "What should the thirty- and forty-year-olds, do? We are poorly educated, we have no 'survival' skills, and hence we have no certainty about tomorrow. It is now not to my advantage to do a good job. As a result of such 'diligence,' people become redundant and hence are out or not certified."[165]

Inconvenience, loss of earnings, loss of dignity all intertwine in worker complaints, as an *Izvestiia* review of readers' letters revealed.[166] One industrial worker wondered why *he* should be told to become a barber, cook, or waiter—service-sector occupations of no great public prestige. Another resisted the notion that he might have to move from southern Kazakhstan to the Caspian Sea area in search of work. A worker from the mining area of Krivoi Rog complained that he and others had long been told that society needed people who produced "material assets"—not "clerks." What of the earlier assurances that mechanization would mean cuts in the length of the working day, not cuts in jobs? The notion of job as welfare entitlement, as something on which the worker has a just claim—one not to be violated—cut deep. In factories or offices, among blue- or white-collar people, plans for staff reduction could be announced, explained, "accepted" as necessary on an impersonal basis ("a 10 percent cut is necessary"); but the near-invariant response of the individuals selected for reduction was "why *me*?"[167]

Less security in employment was not all. For many the new tempo of work, the new pressures that came—or were threatened—via the diffusion of the "brigade method" represented another erosion of the quality of work life. For some workers, this was surely a promising innovation; if it "worked" well, an accurate KTU would link their (presumably above average) efforts and results with advantageous pay differentials. But for others, as various Soviet data and writings indicate, the picture was less pleasing. If "workers who are considered unproductive actually appear to enjoy their jobs,"[168] then the strictures and pressures of brigade forms of operation would come as a disturbance to familiar patterns. Not all workers are ambitious. Not all would like to work harder or better. Few, for good reasons, would be easily convinced that new forms of organization, new tempos of work, if they are forced to adopt them, will yield any real advantage or benefit. To bend themselves with greater effort to their tasks, workers in a steel-plant brigade should know that brigade members in plants producing consumer goods, construction brigades in the housing sector, "brigades" in the service sector, are all doing their part as well. They could not know this. They would be hard to convince. That the potential for envy, disruption of relationships with workmates, and bad feelings in general is coped with so frequently by employing (or ignoring) the KTU to generate *equal* shares, or ones based on welfare rather than work claims, is not remarkable. It is a human response to yet another intervention from above; one that few on the factory floor called for.

On the positive side, less than two years after Gorbachev's accession, workers and employees were offered purported new rights and functions in determining how, and by whom, factories are managed. In January 1987, at a Central Committee plenum, Gorbachev, in line with the developing emphasis on participation, [169] advocated the *election* of enterprise managers. In mid-1987, the new Law on the State Enterprise[170] made several points specifying what seemed a greater "empowerment" of line workers. Two points were particularly important. The new law called for the election of all managerial staff, from directors to brigade leaders, turning what had been a much-publicized "experiment" in certain areas into a nationwide policy. It also provided for a "council of the labor collective" in each enterprise with authority over a variety of activities within the plant—a body to be elected (two- to three-year terms) by balloting at general meetings of the plant work force.

Those familiar with the gap between Soviet paper and reality could, in 1987, project problems with the state enterprise law in general, as well as with its worker provisions. As events since have shown, they were right. If worker participation and enterprise autonomy were to work hand in hand, they had to be real. How real would the manager's autonomy be? It seemed compromised from the start. While the plan directives were to be cut back, with more decision making about production being done at plant level, for "critical" items "state orders" (*goszakazy*) were supposed to guarantee that needed goods would be produced. But from the first, *goszakazy* showed signs of substituting for detailed plan directives: one factory faced a state order that amounted to over 100 percent of its prior year's output.[171] This left little room for managerial choice—one that many managers would not have welcomed, in any case.

Nor did the new law, on close inspection, give much by way of an active role in management, or even an institutionalized veto power, to workers. Directorial elections would take place, but the elected director must be confirmed by the plant's superior "organ." This meant ministry approval—and despite the emphasis Gorbachev placed on paring the personnel in economic ministries, there would be sufficient bureaucrats to manipulate candidacies by accepting or rejecting names. Directors, in turn, were to give approval to those elected to lower supervisory posts. Thus a strong version of *edinonachalie* was preserved, with plenty of room for corrupting the electoral process.[172]

The labor collective councils' mandate had less to do with workers' control than with the control and mobilization of workers, that is, with labor discipline, productivity, and even with the monitoring of pay to see that it was "earned." In the provisions and the surrounding rhetoric, there was no evidence of an intention to promote "the interests and rights of workers as a distinct group," as one Western analyst put it.[173] Persons running for director were not to appeal to shop-floor

interests as opposed to others. The councils could include professionals, engineers, managers, and union officials as well as line workers.
Rights to "participate" were spread broadly within a context empha-
sizing a community of interest in production and efficiency, rather
than division of interest based on one's place in the work process, or
in the setting or distribution of rewards.

Still, much of the Soviet managerial strata had no reason to welcome even these changes, and this may be a reason behind the rationale of an attempt to change their behavior by creating a new situation.
Enterprise directors—bad ones, "typical" ones, traditional ones—
evoked no special love in Gorbachev. Yet if large-scale perestroika
worked, managers would have more autonomy vis-à-vis weakened
mid-level ministerial controls. How, then, to guarantee the quality of
their work, how to control them? To some degree, a procedure
whereby ministries would vet candidates, pre- and/or postelection,
but whereby those candidates must nonetheless *be* electable, should
yield less incompetence and a better utilization of the "human factor."
The very moderate control capacity of the labor collective councils and
the noncontroversial power of unions to defend workers' legal rights
as individuals suggested a desire to maintain and promote some
checks on managers from below. Khrushchev-era encouragement of
trade union intervention at the plant level was aimed at the narrowing
of managerial prerogatives and abuses, as much as at the defense of
workers per se. Such a rationale made sense as well in the Gorbachev
line of 1987–88, though later, as we shall see, unions assumed a
higher profile. In both cases, the role to be played by plant-level party
organizations[174] in directing the work of the organs of participation
and "self-management" was a large and clear one. The balance to be
struck between management's representation of ministerial oversight
in the plant and worker-union participatory representation of broader
policy priorities was not to be a matter of "local option." Workers constituted only one category of players in this game, and not a category
recognized as possessing legitimate interests distinguishing them
from other categories. No room was made in the 1987 law for the
working *class*, however much the emphasis on participation might
show a recognition of the existence of the "new worker," with all the
attributes about which reformers had written.

The law went into effect on January 1, 1988. The results were unim-
pressive. "Enterprise autonomy" remained, largely, a fiction: *goszakazy* in many instances still imposed plan-type discipline from
above. Ministerial bureaucracies retained many levers of control over
managerial discretion. If worker participation in management was the
logical corollary of managerial autonomy, the logic failed in the ab-

sence of autonomy.[175] There were some who not only argued that it was, but that in large state factories working under self-financing it was critical[176] in avoiding the militancy that would rise under the financial and work pressures on the rank and file. A study of views on the election of plant leaders, published in September 1988, showed little difference between workers and senior managers in advocating the electoral principle: workers "absolutely" (25 percent) and "firmly" (55 percent) favored it, versus 21 and 42 percent, respectively, for managers.[177] The "participatory current" had become rhetorical, but the very readiness of managers to give lip service to it under the conditions of their own continuing subordination to ministries suggested less than sincerity. Responses to an inquiry on how well new collective self-management organs worked, conducted in 120 enterprises, were lukewarm to negative. Only 2.7 percent saw them as "very active," while 18.3 percent saw them as inactive and 52.6 percent as "not fully" effective; a substantial 15.3 percent said "don't know" and 11.1 percent said they *had* no such organs.[178] The factory floor was not in the throes of any organizational revolution, and the "new worker" may well have found it expedient to rely on negative control and on the reluctance of many managers to assume autonomy (preferring instead the old relations with ministerial superiors and blue-collar inferiors). One worker, complaining that his factory manager was not elected, admitted that his enthusiasm for the principle was not widely shared. His coworkers were "unwilling to make trouble. Our earnings are high, the bonuses are good, the work is not dirty, housing is available nearby. Who would like to lose such a job?"[179] The mention of livable conditions on the positive side, and some concern about managerial sanctions on the negative, said a good deal about the persistence of older patterns into a new era. It also suggested other possibilities if work and pay conditions were to worsen in the absence of real participatory channels.

Class, Work, and Authority

How does one summarize the lessons of the quarter-century from Brezhnev's 1964 to Gorbachev's 1988? Soviet workers are not particularly satisfied with their jobs. They work in an authority system that diffuses little autonomy in their direction. Work is a performance of rather routine, segmented tasks under orders. For all the long-term persistence of rhetoric about participation, about workers as coproprietors of the national wealth, workers do not feel like they are participating or in charge. Asked whether they would like to participate more and elect their superiors, large numbers answer in the affirmative.

Those are some of the lessons of this chapter. Their professed alienation from the job, even if minor, and the experience of subordination to authority are the sort of shared experiences that should make for working-class identity. Given their desire for greater participation and control, there should also be a certain opposition in a worker-boss, "we-they" image of the plant and work life. How strongly these factors really work depends, *inter alia*, on the degree to which nonwork life compensates for job alienation and displaces from centrality the work experience that classic Marxist theory argued was, or should be, central.[180]

We have not dealt here with nonwork life in any great detail. In any case, there is already a large Soviet and Western literature on the use of free time in the USSR. It indicates that workers spend more time in passive, less "cultured" leisure pursuits than do professionals and intellectuals. All this is predictable enough. But if one thinks of nonwork compensation as involving high levels of consumption of lowbrow goods and entertainments, it is hard to see a major escape route here. One of the dissatisfactions of many Soviet workers is with pay (too low); another is with the goods that pay should buy (too few).

Experience of another type of nonwork life—the work done outside one's state-sector job, in the second economy—as another factor in diminishing the centrality of the job situation suggests two important points. First, most workers do not work in the second economy at all: the escape is not there. Second, it is precisely the workers in classic heavy industry who seem least involved in the second-economy private work that might refocus attention away from the factory job. Lack of opportunity may be a large part of this. It also means that the advantages of relatively high pay scales and bonuses for workers in the favored branches are less decisive, relative to moonlighters from other branches, than the basic statistics would indicate. In all, the positive compensations of nonwork life may not be so significant as to work strongly against the formation of feelings of class identity and opposition. (In a negative sense, both the large-scale thefts from the workplace and working-class alcohol abuse, proverbially widespread and persistent, may represent "compensations" that limit the degrees to which alienation grows beyond the passive, and to which working-class identity and opposition translate into active, collective forms.)

Workers' "negative control" practices certainly show some capacity to act, as workers, in opposition to what management does to impinge on workers' interests. Students of labor dynamics in the West note frequent distinctions between low levels of worker political activism and higher levels of economic activism.[181] They also distinguish between activism that looks for job control (control of the work process, the authority structure), and that which is economistic—action for better pay. Job control is more a class issue, in the general understanding, than are economistic demands: the one has more of opposition, of totality, and under certain circumstances, of alternative consciousness, than the other. This is not, however, a matter of seeing generally economistic labor unions and their leaders as "sell-outs." Capital has been more conciliatory on economistic issues, less on control. Workers take what they can get more easily—money—and reduce the salience of the rest, with the added money facilitating nonwork compensations. Economistic union activity reflects this worker experience; it does not betray it.[182] Job control issues, as pursued by union activity in the capitalist factory, are pursued in a conservative and defensive manner, seeking to preserve practices, to make the *de facto* arrangements management may wish to disturb, *de jure*.[183] The workers do not, typically, make a grab for power.

Soviet trade unions—as should be evident and will become even clearer in the next chapter—have been neither control oriented nor really economistic. This essentially means that workers' negative control practices in Soviet plants, within their limits, do seek some control of the work process, but—at least until quite recently—for economistic ends. After all, this is what pressures for easy, stable output norms, for the supplementing (*vyvodilovka*) of wage-rates that are too low, even in some sense the sabotaging of differentiation through the KTU have been about: an economic result each can live with, and that all can tolerate—though many, as individuals, may see it as less than optimal. Negative control, in this sense, seems a limited but clear manifestation of elements of working-class identity and opposition, if only at the level of the shop, the section, or the plant. The viability of these negative control practices, the likelihood that they might be exchanged for greater empowerment in work organization via the brigade method, in general factory organization via the councils of labor collectives, depends on a complex set of factors. On them also depend some of our class issues.

The brigade method, by design, offers the possibility of more control of the work process. If boredom, monotony, sameness, the segmentation of tasks are critically salient to worker discontent, brigades may offer benefit, may take the edge off oppositional attitudes. But their deep rationale is enhanced labor efficiency, for production purposes. This implies harder work, self-enforced within the brigade, and overall is a departure from an informally recognized right not to work hard. Negative control, as we have seen, can work within the brigade to adapt it to worker purposes. Missing has been the one thing that might make brigades work, that might render less sharp the we-they divide around which worker identity and opposition are likely to focus: clear economic benefits, in consumption, for workers who will go along. Given the general economic picture, harder work, by the brigade rules, may generate more rubles, but not more things to spend them on. Negative control probably continues to represent the best defense of workers' interests.

This was the case in Gorbachev's first three to four years with respect to broader worker participation in management. "Councils of labor collectives" were not, typically, dominated by line workers. They only make sense if there is real enterprise autonomy—if the plant has something to decide. For many plants, whose old plan targets became, instead, *goszakazy*, there was nothing to decide, nothing for management and workers to codetermine, and no economic benefit to be gained by trying. Sound and fury about participation seems more likely than not to strengthen the defensive stance of workers and to enhance elements of class consciousness.

Without anticipating the strikes and worker militancy discussed in the following chapters, it may be well to note a few points that take us back to matters touched upon first in the introduction. It was unlikely that workers would choose to focus on the long-term promise of perestroika and take an optimistic view of that long term. There was plenty for them to react to in a neutral-to-negative fashion in its early stages. Its innovations in the world of work were hardly welcome. *Gospriemka* hurt. The worker's claim to *this* job, on *this* shift, in *this* plant was eroded by policies favoring dismissal and reassignment. Material benefits in exchange for all of this readjusting have been elusive, save for those who have gone to the new co-ops, a destination many workers find offensive. Both the symbolic and real impacts of perestroika could be seen by many as *anti*-worker; the likely outcome would be an intensification of identity and opposition. To the degree that workers come to identify their world, its familiar securities and certainties, its satisfactions and dissatisfactions, as what "Soviet life" *is*, perestroika can appear alien indeed. Glasnost' means unfamiliar voices, new facts hitherto denied, an assault on workers' general sense of their own history. The intelligentsia, the talkers and scribblers, have made this system their own—and made political leaders, to a degree, their own as well. Is the worker, then, the defender of authentic Soviet life, of what is real and supposed to last? For workers who feel this way—and my judgment would be that there are many— the gap between them and the reformist political leaders, economists, and intelligentsia could be, after the seemingly insoluble question of ethnic nationalism, the central divide in Soviet society. It would still be going too far to see this as totality. But much of what perestroika brought—and failed to bring—in Gorbachev's first four years was more likely to intensify working-class consciousness than to enlist workers in a broad alliance with reformist forces.

More broadly, what we have seen in this chapter testifies to the general difficulty the largely unreformed Soviet polity experienced in regulating an increasingly complicated range of activities—production, consumption, thought, and the development of tastes and preferences—in a more complex society, "matured" to urban-industrial status over the Khrushchev and Brezhnev years. As a stratum or class, the intelligentsia, or its dissident segment, seemed a larger, more visible problem to the Brezhnev regime than did the workers. Policy was generally repressive—but not to the Stalinist point, and not entirely successful. Growing corruption, which was not "willed" from the top but was certainly tolerated and engaged many near the top seats of power as well as those lower down—indicated the failure of control in the absence of violent repression and the presence of the desire to live better than the Soviet economy made possible in general. There were new intellectuals, new professionals, new crooks as well as "new workers." The early Gorbachev period was, in this context, one of attempts to fuse new rhetoric and purpose with a mix of new, and old, policy instruments in the pursuit of reform. It worked better with the intellectuals and professionals than with the workers who so outnumbered them.

6

Regime Control and Worker Opposition

> [It's time] to give it to the Poles . . . we live no
> better than they, but we don't strike, we
> don't disrupt defense preparedness.
>   (*A Soviet worker, 1981*)

> *Esli norma budet bol'she, to my sdelaem kak v*
> *Pol'she.* (If the norm is increased, we'll do as
> they do in Poland.)
>   (*Workers' slogan, Pavlovsk, 1982*)

FROM LENIN ON, Soviet leaders have feared the spontaneity likely to emerge in a society not yet (and likely never) sufficiently "conscious," by way of social and economic development and unending political education, to be left to regulate its own affairs. Workers and their families, the core of that society, have been the objects of tutelage and control on a large scale. Today's better-educated, hereditized workers, no less than the ex-peasant factory hands of the 1930s, were the targets of the regime's organizational "active measures"; the difference may be in why and how they react. A prime aspect of this control has been the penetration of Communist party organizations into the plant, down to the shop floor and up to the director's office: political guidance, surveillance, and the discharge of political rhetoric and stimulation over the day-to-day work of production.

Another feature has been the use of the official trade-union organizations to administer various programs of the Soviet welfare system for the workers. Under rather tight constraints, and inconsistently, they have also defended individual workers in claiming the few rights the regime has granted them in their dealings with managers. These unions are grouped under the All-Union Central Council of Trade Unions (AUCCTU) and in the early 1980s numbered thirty-two national organizations comprising more than 130 million members, or some 98 percent of the work force.[1]

Both party and union organizations are the focus of this chapter, as are two kinds of evidence indicating that the total of negative and positive controls has not worked effectively enough to prevent manifestations of worker discontent, opposition, and revolt. Even before Gorbachev, Soviet workers went on strike, sometimes in the thousands; activists attempted, against all the odds, to form independent trade unions. But the chronicle of worker militancy against the Soviet system is a modest one, through 1988. Such militancy and an appreciation of party and official union roles in the plants are essential components of the background against which the USSR today confronts crisis.

Politics: The Party at the Plant

Soviet accounts of the degree of working-class political integration via the CPSU were nearly invariable in style—and almost invariably boring, an alternation of statistics on party "saturation" of various segments of the working class with didactic accounts of various "model" worker-Communists and their exemplary behavior as producers, citizens, and family people.[2] What lies behind this boilerplate of the pre-Gorbachev times?

Both party and Komsomol organizations have been, if not ubiquitous, nearly so in the workplace: a 1984 report proudly noted that more than one-third of the 428,000 "primary party organizations" are located in production *kollektivs*, in which seven of every ten members of the working-age population are to be found; added to this are 450,000 Komsomol primary organizations.[3]

Regime access to the working class was thus assured. More variable over time has been the propensity of workers to join up, and of the party to enroll workers. In the post-Stalin period, the story was, without a doubt, one of expansion in the party's "representation" among workers and of the working-class share in total party membership. While through the period from the 1930s to Stalin's death, the party heavily enrolled those who could boast of a working-class origin, the enrollment of new members who were currently workers was more moderate. In 1952–55, only 28.3 percent of new admissions were workers; with Khrushchev, the change was dramatic, to 44.7 percent for the 1962–65 period. The policy continued under Brezhnev; in 1976, 58.6 percent of the new party admissions were current workers.[4] This latter figure meant that 9 percent of the "working class" was enrolled in the party in 1976, up from 7.56 percent in 1966[5]—an ostensibly modest figure, even taking into account the party's elite, *avangard* status. But this figure assumes the broadest definition of the working class, including state farm workers, and cloaks considerable variation by economic sector, level of skill, urban versus rural location, and so

TABLE 6.1
Workers' Party Membership, by Skill Level (percentage of party members
in each skill grouping)

	Gor'kii (1979)	Leningrad (1970)	Taganrog (1978)	Ufa, Other Cities (1970–72)	Bashkiria (1974–75)
Lowest skilled	7.0	9.0	7.0	3.1	6.3
Highest skilled	16.7	25.0	20.0	13.1	23.9
Number of groups	2	4	3	4	5

Source: Adapted from M. N. Rutkevich, "Sblizhenie rabochego klassa i inzhenerno-
tekhnicheskoi intelligentsii," *Sotsiologicheskie issledovaniia*, no. 4 (1980), pp. 25–34
(Gor'kii); E. V. Klopov, *Rabochiii klass SSSR (Tendentsii razvitiia v 60-70-e gody)* (Moscow:
Mysl', 1985), p. 202 (Leningrad and Taganrog); N. A. Aitov, "Izuchenie struktury rabochego klassa promyshlennogo tsentra," *Sotsiologicheskie issledovaniia*, no. 1 (1974), pp.
60–65 (Ufa and other cities); Ia. P. Ladyzhinskii, "K kharakteristike rabochego novogo
tipa v razvitom sotsialisticheskom obshchestve," *Nauchnye doklady vysshei shkoly,
Nauchnyi kommunizm*, no. 4 (1978), pp. 86–87 (Bashkiria).

on. In 1977, critical sectors such as industry, construction, and transportation had 10–11 percent party membership, less favored areas
(trade, catering, communal services) 6 percent.[6] In all, the party had
become, demographically, more of a workers' party. Worker-mem-
bers and candidates for membership amounted to 32 percent of the
total in 1956, to 37.8 percent in 1966, 40.1 percent in 1971, 43.4 percent
in 1981. In 1986, 59.3 percent of candidates waiting for membership
were workers, and the worker share of total membership reached 45.3
percent in 1987.[7]

The party sought certain kinds of workers; conversely, certain kinds
of workers also seemed to seek party membership. Just as the educated, managerial, "intellectual" strata have been statistically overrepresented in the party, so, among worker members, were the
highly skilled more likely than the unskilled to find a place on the
party rolls (or, among better-skilled younger workers, in the Komsomol). Table 6.1 roughly depicts this persistent pattern, counterposing
the party membership of those categorized as low-to-unskilled workers versus that of "skilled" or "highly skilled," the extreme categories
in each of several Soviet studies. The differences are marked, accentu-
ated, to some degree, by the number of different categories and thus
to the degree to which the "highest-skilled" worker group may include people close to the "technician" category. The party felt little
need to enroll large numbers of unskilled workers—those "in" were
likely among the oldest members in a given workplace. A somewhat
more illuminating if restricted picture is available from research in

TABLE 6.2
Party Membership, Workers and Other Categories, in Three Soviet Cities, 1967 and 1975 (percentage of party membership in each category)

	City	1967	1975
Workers			
in unskilled and low-skilled physical work	K	3.7	4.5
	A	3.8	1.2
	M	3.8	2.2
in skilled, predominantly physical work	K	9.5	7.9
	A	9.6	7.4
	M	11.4	5.8
in highly skilled work combining mental and	K	20.0	15.9
physical functions	A	35.1	41.6
	M	—	—
Employees and specialists			
in low-skilled mental work (nonspecialist	K	7.3	8.8
employees)	A	8.1	7.2
	M	7.8	7.1
in skilled mental work requiring secondary	K	18.9	20.0
specialized or higher education	A	24.2	13.8
	M	29.6	21.2
in highly skilled mental work requiring higher	K	25.9	14.8
education and supplementary training	A	54.5	21.4
(personnel with academic degrees, high-caliber	M	—	—
artistic intelligentsia)			
in highly skilled managerial work	K	61.3	60.7
	A	55.1	48.3
	M	54.5	66.7

Source: O. I. Shakaratan, "Peremeny v sotsial'nom oblike gorozhan," in *Sovetskaia sotsiologiia*, vol. 2 (Moscow: Nauka, 1982), pp. 39–52 (trans. in *Soviet Sociology* 24, 1–3 (Summer-Fall-Winter, 1985–86), p. 114.
Note: K = Kazan'; A = Al'met'evsk; M = Menzelinsk.

three cities in the Tatar ASSR, which gives party "shares" at two dates (1967 and 1975) and places worker membership in perspective relative to that of other social groups in the factories (table 6.2). The differences between the skill levels remain considerable; low-skilled ranks are least penetrated by the party, skilled workers and lower white-collar functionaries (the latter predominantly female) are represented rather similarly and fall well below the very highly skilled workers. On the whole, however, the upper reaches of intellectual/managerial work exhibit much higher membership rates than do blue-collar ranks of whatever skill level. Evidence on the relationship of educational attainment to party membership, available in more systematic form than that on occupational status, runs in the same direction: levels of education likely to guarantee that one is *not* a worker are much more strongly associated with membership than are lesser educational levels.[8]

Thus we have a "working class" whose more skilled members—those predominantly male workers in the more important branches of industry—include a minority, but a significant one, of party members. In turn (although the direction and definition of causality here are debatable areas), worker-Communists and Komsomol members exhibited qualities and behavior patterns which, from the official viewpoint, denoted them as exemplars. In a 1976–77 study in seven machine-building enterprises in Leningrad, worker party members averaged 9.3 years of education (9.9 for the younger Komsomol members) versus the 8.5 years of those affiliated with neither organization. Party members (93.7 percent) and Komsomols (72 percent) participated in various "volunteer" work more than the remainder (54 percent) and in work-related "socialist competition" within the plants (97.8 percent for party members, 85 percent for the unaffiliated in the more "controlled" intrafactory context). Exemplars as well of moral values (or better attuned to giving the right answer), half again as many party as nonparty workers agreed that the "content" of work was more important than the wage.[9]

"Striving" was long part of the approved repertoire of worker behavior, and in its various forms the politically committed outscore nonparty types. A series of 1970s studies of young workers in nine cities and areas, comparing party members and candidates, Komsomols, and the remainder, found, respectively, 29.3, 25.5, and 16.5 percent bending their efforts to the "best in [my] specialty" skill-development program, and 55.8, 24.4, and 20.6 percent already the recipients of the title "Shock-Worker of Communist Labor." Total nonparticipation in these and similar programs ranged from 19.6 percent among the unaffiliated, through 13.1 percent for the Komsomols, and down to a respectably low 4.3 percent for party affiliates.[10] Other studies show that party members among young workers were well ahead of average in observance of labor discipline, commitment to skill development and high-quality output, and involvement in the life of their *kollektiv*—but show little difference between Komsomol membership and the average.[11]

Similar data demonstrate growing worker representation in other, presumably "integrative," political and social activity. Workers were elected in large numbers (in the pre-1989 Soviet single-slate elections) to local and regional Soviets and even to the nationwide Supreme Soviet. Since the mid- to late 1960s, more than one worker in every hundred, in fact, has been a member of one or another level.[12] Worker members of local Soviets grew from 10.6 percent of the whole in 1955 to 28.8 percent in 1965,[13] to 36.5 percent in 1971.[14] Since then, growth of the worker share was steady (39.3 percent in 1973, 40.5 in 1975, 42.3 in 1977, 43.4 in 1980, 44.3 in 1982, and 44.4 in 1985). But "core" workers in industry, construction, transportation, and communications made up a bit less than half of this share, the corresponding figures for 1973–85 being 18.6 19.1, 19.4, 19.6, 19.7, and 19.3 percent.[15] At the ceremonial pinnacle of the Soviet state, the Supreme Soviet, officially the top legislative body, worker shares grew apace in the post-Stalin years. Workers made up 23.5 percent of the body in 1963, 26.6 in 1966, 31.7 in 1970, 32.8 in 1974, 34.8 in 1979, and 35.2 in 1984.[16]

As these data imply, these and other indicators are very uncertain indices of effective *participation*, and say less about the integration of even the involved workers into the official political consensus than is evident at the outset. Effective political power in yesterday's USSR was extremely narrowly concentrated; mere membership in the party conferred little power. "Workers" currently in production made up only a symbolic 3 percent of the party's voting Central Committee members in 1976, far below their share among the rank and file.[17] While the pre-1989 Supreme Soviet was "decorative" and legitimating, lower-level Soviets were more involved in the stuff of local administration, constituting one of the arms of local government. Here, however, the clout tends to be in the executive committees (*ispolkomy*) of these bodies, not in the total of elected members. And, while workers made up, for example, 35 percent of the total in 1969, they constituted only 19.9 percent of the executive committees in the same year.[18]

That the working class was not in a political sense the "ruling class" was never in doubt, and that such statistics indicate no leading role for that class is thus no surprise. But it is a different, altogether more complex matter to ask what else political "participation" of this sort can mean.

To a worker, activist participation in trade unions, social-political activities, or electoral commissions—expected to some degree, especially of party members—meant, in cash terms, about 9 percent more pay than that given an otherwise similar worker without such political commitment. This, at least, is the conclusion drawn from the Soviet Interview Project (SIP) survey research on late-Brezhnev era emigrés.[19] All in all, this seems a moderate return, and only 17.9 percent of workers placed themselves in this "activist" category. Even though the sample is made up of emigrés, the figure does not seem radically

out of line with Soviet data, once the latter's massive figures on participation in trade union and other work-related activities are deflated
for the nominal participation which was the lot of most workers, evident more on paper than in reality.

Such activism in approved channels could not hurt in getting pref-
erential treatment in housing access, vacation scheduling, and the
like. But by itself it did not lead to career advancement, to promotion
from the factory floor to an office, either via sponsored education or
directly, as party membership and other sorts of activism did in the
more dynamic times of rapid economic growth, social mobility, and
fast-changing occupational structure. Career patterns became more
regularized, appropriate education before going to work became more
and more necessary at entry level, and higher education was the correct route to jobs in economic or political administration. The "activist" worker of the Brezhnev period remained a worker: he simply
earned a bit more.

Second, in the SIP sample, former workers who reported activist-
level involvement in "bad" activities (protests, strikes, distribution of
samizdat, etc.)—only 1.7 percent of the emigrés surveyed—were punished more severely than conformists were rewarded. Activist workers on the "wrong" side earned 34–36 percent less than otherwise
identical workers.[20]

Beyond the monetary, the meaning of positive political involvement is mainly a matter for speculation. We can assume that some of
the minority of workers who were party members or other types of
political activists were and are sincere, patriotic, nationalistic perhaps, and satisfied with the Brezhnev-era system on its terms. Activism is an appropriate expression of support. Others, distinguishable
to some degree from the first category, may be people who are psychologically quite comfortable with an authoritarian system that, in
the workplace, bid people to watch for and condemn drunkenness,
"slacking," and petty theft among their fellows; and to take the same
stern line, as a citizen, outside the plant. Those feeling a need for a
"strong boss," a "tough order," for everything being "in its place,"
can express those needs in activist channels as well. Few indeed must
be the Russian-speaking Western visitors to the USSR who have not
met such authoritarian personalities.

It is worth noting that the SIP emigré research draws a profile of
workers which the Brezhnev regime might have found basically satisfactory on the political score, one that might have made campaigns to
increase workers' enrollment in the party, for example, lose some ur-
gency. Workers reported less involvement in oppositional activity
than other emigré groups, as they were also less "mobilized" in pro-

regime organizational activities.[21] Less likely to read *samizdat* and to listen to foreign radio than other, higher-placed groups (though in all groups, a majority did tune in to foreign radio), they were also less likely to work on electoral commissions to get out the vote for Soviet elections, less likely to belong to various committees at work, less likely to read newspapers.[22] They were more likely to vote than other groups (i.e., report a smaller share of nonvoters)[23] and less likely than managerial-level people to attempt to avoid military service.[24] (The majority of young workers go into the military, which may have its own pro-regime political socialization effects. As Victor Zaslavsky argues on the basis of *in situ* but "unofficial" interviews in 1968 and 1969 with 352 geological-survey drill operators, military service was probably the major differentiator between workers younger than 21, only 7.7 percent of whom expressed "strong support" of the Soviet invasion of Czechoslovakia, and those aged 21–30, whose strong support reached 35.5 percent.)[25]

In all, then, the working class was hardly the mobilized, enthusiastic, "conscious" supporter of the regime that early postrevolutionary ideologues had envisioned for the future. But it did not, in the years from Khrushchev's emergence to Brezhnev's demise (1953–82), give very clear signs of becoming the "spoiler," the destabilizer, of the Soviet order either. If the mechanisms of formal political involvement seem to add little to the passive political integration of the workers, it did not mean that massive work remained undone, or needed to be done. Through the years, workers tolerated and supported an order which, for the most part, they did not complain about in a major way. One of the elements they apparently did not give much thought to was "their own" labor unions, but later events would demonstrate that this inattention may have masked some real contempt.

Unions: Workers' Interests, Workers' Rights

Asked about their impression of the impact of factory-level trade union activity on wages and general worker welfare, the Brezhnev-era emigrés who responded in the Soviet Interview Project in the early 1980s provided the data in table 6.3.[26] Such responses obviously add up to neither a ringing endorsement, nor a retrospective overall condemnation of yet another bureaucratic institution left behind with one's exit from Soviet society. Without stressing "continuity" to the point of ignoring real and important developments over the years, one might argue that these attitudes are rooted in fifty years of experience. What John Scott, the American working at Magnitogorsk in the

TABLE 6.3
Impact of Union Activity on Wages and Worker
Welfare, Emigré Sample, 1970s (in percentages)

| | Unions Made | | |
	Better	Worse	No Effect
Wages	15.4	2.7	72.0
Worker welfare	37.3	0.9	61.7

Source: See note 26.

1930s, had to say about his coworkers' attitudes toward their benefits
and their source, makes the point: "The social insurance laws, whose
application was directly connected with the trade unions, worked
well. Paid vacations, sick money, free medical attention, rest homes,
were universally enjoyed and taken for granted. This service was generally appreciated, but usually attributed to the Soviet power in general, to the Bolshevik regime, rather than to the trade unions."[27] There
is a difference between source and conduit, between authoritative decision making and the execution of those decisions. Workers of the
1930s and the 1970s seemed to agree that the unions to which they
belonged did no harm and, if anything, did good, but as the noninde-
pendent instruments of higher policy. Such high votes for "no effect"
would imply a confidence that, were the whole union bureaucracy to
disappear, some other bureaucracy would be charged with the same
work.

Were the unions, then, instruments of workers' welfare, or subjection, or both? Did they mean much to workers who, after all, were
distant in time and space from any experience of independent, combative unions, pursuing "workers'" interests unabashedly versus the
bosses, capitalist or state/managerial? We can offer some brief and
tentative observations here, informed by voluminous Soviet writings
on the trade unions as well as the work of Western scholars who have,
over the years, lavished a good deal of energy, attention, and analysis on a topic that seems, at the outset, to fall short of excitement or
promise.

Soviet trade unions, after all, were victims, along with other quasi-
independent organizations and institutions, of the totalitarian breakthrough accomplished by Stalin. The dualism of the Leninist formula,
wherein trade unions were to "seek both increased productivity and
labor protection, in that order,"[28] gave way to near-total stress on the
former and neglect of the latter. In the post-Stalin period the original
dualism was restored via renewed attention to elements of worker

welfare, but with no intimation that unions should assume a combative stance versus management, or exceed their "mandate" with respect to workers' rights as predefined and circumscribed by the regime.

Soviet trade unions, then, by any Western standard, were a joke. But in the Soviet context, they were not a bad one (at least not until the economic slide of the late 1980s focused attention on their passivity). Paradoxically, the "negative control" that workers exercised in the workplace both rendered the poorly performed general "defense" functions of the unions less relevant and eased demands that might otherwise have been made on the unions: "Indeed, the relative stability of industrial relations in these societies has long been due at least in part to extensive informal bargaining between lower management and solidary work groups. For . . . unions this makes life easier insofar as it reduces pressure coming from the most vocal and best organized groups in the factory. On the other hand, the operation of informal bargaining further reduces confidence in the unions."[29] Unions, then, were not the worker's sole defense. Given the Soviet context, this was just as well. But they are not functionless. If unions were barred by politics and practice from any articulation of broad "workers' interests," at the factory level they did defend and protect in a case-by-case, "personalized" fashion. It was, most likely, the experience of this sort of union activity—which will not directly affect *all* workers—that accounts for evaluations such as those cited above. As Blair Ruble succinctly put it, Soviet trade unions "can only protect lone workers against case-specific abuses by individual managers."[30] Many workers who are neither inclined, nor certainly encouraged, to think of grievances in general categorical or class terms will experience their problems "alone," as discrete abuses, flowing from the manager, not the "system." A union organization that could demand the restoration to work of a fired worker, straighten out the claim to a certain pension or disability payment level, validate the place of a claimant to housing on the priority list for such, could be seen at least as doing something.

Even in the Stalin years, in the small margins of room left to them, unions could operate in the manner of informal personnel departments in various hardship cases. They provided another channel through which an individual might appeal for a room to live in, a pension to live on, or against some particularly egregious managerial behavior that exceeded even the very broad prerogatives of bosses at the time.[31] With Khrushchev, and especially after his consolidation of power in 1957, both the scope for union activity and the resources from which unions could allocate benefits and services increased. This amplification flowed neither from union "power" nor from worker "demand," but from the top down. (The few incidents of worker militancy in this period were, as we shall see, typically crushed with force.) Was it motivated by a leader's desire to do something for the workers, after years of deprivation, or to set the stage for getting more and better work out of them? We may join a student of union activity in the period, and hazard the opinion that Khrushchev combined both motives.[32] Resources, however, were perhaps the more critical element—Khrushchev eliminated some of the worst Stalinist practices, saw economic growth continue at a high rate, and allocated more of the GNP to consumption, both collective and individual. Factory union committees had more services and benefits to allocate, saw housing stocks increase, and thus had more square meters of living space to distribute.

Unions, thus, were able to *do* more, *with* more. At the factory level, their functioning was aided by a basic contextual fact that remained true from the coming of Khrushchev to near the end of the Brezhnev era—a certain commonality of interest between managers, union officials, and workers. Managers were not interested in production or productivity per se, but in meeting and moderately exceeding a plan target. They thus were desirous of securing a slack plan, one easy to fulfill. So were workers. Bonuses for all, and the filling of various factory benefit funds, depended on this. Both had an interest in a large wage fund with which they could finance the various "adjustments" in the *tarifnaia setka* to meet the "needs" of workers in general and in particular. Getting all of this "right" facilitated the retention of a labor force sufficiently motivated to do the work to fulfill the plan. It was not idyllic; it did not always work; but it often did, and there is some nostalgia for such times now. Whatever the deleterious long-term effects in the economy as a whole, this arrangement left little "first principles" material that management and unions could fight over, even if the latter had the mandate to conduct an active struggle on behalf of their constituents.[33]

On the level of individual grievances, there was much work to do for the unions, even without the persistent rhetorical calls for the unions to be active in everything from labor discipline to skill-upgrading and educational-moral-political "uplift"—an "almost infinite number of duties."[34] The pension system is complicated and inefficient, with its noncentralized records, the multiplicity of factors to be computed to determine pension levels, and the many pitfalls and bases for disputed claims. All this kept the paid staffs of plant-level unions, which are usually small, and their unpaid volunteers busy. A lack of training and the general inefficiency made this whole process more time-consuming than it should have been.[35] Union representatives "consulted" in joint commissions with management both in classifying workers by skill (and hence wage) level, and in agreeing to the norming of work in the various sections of a plant. (One student of Leningrad unions in the Khrushchev period noted that unions tended to see given wage levels as entitlements. They would resist any revision of norms threatening current levels, but, given management's generally much stronger hand and their own responsibility for increasing production, were less likely to resist new norms that called for harder work but could still be reached to keep wage levels stable.)[36] "Erosion" was to be avoided—a critical matter, as we shall see, in the genesis of strikes.

As we have seen, firings were no mass phenomenon in the Soviet economy in the years before the current crisis. They threatened few workers. The plant union committee's consent was legally required for a firing to be allowed. Yet there was slippage. Managers did tell workers "be gone," and in this area unions, by and large, defended individuals from "particular" abuses (and individuals found, in the courts, redress from what were unions' irregularities). Research in Moscow and Leningrad in the early 1960s, as well as in some other Soviet cities, indicated that most firings took place with the agreement of the union committee (generally about 75–80 percent). Workers who appealed such dismissals and asked the courts for reinstatements prevailed in about one-third of all cases; workers who appealed illegal dismissals (without union agreement) won all their cases in Moscow and Leningrad.[37] In all, about half of the cases workers brought for reinstatement were successful. Considering the small numbers, we are not dealing with a major grievance here; but it is notable that the union's prerogative to agree or to withhold consent to a dismissal has been treated seriously by the courts.

How much union organizations can do depends very much on resources; branch by branch, city by city, plant by plant, the variation is large. Favored heavy-industry plants, in well-developed urban areas close to the European center, offer services and benefits through their trade union organizations that peripheral factories in light and consumer industry cannot. At the extremes, the welfare-and-leisure resources of the famous Kirov metalworks in Leningrad, which has a "profile" dominated by highly skilled male workers, vastly outclass what a Bukhara silk factory offers its overwhelmingly female work force.[38] (Such differences by branch also affect the pockets of trade union chairmen. With their compensation usually pegged around 70 percent of the director's salary, the actual ruble income will vary—as will that of the director and others down the line—depending on whether the plant is in a high- or low-paid branch.)[39]

If high degrees of participation in union activities are an indication of the value workers place on them, then Soviet surveys of worker attitudes and self-reported activity show their value to be moderate.[40] A great deal of what unions did was done by volunteer "activists" (often party members). To some degree, the union's activities provided a focus for those who, for whatever reason, tended to volunteer for many activities.[41] But most workers seemed neither religious in their attendance at union meetings, nor active in the expression of opinions and suggestions that were theoretically encouraged as a manifestation of worker democracy, participation, and control: there is no evidence that workers regarded the unions as particularly "theirs."

This need not have deprived workers—who would prefer fewer meetings, in any case—nor run contrary to their legally recognized interests. While the Brezhnev era considerably deemphasized the various participatory projects of the Khrushchev period, it did see an amplification of the role of the factory-level union committee chairman, an increase in his clout versus the director, the head of the plant party organization, and others. A "good" chairman thus could defend the "individual rights" of his workers against encroachment; if many fell short, many did defend them. But, with the increasing "professionalization" of union roles, the career and perspective gulf between worker and union official widened; they were not the same sort of person.[42] And, ultimately, the chairman answered upward. The careers of union officials depended more on their superiors in the branch and regional union administrations, on their relationship with factory directors and ministerial officials, on factory, and perhaps on regional or local party bosses than on the workers. Ultimately, this determined their actions.

Whether workers ever had any image of the all-union trade union organization (AUCCTU) as an "advocate" of nationwide worker interests is unclear. To the rank-and-file worker, the AUCCTU—or a branch union—might appear to be an advocate of better conditions, of achievable norms and steady pay, of a certain "just" sharing out of rewards that precludes any widening gap between white-collar and blue-collar.[43] It might even appear effective in its advocacy, especially if it is the union of an economically favored branch. But most evidence leaned against this view, even before the outburst of worker militancy in 1989–90. "Life" is closer to hand in the plant; here the critical issues are played out.

The issues have not, certainly, always been resolved successfully. Neither the political penetration of the worker's world manifest in party and Komsomol organizations, nor the functioning of the trade unions as defenders of individual workers' legal rights and as the channels for allocation of benefits and services, nor informal "negative control," nor, finally, the threat of repression, always contained or diverted the grievances of workers.

From Negative Control to Collective Protest

Too much emphasis can be put on workers' negative control and, secondarily, on trade union activity as stabilizers of industrial relations. They do not always work, do not always protect workers against the raising of output norms, with consequent cutting of pay. They have not protected against price rises. These are matters of high-level decision making. They cannot protect against conditions in the local environment that may be chronic: particularly acute housing shortages, and bad housing conditions; corruption among local managers and officials that is more pronounced than average; managers whose sternness, inflexibility, or indeed cruelty make for unfortunate workers. At various times prior to the loosening of political control under Gorbachev, and in various places, such circumstances have reached a breaking point, one where "strikes, riots and other disturbances" have broken out.[44] The matter here, then, is the failure of controls over labor-management relations, or the transformation of "negative control," organized at best on a group basis, and generally tolerated as an aspect of "informal enterprise politics,"[45] into *collective protest*, episodic or prolonged, violent or peaceful, on a larger scale.

The basic facts about strikes remain elusive. The pre-Gorbachev USSR had no interest in publicizing them and used considerable resources to keep them hushed up. *Samizdat*, word-of-mouth, and reports of emigrés have combined to provide grist for the mills of outside analysts; they mix actual strikes with other sorts of disturbances; they can tell us nothing of what is *not* known. What we can be certain of is that our record of events is incomplete.

The data summarized in table 6.4 (starting on p. 249) refer to 106 strikes, reported with varying degrees of specificity, that occurred between the time of Stalin's death and the advent of Gorbachev. They are drawn, in turn, from four other summaries. Belotserkovsky's chronicle of "workers' struggles" in the early 1960s reports seven instances.[46] Over time, these range from 1959 to 1962. Of the seven, four might be assigned to the category of "other disturbances," ranging from a riot in Dneprodzerzhinsk over deaths in a wedding party due to the intervention of drunken police, through a mutiny on a cruiser in Vladivostok. The three actual strikes proper (nos. 5, 11, 13 in the table) all terminate in police or military repression, with shootings and loss of life. Whether many other Khrushchev-period strikes (on which data are scarce) involved such violence is difficult to say. Gidwitz's 1982 compilation reports thirty-seven strikes, ranging in time from 1956 to 1981, with little overlap with Belotserkovsky.[47] Holubenko's 1975 list overlaps in many places with Gidwitz, and adds several more.[48] Most comprehensive by far is the report by Alekseeva,[49] which lists a total of seventy-five strikes spread over the years 1956–83. Together, the four sources, eliminating duplications, yield a total of 106 strikes. On some, the only information is that they took place at a certain time and place, as when several cities are listed as the locations of strikes in a given year. On others, the data are much richer. We can scarcely hope to do justice to all the instances for which we have a reasonable amount of information; but some description, to provide a "feel" for the phenomena, should be useful.

In Novocherkassk in June 1962 (strike no. 13) nationwide price increases on meat and dairy products coincided with output norm revisions (i.e., lowering of piecework rates), which amounted to perhaps a 30 percent effective pay cut, at a large electric locomotive works employing 20,000 workers, to produce the largest explosion recorded in the USSR until 1989. Workers' protests within the plant merged with protest marches of women and children to local party headquarters. Troops (army, KGB, perhaps both) were called after local officials panicked. Some reports indicate workers "from several plants had taken over" the city: in any case, a massive but peaceful meeting in the town square, involving tens of thousands, was fired upon, in a disputed combination of mistakes (e.g., firing over the heads of the crowd may have killed some children perched in trees) and intent. Deaths probably ranged between seventy and eighty; some sources say several hundred. Curfew and effective martial law followed. A Central Committee delegation visited and found fault with local conditions as well; after they left, more food appeared in the stores. Trials and, evidently, executions and exiles also followed.

Temir-Tau in Kazakhstan (no. 5) in 1959 and Aleksandrov in Vladimir oblast' (no. 11) in 1961 were two other sites of disturbances. In the first, young workers at a construction site, agitated by poor living conditions and low wages (theirs being lower than those of "imported" Polish, Bulgarian, and Romanian workers), marched off the job. Protest acts included burning a dining hall and raiding a *kolkhoz* food market. As may have been the case in Novocherkassk, the first troops may have hesitated, but later ones did not. Workers—perhaps over a hundred—were shot, and local officials sacked. In Aleksandrov a worker in a factory was beaten to death while in police custody—a workers' suspicion confirmed when the factory director pressed the local authorities for an exhumation. The local police rejected demands for an investigation; workers struck and marched on police headquarters. The police fled, workers occupied the building, burned it, and marched on the local prison. After some confused dealings, with troops and with police and local officials taking refuge in the prison, other troops brought to the town opened fire on a large crowd, killing perhaps one hundred. According to one account, the factory director and two of his staff were tried, sentenced, and shot.

The three strikes described above represent a fair range of grievances: in the first case, simultaneous price rises and wage cuts; in the second, the evident buildup of economic grievance; in the third, a "noneconomic" precipitant for workers' protests. But as the record suggests, it was probably economics rather than other causes that precipitated most strikes in the Khrushchev years (1956–64). Likely, price rises nationwide and local wage dynamics in some areas, as in Novocherkassk, generated the largest share of the strike activity peak of eleven strikes (nos. 13–23) in 1962. Wage policy and general economic performance in Brezhnev's first five years (see below), on the other hand, seem to have moderated strike activity after Khrushchev's ouster in late 1964.

Most strikes have been less dramatic and, on the whole, more successful for the workers. For her seventy-five strikes, Alekseeva calculated that sufficient data on success and failure existed for thirty-eight of them: in only six did she "score" workers the losers, and in thirty-two she saw them as clear winners.[50] Aleksandrov and Novocherkassk are among her "losers," as well as those numbered 3, 22, 69, and 90 in table 6.4, for reasons indicated there.

"Winning" strikes range from small to large scale. Only six or seven workers struck in a Kiev printing plant in 1961 (no. 12), but they evidently comprised the whole, small shop. Paid by piecework, they found their norms subject to frequent intervention from management, and in this incident, pay was cut effectively by 50 percent. Sitting at silent presses, resisting a management that threatened them while itself under pressure from those expecting the plant's delayed product, workers saw management cave in and keep the incident quiet. (However, later moderate cuts on the order of 5 percent—too little to provoke militant action and not too large, perhaps, to be overcome—eventually added up, *in toto*, to the original reduction.)

Twelve years later, in 1973, at the Aleksotas woodworking plant in Lithuania (no. 47), two full shifts numbering 660 workers protested low piecework rates with a refusal to work. Local party leaders and

KGB and police officials all jawboned, but to no avail, and finally raised the pay rates, with no evidence of reprisals. Wages are not the only economic issue. In the Brezhnevian twilight, a porcelain factory in the village of Mishelevka near Irkutsk (no. 75) in Siberia struck because no bread had been seen in the town's stores for several days. The bread was delivered.

Such a response may be typical: bread, after all, *is* supposed to be available; workers in a factory cannot be blamed for its absence, as they might be blamed for wage demands. (Alekseeva calculates that such a response is typical, if temporary, in food-shortage strikes, and thus adds to her thirty-two clear successes, eleven more of the seventy-five wherein, even in the absence of "outcome" data, the actual cause of the strike made it likely to be resolved.)

Some strikes have an economic base but not, in effect, an immediate economic goal. In 1977 Baltic port workers (strike nos. 59–64) refused to work overtime unloading imported produce destined not for local stores, but for elite outlets and "closed distributors" in Moscow, and in 1962 Odessa workers (no. 21) likewise refused to load Cuba-bound produce. In neither case was reversal of state policy a realistic goal. Tallinn's work stoppage in 1981 (no. 97) was the only recorded strike in response to Baltic dissident calls for universal thirty-minute stoppages to protest political repression. All in all, Alekseeva characterizes eight of her seventy-five strikes as "symbolic" in this sense.[51] Other strikes involve noneconomic grievances but have proximate ends that are more than symbolic, for example, protesting work on a traditional Latvian national holiday in a Riga factory (no. 4); demonstrating against instances of police brutality (nos. 11, 29); objecting to closings of local churches (nos. 40, 67—two strikes on collective farms in Zarechenka and Znosychi); and voicing ethnic issues: Crimean Tatars protesting repression (no. 51), Moldavian-gypsy tensions (no. 100), animosity between Ingush and Ossetians (no. 95). (As national-ethnic issues emerged in greatly radicalized form in 1988, these were to provide a political impetus for strikes that would amount to many more "man-days lost" than in "pure" economic protest.) Mainly women workers struck in the textile city of Ivanovo in 1977 (no. 66) to demand some "balancing" of industry in the city to bring in male workers; because of its textile specialization, Ivanovo is a city where females dominate the population, and where the abnormal sex ratio makes marriage, household formation, and such difficult.

In general, however, women were less likely to be strikers than men. Heavy industrial plants and construction sites, where male workers predominate, have been more often the "base" for strikes than the food and light industry plants that are much more "feminized." In the latter, where wages are lower, theft of food and goods is a way of supplementing the wage-versus-needs gap, and more effective than strikes. Bus and truck drivers as well are strike-prone groups. Figure 6.1 contains numerous such instances, and driver militancy makes up six of the strike instances (nos. 79–83, 86) in the turbulent year 1981, which saw twenty strikes recorded in the data available. (As we shall see, "driver militancy" also marked the strikes in the Gorbachev era through 1988.) Data on ages of the male strikers are anything but plentiful, but those that are available tend to indicate that participants were young,[52] while leaders, on the other hand, were more typically older workers with families, with roots in the plant, with some sense thus of what is proper, what is "needed"— and, one must assume, a certain amount of authority among their fellows.

Taking the "long view" of the record, and mindful of the perils of interpreting minimal data over a period of thirty years, what might be said about trends? Strikes are few until 1960—though one of the 1956 entries mentions a Sverdlovsk "strike wave," and in Nikolaev in 1958, "several hundred" workers were reported arrested after a failed strike, cause unknown; 1960 saw actions in Kemerovo, Nikolaev, Rostov-on-Don, Kharkov, and Barnaul—the latter the only one "locatable," in a plastics factory. Aleksandrov (1961) and its repression were already detailed. In Kiev, the same year, the six strikers, as noted above fared better.

The price rises very probably figured in most of the 1962 strikes: in addition to Novocherkassk and to the Odessa dockers' action already noted, strikes occurred in Grozny, Krasnodar, Donetsk, Yaroslavl', Zhdanov, Gorky, Moscow, Kiev, and Kaunas; in Kaunas, a shoe factory strike of five hours was terminated when KGB troops, backed by tanks, reportedly threatened workers with Siberian exile (there is no information on the disposition of the other strikes). One shoud recall that the 1962 price rises "held"—the state did not back down—but that they were the *last* open price rises on basic foods before the "fluid" situation that characterizes the economy today. The legacy of 1962 may have had, in its own way, a major effect on the Brezhnevite interpretation of the "social contract."

Quiet years, by and large, follow. Not much is reported about the four 1963 strikes (Ryazan', Baku, Omsk, and Krivoy Rog), except that several plants were involved in the latter and "martial law" was imposed. In 1964, Sevastopol shipyard workers, numbering about two hundred, struck; the local MVD commander was reprimanded. Between 1969 and 1973, the nineteen strikes reported cover a broad range of grievances: of the eight where the outcome is known, six resulted in workers' demands being met wholly or partially, but in protests over wages and living conditions in Dnepropetrovsk involving thousands, some dead and wounded were reported, while dismissals and arrests followed strikes (even some successful ones) in Chervonograd, Kopeisk, Kerch, Baku, and Kamenets-Podol'sk. The only strike of any reported scale between then and 1977 is a three-day stoppage involving four hundred strikers at the Kirov works in Leningrad, with no other details available. The 1977 "spike" of eight strikes reflects six in Baltic ports, including Leningrad, over unloading foodstuffs directed to elite "distributors"; workers who refused to work overtime were replaced by soldiers and students.

The 1980 score duplicates but is more diverse than that of 1977. Of the eight, three were reported in auto plants in Gorky, Cheliabinsk, and Naberezhnye Chelny (KamAZ), involving protest over food shortages, and were swiftly settled. Another involved one thousand workers in a machinery plant in Tartu who stopped working because of bonuses, work conditions, and shortages. Of the eight, positive resolution is reported in five. Is there a "Solidarity" factor here? The four strikes that are dated all precede the Gdansk shipyard strike; the others cannot be placed. But there is no regional pattern that suggests propinquity to Poland or any "demonstration effect" in 1980.

The year 1981, finally, may be a different matter. Reported strikes peaked, Brezhnevian *zastoi* bottomed out. Of the twenty strikes, six took place in Kiev at five different enterprises, some lasting as long as five days. In five of them the workers' demands were reported as met. Vorkuta and Kuzbass coal miners, who would figure heavily in the militancy of 1989, struck as well, with no information on the outcome. In Pavlovsk (the Zhdanov auto plant) and Moscow (the Khrunichev factory), demands—evidently economic in the former case—were met. Reported strikes by bus drivers in Monchegorsk (five in all) and one in "urban transport" in Ordzhonikidze highlight another occupational group that would prove militant at the end of the decade.

If the price rises of 1962 and the attendant discomforts are the precipitants of the Khrushchev-period peak, the relative quietude of Brezhnev's first years have something to do with reasonably solid economic performance (which to some degree undermined arguments that might have been made in defense of the quickly strangled 1965 reform). It may also reflect (though here we are far indeed from being able to gauge the worker mood) increased repression and the fear of a yet more decisive return to the past than actually occurred.

The growth of strike activity in the later Brezhnev times suggests something else. If Soviet diets were, in the Brezhnev period, better than they had been years before, expectations had grown too. In this context, the poor *late*-Brezhnev performance on the food front was, for an expectant public (with the rubles to buy), seen as a time of shortages. The Baltic port strikes that bulk large in the 1977 figure had to do with a "social justice," elite-versus-mass issue, at a time when food was becoming what Brezhnev would later admit was "political problem number one." It remained unsolved and clearly contributed to the peak twenty-strike total recorded in 1981. Wage cuts, through norm/bonus manipulation, played some role in individual instances, exacerbating pains of shortages. But so many strikes, emerging in the late years of a rather "consensual," worker-oriented regime, must involve other factors. Arguably, the cumulating social and political erosion—the weakening and failure of social controls, the partial "escape" from such—in the late Brezhnev years made workers prone to act where they would not have done so earlier and more conscious of threats to their collective sense of fairness, to "social contract" claims. Flat to negative economic prospects in the face of earlier expectations—plus a confidence that, on economic issues at least, harsh responses to collective worker action were less likely—fed into the relative militancy of the late 1970s–early 1980s. There is, in all this, little evidence of any direct "demonstration effect" of Polish Solidarity militancy in 1980–81. If Polish events played a major role, it was likely mediated by obvious Soviet regime concerns about their effect in the USSR, reflected in renewed rhetoric in 1981 on the Soviet trade unions' need to defend workers' rights and welfare: workers sensitive to *this* signal might have been prompted to press harder.[53] The strike record in 1981 likely contributed to the ousting of AUCCTU head Aleksei Shibaev before the year ended.

Despite the various lacunae in the picture, another broad pattern of change is detectable in the record. Under Khrushchev—"viscerally" in some sense a reformer, if bounded by his background and time—there is evidence of violent suppression of worker protest. The workers who protested at that point were, of necessity, often people of peasant and rural origin with what is, by today's Soviet standards, quite low average levels of education. Under Brezhnev—no reformer—there is evidence of a *less* repressive stance: not tolerance, but a conventionalized response in many strike cases. By the late Brezhnev times, workers who downed their tools were much more likely to be second-generation blue-collar urbanites with more education, not necessarily "challengers" to the regime but a more complex problem in terms of their expectations, aspirations, and the state's attempts to manage these.

Pressing further on such limited data is inadvisable—and it is worth stressing that many observations here are ad hoc. For the present, before we examine some other aspects of strike behavior, we might make two observations: (1) conditions not in dispute generated worker protest at a relatively greater rate under "late Brezhnev" than earlier: deterioration was *not* met, overall, with quiescence; and (2) if evidence of any high degree of planning and organizational preparation is absent in these strikes (versus, notably, Poland in 1980 and the USSR itself in 1989–90), then indirectly, at least, there is contrast with the anomie of the more violent Khrushchev-era conflicts; workers' demands under Brezhnev were quite frequently met when put at issue; "symbolic" strikes tended to make their points without evoking reprisals. These developments do not confirm decisive progress toward class identity and class modes of action. But without them, evidence would be even less, and the argument that today's workers represent something closer to a class than at any time since the close of NEP, a weaker one. There was more of what one would expect from a better-educated, urban-origin, hereditary stratum of workers under pressure in the "hard times" of the Brezhnev period than there was during "hard times" under Khrushchev, just as the broad problems of societal management seemed to strain the former more than the latter.

Stoppages and strikes most typically broke out over worsening working conditions or over their long-standing and unacted-upon deterioration; over pay cuts resulting from an upward revision of production norms; over price rises on food and other necessities (or exaggerated supply problems in a particular area). Workers thus "have tended not to strike to secure improvements in their material situation, but to protest against erosion of their existing standard of living."[54] This is an important point. The strike—considered neither legal nor illegal, but simply ignored in the "old" Soviet legislation (since, one presumes, "who would workers strike against, under socialism?")—could not play the role of improving "normal" conditions beyond what policy and performance in the economy allowed. As Alekseeva put it, workers were "not struggling for improvement in the conditions of their existence, but protesting with indignation against their worsening."[55] Defense against erosion, not advance, is the keynote. Certain kinds of erosion seem more provocative of discontent and collective protest than others. In the USSR and in other Soviet-type economies, increases in prices have been due to central policy decisions. Shortages, on the other hand, are "conditions," perhaps localized ones, seen as less anti-worker than price rises. If rationing by price is economically more efficient than the rationing by queue (and bribe, and luck) characteristic of Soviet-type economies, it can be seen as a violation of the "social contract" that promises low and stable prices for basic commodities, which links rank-and-file workers with the state.[56] Nationwide wage and labor policies to squeeze more efficiency out of workers would be as controversial as price rises. Brezhnev clearly avoided these, leaving the issue to be confronted by Gorbachev.

Of course, it is not only the strength of "push" factors that have determined whether conditions will lead to collective protest rather than to individual withdrawal of effort, absenteeism, foot dragging, and the like. To some degree, negative and positive deterrents have varied by region. In the high-priority industries located in major cities, especially in the RSFSR and the Ukraine, the state's surveillance and control capacities may have been the greatest; but so have the resources and the desire to keep workers relatively satisfied. According to one analysis, strikes have occurred more frequently in the geographic periphery than at the European center, though our pre-1985 data offer indifferent support, and the 1989 strike wave hit high-paid but poorly supplied miners in several areas—some remote, some less so. They have taken violent forms there more often as well, perhaps because the state's coercive resources were not so richly deployed, nor is its care for (lower-priority) workers' welfare pronounced.[57]

What strikes "mean" to workers is not totally clear. There is good evidence that Brezhnev-era strikers saw themselves as standing up against violations of a just social contract, barely conscious that they were challengers to the legitimacy of the system. But, to be objective, it is true that striking workers are pressing claims against a state that is their employer and welfare-provider, as well as their political controller—an "omnicompetent" state. As Geoffrey Hosking puts it, "Workers' grievances appear to range over the whole of their life"; in a situation which, nationwide, resembles that of the "company town," the workers "see themselves as being in a total relationship with their employers."[58] The state, then, cannot act independently as mediator between parties in conflict, as it may in labor-management disputes in the West. Here, as employer and paymaster, it is a party. Without a market or the ebb and flow of unemployment to discipline blue-collar workers, the Soviet state must sometimes use what one analyst called "repressive administration" on workers to achieve its ends. This repression, and equally the allocation of differential privilege in the economic sphere, were obviously bureaucratically controlled—the absence of the rules and operations of the market meant that the resultant inequality and subordination could not be "mystified." Hence, the economic demands workers express at the factory level are, at the same time, "demands on the central political apparatus."[59]

Whether or not workers understood that this is what they were "doing," it cannot be said that the state has been unresponsive, or totally unsubtle, in its dealings with workers engaging in collective protest.

If, analytically, the state is party to the dispute, in many cases it intervenes *as if* it stands in judgment of *both* workers and local managers and officials—and, as we have seen, often backs up workers' claims.

Where worker demands were clearly economic—whether related to prices, local supply problems, or wage cuts via the upping of norms—and the action was confined within the factory walls, characteristic state reaction involved three elements: (1) satisfaction of the immediate workers' demands (cancel pay cuts, restore prices, "tap reserves" to fill the shelves of local stores, etc.); (2) disciplining, up to firing, of local managers/other officials deemed guilty of setting off the protest; and (3) later apprehension of strike leaders, with penalties ranging from firing to exile in another part of the country to execution—rumor has usually been the only source of information on disposition.[60] Major priorities have been to cool off the immediate crisis, and, later, to neutralize and remove informal opinion leaders around whom collective protest has coalesced.

When strikes are violent or large-scale and involve the local population *as well* as the work force, *force*, up to the lethal level, has been applied; the classic instance here is the 1962 Novocherkassk revolt, where wage cuts and increases in prices led to mass protest in the streets and a military response that left many dead.

Another priority was to suppress information about the occurrence of strikes, both internally and abroad. For some time, the Khrushchev-period strikes were covered up rather effectively. As one commentator has suggested, there were two reasons. First, the sheer size, control over travel, and lack of telephones in the early-1960s USSR made the diffusion of information difficult in the extreme. Second, these strikes all preceded the emergence of a dissident/civil rights movement among intellectuals and the development of *samizdat* as a means of communication. There was no link to which workers might turn with information on strikes and have it diffused internally and, via dissident contacts with Western journalists, to the West, then *from* the West back again to the Soviet foreign radio audience.[61] Strikes from the late 1960s on were somewhat harder to conceal.

Regularities in the form, rhetoric, and rationale of strikes over a long period deserve some extended consideration. They were short-term, loosely organized, and did not give rise to any continuing type of unofficial organization. When "textual" evidence for the reasons of protests was disseminated through *samizdat*, its tone showed appeals to higher authorities against the abuses, malfeasances, or insensitivities of local bosses: no challenges were presented directly to the system as such. Through 1988 this was quite different from the history of Polish worker protest in 1970 and 1976 and the 1980 strikes, which gave birth to Solidarity. This is not the place for a systematic contrast of the Soviet and Polish situations in the period prior to Gorbachev's domestic and foreign policy innovations, but it is noteworthy that the two differed strikingly in (1) the measure of political repression and state "penetration" of society; (2) the confidence, unity, and readiness of the regime to use force on a large scale to suppress worker resistance; (3) the "political culture" that gave context to worker protest; and (4) the ability of the regime to contain the international political and economic consequences of repression. The differences are such that Soviet workers would be expected, for tactical reasons, to be more moderate in collective protests (unless they rapidly got out of control).

Still, Soviet and Polish situations shared some regularities, themselves rooted in the Soviet-model economy. Centralized bureaucratic nonmarket economies, largely ignoring prices as economic signals and committed to the herculean task of setting a vast number of different wage rates and output norms, moved slowly in these areas, and from time to time found themselves in catch-up situations. Prices were held stable for years on basic foods and other items, while the state's procurement costs rose annually. As the price-subsidy burden on the state budget increased, the discomfort among ministers, economists, and planners grew, finally provoking a large and sudden increase often felt to be "anti-worker." Polish leaderships foundered over these crises (Gomulka in 1970, Gierek in 1980); Hungary, on the other hand, under the 1968 New Economic Mechanism reform, relaxed controls on many prices, allowing for a gradual and publicized upward creep, and managed for a time to convince most citizens that socialism did not, and could not, mean indefinite price stability, especially in a context of rising wages.

In the area of wages, the standard practice of pegging an assumed basic wage to certain output norms, with bonuses for overfulfillment, and leaving it indefinitely in place, created problems. As much as possible, enterprises lobbied for output norms that were easily met; a "learning process" versus the given norms then made for overfulfillment and the automatic bestowing of bonuses, which thus became part of the basic, "expected" wage. The upward drift of the wage bill, the growing amount of money in circulation in shortage-ridden economies, alarmed the central authorities and forced them to choose between output norm revisions that threatened wages or growing inefficiency. The rules and operating procedures of the Soviet-model economy begat such results almost automatically.[62]

The regularities suggest recurrent violations of the social contract between the working mass and the regime that were manifested in the wage cuts and price rises, which, in turn, were "forced" to some degree on regimes. The regime did engage in a nonmarket variety of "mystification" of economic processes vis-à-vis the public: promises of rising wages ("real" income) while prices remained stable exacerbated shortages (which were treated as "problems" rather than a product of basic policies). The public, to some degree, was "taken in." (As an earlier-cited SIP survey of Brezhnev-era emigrés found, the majority saw no reason why meat, sold at below-production-cost retail prices, remained in short supply and expressed little sympathy or understanding of any policy that would raise prices to come near to, or cover, production costs.)[63]

This "contractual" base of protest goes deep. One observer suggests that in the pre-1956 period, and even under Stalin, workers had already acquired a certain amount of "negative control":

> Those who perpetrate the tyranny . . . feel nervous even when unjust demands have long since been accepted. The workers calmly and quietly observe those who exercise power and say, "Well, O.K., the power is on your side but . . . ." The 'but' is significant because it indicates that whilst the workers may accept the exercise of power, there are limits to what they will accept and from these they will not retreat. Thus, for example, the authorities were never able fully to implement the Stakhanovite movement, nor were they able to make widespread use of strikebreakers or informers amongst the workers.[64]

Although these words from a left-wing, pro-worker critic of the system may exaggerate to some degree workers' effectiveness against strikebreakers, he is surely on point when dealing with aspects of the Khrushchev period and the consequences of the cessation of mass terror. Khrushchev's revelations brought understanding and disillusionment about what had gone *before*, and were

> followed by disillusionment in the post-Stalin leadership. Khrushchev furthered this disillusionment in the sixties, with his fraudulent currency reforms, his boastful prattle and his absurd schemes. The absence of overt political repression further decreased the level of fear in the country, and was perhaps interpreted as a sign of weakness on the part of the authorities.
>
> Everyone now understood what the existing regime could offer them and understood all its lies. But nothing could be done about it and a new kind of popular attitude began to appear towards the authorities: you can sit on your soft jobs, while the power is still on your side, and you can play your game called "building communism". But do not overplay it, because the times are different. Enough is enough![65]

The excesses of authorities, a tendency "to 'go too far,' to exceed the limits of the invisible agreement"[66] under the post-terror conditions that left workers some increased insurance, thus catalyzed some reactions into strikes, which would have been unthinkable under Stalin. The strike and protest activity facilitated by Khrushchev's abandonment of terror peaked in the 1959–64 period, and after his ouster evidently fell off until the end of the decade. As the record indicated, the years 1965–68/69 were rather tranquil ones. This was not simply a matter of repression. The wage policies of the Brezhnev-Kosygin leadership and the upward drift of minimum and average wages that benefited workers explain some of this quiescence.[67] The early Brezhnev years—those of the 1966–70 FYP—were good ones economically. Good performance fed the wage policy; food and goods gave some meaning to the extra rubles. But that performance did not last. The subsequent stagnation by 1987–88 would pose the question of potential worker reaction to new policies stressing hard work and the tying of rewards to quality of output, attempting to rationalize the price system, and in other ways threatening the invisible agreement, a major component of which was "the right not to work hard at the factory."[68]

Strikes, however, did not exhaust the repertoire of Brezhnev-era worker activity. It is time to turn to a "failed" variation, interesting for what it reveals about the time: the struggle to form free trade unions.

Organizing Worker Opposition: The "Free Trade Unions"

No Lech Walesa emerged to lead Soviet workers willing to commit themselves to organized struggle. No Orthodox patriarch, or strong, independent church organization provided moral and social support or an alternative, authoritative ideology around which workers might coalesce. No Soviet leadership was "backed into a corner," no General Secretary of the party lost his post because of rebellious workers. Still, it remains a fact that before the emergence of the Polish Solidarity, the late 1970s witnessed three attempts on Soviet soil to establish organizations that would function independently as trade unions.[69]

The first of these was spearheaded by Vladimir Klebanov, an engineer. Klebanov, who in the mid-1960s had attempted to form a free trade union in the Donetsk coal-mining area (and was confined to a psychiatric hospital for his efforts), met some similar-spirited people among visitors to Supreme Soviet, Central Committee, and Prokuratura offices in Moscow, all there to complain (in the legal, *individual* manner) of abuses in work conditions, employment, and so forth. A series of three "open letters," critical of worker living conditions, followed from Klebanov and others on May 20, September, and November 7, 1977. After two Moscow press conferences to publicize these issues among Western journalists (and another nine-day stay in a *psikhushka* for Klebanov), on January 26, 1978, he and four others announced the formation of the Association of Free Trade Unions of Workers in the Soviet Union (Assotsiatsiia Svobodnykh Profsoiuzov Trudiashchikhsia v Sovetskom Soiuze), claiming that two hundred workers across the country were members. Expressions of Western support for Klebanov's initiative helped little in the Soviet internal situation. Ten days after the declaration, Klebanov and the other four, plus two other labor activists, had all been detained. Continued repression effectively ended the organization within two months of its foundation.

In April 1978 came the announcement of the formation of the Independent Trade Union of Workers in the USSR; in this case a small group headed by Vsevolod Kuvakin, formerly on the staff of the official trade union for oil and gas workers, formed the core. Following a somewhat different tack than Klebanov, it requested official recognition from the Soviet government and the AUCCTU as well as the International Labor Organization (ILO) and the International Congress of Free Trade Unions (ICFTU). In response to a general silence, Kuvakin and his allies announced yet another group, the Working Group for the Defense of Labor, Economic, and Social Rights in the USSR, whose major activity over the ensuing months was the *samizdat* publication of several reports on legal and economic problems of worker-state relations. Beyond the name, the group was essentially more of the human rights/dissident variety than a trade union; but the "legalism" evident in its attempt to press the Soviet state for recognition was a departure from the Klebanov precedent.

Finally, October 18, 1978, marked the announcement, in the Moscow apartment of the mathematician Mark Morozov, of the Free Interprofessional Association of Workers (Svobodnoe Mezhprofessional'-noe Ob"edinenie Trudiashchikhsia—SMOT). More ambitious than its predecessors, SMOT disavowed "political" intentions for legal, material, and moral assistance to its members. Organized in "autonomous groups," of which one member of each would serve on a "council of representatives," it claimed a hundred members in eight groups. Only the council members were named publicly, and of the eight in 1978, one was a worker, one an electrician, the rest *not* clearly workers.

The council grew: by November 1979, six more members had been added, the last of them the lawyer Vsevolod Kuvakin, founder of the Independent Trade Union of Workers in the USSR. But neither the council nor the groups implied by the number of council members flourished; by mid-1980, of the fourteen council members, ten had been removed (three by arrest, two by emigration, one under police pressure, and four of their "own accord").[70] An indeterminate number of "groups" may have survived: while one estimate is less than fourteen,[71] a more optimistic one from a SMOT founder exiled to the West in 1982 cited "at least twenty-one" groups, comprising about three hundred "active" members and fifteen hundred supporters.[72]

SMOT's most critical activity was the publication of its *samizdat* information bulletin, of which at least thirty-five issues were produced. Less successful, if more relevant to the mission of an organization that sought to be a trade union, were other services announced at its foundation, such as a credit union, day-care for children, and provision of better medical care. As an organization "forced" into a clandestine route, SMOT may have survived into the early 1980s; it is difficult to tell.

It is certain, however, that none of these attempts at "union organizing" really succeeded. But their emergence—in the same late-Brezhnev years that were marked by an increase in strikes—highlighted some other aspects of working-class politics, pointing to limitations on the nature and style of the demands likely to be made even by those who had crossed the line to independent, organized activity. These are of special interest.

The Klebanov case pointed up elements of a class-based gap that existed between the workers and the "educated," between white collar and blue collar, between two different worlds of perception. When Klebanov emerged in late 1977, the human-rights activist Andrei Sakharov declined to offer the support he had offered so many other dissidents, expressing a belief that the workers "did not understand" the risks of open dissent and doubts about Klebanov's commitment to individual liberties. Klebanov, in his turn, accused the intellectuals of considering themselves "above" the workers.[73] When, a short time later, Sakharov's wife Elena Bonner joined with some other dissident intellectuals to express support of the activist workers, one of Klebanov's worker allies denounced these would-be supporters as "swindlers."[74]

Thus, on one side, there is evidence of a *de haut en bas* attitude in the Moscow "human-rights" intellectuals' view of the workers—conditioned by a long-standing self-image of Russian intellectuals as combatting a repressive regime while standing athwart a "social base" of chauvinistic, unthinking "dark people" (the then-peasant, now-worker Russian mass). On the other side is the long-standing distrust and incomprehension, from those at the "bottom," of the life and attitudes of the educated, of those who do not work with their hands.

There is a suspicion that the articulate harbor a "patronizing prejudice" (of which then *New York Times* Moscow correspondent David Shipler accused Sakharov in connection with the Klebanov group), an attitude that, "for their own safety, these backward people should drop such unimportant matters."[75] "Importance," of course, depends on the activist: the work-related, bread-and-butter concerns of the worker-advocate Klebanov were not in the Brezhnev era the typical grist of the intellectuals' mills. Klebanov, who sought Sakharov's support initially, was probably right when he concluded that even a dissident academician knew "very little about how average people live."[76]

Working-class views of the intelligentsia present a mix of envious fascination, contemptuous rejection, and the consciousness of a growing gulf between those few who have "succeeded" and the rest, within a culture where the rules that would legitimate both success and failure are not all that well articulated. The late Anatoly Marchenko (of "pure" worker background), whose adult life, spent mainly in prisons and camps, also brought him into contact with intellectuals, is most penetrating in his vision of the gulf and what it means to workers. His childhood ideas of the intelligentsia had been, in his own words, "typical of a backwoods yokel": "I grew up among the children of railway workers. Our parents weren't called mechanics or conductors. There was one name for all railway workers: greasers. Winter and summer, heavy black grease literally dripped from their clothing."[77] But in these relatively early years of the Soviet period, parents were resigned at their lot but also had hope—if qualified—for their children:

> We constantly heard the same warning from our parents: if you don't want to end up a greaser like your father for the rest of your life, then study! For us kids, the life and occupation of our parents was a curse. To live meant to suffer, to work meant to toil. That was the only philosophy of life our parents knew.
>
> As good examples for us, my parents would point to the few people in our town with "clean" professions; teachers, doctors, the stationmaster, the director of the bread factory, the regional party secretary, the state attorney. They were all considered members of the intelligentsia. It's true that teachers and doctors did not live better than we did and many were even worse off. But their work was clean and easy. The others represented the height of prosperity and contentment in everyone's eyes.[78]

Intellectuals, then, were not exactly role models for the young Marchenkos of the time. The distance between the observer and the observed often seemed too large to be the stuff of realistic aspirations. The alien quality of intelligentsia life and rewards surely helps explain why Marchenko, in his own words, "entered adult life with a firm prejudice against intellectuals. They were people who didn't work very hard and got paid for doing nothing. You can imagine what people thought of those whose names were decorated with hypnotic titles: 'Ph.D.,' 'Professor,' 'Dr. of Science.' Such a title seemed like a magic wand. We imagined their life to be a continuous feast."[79] For the "creative" intelligentsia, whose work was not only clean but immensely remote in its focus from the concerns of grass-roots life, workers entertained an especially "ambivalent attitude": "On the one hand, everyone knew that academics and writers were involved in absolutely useless, even ludicrous work: writers scribble lies, scientists breed some kind of flies. In conversations we joked about them. On the other hand, everyone worshipped their omniscience and omnipotence, except when it came to everyday life."[80] That even the quite atypical Klebanov and Sakharov had difficulty in finding a common language is not so remarkable, given the persistence of such deep stereotypes over a long period of Soviet history, wherein the emptiness of the "working class = leading class" formula is brought home to workers daily.

Workers, of course, have and do diverge in their assessments of the situation. Many workers—perhaps even most—as we have seen in some earlier data, accepted and supported a system that provided job security, price subsidies, poster art glorifying *them*. These things were valued, while "negative control" on the shop floor blunted, to some degree, demands the system might otherwise make. But strikes, and even the "failed" free trade unions, indicate that not all saw it this way. Fewer certainly did as the Brezhnev era ended. At the dawn of Gorbachev's rule, a worker's letter sent to the French Embassy in Moscow decried the situation where he is "in effect tied to the enterprise he entered on completing his military service. He has to work ten to twenty years to get an apartment."[81] Pensions whose magnitude is linked to length of service in the same factory similarly incline the worker to "keeping quiet, not jumping in with his own opinion, for which he might lose everything."[82] But the same worker shows some sympathy for the intellectuals, in a period when Sakharov was already some years into his exile in Gorky: "If all norms of behavior are infringed in the treatment of Academician Sakharov, how much more those of an ordinary person who dares to speak openly."[83]

If the gulf between workers and intellectuals weakened worker protest and organization, so did another factor, which under the circumstances was probably unavoidable: the tendency of workers to couch their appeals to higher authority in terms that suggest that the authority and workers are *united* in spirit and values against whatever action by local authorities was the basis of the grievance. Higher party and state authorities were projected into the position of arbiters, manifesting, perhaps, a worker tendency to engage in a "mystification," after all, of the role of their distant bosses. A 1969 letter sent by a group of protesting workers at a Kiev hydroelectric construction project to the Central Committee of the CPSU, detailed the long grievances over abominable housing conditions, workers' meetings that were denounced by local authorities, the sending in turn of an (unofficial) workers' delegation to the Central Committee in Moscow, and the later arrest of workers' delegates at a local meeting ostensibly called by management to "put things right." The letter, circulated in *samizdat*,[84] is more important for its mood and the mode of approach to the authorities than for its recounting of details:

> Comrades! What is this??? Who ever saw the like? One gets the impression that these puffed-up and presumptuous so-called leaders were provoking a riot.
>
> Is it possible that they do not understand the basic truth that our enemies are waiting just for this, for something to happen in our country? Why then do we simple workers understand this? We did not fall for this provocation.[85]

Thus the worker-authors put themselves on the side of the regime, *with* the regime against that pervasive presence, "our enemies," those outside the USSR whose purposes have always made it advisable "not to wash one's dirty linen in public."

> Comrades! We do not believe that this arrest was made with the knowledge of those above, and we earnestly ask that you take under your protection the delegation which has come to you with this letter. As to our demands, we will express them when your representatives come to us. Do not believe those who call us rebels, do not believe when they tell you that we are demanding that dwellings be given us today on a silver platter. We want to wait our turn honestly and know that that turn is real, that each of us, regardless of whether this be in a year, or two, or five, will receive quarters, and that no one will make any rearrangements in the order. We are not afraid of work, if necessary we will roll up our sleeves and we will build dwellings after working hours.[86]

"Simple workers," then, appeal here to authorities. Implicitly at least, they lay claim to a closeness to the worker-based power of party and state, a closeness that may be denied in the case of intellectuals. Workers are "simple," workers are honest, blunt. Workers are thus not rebels; they trust in the system. Not dissident, but deprived, they claim justice, seeking it not in systemic overhaul, not in alternative political arrangements, but in the expected actions of central authorities.

> Behind these [worker] protests, there generally stands a tacit conviction that there is some unwritten agreement between workers and leaders. The former work, the latter secure them the elementary conditions for life: wages, food, housing, etc. The state, as the single and monopolistic boss answers for all, and workers understand that stopping work is the only weapon that they possess to draw attention to a crying injustice.[87]

When, nearly a decade after the Kiev protest, the organizers of the "free trade unions" emerged, the self-images they projected were consistent with these patterns. Evgenii Nikolaev, in a 1978 *samizdat* communication, expresses the sense of "difference" he and other worker activists felt against typical "dissidents":

> These petitioners, who were trying to exercise their rights, were not "dissidents" in the generally accepted meaning of that word. They were ordinary Soviet citizens whose only aim was to restore their violated rights. They were trying to get back into the official Soviet way of life, from which they had been displaced by the arbitrary actions of local authorities. They had no intention of engaging in human-rights activities or politics on a national or international scale. But the arbitrary actions of local authorities, supported in turn by high officials in Moscow, compelled those people to come together and announce the founding of a Free Trade Union. The authorities responded by stepping up the repressions.[88]

This assessment was supported by the authors of a *samizdat* review of the free trade union movement dated May 1980, who link the patriotic, "pro-system" aspect of worker protest to the earlier-noted failure to gain support from dissident intellectual circles:

> The human-rights movement did not provide any real support for Klebanov's group. The objective reason given for this was that the mandate of the Moscow Helsinki Watch Group, the leading organization of the human-rights movement, precludes support for any national, religious, functional, or other groups or associations. It would seem, however, that it was largely subjective considerations which were responsible for the coolness toward Klebanov's group on the part of dissident circles. Klebanov himself, along with many members of his "Free Trade Union," repeatedly stressed that they "had nothing in common with the dissidents," and that their goal was "to help the successful construction of communism and to combat bureaucracy and red tape." The dissidents' reaction to this "program" of Klebanov's group needs no comment.[89]

One runs a risk here, of course, of overinterpretation. We have a better record of words than of actions. The quotes are long, they seem to speak for themselves, yet what precisely *do* they mean?

One could argue—and such an argument is hard to counter—that Klebanov and others, far from being "mystified," were using a verbal *tactic*. Even smot, in a 1983 statement that refuted the state's argument that it was a "political" organization,[90] argued that its founding as an independent trade union was justified by the "merger" of the official trade unions with the party and state apparatus. smot thus claimed a different function—and, in pursuit of that function, it reminded readers that strikes, per se, were not illegal under Soviet law. smot thus defined itself as an "economistic" union.

Distancing one's claims and social base from those of intellectual dissidents might thus have seemed a way of increasing the chances that authority might listen (as it had, after all, to striking workers in certain circumstances). Over the longer run, this might also increase (and here tactics merge with strategy) the chances of recruiting "pro-system" workers: we may have an activist as "disloyal" as any Moscow intellectual dissident, but one who seeks to use "worker" identity as a resource that is unavailable to the intellectual. (If, in an earlier, mid-1970s article, I read the broad political culture of Soviet "welfare-state authoritarianism" correctly, in that the culture "links the bureaucratic elite and the masses more closely than it links the [intellectual] dissidents to either,"[91] then the appeal of workers, representative of the masses, might have seemed the most promising path to follow for an activist aiming at the unconventional step of *organizing* an independent body to defend and assert workers' rights.) In the event it did not work. Klebanov and others paid the price.

Alternatively, assuming that the Soviet system of the mid-Brezhnev era was still "legitimate" for the majority of Soviet citizens through most of the period, both because it was perceived to deliver enough of the modest amount Soviet citizens expected and because of their lack of any clear idea or experience of other systems, it may be that Klebanov-type approaches were quite sincere and visceral reactions to frustration. We are then dealing with a species of what Reinhard Bendix has called "populist legitimism": protest which, while accepting the established political *order* (the system), appeals to highest authority against abuses systemic in their roots but attributed to lesser, local authority. Bendix, discussing this in the context of various types of social unrest in preindustrial polities, cites peasant rebellions in eighteenth-century Russia as a major example: "The rebels appeal to the official creed of the Tsarist order, when they interpret their massive deprivations as evidence that the Tsar's authority has been abused.

For a rightful Tsar would protect his people against oppression; he would safeguard the just claims even of the lowliest peasant."[92] So, too, the workers in Kiev in 1969 appealed to the Central Committee: "Such an appeal to expectations that are justified by ancient custom probably serves to minimize the psychological burden of revolting against a social order that is accepted as legitimate but has become intolerable by specific abuses."[93] Again, if we substitute the ruling ideology or "social contract" for "ancient custom," and understand "psychological burden" in a broad enough sense, the process of justification that Bendix describes is no great distance from what the regime may face where workers are driven to strike over some last straw in a process of erosion. Of course, revolts or protests of this sort do test "reality": "The peasants justify their rebellion on the ground that the Tsar's authority has been abused; and if it is proved to them that the Tsar has personally authorized the measures they regard as oppressive, they conclude that such a Tsar must be an imposter."[94] Such a dramatic conclusion is one thing; acting on it is another. What eighteenth-century peasants concluded of tsars, what Kiev workers concluded about the Central Committee, may have been "delegitimizing." Still, the chronicle of eighteenth-century Russia is one of revolts lost by the peasants and won by the tsars. So, too, of Kiev workers. Moving beyond "populist legitimism" would have been an important development in Soviet labor militancy, but only one step—and doomed to fail—so long as the Soviet state remained what it had been.

Much of the writing on the free trade unions—by Western specialists, dissident emigrés, and activists still in the USSR—had assumed a post-mortem tone by the end of the Brezhnev period. An appraisal of the fate of SMOT noted that from its fourth *Bulletin* on, the contents had consisted mainly of reports on arrests and trials of activists, frightening off potential supporters and thus further reducing the organization's chances of survival. This was not simply a public relations problem; repression was a fact, activists were jailed, and SMOT could hardly fail to report this. It is not clear whether it might better have published, for the help of proletarian activists, "models of complaints about 'typical' situations: violations in the fields of transportation and trade; housing violations, complaints about unlawful acts by management,"[95] but this could not have been its only content.

The core dissidents of the broad human-rights movement were *not* workers. Alekseeva, in a review of worker participation in the movement, characterized it as "strictly a creation of the intelligentsia . . . launched by humanist intellectuals from Moscow."[96] Workers did join, but, like Iuri Galanskov and Aleksandr Ginzburg, who were tried for dissident activities in 1968, many had blue-collar occupations because of their nonconformist activities; by family background and/or education, they were not likely working-class material. Indeed, of seven hundred persons who signed appeals in defense of Galanskov and Ginzburg, only about 6 percent, according to Alekseeva, were blue-collar workers. Workers arrested in 1978–79, in connection with the free trade union movement, however, better fit the blue-collar mold. None were Muscovites; none had completed a vuz; their average education was eight years.[97] Still, the fact that the founding members of the various free trade unions were not, in many cases, typically proletarian themselves—whatever the nature of the language and approach they used—placed them in a peculiar position versus their potential audience of Soviet workers. smot's founders, its first "council," numbered fourteen; previous histories of oppositional activity meant that eight of these were not employed at the time.

> This situation provoked a negative attitude toward smot, since a perfectly reasonable objection was raised: "What kind of workers' association is this, if it is run by people who have never worked anywhere?" The fact that a human-rights activist may be unemployed for various reasons (including the impossibility of finding work in his profession) is something that dissidents can understand. But the ordinary Soviet citizen cannot understand such a situation, and does not want to. And when he learns that smot was founded by and is directed by people who never worked anywhere—by "parasites"—that citizen will refuse to join smot.[98]

There were, of course, exceptions. In a 1978 *samizdat* "letter to American workers," Vasil' Stasiv, a Ukrainian worker, asserted that the October revolution had been a Bolshevik "countercoup" launched by people whose "alpha and omega" was power. For capital in the 1930s industrialization, they had substituted the "cheapest labor possible"; the workers' situation was that of "working cattle."[99] Another radical stand was that of the smot activist Valeri Senderov, who after his 1982 arrest demanded to be tried "as a member" of the Narodno-Trudovoi Soiuz (nts), an anti-Soviet emigré organization founded in the Stalin era which made no bones about its commitment to the end of the system and remained a bugbear of the regime.[100] But on the whole, the record of worker action under Brezhnev has more of legitimism than systemic rejection about it.

Reasons are not hard to discern. Brezhnev-era policies of allocation were pro-worker—some credit for quiescence must, of course, go here. But beyond this, the extraordinarily tight political control maintained in the USSR, even without the mass terror of the Stalin era, imposed limits which, as we noted before, went well beyond those faced by workers in their revolts (1956, 1970, 1976) and in the formation of Solidarity (1980) in Poland. Also, not even the oldest Soviet workers could have any effective memory of any truly independent trade unions. Nor was the element of nationalism unimportant. In Eastern Europe, worker militancy easily took on an element of protest against a political system imposed from above and from abroad. The Soviet and Russian provenance of the system, whether made explicitly a matter of protest or not, helped motivate worker discontent. In the USSR, patriotism, the fact that the rulers were not ethnically and culturally alien to the mass, at least to the Russian one, and the "domestic" nature of the various symbols of Soviet power all helped deprive worker militancy of this spur. Indeed, evidence suggests that many Soviet workers, especially Russians, viewed demands for "democratization" in Eastern Europe, and even labor militancy, through a prism of nationalism, one hardly discouraged by their own media until the late 1980s. Little support of any sort existed for the Czechs during the Prague Spring of 1968, and, as a *samizdat* document from a Soviet worker quoted at the beginning of this chapter testifies, *his* fellow workers showed little sympathy or understanding for Polish workers during the Solidarity ascendancy, even if others may have admired Polish militancy, as the quote paired with it indicates.[101] Soviet workers did not yet, in any case, face in the late 1970s the raw sort of economic crisis that contributed to the founding of Solidarity in Poland; stagnation did not yet mean crisis, and the discontinuity between expectation and delivery was not so sharp. But that fragile balance did not last long.

Enter Gorbachev

Fewer than three years separated the end of the Brezhnev era in 1982 from the coming of Gorbachev in 1985; for workers, it was a period marked by little real change. The much ballyhooed discipline campaign under Andropov petered out. Andropov's term was short, and Chernenko's, on the surface, an interlude of low-key Brezhnevian stagnation.

Gorbachev, as we have seen, brought new wage policies as well as the unfamiliar discipline of *gospriemka*. With respect to the party's role on the factory floor, the period after his 1985 accession shows no great change. The dual themes of greater worker involvement in self-management schemes and enterprise independence assumed high profiles, but in Gorbachev's first three years issues of the party's role were posed in broader terms involving the "restructuring" of major elements of the political system.

On the whole, over 1985–88 leadership rhetoric and indications of current and future policy turned heavily on major economic problems and the grim prospects looming if long-term trends were not reversed. With little economic progress to show after nearly two years in power, in a speech in Riga in 1987, Gorbachev laid out the necessity for a transitional period of belt-tightening before his new economic measures were likely to confer benefits in the 1990s.[102] Perestroika, to succeed, would require support, or at least compliance, from various elements of the Soviet population. The near-revolution in freedom to discuss and publish, the vastly expanded parameters of past and present Soviet life that could be made matters of open controversy, had brought much of the intelligentsia to Gorbachev's side under the banner of glasnost'.

But, more than any other of the "reform" schemes tried in previous Soviet economic history, perestroika depended on workers: on their forbearance and conscientious attitude toward work, on their readiness to invest extra effort now to create the base of efficient economic growth later. Even leaving aside the potential for a "social justice" controversy in the leadership's encouragement of cooperatives and "individual labor activity," with its predictable disparity in earnings between privateers and the blue-collar work force, evoking that effort voluntarily was bound to be difficult. If some workers chafed under wage leveling and equal rewards for the industrious and the lazy, others were quite comfortable with this low-effort security system. More importantly, there was increasing recognition that more, and better, goods and services available for one's earned rubles were the real motivators of effort. Could they but be provided "up front," effort might follow. But perestroika could only call for the effort to be invested first, to produce the goods and services. The start was not an easy one.

If workers in many factories labored harder under the new discipline of *gospriemka* and in the context of the "brigade method," they were also earning more, according to the official statistics. Average "worker and employee" wages in the first half of 1988 were reported as up 5.7 percent from the same period in 1987,[103] setting off a trend that has continued since. But it was doubtful that the increases had been financed by the kind of enhanced earnings and profits the factories were supposed to achieve, or reflected the production of more and better goods. Newspapers complained of factories abusing the freedom of new pricing flexibility to charge too much for unimproved goods (for example, a type of sausage irreverently nicknamed "dog's delight" now being sold at "gourmet" prices),[104] or by cutting the production of unprofitable but necessary goods for children and old people in favor of higher markup terms. Profits were supposed to be achieved by cutting costs, by raising quality, by producing more, not by the jacking up of prices alone.[105]

Neither for those whose raises brought low wages nearer to a necessary minimum, nor for those whose raises added to really "discretionary" income could the extra rubles make much difference if prices continued to rise and if there were not more goods, in effect, to consume; and by 1990, the public conviction was that there was less. In the freewheeling drama of the extraordinary Nineteenth Party Conference in 1988, V. A. Iarin, a metalworker in a Nizhnyi Tagil' plant who would later become a major figure in "worker" politics, said that workers were asking, "Where is perestroika?" There was "no meat before, and none now." Durable goods had "vanished" to who knows where, while state orders for 100 percent-plus capacity output reduced his plant's promised independence.[106] Perestroika had imposed effort, but conferred no reward, in Nizhnyi Tagil'.

Nor, evidently, in Kiev. As Western and Soviet newspapers reported a sorry tale of continuing shortages and creeping inflation, the reform-oriented paper *Sovetskaia kul'tura* sponsored, on May 17, 1988, a meeting confronting some of the paper's representatives and others of the intelligentsia with the local public. The words of one member of the audience indicated both dissatisfaction with results and the gap between the man in the street and the intellectuals: "All this talk about restructuring is for the intelligentsia. They have been given the opportunity to talk and talk, but we still have no meat or butter."[107]

The lack of goods to give meaning to rubles was an obviously weak link in the chain forged to bind the worker to perestroika via self-interest. In the late Brezhnev times, in 1981, the writer-economist Vasilii Seliunin had suggested that wage-fund increases should be linked to plants' output of consumer goods rather than to their total production, in order to counteract the tendency to put more wage rubles in circulation than the consumer output of the economy could meet.[108] In 1986, a few months before the introduction of the new wage policies, another writer criticized the use of material and labor in making things "no one" wanted. The judgment of the consumer gave a product its value, not some calculation of expended labor and wages that is reflected in its price.[109] In January 1988 Seliunin observed in a pointed article that the economy was "still working more and more for itself, rather than for man."[110]

What of the labor union, the AUCCTU, and its place in the public mind? With glasnost' came the possibility of testing whether the dominant image was that of a subordinated and "harmless" organization. In July 1988 the irreverent *Moscow News* published results of a poll of 544 Muscovites on the fairness of high salaries and privileges for executives of various organizations. On a 5–2 scale (5 = all privileges deserved, 2 = none deserved), trade union officials received 2.7, versus 4.3 for national political leaders. In all, 54 percent of respondents felt that union leaders' privileges were "undeserved" or "largely undeserved," prompting *Moscow News* to express the idea that respondents (ranging from students to retirees) felt that "rather than protecting workers from the administration, [unions] protect the administration from workers."[111] One could not, of course, readily tell whether this image was a recent one or long-held but unexpressed in the pre-glasnost' period.

Certainly, the late Brezhnev years and the transition to perestroika had seen some indication of sensitivity to worker issues, at least in rhetoric. In 1981, with Polish labor militancy on some minds in the Soviet Union, AUCCTU head Shibaev had been replaced by Stepan Shalaev; unions in other East European states had also seen such personnel shifts. Now, with Gorbachev in place and his economists calling for a tighter linking of pay to the results of work and for redeployment of the labor force, union officials began to stress the defense of workers' legitimate interests in these new and unfamiliar situations (without, however, offering what might be regarded as straightforward criticism of the new policy lines).

In February 1986[112] Ivan Gladkii, who had recently made the transition from a secretaryship on the AUCCTU council to the chairmanship of Goskomtrud, stressed (in an article evidently written while he was still in his trade union post) that the law must be observed in implementing new policies. The release of redundant workers was necessary but had to be accompanied by the finding of new jobs, maintenance of pay levels, and retraining when necessary: union organs were admonished to exercise constant checking (*kontrol'*) to see to this. Regulations on the revision of output norms were to be observed meticulously, since a cutting of wages "without foundation" led to "dissatisfaction, conflict situations, and affected labor productivity negatively." A year later, as the new pay system was being introduced, K. Turysov, another secretary of the AUCCTU, stressed the union committees' role in ensuring that regulations were observed in implementing it at plant level and their responsibility to criticize managements that strayed. Like Gladkii, he asserted that worker failure to meet output norms was mainly due to unsatisfactory organization of the production process by their superiors.[113] Later in the year, he called for unions to act as "fully empowered representatives of the labor collectives," to express their "interests and needs," as plants moved toward financial independence—and he also admonished unions that they should watch for unjustified price increases. (Presumably among them were increases on the products made in the factories where they operated—although pay raises might be linked precisely to those rises.)[114]

If the *Moscow News* poll cited earlier reflected nationwide perceptions, there was evidence in 1988 that top-level trade union leaders sought, especially as the Nineteenth Party Conference focused so much public attention on current economic issues, to change those perceptions and, within limits, the reality as well. At the conference, AUCCTU head Shalaev[115] asserted that perestroika must be pursued in working people's interest, not at their expense, and expanded on a number of welfare and consumerist concerns. Rejecting notions that the roughly 73 percent of national income going to consumption in 1971–85 should be reduced to 70 percent, given the current economic problems, he argued for raising it to 78–80 percent. Industrial production of consumer (group B) goods needed a lift from the 25 percent they currently represented of the total to at least 35 percent. He cautioned that the retail price reform slated for the early 1990s must include full compensation for price rises to the population and answer the principles of social justice.

Shalaev criticized managerial abuse of workers' rights and placed the unions squarely in defense of self-management (presumably, including the councils of labor collectives), observing that the law supposedly defending the collective's rights was "itself in need of defense." Finally, having argued that plant-level unions needed defense from intervention by ministerial and local organs, he staked a claim to union independence in internal affairs, against the tendency of "some party organs" to intervene, and to transfer functionaries who had failed at party, government, and economic jobs into positions in the union apparatus (an interesting admission on the part of one who was atop the whole hierarchy).

Other union spokesmen were to follow up. Turysov spoke of a system of union-provided legal aid to workers whose rights had been violated,[116] while Lomonosov, number two in the AUCCTU, responding to criticism of the unions' "do-nothing" past, noted, like Shalaev, the union's proposal to raise the consumption share of national income to 78–80 percent and its call for more consumer goods.[117]

Was this all smoke and mirrors? Unlikely. Surely, at a time of increased work pressure on blue-collar Soviet citizens, Gorbachev et al. were unlikely to want the AUCCTU to take on any role—however historically anomalous—as an independent defender of those worker interests—however strongly felt and widely shared—that perestroika necessarily aimed at violating. Still, the implementation of new wage and employment policies called for finesse and sensitivity to "social justice" concerns in a tough situation. The unions were asserting, with a certain degree of top leadership approval and with a certain opportunism in the new political game, their responsibility for seeing that managers did not exceed their mandates, imposing excess costs on workers beyond those implied by the broad policy itself.

Militant unionists were not what Gorbachev wanted. Neither, however, could he use the old-style economic and political officials who were likely to meddle in or ignore the unions, thus risking offense to the worker interests that the unions were supposed to defend. But the unions would prove weak reeds indeed, with their sense of mission, their personnel qualities, varying broadly from enterprise to enterprise.

And worker protest there surely was. Though dwarfed by what was to come in the coal fields in summer 1989, the Gorbachev period, through late 1988, saw a number of strikes, covered with increasing glasnost' by the press. They indicate both worker combativeness and the new pressures of the early perestroika mix of "administrative" and economic measures.

> *Zelenokumsk (Stavropol')*, May 10, 1986: At an electronics factory. A brigade leader refuses to bring his brigade to work on Saturdays. Management does not consult with the plant-level union committee, but has ministerial-level union authorization for some working Saturdays, which it does not explain to workers. Conflict leads to depriving the brigade leader of his post and applying to the union committee for approval for his firing. Both sides are seen as at fault.[118]

> *KamAZ truck plant (Naberezhnye Chelny)*, Nov.–Dec. 1986: At a giant "model" complex of imported technology. Workers protest over the introduction of a *gospriemka*-type system of independent quality control. "Stormy protests" reported, without details on results.[119]

> *Moscow*, April (?) 1987: Strike in a wooden-structures plant, with generally obsolete equipment, poor environment, old-style management. *Moscow News* characterizes the television coverage of the conflict: "The enterprise's trade union leader was babbling something incoherent into the mike and the plant's director glared like a bull at the camera." Workers apparently struck when one was seriously injured "on account of faulty machinery." The plant director is replaced.[120]

> *Chekhov (Moscow region)*, summer (?) 1987: Bus drivers strike against a system linking pay to meeting bus timetable. Drivers are working on a "bri-

gade contract," with a common bonus fund to be divided by the KTU (coefficient of labor participation). Varying quality of buses and the frequency of breakdowns, however, lead drivers to distribute bonus funds as compensation for the "unlucky," to a degree. The director is reprimanded, but outcome is not entirely clear.[121]

Yaroslavl' auto plant, December 1987: A conflict over shift scheduling; requirements of "working Saturdays," and management failure to take into account sixty workers' meetings. Management wants a 7-hour, 50-minute shift and fifteen working Saturdays (versus previous 7-hour 40-minute, twenty Saturdays); workers express desire for 8-hour shifts and eight Saturdays. Trade union committee head agrees with management without consultation. Workers' protest placards read "perestroika i glasnost'." A meeting of 660 elected delegates finally agrees (359–298) to management's schedule for 1988, with the understanding that 1989 will see a schedule more to the workers' liking.[122]

Likino bus plant, 1987: Workers shut down assembly line for three days. Shifts had lengthened early in the year, "most" Saturdays and Sundays had become work days. Gospriemka in the plant caught "every little flaw" in production, which was hardly avoidable since some of the machine tools were forty years old. Bonuses disappeared as accepted output fell behind. Protest focuses on poor technology, general backward condition of factory. Manager is removed, ministry provides 800,000-ruble addition to plant's wage fund for emergency measures; new technology and equipment are promised.[123]

Omsk, December 1987: About 140 cement truck drivers refuse to truck loads to building sites because of lack of return loads and return-trip pay for them. Manager calls the protest meeting of the labor collective "strike, mutiny." Trade union and party official of enterprise side with workers, district party official with manager.[124]

Moscow, 1988: At a housing construction organization. Workers protest wage reduction (possibly due to the 1988 introduction of gospriemka in some parts of construction industry), go to court versus management. Organization's trade union committee offered no help to workers in face of management's unexplained pay cut.[125]

Kharkov, late 1987: At a glass works. Workers protest the firing of their manager by the ministry; manager is restored to his position.[126]

Klaipeda (Lithuania), April 1988: Bus drivers strike against new pay scheme (wage rates higher, but bonus fund cut by 40 percent). Management had guaranteed new total pay would be higher, but after one month, wages are cut, from "a few" to 60 rubles, with cuts averaging 18 rubles (drivers' base salaries were about 330 rubles). Local and republic officials intervene, director agrees new bonus rate is too low (though conflict derives from general organization failure to meet ticket-sales plan, eliminating overall organization bonus). Drivers make various proposals (including raising fares). The final agreement is to revert to old pay system until new one is offered and approved.[127]

Chernovtsy, May 10, 1988: Trolley bus drivers refuse to roll, demanding extra pay for operating alone (without a ticket taker). They are informed that such extra pay will be authorized only when the whole organization fulfills its plan, which it failed to do in April. The "collective contract" specified this condition, but workers were ignorant of its details. Outcome is unclear, but the implication is that the strike was successful.[128]

Volgograd, June 1988: A team of bus drivers refuses for two weeks to drive a route with notoriously bad roads; within a few days, roads are repaired.[129]

Kishinev, July (?) 1988: Bus depot's drivers protest 5–7 hours on several issues (large amount overtime needed to maintain relatively high wages; introduction of "team contract," extra ticket-sales responsibilities). Settlement of main demands is made or promised.[130]

Lipetsk, 1988: Bus drivers, in conflict with management over working conditions and housing and child-care problems, form their own labor union as an alternative to strike; reject official union.[131]

Overall, the reaction to these strikes was tolerant, and repression was not in evidence. In Yaroslavl' blame was basically attached to management's failure to consult, and in Omsk to an unjustified overreaction by a bad manager to "a meeting of the labor collective—not a mutiny."[132] In Klaipeda, Omsk, and Kharkov, workers seem to have achieved their objectives, as did the drivers in Chernovtsy, Volgograd, and Kishinev.

One step removed from the fray, the rhetoric of leaders and official commentators hinted at a readiness to change, but also at resistance to growing worker militancy. The growth to some degree surely derived from the success that strikes were having, which was partially a product of political liberalization and increasing divisions of leadership opinion at local levels. Gorbachev, discussing the Yaroslavl' strike, struck a tone that attributed the conflict to a failure to "consult" on the problem of working Saturdays, implying that consultation was good practice and something workers had a right to expect.[133] In a speech in Gorky on August 5, 1988, Yegor Ligachev, then Politburo "second secretary" and the follower of a consistently harder line than Gorbachev, made a somewhat different point: there were simply too many strikes:

Misunderstanding democratization, people in some places are trying to solve the emerging problems by means of strikes. Socialism is the system of the working people, and to strike against oneself is absurd. In our society, there are other ways—democratic, constructive ways—of resolving conflict situations. An atmosphere of contempt must be created around the instigators of strikes and unlawful rallies and demonstrations that are extremist and antisocialist in nature. Leaders who connive at illegal actions must bear full responsibility for this. As far as Communists are concerned, their participation in strikes and unlawful assemblages is simply incompatible with membership in the party.[134]

There was much of the "old-time religion" in the tone, in the assertions about "socialism" and "Communists," in Ligachev's general approach. This tone was not to be found in a *Pravda* piece, simply entitled "Strike" (*zabastovka*) in July 1988.[135] Noting that the process of restructuring had begun not in abundance (if so, of course, why restructure?) but in stagnation, it stressed the costs of strikes, even when workers had a legitimate gripe. Not hysteria but bravery and restraint were called for. When the Kishinev bus drivers struck, five to seven hours were lost before the buses rolled: the bus enterprise, already subsidized, lost income; factory workers were late, production suffered; mothers and children lost time, missed lunches. All in all, in striking, workers "robbed themselves" (an old theme). Strikes themselves suggested that party members in the work force were silent, inactive—or that they might even be joining in the strike chorus.

If political decompression removed a deterrent to striking, it should still be noted that the strikes recorded in this period had little to do with gains. Much as in the pre-1985 period, they had to do with perceived and real erosion. What was at issue, frequently, was a change in work and compensation rules. For all the fact that the food and goods situation had shown no great improvement under Gorbachev, it was the work and wage rules rather than local shortages and living conditions that generated most of these strikes. Workers were, in 1986–88, beginning to contest policies of nationwide aim and application that were integral to early perestroika. Less pay for the same work, the same pay for more work, or worse permutations, were part of the "shakedown phase." Few more goods available for any extra rubles earned added to the problem. Linking pay to performance indicators when, in the workers' view or in reality or both, those indicators are determined by many factors beyond the workers' control, was perceived as unjust. As *Moscow News* put it, *gospriemka* was "now being applied on an ever greater scale in industry. The workers most of all suffer materially from this. But are they to blame for having utterly worn out the machinery and the tools, or for not getting the measuring instruments in time?"[136] On the whole, in fact, the press

was moderately pro-worker, and certainly anti-"old-style manager."
The abuse of managerial *edinonachalie*, the resistance of managers to
worker claims based on new rights and laws on self-management,
was a major topic of condemnation. *Izvestiia* titled its article on the
Zelenokumsk incident "Between the Law's Lines," noting that the activist brigade leader, referring to the new law on labor collectives and
to pro-participation articles in the press, had been advised to "read
between the lines"—and, presumably, draw the conclusion that management would still call the tune, in the old way.[137]

Notable were the attempts to project an alliance between the "high
policy" of perestroika and its protagonists, and the worker, fed up
with inefficiency, mismanagement, the old do-little, collect-salary directors of plants and enterprises. *Moscow News*, again, quoted a
worker reflecting on the strike in the wooden-structures plant, after
the manager had been dismissed and others were sharply criticized:

> We were even a bit sorry for them. Though objectively—judge for your-
> self—do they merit a place in our life today? The decisions taken by the
> government press on them from the top. And we press from below, we, the
> formerly silent majority. You people tactfully define their behaviour in the
> newspapers as a "discrepancy between the word and the deed." But we call
> this simply stagnation and quagmire. We're fed up with them. Therefore,
> being inactive today means to be a traitor.[138]

All very well, and no doubt some workers did line up, naturally, with
the new policy. But thus to link the worker majority with Gorbachev,
both of them squeezing recalcitrant management, was even at this
time an overly simple attribution of a working-class pro-reform sentiment to a very complex reality. It would prove to be even more so the
case in 1989–90.

Certainly, in the complex situation of 1988, Gorbachev understood
that things were uncertain. He wanted and called for worker participation and support for perestroika as a set of economic goals; he
would have "liked" worker pressure in this sense to be exerted, effectively, through new schemes such as managerial elections and labor
collective councils. But this was not really happening. Instead, he
faced strikes he cannot have welcomed, given the parlous state of the
economy, from some workers. From others, there was evidence of
general discontent and frustration combined with passivity, prompting him at one point to denounce (populist legitimist) expectations for
the "good tsar" to intervene, the all-powerful "center" to step in and
resolve local management problems.[139] The worker mood was becoming increasingly difficult to manipulate, even to predict; worker militancy could cut several ways. In September 1988 it was partially a

realization that the trade unions could neither channel nor suppress worker discontent, partially "public relations" that led AUCCTU head Shalaev to suggest that the USSR might find it necessary to legalize the right to strike.[140]

Strikes, pre-Gorbachev and in 1985–88, gave evidence of a worker capacity to "act together," though still at low levels of organization, and for short times only. "Defense against erosion" was, before and after 1985, a dominant motif. Though it is impossible to be exact here, protests against living conditions as such seem more pronounced in the chronicle of pre-1985 strikes than in those that came later, when new work disciplines and related risks of pay cuts more often set off action by workers "as producers." If to some perestroika was promise, to others it meant an acceleration of erosion.

Thus, under the post-1985 political conditions that lowered the costs of militancy, what were expressed were probably two varieties of worker "interest." One was pro-perestroika, articulated in militant fashion by workers fed up with managerial immobilism, inefficiency, and foot dragging—workers who see their interest in the success of reform, in linking pay to work, in de-leveling and greater "meritoc-racy." This can be seen, partially, as a "class" attitude. Activists of this sort, quite conceivably, may have seen all workers as witting or unwit-ting victims of the old ways, the old "social contract." They are, likely, a minority. The other worker interest is viscerally linked to mainte-nance of the old ways, the old "contract," the rough egalitarianism and certainty of predictable reward for predictable—and sometimes minimal—efforts. For many, especially low- and semiskilled workers, and in the traditionally favored but often loss-making industries, *this* remains the critical "class" interest. They are probably more numer-ous than the former variety of activists.

Militancy and Class

This chapter's subject matter links directly with the broad concerns about class—identity, opposition, totality, and alternatives—ad-dressed in preceding chapters. What it offers, however, probably complicates our judgments as much as it facilitates solid conclusions about the situation from the Khrushchev period through "early Gorbachev."

The party's presence in the plant, the limited welfare functions of factory-level trade union organizations, were not likely to affect devel-oping consciousness of class identity very much. To the degree they did, it probably was to promote greater identity. Party membership by a minority of skilled male workers neither reidentified them as something else, nor deprived the nonparty members of their worker status. Trade union rhetoric and activity carried no effective symbolism that looked capable of diluting class identity (beyond the obvious one that Soviet trade unions are branch/industrial, and therefore unite blue and white collar, supervisor and order taker, in the same union).

Both party and union organization, however, gave priority to blocking the development of an oppositional worker consciousness, and *a fortiori* totality, or worker awareness and adoption of an alternative design of economy and polity. Did they succeed in the years of our concern? The party in the plant represented power—power ready, by and large, to punish politically deviant behavior and other manifestations of opposition. We must ascribe to it partial effectiveness, simply because without such controls, we have little reason to think that more strikes, however loosely organized and episodic, would not have occurred in those late Brezhnev years. Force or the threat of force works against behavior. Whether the party really was effective against the development of oppositional attitudes is a different question, and events to be covered later in this book suggest that it has a different answer.

The unions, representing employees as well as workers, were not there to blunt a sense of workers' class *identity* per se—nor, obviously, to promote it. But their whole rationale was antithetical to the development of an oppositional consciousness. The defense, case by case, of individual workers' rights versus managerial abuse, even if active and honest, in no way contradicted a doctrine that the true interests of workers and good managers were the same. Did it work? Certainly not totally: but, at least up to 1989 it would have been hard to show that the unions' failure to broaden their mandate and to seek broader shop-floor class interests to defend had fed the growth of oppositional attitudes. It was more a matter of evidence of some contempt for unions as part of "authority" on the one hand, balanced by a kind of rough tolerance on the other. The negative control on the shop floor did testify to something oppositional in the production situation. To the degree that it worked, it provided a vehicle to advance workers' interests; it did what a "real" union local might have done and to some degree made good the plant union's deficiency. Later evidence would change this generally accepted picture somewhat.[141]

All this, at least, so long as negative control itself worked. Our chronicle of strikes offers eloquent evidence that it often did not. And it is in the strikes and the experience of the free trade union organizers that we deal more explicitly with the totality and alternative stages of class consciousness before 1989.

Totality signifies that workers come to accept class identity and opposition as *the* defining characteristics of both their own total situation and of the whole society in which they live.[142] It is worker versus capitalist under capitalism, and worker versus, generally, the state-socialist system that employs the bosses and managers in the USSR. Totality as an element of consciousness has not been evident in what we have seen in this chapter, at least not in the sense of a fundamental, total social divide running between worker and boss. Strikes on economic issues may be evidence of identity and opposition, but they made claims *on* the bosses, *on* the system. They did not reject it nor express the kind of irreconcilability that would seem to be evidence of totality. The "populist legitimist" appeal to higher authority versus plant-level or local abuses, the assertion of a commonality of interest, perception, and morality with the "bosses of one's bosses," denies totality in worker-system confrontation. To what degree this was tactical, "masking" a more antisystem deep consciousness, we cannot really tell. In the absence of evidence that it was *only* tactical, it is better to assume that it was not, in the years before real crisis hit Gorbachev's USSR.

This is all the more so since our record of strikes and free trade unions gives little evidence of a consciousness of any systemic alternative that motivated militant workers. With the exception of earlier Baltic strikes employing work stoppage as political protest and of individual militants who clearly rejected the Soviet system, there is no indication that workers sought to replace Soviet socialism with something else, much less with any fully articulated "something" amounting to an alternative political and economic order. If Western workers find totality and alternative consciousness much more elusive than class identity and opposition, it is no wonder that, under much greater political and informational constraints, Soviet workers fell short as well. If anything, the broad drama of perestroika, and the workers' role in it, seemed more likely to turn on the elements of the still-vague but radical alternative that Gorbachev's reform seemed to present to Soviet society. It also depended on how workers perceived and reacted to it, as the economy failed to show any signs of real improvement, and more political demands, especially those from disgruntled nationalities, made themselves felt on the leadership.

The year 1989 would raise issues, for both politicians and analysts, that reflected the tentativeness of the conclusions in this chapter. How much of the relative quiescence of workers in previous years had been the result of repression, how much the product of the state's adequate economic performance and honoring of its "social contract" commitments? Attributing it mainly to the latter factor would not in

any way really exculpate the Brezhnev-era system: analysts and reform politicians alike saw it as radically flawed, as much by what it
had delivered (and thus created dependence upon) as by what it had
denied the populace. But now the slackening of political repression
had come, simultaneously, with a decline in economic performance
that pained and confused many citizens. When workers proved to be
angry—as they soon would—it would be rather late to ask whether
this was a long-suppressed anger released by political liberalization or
a new one spawned by deteriorating economic conditions. The leadership would simply try to cope, as it had to with so many other items
on the political agenda.

TABLE 6.4
Strikes in the USSR, 1956–83

Location	Date	Type	Source	Duration/Results	Comments
1. Sverdlovsk	1956	"Strike wave"	G., p. 32	—	—
2. Moscow	1956 (Oct)	Ball-bearing plant	A1	—	—
3. Nikolaev	1957–58	Unknown	A2	Strike fails; several hundred workers arrested	—
4. Riga (Latvia)	June 1960?	Radio and car plant	A3	—	Workers protest working on a traditional Latvian national holiday
5. Temir-Tau (Kazakhstan)	1959 (Aug? Oct?)	Construction site living conditions/wages	G., p. 32; B., p. 38, H., p. 11	Several days (?); 2,000 to 20,000 involved; troops repress with force; deaths, arrests	Perhaps 100-plus dead; later, CP/MVD/KGB officials sacked
6. Kemerovo	1960 (Jan)	Riot	H., p. 11	—	—
7. Barnaul	1960	Plastics factory	A4	—	—
8. Nikolaev	1960	Unknown	A5	—	—
9. Rostov-on-Don	1960 ('61?)	Unknown (currency reforms?)	A6; H., p. 11	—	—
10. Kharkov	1960	Unknown	A7	—	—
11. Aleksandrov	1961	Factory	A8, B., p. 38	Mass demonstration, shooting	About 100 dead (?); 3 death sentences carried out
12. Kiev	1961	Book/journal plant	A9	2 days; management meets workers' demands	6 strikers involved

TABLE 6.4 (cont.)

Location	Date	Type	Source	Duration/Results	Comments
13. Novocherkassk	June 1–3, 1962	Citywide strike on prices/wages	A10; G., p. 32; H., pp. 11–13; B., pp. 44–46	—	—
14. Grozny	1962	Price rise?	H., p. 12	—	—
15. Krasnodar	1962	Price rise?	H., p. 12	—	—
16. Donetsk	1962	Price rise?	H., p. 12	—	—
17. Yaroslavl'	1962	Price rise (tire factory)	H., p. 12; A11	—	—
18. Zhdanov	1962	Price rise?	H., p. 12	—	—
19. Gorky	1962	Price rise?	H., p. 12	—	—
20. Moscow	1962	Mass demonstration, Moskvich auto plant	H., p. 12	—	—
21. Odessa	1962 ('63?) (Summer)	Dockworkers; food shortages, prices	H., p. 13; G., p. 32; A12	—	Refusal to load butter on Cuba-bound ship
22. Kaunas	1962	Shoe factory strike	A13	5 hours; KGB troops/tanks threaten Siberian exile; workers return to work	—
23. Kiev	1962	Motorcycle plant/food shortages	H., p. 13	—	—
24. Krivoy Rog	1963 (Oct)	Several plants	A14; G., p. 32	—	Martial law/curfew imposed
25. Ryazan'	1963	Unknown	G., p. 32	—	—
26. Baku	1963	Unknown	G., p. 32	—	—
27. Omsk	1963	Unknown	G., p. 32	—	—

Location	Date	Place/Description	Ref.	Details	Outcome
28. Sevastopol	June 25–26, 1964	Shipyards	A15	Leaders came from Moscow; local MVD commander is reprimanded	200 strikers
29. Priluki	1967 (Nov)	Citywide strike	A16	2 days (?); workers' demands are met	Protests about local police abuses
30. Kharkov	1967	Tractor plant	H., p. 14	—	—
31. Nakhodka	1968	Unknown	A17	Arrests (?)	—
32. Kishinev	1969	Two garages	A18	On second day, ministerial commission comes from Moscow/ director, deputy, chief accountant all get prison terms	—
33. Sverdlovsk	1969	Rubber plant; wage cuts/food shortages	A19; H., p. 16	One shift; MVD, party officials grant workers' demands; dismiss director	Later some strikers fired; dismissed director given promotion, Moscow job
34. Kiev	1969 (May)	Hydroelectric station; housing	H., pp. 16, 17	—	Workers confront KGB troops in veterinary vans
35. Chervonograd	1969 (June)	One plant; wage raises and complaints vs. managers	G., p. 33	8 days; most demands granted	—
36. Kiev	"Early 1970s"/'72?	Machine plant	G., p. 33; H., p. 15	—	Later, strike leaders fired; one receives one-year sentence
37. Vladimir	1970	Several plants	G., p. 33	1 or 2 days	—
38. Sverdlovsk	"Early 1970s"?	Unknown	G., p. 33	—	—

TABLE 6.4 (cont.)

Location	Date	Type	Source	Duration/Results	Comments
39. Kopeisk	1970/71?	Machine factory	G., p. 33; A20; H., p. 15	—	KGB arrests strike organizers
40. Zarechenka	1970	Collective farm	A21	3 days; demand that church used for grain storage be returned is met	—
41. Kerch	1971	Unknown	A22	—	Arrests; sentences to 4 years; imprisonment plus exile; psychiatric hospital
42. Baku	1971 (Dec)	Mass meeting/oil refinery/working conditions	G., p. 33	200 workers involved	10 workers, 3 engineers arrested and sentenced
43. Kotovskii raion	1972	State farm	A23	Demands met same day	—
44. Dnepropetrovsk	1972 (Sept)	Wages/living conditions	G., p. 33; H., p. 15	Thousands strike; repressed with force	Some dead, wounded
44. Dnepropetrovsk	1972 (Oct)	Riots	G., p. 33; H., p. 15	—	—
46. Kamenets-Podol'sk	1972 (Dec)	Agric. machinery plant/ norms and pay	G., p. 33	—	30 workers fired as instigators; 2 later sentenced to 3 years
47. Aleksotas (Kaunas)	1973 (Oct)	Woodworking plant/ wage cuts	A25; G., p. 33	2 days; KGB, MVD, Soviet and ministerial officials grant workers' demands	660 strikers

Location	Date	Description	Reference	Worker demands satisfied	Organizers sought, but not found
48. Vitebsk	1973	Large plant/wages	A24; G., p. 35; H., p. 15	Worker demands satisfied after KGB intervenes on second day of the strike	Organizers sought, but not found
49. Moscow	1973 (Winter)	Construction/"scores of stoppages"	H., p. 16	—	—
50. Leningrad	1973 (Winter)	Construction/"scores of stoppages"	H., p. 16	—	—
51. Novoalekseevka	1974 (Aug)	Unknown	A26	Demands met same day	About 100 strikers
52. Shauliai	1975	Bus drivers	A27	Demands met in 3 hours	—
53. Baikal-Amur (railroad)	1975	Walkout/poor work organization	G., p. 33	—	—
54. Leningrad	1976	Kirov machine factory	A28	3 days	400 strikers
55. Riga	1976 (Summer)	Port factory workers/dockworkers?	G., p. 33	Demands met that "meatless days" in restaurants be canceled	4 arrests for anti-Soviet slander
56. Sinelnikovo	1976	Unknown	A29	—	Arrests?
58. Dnepropetrovak	1976 (Aug)	Machine factory	A32	—	—
59. Leningrad	1977 (May)	Dockworkers	A33	Workers refusing to work overtime replaced by students and soldiers	Issue: unloading of imported foodstuffs not destined for regular stores, but for "elite"
60. Vyborg	1977 (May)	Dockworkers	A34	Same as no. 59	Same as no. 59
61. Tallinn	1977 (May)	Dockworkers	A35	Same as no. 59	Same as no. 59
62. Riga	1977 (May)	Dockworkers	A36	Same as no. 59	Same as no. 59
63. Ventspils	1977(May)	Dock workers	A37	Same as no. 59	Same as no. 59
64. Klaipeda	1977 (May)	Dockworkers	A38	Same as no. 59	Same as no. 59

TABLE 6.4 (*cont.*)

Location	Date	Type	Source	Duration/Results	Comments
65. Kaunas	1977 (Dec)	Rubber plant/wage cut	A39; G., p. 33	12 hours; demands met; one worker taken by police and beaten	Several officials fired, manager reprimanded
66. Ivanovo	1977	Textile plant	A40	—	—
67. Znosychi	1978 (Spring)	Collective farm	A41	Demands met	Church later demolished
68. Stavropol'	1978 (Aug)	Grain truck drivers	A42	—	—
69. Kokhtla-Jarve	1979 (June)	Gas/shale plant	A43	MVD attacks strikers with clubs; 1st secretary Estonian party threatens them	—
70. Togliatti	Aug 10–11, 1979	Bus drivers (managers/work conditions/wages)	A44; G., p. 33	Demands met, including managerial firings, wages	No arrests, but some interrogations/200 strikers
71. Togliatti	May 6–7, 1980	Bus drivers and auto plant	A45; G., p. 33	3 hours; demands met	—
72. Gork'ii	May 7–8, 1980	Auto plant/food shortages	G., p. 34	Food supplies improve immediately	4 leaders arrested
73. Cheliabinsk	June 2, 1980	Tractor plant/food shortages	G., p. 3	—	—
74. Naberezhnye Chelny	1980 (June)	KamAZ truck plant/food shortages	A46; G., p. 34	4 hours; food supply improves but not for long	—
75. Mishelevka	1980	Porcelain plant/bread shortage	A47	One day; bread is brought to settlement	—

Location	Year	Description	Ref.	Outcome	Notes
76. Tartu	1980	Agric. machinery plant (norms/bonuses, shortages)	A48; G., p. 34	Commission from Moscow grants demands	1,000 strikers
77. Nikel'	1980	Unknown	G., p. 34	—	—
78. Vyborg	1980	Unknown/protest vs. police	G., p. 34	—	Issue: police brutality (?)
79. Monchegorsk	1981	Bus drivers	A49	—	—
80. Monchegorsk	1981	Bus drivers	A50	—	—
81. Monchegorsk	1981	Bus drivers	A51	—	—
82. Monchegorsk	1981	Bus drivers	A52	—	—
83. Monchegorsk	1981	Bus drivers	A53	—	—
84. Vorkuta	1981	Coal miners	G., p. 34; A54?	—	—
85. Kuzbass	1981	Mines	A55	—	—
86. Kuldre	1981 (Mar–Apr)	Bus drivers, state farm	A56	Some demands met	50 strikers
87. Kiev	1981 (Mar)	Machinery/design plant (work norms)	A57; G., p. 34–33	1-5 days; demands met	—
88. Kiev	1981 (Apr)	Same plant	A58; G., p. 74	1-5 days; demands met; director removed, staff of local Soviet/party committees changed	—
89. Kiev	1981 (Mar–Apr)	Concrete plant	A59	2 days; demands met	
90. Kiev	1981 (May)	Tool and die plant	A60	Several hours; Moscow commission rejects demands	Workers called in one by one, threatened
91. Kiev	1981 (June)	Construction assembly line	A61	1 or 2 days; all 15 strikers taken to police station for several hours; demands met	One brigadier (worker) sentenced to 15 days; "hooliganism"

TABLE 6.4 (*cont.*)

Location	Date	Type	Source	Duration/Results	Comments
92. Kiev	1981 (Aug)	Motorcycle plant (norms/bonuses)	A62; G., p. 35	Management meets demands	—
93. Riga	1981	"Labor disputes"	G., p. 3	—	—
94. Pavlovsk	1981 (oct)	Zhdanov auto plant	A63; G., p. 35	"Several days"; demands met, bonuses paid out	600-plus strikers
95. Ordzhonikidze	Oct 24–25, 1981	Urban transport	A64	2 days; Solomentsev (prime minister of RSFSR) promises improved conditions	—
96. Volinsk	1981	Painters/auto plant	A65	—	20–30 strikers
97. Tallinn	1981 (Dec)	Road crew	A66	30 min; part of a planned political protest strike	—
98. Moscow	Sept 9–10, 1981	Khrunichev plant	A67	Demands met	—
99. Riga	1982	Motor transport	A68	—	Ethnic tension; Moldavians vs. gypsies
100. Atari	1982	Unknown	A69	Several hours; demands met after call from city CP and KGB	Organizer threatened, but not fired
101. Vyborg	1983	Electric tool plant	A70	One day; demands met, workers paid for strike	Commissions blame administration, criticize workers
102. Narva	June 1, 1983	Taxi garage	A71	Demands met	—

103.	Kiev	1983 (June)	Meat packing plant/ sausage plant	A72	Demands met
104.	Krivoi Rog	1983	Several plants	A73	—
105.	Sverdlovsk	"1980s"	"Uralmash" plant	A74	—
106.	Sverdlovsk	"1980s"	Verkhneisetskii tool plant	A75	—

Source: Adapted from Liudmila Alekseeva, "Zabastovki v SSSR (poslestalinskii period)," *SSSR: Vnutrennie protivorechiia,* no. 15 (1986), pp. 80–145 ("A"); Betsy Gidwitz, "Labor Unrest in the Soviet Union," *Problems of Communism* 31, 6 (November–December 1982), pp. 25–42 ("G"); Vadim Belotserkovsky, "Workers' Struggles in the USSR in the Early Sixties," *Critique,* nos. 10–11 (1979), pp. 37–50 ("B"); M. Holubenko, "The Soviet Working Class: Discontent and Opposition," *Critique,* no. 4 (1975), pp. 5–25 ("H").

7

Worker Politics and Economic Crisis

> During the second half of last year [1988]
> trade started to collapse before our very
> eyes. . . . We are promised that no further
> rises in retail prices will be permitted. . . .
> But . . . has anyone ever seen prices remain
> stable while economic affairs go poorly?
>   (*V. Seliunin, April 1989*)

THE JOURNALIST-ECONOMIST Seliunin would have words even more grim than these as 1989—a bad year in the economy—faded into 1990—a much worse one. From 1988 to the autumn of 1990, the Soviet political scene grew more dynamic and "democratic" but also inchoate, as more actors—groups, "movements," charismatic individuals—crowded a stage that for so many years had been carefully managed. A complex society, woven of many groups and categories representing conflicting political principles, economic and ethnic-territorial interests, had emerged into a politics that was much more than "post-totalitarian," much less than that characteristic of a civil society.[1]

The political drama proceeded against a backdrop of an economy sliding into crisis—the crisis Gorbachev and the reformers had set out to avert. By mid-1989, the tones of Soviet commentators resembled those of Western observers. At a news conference, major reform economists—Abalkin, Shmelev, Bogomolov, Popov—hit the note of an economy on the verge of explosion: a possibility of "famine," a collapse of supplies that would produce shortages as severe as any in the postwar period, a state deficit already huge and escalating while the state printed yet more rubles. Abalkin, recently named to a deputy premiership, foresaw, in the absence of improvements in the "next two years," a destabilization of society "unpredictable" in form but "inevitable."[2]

Subsidies, Prices, Poverty

By early 1989, Soviet society faced an economic situation that combined deprivations with continuing and perplexing changes in direction; perestroika had not yet achieved a coherent quality. If some people benefited, many more were not so well positioned to locate or take advantage of opportunities afforded by the developing scenario of change.

Among the latter, on the whole if not universally, were the workers. New policies, in prospect if not yet in execution, agitated them. The economic past was being reevaluated; the process threatened to upset a familiar world, a sense of what the Soviet system was "about" and what its real accomplishments—in which, as workers had always been assured, they had played a major role—had actually been. The ground was shifting.

Among the most controversial points was retail price reform—for economists, the long overdue rectification of the abnormality of massive subsidies on the state retail pricing of bread, meat, other foods and goods. Within a year of Gorbachev's accession, the press was constantly reminding Soviet citizens that bread and meat were priced at less than half their production costs, placing a massive burden on the state budget, absorbing funds that might go to other purposes.[3] The state's "take" from the rental charges on housing—at per-square-meter rates unchanged for decades—covered less than one-third of putative maintenance costs.[4]

Price reform, then, meant price rises on these basics in the future, as well as possible price reductions on some big-ticket durables. The economists who advocated the reform were, in general, quick to assure the public that compensation would be provided: that the billions of rubles the state budget would recover with the end of subsidies would provide supplements to those who were low-paid, had many dependents, and so on, so that they would not be "hurt" by price rises.[5]

Economically, bringing prices up to their "real" levels made sense. Demand for underpriced bread was artificially high, given how cheap it was: farmers even fed their pigs bread, since feed was more expensive, and schoolboys used stale loaves as soccer balls. But social moods and expectations were to prove as critical—or more so—than economics. The proposals ran profoundly against the ingrained public expectations of accessible, stable prices on basic goods. They seemed insensitive, as well, to the painful daily experience of shortages. If bread was still plentiful, dairy products and, especially, meat were anything but readily available in the state stores. Meat in the *kolkhoz* markets sold for a large multiple of its state retail price; but even in the state retail network *at* state prices, meat was not cheap relative to disposable income for the vast majority of Soviet citizens. Nor was it clear that the Soviet public was universally aware that many food prices were subsidized, any more than they understood that large appliances, cars, and the like were not only very expensive because they are big and rare, but because the state's hidden markup on these items is enormous.

Public reaction to the proposals of price reform had been sharply negative. Readers' letters in *Izvestiia* in September 1987 complained about many things: that prices *had* risen, but one only learned this "in the store"; that the quality of meat and dairy products, whose price had been stable since 1962, had suffered greatly; that, in Novosibirsk, it was "impossible to buy goods at state prices."[6] A reader from Belgorod complained that "no meat" is available, and that it is rumored that prices would rise soon: the "city is literally seething, passions are at boiling point." Another, citing the generalized fear of what the government might do, pleaded "don't let people suffer in ignorance." Later, an *Izvestiia* reader, reflecting what would be a common Soviet view, argued that a ration card system would better serve "social justice" than would price increases.[7] In January 1988 *Literaturnaia gazeta* summarized its mail and noted that of about fifteen hundred readers' letters, only about a dozen had favored price increases. One of its readers noted that meat at the state price was available locally, but only "to leaders of organizations."[8] (This point, which was also made by advocates of price reform who continued to argue that subsidized low prices mainly benefited those with large incomes and bureaucratic privilege rather than the poor, never really became an accepted argument in defense of price reform.)[9]

In Estonia, a republic marked by both political and economic reformist initiative, some indication of what price reform might bring came from the "leak" of a republican price reform plan—via a secretary of the republic's trade union organization—to some workers. The plan would have seen beef prices rise (from a "state" price of about 2 rubles) to 7.90 rubles per kilo—higher even than the 5–6 rubles price in the *kolkhoz* markets. "Compensation" was planned, but workers felt that the price rises would move diets in the direction of "more groats, fish, potatoes," and with *these* in short supply too, price hikes on them would be likely as well. A point of criticism was that "reform" on the basis of production costs, reflecting massive inefficiency and waste in the agricultural sector, was no incentive to greater efficiency and offered no real promise of improvement in supply.[10]

The "Estonian affair" ended in the withdrawal of the draft plan: although, in 1990, it would be the first republic to reform food prices. It echoed the earlier-expressed concerns of two economists about raising prices when so many commodities were in a state of chronic shortage. Chiding their colleagues for an insensitivity that equated "demand" with *effective* demand (having the wherewithal to pay the price), they noted—much as had the Estonian workers—that price rises would compel underconsumption and put basic necessities quite beyond reach. Price rises would, as a social policy matter, have to await somewhat better supplies. Otherwise, to raise prices would resemble the carrying out of heart surgery "by a blindfolded surgeon while the patient was having a massive attack."[11]

In the face of public reactions, top reform economists still insisted that price reform was necessary, and would come. Some emphasized, as Leonid Abalkin did in July 1987, that people had to be "psychologically prepared" for the necessity of such increases.[12] But the radical difficulty of such preparation was clear in the selective memories many expressed about the Stalin era. What readers "remembered," in many letters to the press, was that under Stalin, prices had been lowered several times in the postwar period; that food *was* to be found ("caviar in the stores"); that life had not been so expensive. Economists, admitting these "facts," were quick to put them in context.[13] Caviar had been in the stores—so few could afford it, that it was always visible on the shelves. Per capita meat consumption in 1950 had been only about 40 percent of that of the late 1980s. Prices had been lowered—but from 1947 levels, set when wartime rationing ended, that were 3.6 times higher for food items than they had been in 1940, well more than wage rises. Incomes were low, but in the early 1950s the state retail network was still charging six times the procurement price for beef, eight times for milk. Only in 1965, after several adjustments, did procurement prices on meat and dairy products exceed the retail prices last raised in 1962 (the year of the Novocherkassk strike/massacre) and stable since. In 1965 all food and nonfood subsidies amounted to only 3.5 billion rubles, and were growing apace.

The economists were right—but it made little difference. Evidence of a backing away from the explosive potential of broad, regime-backed price rises amid shortages was growing in early 1988.[14] Certainty gave way to statements that "we have still not decided *whether*" to raise prices, to emphasis on cutting costs rather than raising prices, to denials, as 1988 went on, that prices would be raised before a draft plan was "fully discussed," to denials that the state envisaged *any* rise in consumer-goods prices.[15] The grim picture convinced even the hardest marketeers. Shmelev, in late 1988, expressed the view that an all-at-once reform "might prove to be too much for perestroika."[16] He later placed possibilities of reform at least six to seven years in the future, more likely at the end of the 1990s[17]—while earlier plans had been for reform at the beginning of the decade. Even convinced reformers saw the possibility of disaster and social unrest if price reform were to be pursued. Otto Latsis, the deputy editor of the party theoretical organ *Kommunist*, observed in January 1989 that, while a year and a half before he had said that price reform was "necessary and possible," he now had to admit that it was still necessary, but impossible.[18]

Still, conditions worsened; 1989 was a year of growing shortages, of grim economic statistics. Sensitivity to the possibilities of social explosion was manifest in a late-1989 reform plan that was lackluster and apprehensive, with no real answer to shortages and no surgery on prices. A grim bottom line on production in early 1990, combined with increased ruble wages in the face of near-universal shortages of many necessities, would finally force Gorbachev, possessed of new presidential powers, to consider harder reform options. As Deputy Prime Minister Abalkin would put it, the 1989 program, authorized by the Congress of People's Deputies to cover a six-year period, had lasted only four months before worsening conditions forced its abandonment.[19]

Prices *had* been rising, reform or no reform. Some of it was due to long-term trends that were never publicly admitted but still felt by the public. The interested Soviet citizen, in 1987, could consult official statistics that told him that the "state retail price index" had increased only 10 percent between 1960 and 1986(!).[20] But the state price statistics were unreal. Under glasnost', economists made more sober estimates. Bogomolov calculated that the price of a standard "urban market basket" had risen between 1.5 and 2.5 percent annually from 1961 to 1987,[21] and the State Committee on Prices (Goskomtsen) estimated 2.8 percent annual retail price increases as an average for 1971–83.[22]

No one really knew, but many "felt," the dimensions of inflation. In 1989 the USSR admitted to a massive budget deficit. Its propensity to print rubles unbacked by consumer goods and food was also clear: in the fifteen years up to 1988, consumer production had perhaps doubled, and money in circulation had increased by 3.1 times.[23] Under perestroika, while goods production *might* be up, wages were up by more; 1988 national income rose 4.4 percent over 1987, and wages rose 7 percent.[24] Both trends worsened through 1989, and in 1990, wages rose while production fell, as the crisis deepened.

Many factories, however limited their autonomy, used their near-monopolistic power to raise prices on supposedly improved products and cut production of cheap items in order to finance the wage raises the 1986–87 authorizations foresaw. The state jawboned against such practices, but there was little relief.[25] Some workers got raises, others felt the negative side of new discipline; for those whose pay packets were fatter, goods were still short. One economist calculated the overhang of excess rubles in savings banks and people's hoards of cash at

370 billion—a possible underestimate, but enough to cover a year's worth of state, co-op, and *kolkhoz* market retail trade.[26] It was unevenly spread; while some had money, many could scarcely get by. One study estimated that seven-eighths of the population had no savings, and that a quarter could not save, given their low per capita incomes, while the 150 billion-plus rubles in savings accounts alone in 1988 were held by only one-eighth of the citizenry.[27]

People also did not have equal chances to alter their situations. Workers with skills marketable in the new, consumer-oriented cooperative sector began to command a premium to remain in state-sector plants, and a Council of Ministers meeting complained of the hefty raises awarded to retain them.[28] Others, including traditionally high-paid heavy and extractive industry workers, lacked these opportunities. Soviet citizens could also learn that their "real" per capita incomes probably ranked them fiftieth to sixtieth among the world's nations;[29] that "free" services and minimal rents now under attack were the reflections of a Stalinist economic design that *paid* people very little and thus had to promise a large number of free items—deliver or not.[30] Shmelev, in a speech in the Congress of People's Deputies in June 1989, asserted the working class's "moral right to increase its share of our GNP."[31] But the worth of a share of GNP would depend on goods available, and on their prices. Here, the picture remained bleak. "We are working harder, as it were, but our life has deteriorated, especially if we judge it by what is available in the stores."[32] Public opinion polls reflected general pessimism. Muscovites polled in 1987 and 1988 about expectations for the following year showed this: 70 percent had expected 1988 to be better than 1987, but only 55 percent anticipated 1989 to exceed 1988; 22 percent had expected "economic prosperity in 1988," 12 percent in 1989.[33] A Komsomol survey of 9,600 young people in 1988–89 showed that 8 percent thought living standards had improved, 20 percent thought they were worse, and 53 percent said standards had changed "only in words."[34] Later polls showed an even darker picture. "Average personal incomes are by no means excessive. They are not large in relation to our needs, they are large in relation to the available mass of goods,"[35] as Latsis put it in spring 1989. A year later, the imbalances were worse, and the situation was one of greater public desperation.

Entitlement and Entrepreneurship

Under perestroika workers faced a general deterioration of supplies and living standards. To this pressure was added, from 1987 on, a controversial unleashing of private (cooperative) enterprise and "individual labor activity." Since the late 1920s, socialism had been "about" the worker. Silhouetted in the poster art standing tall with his jackhammer against the smokestacks of the giant factory, the worker symbolized the old-style "human factor" in the large-scale industry on which the economy was centered. Though a conscientious, disciplined, highly skilled worker on the poster, he was, of course, something different in treatises on labor discipline problems. But he was our accidental proletarian, the accomplishment of sixty-plus years of Soviet power. Those years had seen the supposedly permanent abolition of the trader, the merchant, the middleman, the money grubber, the speculator as factors of any account in the economy. The peasant selling his private-plot produce in the *kolkhoz* market remained, but as a marginal figure against whom history's currents ran. The worker, and state industry, were the victors.

With perestroika, the moral meaning of the story was reformulated. Policies that had wiped out small-scale private enterprise had been wrong,[36] doctrinaire, misguided—and had deprived citizens of services and goods the state sector had not then provided, even though it "overemployed" people. Moral and economic factors were thus intermingled—the economy as a whole was retarded by the lack of benefits co-ops might provide, and (secondarily, given the potential scale of the problem) the need to cut the vast numbers employed, uneconomically, in material production made an expanding cooperative sector attractive as a source of alternative employment.[37]

The story of the cooperatives, interesting in itself, would require more space for the full telling than we can give it here. The beginnings were not auspicious. While late 1985–early 1986 saw discussions that indicated "enabling" legislation might be under way, the first fruits came in a decree and resolution in May 1986 against "deriving unearned income,"[38] which led, in the summer of 1986, to what one economist called a "pogrom against private hothouses, gardens and feedlots"[39]—activities in the farm sector that were generally legal. This phase probably reflected a combination of compromise on matters of policy conflict and, for the reformers at least, a clearing of the decks for pro-enterprise moves to come. They indeed followed—a draft on cooperatives in October,[40] a degree on individual labor activity in November.[41] Cooperatives got under way under the draft legislation. At the local level, where licensing took place, there was evidence aplenty of bureaucratic resistance and restriction,[42] leaving the central authorities in the uncharacteristic posture of demanding legal support for the rights of entrepreneurs[43] and reminding local authorities that the enabling rules meant that all business that was not specifically prohibited was to be permitted.[44]

The final law on cooperatives (more liberal than the draft, though later to be hedged by various restrictions in 1989 and 1990), was published in June 1988.[45] It came at the end of rather complex wrangling over taxes—both those to be paid by cooperatives as "corporate" entities, and by the members/workers of such as individuals. Concerns to promote the development of cooperatives, via low tax rates on retained income (after wages to members and workers) conflicted with finance ministry concerns about increasing tax receipts. Varying conceptions of "social justice" warred in setting tax rates for individuals.[46] Eventually, a corporate tax regime, setting a maximum of 40 percent of the gross but leaving the individual republics to set rates lower if they wished, was adopted.[47] Still too high in the view of many reform economists, it allowed for the possibility, as one source wrote, that the Baltic republics, whose Western traditions and front-line status in both political and economic reform made them favorable to entrepreneurship, might well set their rates low and become tax havens for cooperatives doing business in several republics.[48] With regard to individuals, a new draft income tax law published in April 1989 established a parity of rates between state-sector and cooperative workers, leaving the very modestly progressive old rates in effect up to incomes of 701 rubles per month, and then escalating in a series of steps to a marginal top rate of 50 percent for "super-earners" in the 1,500-plus rubles per month category.[49] (This replaced an earlier-rejected version that had—significantly—singled out co-op workers earning over 500 rubles per month, imposing on them a higher set of rates that escalated to a top marginal rate of 90 percent on wages over 1,500 rubles monthly.)[50] With average blue- and white-collar state sector pay at around 215 rubles in 1986, only a smallish segment of the population was likely to be affected; but the parity of rates signaled a victory for reformers, and for those in cooperatives and individual labor—a number that, counting some 1.6 million moonlighters who also held state-sector jobs as half-time privateers—reached an estimated 3.5 million full-time equivalents in 1989.[51]

Expansion did not betoken resolution of the moral ambiguity of the cooperatives. Those in cooperatives—whether they were well-publicized restaurants with high-priced menus, small plants producing goods, people engaged in "middleman" activities, or honest cooperators versus the previously illegal operators who laundered rubles by declaring them as cooperative income—all ran up against a public attitude criticized by *Izvestiia*: "Don't anybody dare live better than I do."[52] Many workers, never exposed to market decisions on their products, which were paid for whether consumed or not, found it strange that others were given the opportunity to make a profit by meeting a demand sharpened by long-term shortages. Typical was the complaint of a tractor driver on a state farm: when his tractor was out of order he received only 2–3 rubles a day for compensation, while "someone making bra-fasteners" could earn 100 rubles in the same day![53]

Given the shortages, big returns on cooperative activity and public concern about them were natural. A plastic costume jewelry co-op earned nearly 500,000 rubles in its first four months. Nervous local officials declared the earnings illegal and closed it down.[54] Another made pantyhose, and did so well that its four workers generated 200,000 rubles over a four-month period—Croesus-like returns compared to Soviet wage and salary scales—and then shut down voluntarily in anticipation of police attention. They received a clean bill of legal health, prompting a pro-perestroika commentator to observe that the "main 'culprit' was the shortage."[55]

Deep-rooted feelings are involved here, however, and many would not agree with such observations. The tractor driver, if he is typical, is paid "by the furrow," by the acreage plowed (well or poorly), not by the food produced and marketed. He may earn more by plowing more but shallower furrows. This is normal, "the way it is." That the co-op must produce the bra fasteners, that it does so because there is a market and earns money from the market demand, is strange, not really normal, nor immediately self-justifying. Demand in many minds does not justify high prices and high incomes from those prices, at least not to people whose social studies lessons in Soviet schools never explained the functions of the market, except to condemn them.

Even some reformers had trouble with the unleashing of entrepreneurs and the resultant high incomes.[56] Workers could hardly be expected, then, to cheerlead. They had signed on to the social contract. The state provided the job, the materials, and set the pay rates. It rendered the workers protected, but dependent, as the logic of Soviet industrial organization dictated they were supposed to be. It did not encourage initiative; it tolerated sloppy work; it insulated workers from the consumers of their product. There certainly were, and are, abuses in the cooperatives. Many will benefit, after the long drought, from the effective monopolies they enjoy in their area of enterprise. Some *are* run by crooks; some *do* sell, into the economy of shortage, goods as shoddy as (unavailable) state manufactures at several times the state price or re-sell state goods at "speculative" prices. But grievances against the cooperatives go deeper.

Soviet citizens were taught for a long time that entrepreneurial skills and their exercise are "wrong," morally inferior. They are "capitalistic," "bourgeois." Many still believe this. They believe that family-contract lease farming in the countryside will bring back the kulaks, that "cooperatives in cities will revive the bourgeoisie."[57] They do not like this. Many fail to make the connection between the very hard work and the long hours that many cooperative workers put in, and their earnings. The understanding of the work-reward nexus is weak. Some may not even envy the higher earners: as one economist put it of reactions to *gospriemka*'s attempt to bring discipline to the state sector, some people "obstinately believe that it is better to be poor and live a quiet life, without all those capitalist 'acceptance officials.'"[58] (The use of the word "capitalist" is revealing.)

How much inequality can be tolerated by those formed under Soviet socialism? How much is consistent with broad notions of "social justice" in workers' minds? One cannot be precise, but a likely answer is "not too much." Many of those who have relied on state-sector employment for their security and rewards have also relied on the state— indeed *expected* it—to make sure that, in their field of social vision, no "regular" people made a great deal more than they did. Economists might argue that "justice" requires differentiation of reward, that much state-sector income is "unearned," and they might equate high cooperative earnings with the quality and quantity of *result*-producing efforts involved—but find that their words fall on deaf ears.

An envious leveling-down egalitarianism showed by many workers surely complicated perestroika's rocky course; economists dismissed it at their peril. Those who, like the sociologist V. Z. Rogovin, *are* egalitarian in their sympathies understand how deep such feelings go, and how difficult they are to reconcile with perestroika. He quotes the revealing words of a middle-aged woman, employed in the state sector at a presumably modest income, about a contemporary who earns a larger share of things by "growing spring vegetables" for sale (a commentary in itself on perceptions of affluence and how it can be gained): "I don't want to live like her; I want her to live like me."[59] Fourteen words that speak volumes.

Populism and Social Justice

If Soviet public consciousness, on the whole, valued a rough equality, in the sense that no one should be *seen* to be doing much better than the average, then charges that perestroika amounted to elitism had a certain bite. Glasnost' was there "for" the intelligentsia, as producers and consumers of ideas and information. But wage and salary policies favored managerial and engineering-technical personnel in industry over workers, in a conscious compensation for what were now seen as years of unjustified leveling. Cooperative entrepreneurship threatened common folk with the development of a new economic elite, not remote like high officials, but in their very midst.

This is not to argue that workers *in toto* see themselves as the orphans of perestroika. Though we cannot be precise about group differentiation within the working class, we may allow that some segments of the skilled-worker population, in branches with an economic future, the "worker-intelligentsia" as it has been sometimes called, probably have a stake, which they understand as such, in reform. But over the shorter run, workers as a whole have hardly been beneficiaries of changes in economic policy, to say nothing of performance.

The economic times are harsh. While this might normally call for encouraging words, rhetoric has instead been harsh. Gennadi Lisichkin, the reform economist and foe of egalitarians, draws sharp distinctions, condemning the paying of workers who make television sets that explode, and the persecution of *shabashniki* who do good work for good money. On the other hand, he allows that workers who could produce goods salable on the world market would be underpaid even at 400 rubles per month[60]—cold comfort to that vast majority of workers who are far from producing anything the world market would accept. Some broad-brush comments seem likely to cut deep into Russian workers' sense of self and increase convictions that the intelligentsia find them contemptible. Suggestions that "Russian national character" itself may stand in the way of perestroika surely point in such a direction.[61] They reflect in a crude way observations that earlier could only have been made in the prose of academic journals: observations, for example, about "concrete historical circumstances" that had produced in the ("Nordic," "Western") Estonians and Latvians "high accuracy and care in work" that gave them productivity well above average.[62] However accurate, such judgments are unlikely to be true to the Slavic majority of the working class— "blame" they do not deserve, implied praise for the Balts who dislike the Slavic migrants to their republics, who gave enthusiastic reception to the entrepreneurial side of perestroika; and who wish, in any case, to secede.

During shortages, populist-egalitarian concepts of social justice naturally favor rationing as fairer than allocation of goods by ability to pay. Rationing brings the state back in—and the experience of citizens is that the state *is* supposed to *be* in, to "manage" such things. But it is not perestroika, and writers of pro-rationing letters to the editor got little comfort from the economists typically invited to answer them—at least until rationing became necessary in the crisis context of 1989–90. What is rationing but another aspect of the "command-administrative" economy that perestroika means to leave behind? For the economists, the economy was one with too much rationing and administration, too little exchange and market.[63]

Adaptations at the strained margins of the Soviet economy, strange to Westerners but long a part of daily Soviet experience, indicate how long practice can make market principles even more alien. They can impose burdens on people, or appear as creative responses to needs keenly felt. In the first category are the seasonal drafts of urbanites to help with the harvest—in a country with an overabundant agricultural population! In the second are industrial plants' sponsorship of "their own" farms, whose produce, allocated through internal factory channels at state prices, goes to help fuel the factory's work force and cut time spent in lines at food stores. Also in this category are arrangements whereby housing construction for a plant's workers might be made a responsibility of the plant itself—using its excess labor capacity or even the "sweat equity" generated by would-be house builders who work part-time at the brick plant to help make the bricks in which they, then, are paid.

That there is something archaic, something of the "manorial economy" about this—that industrial workers *should* be able to buy food in food stores, delivered from farms factories should not have to sponsor—escapes many Soviet citizens, and leaders too. Official decrees have encouraged just such "home farms";[64] editorials were still doing so in 1988.[65] The idea is not illogical in the short run; such facilities, at a time of shortage, can well make a difference in workers' morale. But as the economist Pavel Bunich put it of the "civilian" brick makers, such arrangements could logically lead to a conclusion that meat packers should keep the meat, automakers the cars: rational economics requires that people should be able to buy a diversity of things with the money they earned as wages.[66] In 1990, three years after Bunich's statement, they could often do no such thing. (By that time, indeed, republics, regions, cities were embargoing exports of their local products, starving the state distribution system which could only offer rubles in return, and bartering directly with other regions for needed supplies.)

Policy crafting was also complicated by a lack of clarity about the public mood in 1987–89. There was little reason to think that the public as a whole and workers in particular understood the economic problem as the economists understood it (to say nothing of understanding their proposed solutions). As one Moscow academic told me in early 1988, in his view "too many" citizens, earning around the then-average 200-plus rubles per month and (finally) allocated an apartment, were—then—satisfied, and found it hard to conceive of much more, or to understand why economic problems were so much on the agenda—qualitatively and quantitatively, the "demand" side was weak.[67] But, even as the "supply" side worsened, in April 1989 *Pravda* reported a poll of 13,000 people, asked essentially, "Is everything OK—at home? at work?" In all, 71.1 percent responded yes. Three-quarters of the sample were "not involved" in perestroika, two-thirds "expressed no interest" in the state of glasnost'. The article concluded that "many of our compatriots are completely satisfied with what has been achieved," showing the effects of the "ideological narcotic" of Brezhnev-era stagnation.[68]

It is difficult to square these indications with those of earlier polls showing growing pessimism, and with growing labor unrest. Asking questions is, perhaps, one thing, observing behavior another. But poll results of this sort may indicate a still weak demand for the fruits that perestroika might ultimately bring. They may testify to a rejection of the "adjustment" that near-term perestroika calls for ("things are all right in *my* life, so why . . . ?"). Some who feel that life *is* bad say the deterioration started in March 1985 and blame Gorbachev and the reformers for all that is new and negative, as in these quotes from letters to *Izvestiia* at the end of 1988:[69] "Reading newspapers and watching television, one feels he is living in a nightmare"; "today's heroes are strikers, informal [group members], homosexuals, and Riga market bingo players"; "Stalin issued orders only once. There was never a second time"; "the time has come for arrests." These represent a visceral authoritarian tilt. But those who may have wanted perestroika and glasnost' to move even faster were also a problem to leaders as delicately poised as Gorbachev and his collaborators. The working class contains, certainly, people who found perestroika wanting from both right- and left-wing perspectives, but such cross-pressures did not cancel each other out.

It is politically realistic to recognize, and try to deal with and moderate, these feelings. But this requires accommodation to them as well, which runs counter to the logic of perestroika. Gorbachev's then ally, Aleksandr Yakovlev, cited among the brakes on reform the fear of social disruption people felt from perestroika.[70] Gorbachev, in a much-publicized meeting with workers in Moscow in February 1989, enumerated many problems: shortages, unjustified price hikes by factories, the "ruble surplus," the excesses of some cooperatives. He encouraged workers to use the labor collective councils to assert themselves. He effectively projected onto the workers "class" support for perestroika and disgruntlement with its slow pace.[71] Beyond this sort of optimistic reading of the worker mood, however, other moves in 1989 seemed to cater to a perception of a vengeful working class. In May the trade union daily *Trud* published a new statute on the "workers' control" arm of the union: a watchdog organization to police price and other abuses in the consumer goods and services sphere in the state and cooperative sectors.[72] The text, though somewhat dry, was distinctly populist in its tone and offered yet another administrative "lever" in a situation where economic levers were not seen to work. Gorbachev, in the speech to the Moscow meeting with workers, had "telegraphed" the coming of the statute and condemned the "rogues" it was meant to deal with.[73] In workers' control, there was an echo of the Khrushchev style of simultaneously unleashing and channeling public ire against "bad characters," from stand-pat bureaucrats to entrepreneurial profiteers—a two-way squeeze of the recalcitrant between a reforming leader and an aroused, supportive working class. Typically little comes of such opportunistic flourishes, but they broadcast the message that the government is sensitive to grass-roots concerns about hoarding, profiteering, self-enrichment. The government could hardly avoid doing such things. But rhetoric and action at this level would not keep the reformers ahead of events. In its early months, the year 1989 proved to be one in which some segments of the working class would become militant to an alarming degree, testing the capacities of party *apparat*, state and managerial officials, and union bureaucrats to deal with long-term consequences of social change, and short-term economic grievances expressed in new ways.

1989: Winter of Discontent . . .

Strikes were rather widespread in early 1989.[74] They were now treated openly and in a matter-of-fact way by a press that admitted there were more incidents than they could report (less from any self-censorship, one gathers, than a lack of space or particular interest).

Near the end of February, workers in a coal mine in the Ukraine's Donbass region refused to sign the standard "collective agreement": demands included improved working conditions and housing and cuts in the size of the administrative staff. Complaints were voiced about transfer of the mine's revenues, via the coal-industry bureaucracy, to support mines operating at a loss.[75]

At the Severnaia mine in Vorkuta in the north, four shifts, numbering over one thousand people, refused to work at the beginning of March; they were hurt by the failure of transport to move the coal. Miners demanded a 40 percent cut in administrative staff and bonuses for night-shift work. Here, the trade union organization was totally bypassed by the miners—indeed, an official quoted with reference to this case was unaware of *any* instance in which the coal-industry union had ever gone against management.[76] (A foreign report on the same strike suggested that three thousand miners had been involved, and that their proto-organization had called itself "Solidarity.")[77]

Coal miners in Karaganda in Kazakhstan struck later in March: one shift demanded a cut in administrative staff by 40 percent and a 40 percent pay increase on the night shift. After twenty-four hours, management conceded.[78]

Above the Arctic Circle in Noril'sk, thousands of miners struck below ground for five days in early April. They presented demands for a 30 percent pay increase and complained of an authoritarian management, too-large ministerial claims on the mine's earnings, and inequitable division of bonus funds between miners and white-collar managers.[79]

At essentially the same time, in Kemerovo *oblast'*, in the Kuzbass area of western Siberia, a wave of strikes hit mines in Kemerovo, Mezhdurechensk, and Kiselevsk, as well as in a shop in a metallurgical combine, where demands included extra pay for evening and night shifts, and a mining-equipment enterprise. The press report noted the difficulties of shifting over to new pay and bonus systems, and that the large percentage of mine income was still controlled and claimed by the ministry.[80]

Bus drivers—like miners, rather highly paid by average Soviet standards—struck in Ivanovo on February 13[81] and in Frunze in the Kirgiz SSR on May 16.[82] In both cases, introduction of a new pay system was an issue. In Frunze, according to the report, part of the settlement included the government's agreement to allot land for the construction of apartments.

The general loosening of political control that accompanied economic reform allowed workers to be more assertive about problems they previously suffered silently. This put a premium on showing economic results to workers, results that were not forthcoming. Both perceived and real economic deterioration drove the strikes. Newer economic policies in the wage and enterprise-guidance areas, even if supported by the workers, created problems. Miners agreed that staffs were fat and demanded reductions. Even though this was Moscow's policy, cuts came slowly. Policy also dictated enterprise independence, less ministerial prerogative—ministries produce no coal, mines do. Miners complained that too much was claimed from their (presumably profitable) mines to support loss-makers—a conviction in line with reform thinking. What might the leadership expect from miners in pits that are due for closure because they are loss-makers? Were the strikers sure that their mines were profitable? Could anyone actually know this, given coal-procurement prices so far below world levels?

Strikes over extra pay for night shifts aimed at supplements decreed by the 1986–87 new wage policies. There was little reason to think that many strikers recognized their being conditional on adequate "self-financing." Strikers were demanding benefits their enterprises had not "earned," and in many cases, given low state procurement prices, could not earn. The calls for cuts in managerial and engineering-technical staff, beyond showing a general contempt toward white-collar types, drew some of their sharpness from the larger bonuses these functionaries derived from good economic performance. What seemed to be at issue was worker rejection of the rationale of meritocratic adjustment, of enlarging pay differentials between managers and professionals on one side, workers on the other, thus correcting the creeping egalitarianism of the Brezhnev period.

Along with the strikes, early 1989 saw the bureaucrats of the AUCCTU taking a somewhat higher profile with statements that would have seemed incongruous not long before. The national union head, Shalaev, had hinted in late 1988 at the possibility of legalizing strikes. As the new year began, union officials were being publicly critical of union inactivity in the past, and they were defensive to assertive about the increasing role they were playing under perestroika. The Moscow union head, Shcherbakov, talked of abandonment of the unions' "passive role" as a "transmission belt."[83] The editor of *Trud* claimed credit for the AUCCTU newspaper's having been the first to inform the Soviet public of inflation, and for its protective role "for the ordinary man."[84] On a Moscow radio phone-in show, Shalaev stressed that the complexities of perestroika meant more people were bringing their complaints to the unions, and that the unions, in the platform their organizational delegates were taking to the Congress of People's Deputies,[85] would call for a number of social measures. These included pension increases and holding the line on prices for such items as children's clothing—a low-markup line that many factories, with an eye to profits, were now ceasing to produce.[86] Another top union secretary cited union involvement in crafting the new personal income tax law, and claimed credit for making 700 rather than 500 rubles the cutoff point before escalating marginal rates set in. More and more workers, over the next decade, would be making over 500 rubles monthly, thus being spared the prospect of "bracket creep."[87]

The rhetoric of trade union reactivization also focused on the issue of strikes. Shalaev admitted that strikes were a reality and that they

were not prohibited by the law.[88] Earlier, Estonian unions had acknowledged that the shift to self-management had generated conflict
between management and labor collectives that led to work stoppages, which suggested that union-government collaboration in the
republic was needed to draft a law to regulate such disputes.[89]

At the end of April, the new draft law on trade unions was published—with a provision giving plant trade union committees, representing "the interests of the labor collective," the "right to stop work"
under certain specified circumstances in labor disputes. It was the
"right to strike," of a sort—given not to workers, but to the unions.[90]
But it was not to be abused. Shalaev stressed that bringing production
to a halt should not be seen as a "normal" phenomenon. Given the
economic losses caused by strikes, unions and management should
use all the other rights and procedures they possessed to avoid reaching this critical point.[91] The head of the coal-mine workers' union,
noting that January through March 1989 had already seen eleven
strikes in the coal industry, lined up in favor of legalizing the conflicts.
The strike experience had shown union organs "smothered and transformed into an appendage of the management and party organs. They
have long forgotten that they are within their rights not only request-
ing, but also demanding."[92]

The critical tone was not far short of that of SMOT communiqués in
an earlier time. A writer in Sotsialisticheskaia industriia likened the unions to "a granny in the family who fusses a lot, interferes in everything, but to whom nobody listens." The social benefits that unions
distributed were distributed in "some countries" by other organizations, while the AUCCTU's defense of workers' "interests" was evident
to all in terms of overtime Saturdays, last-minute storming, unpredictable days off. The AUCCTU was, in fact, a "servant of the state," its
business "maintaining mass calm and imitating 'mass support' rather
than defending the interests of toilers."[93]

The union politics of winter-spring 1989 indicated the increasing
incoherence of Soviet domestic politics in general, as political liberalization, driven now from below as well as from above, moved forward
in no particular coordination with economic reform measures that
had, for the most part, failed to yield results. There was every reason
to be sensitive to blue-collar grievance; sheer opportunism, if nothing
else, demanded it of the AUCCTU leaders whose rhetoric was changing
so rapidly. Reformers with real convictions may have also hoped that
the new trade union law would both help the unions channel worker
protests that were already rising spontaneously, and provide another
mechanism of pressure on recalcitrant managers and bureaucrats who
were sabotaging even the modest provisions of the 1987 law on the

state enterprise. Neither the opportunistic nor the sincere would see their hopes justified.

In the context of revolutionary changes in the political system itself, other sensitive issues of substance and symbol in worker politics were raised in spring 1989. The old-style "decorative" Supreme Soviet, produced by a nationwide choreography of noncontested elections and yielding the predictable representation of workers and farmers, drill-press operators and milkmaids, cosmonauts and academics, in addition to the officialdom of state and party, gave way to something new. The Congress of People's Deputies, 2,250 strong, would be created of 750 representatives of organizations, from the party (and the AUCCTU) all the way to the Soviet philatelists' organization, plus 1,500 elected from the old districts of the bicameral Supreme Soviet. Within the organizations, elections could be competitive or not (the CPSU and the AUCCTU were not); outside, many elections were competitive, hard-fought, conflictual. For those who thought numbers counted, for those who felt that "democratization" should yield *greater* worker representation among Congress deputies than in the old Supreme Soviet, there was little comfort in this first democratic exercise since 1917. The Supreme Soviet "elected" in 1984 had contained a 35.2 percent worker share among its deputies; their share among the Congress deputies of 1989 was only 18.6 percent.

Whether this was an insult to the working class was a matter of perceptions, and these clearly differed. Certainly, some populist feelings were expressed. At his February meeting with workers, Gorbachev heard one worker from a machine-building plant complain that "some" said the Congress was not the business of production workers, who should "stay at their benches" and let the intelligentsia take the lead.[94] (Others, later, would argue that an honest economist might better represent worker interests than a machine-tool operator.)[95]

As the election results showed, economists were more likely than machine-tool operators to be representing constituent interests. Solov'ev, the Leningrad party secretary (whose unopposed candidacy had itself been rejected by the voters), explained to a workers' meeting that worker candidates in Leningrad did badly because their work schedule gave them less time flexibility for campaigning, but that they also suffered from views that, without legal knowledge, etc., they would have little to do but (in the old style) "raise their hand" in political assemblies.[96] He was to make similar points in a speech at the April 25 Central Committee plenum, where he passed on the proposal of "many Leningrad workers" that an all-union congress of *workers'* delegates be convoked and asked the plenum to support it.[97] A newspaper reported that in Leningrad run-off elections for the Congress, party-member worker candidates faced leaflets and slanders calling them *apparatchiki* and functionaries, even if they were still genuine workers.[98] A. G. Mel'nikov, *obkom* secretary in Kemerovo in the strike-prone Kuzbass region, complained that voters had rejected all the party and state functionaries, and women candidates as well. Even workers who had joined the party in the perestroika period were likely to be seen in a negative light. Mel'nikov suggested some special representation of workers on a commission investigating economic problems.[99] Another *obkom* secretary decried the removal of workers from the "sphere of political activity," blaming in part the emergent style of "meeting democracy"—a slap at public forums in which the intelligentsia had been dominant.[100]

What was "fair"? Workers had voted for intellectuals, for other public figures. *Should* they have instead voted for "their own?" There was, probably, some sincere confusion, but complaints also expressed a rear-guard criticism about the reform, an anti-intellectual, *ouvrièriste* posture. The union daily *Trud* insisted that worker delegates—of which there were so few—were "representatives of the leading class of society," and that a weakening of their "influence" in the highest organs of power could not be allowed. It was suggested that worker delegates to the Congress be given special preference in election to the new Supreme Soviet the Congress would produce—and for the whole term of the Congress; this would markedly increase the "authority" of the Supreme Soviet.[101] Another view, in *Sotsialisticheskaia industriia*, was precisely the reverse. The rhetoric of "leading class" was all of a piece with general ideological myth making. Workers, far from being excluded from politics *now*, were showing a new political consciousness to complement their economic clout. Their strikes and demonstrations were "the normal course of the democratically organized life, a normal struggle for rights." Loss of their symbolic majority was no tragedy—workers *had* chosen their representatives, and chosen intellectuals, economists, sociologists, jurists, and others. A return to a guaranteed quota was a return to what had been and was not worth the trip—a newly conscious working class "would not allow manipulation by the use of its name."[102] As it would turn out, this was true especially of the coal miners spread across Soviet territory from the Polish border to the wastes of Kazakhstan.

. . . and Hot Summer

On July 10, 1989, ten days after they had issued a warning (unanswered) citing their long-accumulating grievances and their intent to strike on that date, coal miners of Mezhdurechensk in the Kuzbass struck. Over the two weeks that followed,[103] virtually the whole of Soviet coal mining would come to a halt. A wave of miner militancy threatened to paralyze a shaky economy, monopolized the attention of top officials, and challenged the old system with worker action unprecedented in scale and organization.

The strikes of earlier 1989 had hardly been a taste of what would come in July. In Mezhdurechensk, the strike begun at the Shevyakov mine spread within two days to at least four other pits in the town. Forty-two demands were presented as miners, joined by others, occupied the area in front of local party headquarters. Demands included the 20–40 percent swing and night shift bonuses many miners were not receiving, economic independence for their mines from the financial manipulation of the coal ministry, and a host of specific demands—essentially, that food, medical supplies, soap, and other necessities be made available again.

Such demands would figure in other strikes as well. Coal minister Shchadov and head of the national mine workers' union Srebny arrived in Mezhdurechensk to negotiate, as other Kuzbass mines and towns went "out." By July 15 nine coal towns in the area were wholly or partly shut down, including what would turn out to be the "tough" town of Prokopevsk, and Kemerovo, the *oblast'* center. Eighty thousand miners were out. Shchadov's settlement of the Mezhdurechensk demands—in negotiations with a strike committee that united the town's miners—and the miners' return to work were reported on July 14, but turned out to be premature. The line taken by the Soviet press and cable agencies had shown itself to be quite sympathetic toward the miners and more critical of the local economic bosses and party, state, and trade union officials who were coming under fire; this attitude remained for the duration. Although the strike committee was reported to have voted a return to work after Shchadov's assurances, covering most of the demands, the miners refused to do so. The other Kuzbass mines struck partly because of a lack of assurance that the Mezhdurechensk accord would cover them also. Out of this mass action, horizontal links developed among the mines, leading by July 16–17 to the formation of an *oblast'*-wide strike committee. At its head was Teimuraz Avaliani, deputy director of the Kiselevsk mine and a member of the Congress of People's Deputies.

With distrust of local authorities obviously near-total and the results of the talks in Mezhdurechensk only partially taking hold even there, Prime Minister Ryzhkov made sympathetic noises in the Supreme Soviet on July 17. The same day, a high-level commission (Nikolai Sliunkov of the Politburo, First Deputy Prime Minister Voronin, and head of the AUCCTU Stepan Shalaev) arrived in the

Kuzbass, meeting strike leaders in Kemerovo and then moving on to Prokopevsk to meet with the *oblast'* strike committee under Avaliani. At this point, 100–110,000 were on strike in the Kuzbass alone, and a new chapter was beginning.

On July 17 strikes moved westward to hit the Donbass region in the eastern Ukraine, the USSR's most important coal region. Six pits in the town of Makeevka quit that day, joined by two more the next. Strikes spread all over the Donbass, to thirty-nine mines by July 19.

The USSR's two major coal regions were thus in paralysis, with industrial coal stocks running down and empty railroad cars waiting to be filled for transport. Talks proceeded between the Moscow commission and the Kuzbass strike committee, which was already transforming itself into a *"workers' committee"* in anticipation of continued existence, both to oversee implementation of the state's commitments, and to act as an organ of popular power. With a reported 150,000 workers (possibly including some nonminers as well) still striking in the Kuzbass on July 19, the talks there neared completion. Most demands were conceded by a government in the unaccustomed stance of across-the-table negotiations with what a *Novosti* correspondent said would have been called "a rebellion of socially dangerous elements" four or five years earlier.[104] On July 20–21, the Kuzbass went back to work, with Kiselevsk and Prokopevsk the last holdouts.

This return to work in the Kuzbass, however, was no automatic signal to do the same in the Donbass region. Some sixty-seven mines were striking there on July 20, a number that, as the miners awaited a delegation from Moscow and found no Ukrainian SSR government or party officials to deal with, would grow to 109 of the 121 mines in the region by July 23. And things grew hotter in other areas. On July 19 a mine in Vorkuta in the Komi ASSR—the Arctic Circle region whose Stalin-era labor-camp heritage still permeates it—struck, as did one in Rostov-on-Don. In Dnepropetrovsk, in the western sector of the Donbass, all eleven mines of the Pavlogradugol association went out.

By July 20 the arrival of another government commission to deal with the Donbass strikers was announced. It was led by deputy USSR premier Lev Ryabev and the head of the Ukrainian SSR trade union council, V. Sologub. As these talks opened in the far north, strikes expanded in Vorkuta to nine of thirteen mines. Well to the east, in the Kazakh republic, seven or eight mines quit on July 20 in the Karaganda coal complex, idling 16,000 miners. The Karaganda miners, told that many of their forty-five demands had been incorporated into the Kuzbass settlement, whose terms were to run to the whole coal industry, returned to work on July 22. Two days later, the Inta mine near Vorkuta joined the other striking polar mines. The Komi *obkom* secretary, whose purview included Vorkuta and Inta, attributed their strikes to their failure to understand that the deals cut in the Kuzbass and nearing conclusion in the Donbass applied to them as well.

Things, however, were winding down. The Supreme Soviet and the press, radio, and television had lavished a great deal of attention on the strikes—on the justice of miners' material grievances, on their presumed pro-perestroika positions, "defending reform" against recalcitrant officialdom—but also on the damage done to the economy by the idling mines. Talks proceeded in the Donbass; a Gorbachev speech to the Supreme Soviet furthered motion toward settlement. On July 24 the Vorkuta miners voted to return to work, though the mine in Rostov remained out, awaiting a visit from Shchadov. On July 25, effectively, Vorkuta, Inta, and the Donbass returned to work.

Over a two-week period, hundreds of thousands of operatives in a critical Soviet industry had struck, threatening knock-on effects in critical power-generation and metallurgical sectors. A Moscow government that had been facing strikes on *political* grounds among Russian workers in the Baltic, prompted by residence and voting-law changes pressed by leaders of the indigenous Baltic national movements, had also negotiated with strike leaders in the coal fields and made many concessions to them. No violence had been threatened, and Moscow had expressed no reluctance in meeting with the strike and workers' committees. These organizational initiatives of worker spontaneity were surely more ominous than the intermittent strikes of the previous years had been. Moscow had negotiated with half a million citizens,[105] whose leaders, if still seeking something from the "center," had not behaved as populist legitimists. They had demanded, not petitioned.

Labor unrest continued for the rest of 1989 and into 1990. Strikes remained a major weapon in the arsenals of national and ethnic protesters, engaging large numbers in prolonged work stoppages and causing local economic paralysis.

Short-term "warning strikes" proliferated in the coalfields as strike committees found much to criticize while monitoring the implementation of the Council of Ministers' "Decree No. 608" of August 3, 1989, which proclaimed the blanket settlement of the mine-strike issues. In early September, the regional strike committee in Donetsk *oblast'* asserted that the government's slowness was "pushing us toward new strikes."[106] In Vorkuta, the city soviet refused to register the strike committee as a legal body.[107] In October, short warning strikes came in coal pits in Lvov in the western Ukraine,[108] in Mezhdurechensk,[109] and in Vorkuta.[110] But in Vorkuta, the old labor-camp area where earlier strikes had taken on political overtones, what was intended as a twenty-four-hour "warning strike" on October 25–26 extended into a lengthy, bitter stoppage that lasted until December 2, when the diehard Vorshagorskaia mine voted to return to work. Overall, the issues, as they emerged, combined economic questions (were government commitments being honored?) with legal and political ones (was the strike legal in the light of new laws instituted in October? Had the Komi ASSR supreme court dealt correctly with the strike committee?). Premier Ryzhkov traveled to the area in the wake of a visit to the miners by the top leaders of the nationwide cooperative union, which led to a document supporting the miners and their demands. He impugned the cooperative leaders' motives—"reckoning on destablizing society," "using the strength of the working-class movement as a lever, a tool"—and confessed some confusion. Why did the Vorkuta miners cheer their cooperative allies, when one demand in Karaganda had been to *close* the high-earning co-ops?[111] After the strike ended, the party secretary at the Vorshagorskaia mine concluded that "communists lost their heads and informals ['political' activists] seized the initiative."[112] True enough. But it also showed a government increasingly limited to *reacting* to worker initiatives, now clearly politicized, with little evidence that the government could muster the resources to increase its own room for maneuver.

In January–June 1989, 2 million workdays were lost to strikes: statistically, 15,000 workers struck each day. Between ethnic and economic protest, from July through November, 5.5 million days were lost; the daily statistical striker total reached 50,000.[113]

July and the following months thus saw intensification of the trends that had started the year. There were many lessons that year in regime-worker relations, and they deserve extended consideration for what they tell us about the dynamics of a polity in decay before a society that was growing stronger and more assertive, if not yet organized, or reliably "civil."

The Collapse of Local *Apparats*

Confronted with strikes, the local structures of authority—party, soviet, trade union—as well as the supposed mechanisms of worker participation, the labor collective councils (STK), proved incapable of either suppressing the actions or of coping with the grievances. They failed at this task as they had failed in their earlier tasks of ensuring a bearable working and consumer life in the coal areas, and in keeping the "center" informed of the explosive situation on the periphery.

In Mezhdurechensk, when the strike wave began, both the city party (*gorkom*) and local soviet (*gorispolkom*) heads, in a classic blunder, failed to return from vacations when the strike broke out.[114] In other areas, similarly situated officials found themselves "at sea" and unsure about how to react, especially in the new era of glasnost' and democratization. They had felt rhetorical pressure from Moscow to mend their "command-administrative" ways, and were alarmed by the spectacle of many local party leaders who had been up for election earlier in the year for seats in the national Congress of People's Deputies and had gone on to ignominious rejection. In Prokopevsk the chairman of the local soviet came to the microphone in the town square to address the strikers, only to be greeted with calls of "Who's he?" In Donetsk, similar catcalls met the local union leaders on the city square.[115]

The limited autonomy of local authorities *was* a fact, but it also had bred a style of passing the buck toward Moscow. In confrontation with the strikers, they tended to ignore or deflect the complaints addressed to their own performance, and instead transmitted the broader demands to the capital.[116] "Waiting for orders" from above was a standard response. For local party leaders, the general guideline seemed to be that, as in the spring strikes, if grievances were real, strikes were still "bad," and it was especially bad that party members took part in them. Still, in Donetsk local party committees were cross-pressured between this line and rank-and-file demands that they not turn against the strikers. In Prokopevsk the strike committee told the local trade union committee that its job was to defend the workers, as it waited for orders from the next level up in the union hierarchy.[117]

Within the mine work forces, the STK also proved its essentially decorative nature—they were generally overtaken by the strike committees, having played no active role, as "workers'" bodies, in the strikes. The "elections" to such bodies had been of the old style; they were not leaders with a natural authority among their fellows. They were, in Donetsk, "actively disliked."[118]

Worst of all, though, was the performance of the trade union organs themselves. Their failure at all-union levels would accelerate the effort under way to redefine the whole AUCCTU as a "populist" body which, having learned bitter lessons, would now play watchdog over workers' interests in the complex politics of economic sacrifice that perestroika would demand.

When the strikes commenced in the Kuzbass, the nationwide mine union head, Srebny, "supported" the miners' demands.[119] This was of little help to local union organizations, caught flat-footed and now in a catch-up situation, well behind events. In Prokopevsk, as in Donetsk,[120] the local union heads essentially entered the strike process only by setting up field kitchens for the strikers already sitting in the town squares. The press generally condemned the unions, generalizing that they had been for some time toothless organizations, that they supported management "everywhere," that in the Donbass "no" union leaders took taking part in the strikes.[121]

The generalizations were broad, but generally accurate. As *organizations*, the soviets, party and trade union committees, and STKs proved to be part of the problem, not the solution. But another evidence of their debility *qua* organizations was their general lack of control over individual members and activists who broke the pattern by assuming leadership roles in the strikes. "Some" trade union leaders backed the strikers,[122] though most did not. Management personnel, too, took active roles in some cases (for example, Avaliani, chair of the Kuzbass regional committee, was a deputy director). At the Abakumov mine, one of the first to strike in the Donbass, the party committee secretary was a member of the strike committee.[123] More commonly, it was rank-and-file party members who joined in Donetsk. One quarter of the strike committee was in the party, though those who had been activists in party affairs were generally no longer so. In Gorlovka, "almost half" the committee were Communists.[124] In the Kuzbass, of the 339 members in eleven strike committees, 38.3 percent were in the party. The 339 included four secretaries of primary party organizations, three trade union chairmen, and eight STK chairmen[125]—formal "activists" in this sense thus making up 4.4 percent of the committees.[126]

Amid the evidence of organizational bankruptcy, national-level trade union leaders began to speak out, in an increasingly familiar mixture of self-criticism and self-defense. Along with Sliunkov, AUCCTU head Shalaev addressed the crowd in Kemerovo, affirming that the AUCCTU supported the coal miners' union in its endorsement of the Kuzbass miners' demands.[127] In a *Pravda* interview, he admitted that "since V. I. Lenin's death" (!) the unions had gradually become organs subordinate to the party. But, rather than endorsing "alternative" unions, he called for electing to plant union committees "real leaders" who enjoyed authority among their coworkers.[128] In another interview Shalaev reacted strongly to the implication that he had traveled to Kemerovo as part of a governmental commission (with Sliunkov and Shchadov), rather than having acted in a "logical" role as *presenter* of the miners' demands from the other side of the table. He argued that the commission was a joint party-government-union commission, and that it could not in any case be a "government" commission since Sliunkov, of the party's Politburo, had been its head.[129] Earlier, he had suggested that trade union committees should close down "executive canteens" in plants. As the fall went on, other union leaders would take similar populist positions, with the AUCCTU plenum in Moscow in September calling for selective support of those cooperatives where prices matched those in state stores.[130]

Why did local leaders so quickly lose control and find it impossible to regain? One answer is that they had simply never faced a worker revolt of the magnitude of July. But the militant expression of worker discontent was facilitated by a second factor affecting local soviet, trade union, and party leaders as well, especially the latter. "Politics" in Moscow had become tumultuous, disorganized, confusing: Gorbachev was exposing the party *apparats* to public ire, distancing himself, it seemed, from the CPSU as his main base. (That this would lead to forsaking the party's constitutional "leading role," in February 1990, was as yet unforeseeable.) *Obkom* and *raikom* secretaries were to work in a new way and abandon, along with their governmental colleagues, command-administrative methods. But such methods were, in fact, their *functions*: with what to replace them? By mid-1989 local authority was in many cases unsure of its authority, of what was to be controlled, and how to control it.

Perhaps most important, a deeper rot affected primarily the local party *apparat*, but translated itself to the soviet and trade union leaders as well. Over the long Brezhnev years, the "tenure" granted to officials (stability of cadres), the routinized politics (the "developed socialist society"), and the general tolerance of slackness at the local levels had developed into what Ken Jowitt identified as a corrupt "neotraditionalism."[131] The CPSU, once a collective hero, a charismatic yet impersonal organization that could readily subordinate its cadre "agents" to its organizational interests via the identification of "social combat tasks" (however, like collectivization a half-century earlier, cruel and ill-advised they may have been), had lost the ability to do so. "Unwilling or unable" to identify such tasks, the party had turned not into an entrepreneurial-capitalist organization, nor a rational bureaucracy graduated from earlier "heroism." Instead, the particular "status" interests of elites at various levels had come to be distinct from, and controlling over, any general organizational interest. *Apparatchiks* had come to emphasize their status rather than function. In a neotraditional way they had become the recipients of favors, tributes, bribes, and deference in return for their benevolent and protective attitudes toward subordinate clients outside the charmed circle of party elites. They were hardly suited to the combat task, when it arose, of dealing with the militant miners.

Neotraditionalism infected managers as well. At one Donbass mine, up to 30 percent of its recorded work force were *podsnezhniki*, not engaged in mining at all but used as servants, gardeners, and home repairmen for the local bosses. They were even deployed as members of the STK—reliable agents of the very bosses the STK was supposed to control.[132]

Neotraditionalist corruption was pervasive. At these local levels, even a committed Gorbachev could not eliminate it. But in the July 1989 crisis, the failure to back local leaders, to offer a credible threat of repression to challengers who at an earlier time would have been seen as "socially dangerous" rebels, left them with little defense. Gorbachev had no interest in bailing them out. Not ready to deal with a militant, self-organizing challenge, they went down, in large numbers.

Against the new background, some national labor-related issues lost their salience. The new draft law on trade unions, published at the end of April, included what had earlier been hinted at—the "legalization" of strikes—in its provisions that union organizations would call work stoppages under certain circumstances.[133] The strikes outran the provisions; local unions clearly did not move under the draft to take any active role in July. In the context of the warning strikes that continued through the fall, what a trade union law might or might not contain seemed to matter little.

More pointed was the move toward a ban, or limitation, on the strike weapon itself. At the beginning of October, Gorbachev asked the Supreme Soviet for a fifteen-month general ban on strikes.[134] The legislators rejected this,[135] but did authorize new legislation[136] that, in effect, legalized some strikes while hedging this with various provisions for conciliation stages and cooling-off periods, and bars on strikes in the health and safety sectors as well as in transport, energy, communications, and defense.[137] The exclusion of these sectors was logical, and the provision for negotiation stages before a strike became "licit" was not uniquely Soviet. But the general attempt was to deal with a situation already beyond direct government control.

Claims and Demands

What did the strikers want? In a sense, a great deal. Mine by mine, region by region, the lists of demands grew long, reflecting, to some degree, variations in the local situations. Where food and consumer supplies were especially bad, where the lack of soap was seen not only as a practical difficulty but an insult to a segment of the working-class aristocracy that got very dirty at work, where housing conditions were atrocious, direct government intervention was demanded. The "residual principle," whereby local needs had to be financed by the net earnings of the coal associations, gave way to commitments from the state to improve situations long ignored by local and central officials.

Several broad demands commonly arose. Delivery of the 20–40 percent swing and night-shift supplements had been conditional on the enterprise—not the state budget—financing it. This was a condition not acceptable to the miners. The government gave in on this point; the state budget would provide the supplements. Pay for travel time down to the coal face and up again was another demand: hours per day had been spent in this work-related activity, but left uncompensated. Again, these demands were met, as were grievances about pension policy and administration. "Met," in the context of July–August 1989, meant the government was to fulfill such demands— "promissory notes" on whose delivery many miners would later take a very different line from government spokesmen. Broader and more general yet—and going to the heart of the economic context of miners' more specific grievances—were demands for the independence of mines, or small groups of mines located close to one another, as free-standing "state enterprises."

"Enterprise independence" as a general proposition had been a prime element in perestroika as it began to assume a more structured shape.[138] But moving toward it, despite a long set of enabling decrees that accompanied the 1987 state enterprise law, proved very slow and difficult. Most mines were components of associations or amalgamations encompassing many mines, which in turn answered to the coal ministry. A "successful" mine—one that met and exceeded its target for tons of coal delivered—was not necessarily a happy mine. Wages, and the funds to finance welfare, housing construction, and the local infrastructure were, supposedly, dependent on "results."

Ministries and associations, however, took a good deal of the "results"—results to which they had made, in the miners' eyes, no contribution. In Kemerovo, for example, five mines earned 39 million rubles through the first half of 1989. After taxes to the state, and the excision of further funds by the Yuzhkuzbassugol association to which they were subordinated, and by the Kuzbassugol amalgamation to which the association answered, the mines were left with only 2.2 million rubles.[139] Successful mines saw their earnings creamed off to support weaker, less productive mines.

Thus the strike committees generally demanded "independence"— which in this context had multiple meanings. Independence required at least the possibility of self-financing; but the state's low procurement price for coal in many cases did not offer this. Avaliani complained that mines that were being paid one-third the world price for the coal they mined were being told they were unprofitable.[140]

Independence, then, meant the mine's ability to deal with the state on a more equal basis (that is, get more for its product) and to decide to whom it would sell at least part of the product. Cutting back on the volume of fixed-price state orders (goszakazy) was critical. In Donetsk such orders accounted for 95 percent of production and were to be cut back to 90 percent for 1990. Avaliani demanded that mines be allowed to sell 30 percent of their coal abroad at world prices.[141] But state orders would necessarily remain large—domestic prices had to rise. The settlements raised the procurement price by almost 50 percent generally. Still, many mines would need a 100–200 percent increase to become "profitable" and hence independent.[142]

Strikers had called for a cutting of the administrative staffs at the mines and associations. This demand was in line with the streamlining emphasis of perestroika, but also, presumably, came out of a conviction that administrators had nothing to do with the production of coal. Two months after the strike settlement, coal minister Shchadov claimed that a cut of 20 percent at the mines and 30 percent at the associations, combined with the dismissal of many directors and engineers at the demand of strike committees, had made for general disorganization.[143]

If Shchadov was dissatisfied, so, even earlier, were the miners. On September 11, forty leaders of the strike committees had met in Moscow to form a national union of the committees and to present their demand to the miners' union plenum for a national role similar to that gained by local strike committees in many local unions. The official union offered the strike leaders ninety-seven votes; current members of the union's Central Committee had another ninety-seven votes, and five "swing" votes would be held by members of the Council of People's Deputies. This solution made it clear that union officialdom had a hard time letting go, and strike leaders debated whether to strike again on October 1 to protest the slow implementation of the agreements.[144]

Political demands were evident as well, though the Soviet press, at first, soft-pedaled them (and indeed, out of prudence, confusion, "populist legitimism," and honest disagreement, many if not most miners avoided them). The dominant Soviet press theme was that miners had "sent packing" the out-of-town dissidents who came to the strikers' meetings in the town squares with political agendas to broaden the base of miner protest. This according to the media, in Makeevka, in Karaganda, and in the Kuzbass overall.[145]

But this was not the whole story. If the measure of a political demand is that it goes beyond economic concerns per se, or raises economic demands that are, in the context of perestroika, opposed to articles of the reform, then we have evidence of both. Strikers frequently complained of cooperative stores and their practices: in Donetsk, for example, the demand that the co-ops be closed was the first one the local powers granted, and, given their anti-enterprise prejudices, granted quite readily. At times of shortage and inflation, retail-trading cooperatives offend workers most. It is not clear that market principles are accepted in general; but their rejection need not preclude demands by miners to sell *their* coal at a profit, while the profits of cooperators are cut. This is "politics," and political demands need not be consistent.

Some demands suggested that some strikers tied the source of their economic deprivations and grievances to aspects of the political system itself. In Chervonograd in the more "nationalist" western Ukraine, miners apparently called for the establishment of an independent, Solidarity-type union—a rather different proposition from taking control of AUCCTU organs.[146] (It was, indeed, to a representative of the Ukrainian "Helsinki Group" from Lvov—the main city of the western Ukraine—that miners in Makeevka, in the *east* Ukrainian Donbass, gave their rebuff.)[147] The strongest political demands arose in Vorkuta in the arctic Pechora basin, an area essentially first settled as part of Stalin's *gulag*, about which a journalist, after the long Vorshagorskaia strike, wrote that "an historic tradition—a division into those who produce and those who guard—is felt even now."[148] Moscow television made it clear on July 24 that the strikers in Vorkuta were demanding "power to the soviets, the factories to the workers, land to the peasants" and calling for the abolition of the 750 nonelective "organizational" seats in the Congress of People's Deputies, direct elections to all offices, and the abolition of Article 6 of the Constitution, which guaranteed the party's leading role in Soviet politics.[149]

Were these really political demands, or were they emotional expressions of an overall "rejectionist" view of the system, using controversial symbols? For our purposes, it matters little. *Some* workers, at least, were finding distinctly political voices, speaking, without evident prompting by the "intelligentsia," the same way as radical deputies were speaking in Moscow. As much as can be judged at this distance, the striking miners were divided in most areas over *how* to characterize their demands and about the organizations they had created. While one miner in Novokuznetsk declared that "we are the new Solidarity," the chairman of his strike committee demurred, noting that the Gdansk shipyard workers of 1980 had political demands, while the miners' demands were economic.[150] In Donetsk when the strikes began, the miners were afraid of being perceived as trying to establish a new "party" or an independent trade union; they did not want to behave as some people did in the Baltic republics.

But a fear of appearing provocative vis-à-vis the authorities suggests that the "populist legitimism" is more "tactical" than real—that workers (miners, at least) were moving beyond the constraints, psychological as well as physical, of previous times. Miners' demands, actions, and organizational innovations were eminently political. What could be more political than a spontaneous, concerted, self-organization out of which an occupational group, in the Soviet context, made claims on the state, negotiated promises from it, and stayed organized to monitor the state's compliance?

Worker Power

As the press emphasized in July, in coal town after coal town, the miners were "in control." In most mines, strike committees detailed skeleton crews below ground for safety and maintenance purposes. Above ground, workers patrolled the streets to keep public order, often jointly with the police. The strike committees typically demanded closure of liquor stores. It was reported that the strike committee was "keeping order" in Mezhdurechensk; that in Dnepropetrovsk the "mine workers themselves maintain[ed] public order"; so also in Karaganda, while in Vorkuta, the miners' committee had "already largely supplanted the organs of official power."[151]

That the press could blandly offer such a factual description, that the tone could be so approving, said something of how far the press had come, how far the Gorbachev reformers had gone in making their own program hostage to grass-roots forces they did not wish to, could not readily criticize, and how powerful those grass-roots forces were in July. Gorbachev noted in addressing the Supreme Soviet that the miners' manner was "responsible, disciplined, and organized. . . . The working class is displaying a very high level of organization."[152]

The spin on the story, then, emphasized the maturity, organization, and moderation the miners showed in managing strike activity, as well as the alignment of miners' grievances and objectives with perestroika (much similar to the line taken on the late winter-spring strikes), even as the damage of strikes per se to the economy was also noted. As the miners established cross-mine and cross-region linkages, and as strike committees became *workers'* committees to oversee the implementation of the settlements, the projections grew broader: the future political role of organized workers was presented in the press as both welcome and inevitable.

Moscow television on July 26 reported the "certainty" that those who had distinguished themselves as strike committee leaders would be elected to union, party, and local soviet posts.[153] *Sovetskaia Rossiia* predicted that the strike committees would not yield their power to local soviets "elected" under the old system: who, it asked, could now remember whom he voted for then?[154]

These predictions were safe enough, and accurate. In the Donetsk area,[155] the party (*gorkom*) secretaries in three cities were replaced, their successors elected in competitive elections. In the Gorkii mine, a new STK was elected, with only two of its sixty-two members being "held over" from the pre-strike council, and twenty-three of the new members also being members of the strike committee. The new STK, as foreseen in the provision introduced in the 1987 Law on the State Enterprise, organized elections for a new mine director—nearly the whole administration was replaced. In the Kapital'naia mine, the new STK voted no confidence in the top three bosses and held elections for new ones. Trade union committees fell as well. The Gorkii mine, having cleaned out its STK and management, retained only four of thirty-five members of the old committee; another area mine elected a totally new committee.

Much of this revealed miners' relish for the exercise of the working-class power they were always supposed to have possessed. The old poster-art proletarian was acknowledged as a fake. *Pravda* declared that "the working class has boldly, exactingly, and unambiguously declared its existence."[156] To a degree, a worker anti-intelligentsia contempt for those with "clean hands" was evident. In some STK elections, workers showed a disinclination to elect *any* "engineering-technical personnel." However broadly such manifestations of class "identity" and "opposition" might be exhibited, one rather clear result was that the *nomenklatura* system's monopoly on designating persons for the various management, union, and even STK posts had been severely weakened. *Sotsialisticheskaia industriia* also noted a certain amount of anti-elitism on the workers' part, and made the point with some surprise that virtually all the leaders had "no more" than secondary education. This statement missed the point that earlier generations of workers had fallen far short of that much education, and that some miners, however anti-elitist, had called in consultants with specialized expertise: the paper did not draw the parallel between this and the similar move of the Polish shipyard workers in Gdansk in 1980.[157]

Everything pointed to greater political "clout" for the workers as summer gave way to fall. The question was whether, in the pursuit of what more and more workers were coming to see as class interests, those capacities would be lined up in the support of reform (as the press generally emphasized) or directed (manipulated?) along lines of a conservative/populist critique of the reform's ultimate social goals and "Russian" objections to several facets of contemporary politics. Both the AUCCTU and a new political organization would seek roles in creating an answer.

The Unions: "Activism" Reasserted

In the wake of the strikes, while local trade union committees in the coal towns were being taken over by the strike committees, the national AUCCTU leadership, still in place, asserted anew its intention and claim to wear the mantle of the defender of working-class interests. If there was still something vaguely amusing about this conversion, given how little the spring rhetoric amounted to compared to the July strikes, there was also some real basis for the move: declining economic performance was indeed hitting the workers hard and demanded, potentially, especially much of workers in traditionally favored industries. Did large numbers of workers tend to connect perestroika and economic decline as cause and effect? Was the union leadership attempting to exploit such feelings in order to block reform and to claim a larger role in the changing political context? The September AUCCTU plenum took a hard line on cooperatives, endorsing them in principle but limiting that approval to those that sold their goods at prices equivalent to those in state stores.[158] The new draft statute for the AUCCTU, sent to the Supreme Soviet later that month, proposed giving the union not only oversight rights over co-op practices, but also powers to veto plant closings, reverse "unjustified" price increases, and play a major role in deciding how a plant's profits were to be spent, while a top AUCCTU official argued that the union body should have the right to veto Moscow decisions that ran counter to the social and economic interests of workers' collectives.[159]

Through the fall, and into the 1989–90 winter, AUCCTU and republican union spokesmen and leaders concentrated on economic issues, taking a combative stance in a claim for credibility. A new note was that of unions (and, by implication, workers) embattled, but now going on the offensive. A *Trud* writer attacked the reform economist Shmelev's accusation that the unions were leaning backward to favor the "administrative-command" system. It was, in fact, union defense of workers' *rights* that was scaring some people, who might otherwise more easily impose on them a near-wage freeze while prices continued to rise.[160]

Retail prices were not the only issue. Beginning January 1, 1990, state-set *wholesale* charges for goods transport, diesel fuel, electric power, and other industrial inputs rose sharply—with no authorization for enterprises to "pass on" their increased costs. As *Trud* put it, the funds for wage supplements, as well as other benefits associated with a plant's profit, would thus be cut—"for this reason . . . serious labor conflicts are coming to a head that could entail unpredictable social consequences, substantial losses, and a further worsening of the economic situation."[161] The AUCCTU protested the price hikes to the Council of Ministers, as did the Ukrainian union council.[162] On February 9, four days after a promised deadline for a ministerial decision on the union protest, the Council of Ministers rolled back the price increases and offered various forms of compensation. *Pravda's* coverage depicted a government apologetic to the unions for an ill-thought-out move, and along the way credited the AUCCTU with less publicized but real, "principled" disagreements with the government in the recent past, on which the spotlight of glasnost' had not been turned.[163]

Was this authentic worker/union "clout"? To a degree, certainly. With no wholesale market, but massive and growing problems, it fell to the government to declare higher prices for what were loss-making goods and services. Minister of Finance Pavlov was left to explain the measures, to say (five days before the rollback) that "we cannot cancel" the rises, and to claim that the AUCCTU had participated in all stages leading to the price-hike decision. Later it was asserted that the AUCCTU had disagreed all along. It got its way, backed or spurred by spontaneous worker protests about the impact of the price rises on the pay packet.[164]

But there was a fair measure of fakery and demagoguery as well. The Moscow city union council organized a mass public rally to back the position taken at the September AUCCTU plenum. At what *Izvestiia* characterized as a "stormy" session, speakers denounced reform economists and cooperatives. Anti-elitist and "leveling" sentiments were expressed in calls by some for a currency reform that would exchange only a maximum of 10,000 rubles and treat the rest, *ipso facto*, as "unearned." The newspaper itself had been one of the institutions called on by a union rally organizer, who requested that it send—in the old style—a certain number of participants to the rally. *Izvestiia's* verdict: the unions were seeking to regain mass trust by appealing to emotions and sentiments "in the public square."[165]

"Union politics," then, cut two ways. There *were* authentic worker issues and grievances that the AUCCTU, in the post-July atmosphere, was free to support and articulate—indeed *had* to—to justify its new claim to defend the blue-collar population. On the other hand, and allowing for the increasingly chaotic political atmosphere in which economic decisions were being made, the unions were coming down against elements of reform, pushed by a government cross-pressured by various forces with which perestroika had not really come to grips. Energy supply and transport could not be left, indefinitely, in a loss-making situation (especially as, in the settlement of the July strikes, the cost of the coal to make the electricity had already increased). Thus prices for these were raised to consuming plants, whose options were either to live with higher costs and less profits or (hypothetically) to raise their prices, creating a knock-on effect of further inflation in an economy where rising retail prices were straining popular morale. For the government, for the unions, the situation constrained decisions to the relatively short-term, the "reactive." It would have been hard, indeed, for the AUCCTU to adopt the long view—especially since, as it turned out, the government caved in so easily on the price issue.

Internal union politics, and perhaps an attempt to enhance credibility, led to a turnover in the AUCCTU leadership in April 1990. Gennadi Ianaev, who as no. 2 in the union had said that the unions either "radically reorganize or workers would create different structures to uphold their rights and social interests,"[166] was elected on April 17 to replace the retiring Shalaev. There was, however, little evidence of a democratizing revolt in the changeover. As *Izvestiia* somewhat ironically reported, it took only thirty-three minutes at the beginning of the AUCCTU plenum for Shalaev to express his wish to retire, for this to be accepted, for four candidates for the succession to be presented, three of these to withdraw, and Ianaev to accept election—and then, after ten minutes, to deliver an hour-long report on plans for the next union congress.[167]

From April on, Ianaev and the AUCCTU—facing increasingly volatile union politics in the provinces independent of the official union, including the founding of a broad Confederation of Labor in Novokuznetsk at the end of April[168]—continued much the same worker-defense line. This involved the explicit defense, while denying that the union was anti-market or pro-leveling, of a "social contract," which would do the utmost to protect full employment, a minimum income, index wages to the broad price rises anticipated from a reform expected to take a tougher turn, and maximize compensation to vulnerable groups. The difficulty was that the "tough" reform rhetoric to which Gorbachev gave voice in May 1990, though his major advisers made it clear that it was not the "shock therapy" the Poles had endured since the beginning of the year, did come as a shock to the Soviet public, and set off a wave of panic buying in late May. No AUCCTU "social contract" was really reconcilable with it. Gorbachev's new chief economic adviser, Petrakov, accused the unions of wanting "to accumulate political capital at the cost of socioeconomic demagoguery."[169] Ianaev rejected the accusation, and claimed that mass strikes would have occurred earlier in 1990 had it not been for the union's intervention with the government over the wholesale price issues noted earlier. He presented the unions as now quite independent of the party and ready to encompass both leaders and members of "various party allegiances."[170]

"Proletarian" Conservatism

Few developments in working-class politics in 1989–90 were so interesting—and potentially alarming—as the emergence of what looked like worker movement against elements of political and economic reform on a broad scale, whether it was authentic or manipulated.

There certainly was growing worker discontent with the deteriorating economic situation, and just as certainly there were some anti-reform leaders who made assessments of how that discontent might be used. The current that would see the founding in September 1989 of the United Front of Workers of Russia drew on deep-rooted political strains and symbolism, as well as more free-floating resentments.

The spring 1989 campaign and elections to the new Congress of People's Deputies had taken place in hard economic times—especially hard for workers and rank-and-file citizens. They had produced a smaller percentage of worker and peasant representation than in the old-style, uncontested Supreme Soviet elections. This became a populist talking point, a focus of anti-elite, anti-intelligentsia (and hence, to a degree, anti-reform) sentiments. (Such sentiments had some real base on the factory floor. A 1987–88 survey of two thousand workers and six hundred technical and managerial white-collar employees in the machine-building industry showed that only 19.4 percent of the workers felt the latter were entitled to higher pay than they, while fully 72.6 percent thought white-collar people deserved less, or at most [25.3 percent] *equal* pay.)[171] Leningrad, especially, was a locus of such complaints, and Solov'ev, the party leader rejected by the voters for a seat while running unopposed, had reason to be unhappy. It was in Leningrad, in June, that a "United Workers' Front," drawing delegates from six republics and eighteen cities, established itself[172] on a predominantly ethnic Russian basis. The agenda was *ouvrièriste*: anti-cooperative, vocal on worker discontent, anti-worker "prejudice," and favoring guarantees of worker representation in legislative bodies.

The Leningrad worker front was created at virtually the same time as a pro-perestroika "Popular Front." The local party leadership backed the former and opposed the latter, as did conservative newspapers and some Russian nationalist organizations.[173] The workers' front, touching both on the economic interests of workers and on the symbolic politics of representation, called for the upcoming 1990 local soviet elections to be based on "production districts"—that is, to assign two-thirds of the seats to factory-based constituencies as a way of ensuring the workers' leading role. Later in the year, at a session of the RSFSR Supreme Soviet, Leningrad workers, with the backing of the trade union committees of many large plants, supported the production district idea for the 1990 RSFSR republican, as well as local, elections.[174]

The issue, however much it may have tapped the authentic concerns of some segments of the working class, proved to be a loser. Against AUCCTU endorsement and politicking at the RSFSR Supreme Soviet session, the idea was generally rejected in favor of territorial constituencies and allowed only in a few districts on an experimental basis; nor was it, ultimately, included in the Leningrad party organization's platform.[175] How broad the support, in worker or general public opinion, may have been for production districts is unclear, but on the whole appears low: one poll found 40 percent in favor, 37.2 percent against, and 22.8 percent expressing "no opinion."[176] In a review of its mail, *Izvestiia* acknowledged widespread anti-intelligentsia feelings among workers, but—similar to arguments made earlier in the year after the Congress of People's Deputies elections—dismissed the idea that automatic representation of workers *by* worker delegates had given workers very much. The miners' strikes were evidence of this, and had also shown "how organized the workers are and how able they are to defend their interests in the square."[177]

More volatile was the action in that part of the expanding political arena where national-ethnic concerns of Russian blue-collar workers meshed with socioeconomic grievances. The "servicing" of the RSFSR by some all-union institutions rather than its own—taken in the past by some as evidence of Russian domination and a tendency in Moscow to equate "Soviet" with "Russian"—now, in the case of the absence of an RSFSR republican party organization, and similar absence of an RSFSR Trade Union Council, was taken as evidence of discrimination. The AUCCTU September plenum approved a call for such an organization, so that 76 million workers "unrepresented" by a republican council now would be represented.[178] While the technical issue was territorial rather than ethnic, the vast majority of the RSFSR population is ethnically Russian, and the percentage of the republic's workers and employees is similar—82.6 and 82.0 percent, respectively.[179]

Two broad streams were feeding into Russian worker discontent. The less questionable in its authenticity was the political resentment of large numbers of Russian industrial workers outside the RSFSR of the independence/autonomy-oriented popular fronts in the republics where they live. In the Baltic republics and in Moldavia, the moves toward making the indigenous languages the official languages, and toward local election and citizenship statutes that might relegate nonindigenous people to second-class status, agitated Russians (and, one can presume, the smaller populations of Belorussians and Ukrainians in non-Slav republics whose identity tends to merge with the Russian). In the Baltics especially, while governmental/cultural/academic positions were in the hands of the indigenous nationalities, large-scale heavy industry was manned by large cadres of Russian workers, their availability having been part of the economic rationale for building large industrial complexes in the small Baltic nations. Far from being the colonial "elite," the Russian workers came to see themselves as rank-and-file citizens, whose "right" to work and residence in other SSRs, long taken for granted, was now an issue. Added to whatever discomforts economic perestroika might impose on them as workers, the local political environments, with little intervention from Moscow, had turned hostile. Symbolic and real political "insult" led to the formation of essentially ethnic Russian- or Slav-based "international fronts" (Interfronts) to counter the Estonians', Latvians', and Lithuanians' ethnic-based "popular fronts." Strikes and protests became part of the Interfront repertoire, although the strikes were political rather than "economic" in their underlying rationale. Nothing in the political developments of 1989 or 1990 in the non-Russian SSRs gave such workers much to take comfort in. Those developments *did* spur support for Russian self-assertion, RSFSR "secessionism" and autonomy.

On the other hand, within the RSFSR (and the heavy-industry, heavily Russian and "Russified" eastern Ukraine), more purely "class" and economic grievances were evident. While in the Baltic, in

Moldavia, in other republics, shared ethnic-national concerns moderated any "intelligentsia vs. working mass" conflict, in the RSFSR a working class that was on the whole less entrepreneurial than the one in the Baltic found more to complain about in a reform driven by Russian leaders. They faced economic problems at least as acute as in any other republic, and *could* blame a Moscow-initiated reform for them. It was as well an erosion of the Russian nationality's place in the scheme of things, an erosion in which a General Secretary "tolerant" of disorders seemed, along with his elite/intelligentsia allies, to connive.

Out of this complex of issues emerged the United Front of Workers of Russia (Ob"edinennyi Front Trudiashchikhsia Rossii, or OFTR), in a founding meeting in the Ural heavy-industrial heartland city of Sverdlovsk on September 8–9, 1989.[180] Representatives of labor collectives from twenty-nine different RSFSR cities and of international-front organizations from Estonia, Latvia, Moldavia, and Tadzhikistan—110 in all—gathered in the city to declare a program that stood against "developing completely unjustifiable market relations in the economy." Cochairman of the front was Veniamin Iarin, a Nizhnyi Tagil metalworker, a charismatic and telegenic member of the Congress of People's Deputies and the Supreme Soviet. Iarin had been critical of cooperatives, the black market, inflation, and other pains of perestroika: open in asserting that workers were worse off under the reform; insistent that the new legislative institutions underrepresented workers and their interests (OFTR, of course, supported "production district" elections); and combative in his rhetoric in a "class" sense. Against those who argued that groups and classes in Soviet society did not, or should not, exist in a context of conflicting interests, Iarin asked, "Who today will defend the working person if not the working person himself?"[181] That anti-reform politicians were manipulating the OFTR for their own purposes was clear enough: as the sociologist Yuri Levada put it, they were trying to give conservative populism a proletarian overtone.[182]

Yet OFTR did articulate some deep, if inchoate, feelings of Russian rank-and-file workers: egalitarianism, anti-elitism, and suspicion of "foreign capital" and fear of exploitation by it as the world penetrates the Soviet economy. (OFTR was instrumental for a time in forcing a reversal of the decision to turn the city of Novgorod into a "special economic zone," playing on local fears and hinting that the capital investments required might be drawn from locals' pockets rather than from Western investors.)[183] There *is* a feeling of "Russia and Russians last" in the minds of those confused by *perestroika*, political reform, and ethnic separatism. Economic and political themes merged in the words of one worker from an aircraft plant in Kuibyshev, at a meeting of Central Committee worker members and Gorbachev in September: "We started to talk about Russia only recently when the strikes began." He observed that Kuibyshev *oblast'* was, after all, economically larger than the whole of Estonia, yet it had been much deprived, like all the strike-prone regions of the summer. "Socially, however, the population's living standard is considerably worse than it is in the Baltic republics. That's not right."[184]

In December 1989, in anticipation of the March 1990 RSFSR elections, the OFTR joined with other Russian nationalist organizations to construct a platform for the Bloc of Russian Public-Patriotic Movements, which was published in the conservative *Literaturnaia Rossiia*. Among its economic planks were condemnations of the "uncontrolled market mechanism" and "legalization of private property," and demands that the RSFSR cease subsidizing other republics to elevate their living standards; that interrepublic "fair trade" be established; and that subsidies be made to the RSFSR for the use of its territory to house USSR governmental bodies and organizations. It stood firm for "socialism": "The economy of Soviet Russia is founded on public ownership. That choice was made in 1917 by the people themselves, and no parliament and no government is legally entitled to change it."[185]

The bloc failed to make any headway in the RSFSR elections.[186] Elections, however, are only a partial index of the volatility of "worker politics" and their linkage to the concerns of the Russian majority. Gorbachev, in assembling his Presidential Council after assuming the new office of USSR President and being sensitive to the worker issue, brought Iarin on as a member of the body. Was he co-opted as "decoration" to protect Gorbachev's flank? Or as a counterbalance to the thoroughly reformist economist member, Shatalin (who asserted that the people did *not* "choose" socialism in 1917)?[187] Iarin made it clear that he saw his role as more than symbolic;[188] all in all, he seemed little fazed by the failure of the bloc at the ballot box, attributing it to "natural political life."[189]

Against the conservative populism, other organizations arose whose working-class pedigree was less suspect. They ranged from the Union of Kuzbass Working People founded in late 1989 on the basis of the earlier miner militancy, to the Confederation of Labor created in Novokuznetsk in May 1990 by 268 delegates of about fifty organizations at the first all-union congress of independent workers' organizations, a congress to which the AUCCTU had refused to contribute any travel funds.[190]

The year 1990, on the whole, was one of continuing descent into economic crisis and political disorder. The government narrowly averted a strike in late March–early April in the critical Tiumen' oil and gas fields in western Siberia, which could have idled 700,000 workers producing 60 percent of the USSR's oil and gas. At issue were much the same concerns as in the miners' strikes: food supply, housing, control over the sale of the valuable resource to finance improvements for its extractors.[191] This would have added to the burden borne by an economy which, according to one report, had already lost 9.1 million man-days in strikes, "ethnic" and economic, in the first two months of 1990, compared to less than 8 million for all of 1989.[192] Production was down, in absolute terms, in 1990; "income" was up, as unspendable rubles were added to the already massive overhang.

Gorbachev's leadership had before it evidence that tough reform could work. An example was the Polish "shock therapy" of the Balcerowicz plan, which finally broke excess demand by letting inflation rates ride astronomically from the first of the year via price decontrol, and saw prices then stabilize at the beginning of spring. But, as Gorbachev's economic advisers and spokesmen made clear, this action was not to be pursued in the USSR. The Poles had, after all, *chosen* their post-Soviet-bloc government, and Poles, in Petrakov's words, find it easier to "accept high prices rather than empty shelves," while all the data indicated that the majority of Soviet citizens stood at the "exact opposite" point: they would "accept rationing and waiting in line, especially during working hours, as long as prices do not rise."[193]

Gorbachev, on a trip to blue-collar Sverdlovsk and Nizhnyi Tagil in late April (accompanied by Iarin), assured the workers at the giant Uralmash complex that no precipitate increase in retail prices would come without prior, extended discussion: otherwise, said the president and general secretary, "You will simply throw us out in a couple of weeks."[194] Several days later, Gorbachev made sympathetic comments in a visit to a Moscow clock factory, connected with his candidacy for delegate to the Twenty-eighth CPSU Congress in July in the city's Frunze district. He was elected, with a very lukewarm 61 percent of the vote. A month earlier, the Supreme Soviet had been presented a draft law to cancel the "elective principle" for enterprise directors: for in "civilized countries," as one official put it, the selection of directors was "determined from the standpoint of the owner's interests," and the USSR was now looking toward a multiplicity of *non*state ownership forms.[195]

For all the talk of no "shock therapy," of a transition, instead, to a "regulated market," the news for the population in late spring turned hard again. What was billed as Prime Minister Ryzhkov's reform plan—rather than Gorbachev's—specified that prices must, and would, rise, still under state control, but enough so that the prices of many food items would double on January 1, 1991, and bread would triple in price on July 1, *1990*. Would the compensation to the public, to be paid out of funds saved from the reduced price subsidies, be sufficient? Ianaev and the AUCCTU threatened the use of the strike weapon if wages were not indexed to inflation and if employment was not guaranteed. In the event, the Ryzhkov plan was rejected by the Supreme Soviet, leaving competing reform designs to be debated through the summer, and messily compromised in the fall.

At the Twenty-eighth Party Congress, Gorbachev emerged a "winner," in that he laid claim to the General Secretary post and was confirmed in it. The need to keep hold of—and submit to the continuing hold of—the party, however, signaled the partiality of his victory. The party was hardly an instrument of reform. It was rather an obstacle that he could not afford to walk away from. The party no longer enjoyed a constitutionally mandated leading role; the Politburo was not what it had once been, but it was still organized and possessed of significant resources. At the Congress, Ianaev of the AUCCTU was elected to the Politburo and as a secretary of the Central Committee and resigned his union post, leaving a vacancy to be filled at the October congress of the AUCCTU. Within the party, Ianaev, together with RSFSR General Secretary Polozkov and the Leningrad party leader Boris Gidaspov, also elected as a secretary of the Central Committee, looked like a potential leader of a "worker-oriented" faction, backing reform to be sure, but pushing precisely the sort of moderation in its introduction that would in fact complicate it. Polozkov's conservative views were clear, and Gidaspov had played his politics in a way not unlike his predecessor Solov'ev, although he had been vociferous in his support of Gorbachev as general secretary and president.

During the party congress, workers had once again dramatized their presence as a political force. On July 11, the coal miners of the Kuzbass, Donbass, and the Far North mounted a one-day, previously announced strike on the first anniversary of the onset of 1989's hot summer. The style was more "controlled," but also more political, than a year earlier. Demands included the resignation of the Ryzhkov government, the ending of party penetration of mines, other enterprises, the army police, and the KGB. The party's assets, the miners demanded, should be nationalized. In Donetsk, the strikers adopted national slogans and demanded Ukrainian independence. Such demands had been absent in this Russified eastern Ukrainian area in 1989.

Given what seemed to be a combination of alarm and paralysis among the leadership, the alteration between recognition that tough economic measures were necessary ("prices must rise") and fear of mass militant reaction to those measures ("society will explode"), hard decisions on the how and what of reform did not come easy in the autumn of 1990. In September the Supreme Soviet debated reform options—a modification of the earlier-rejected Ryzhkov/government plan versus the reform economist Shatalin's "500-day" plan. Aganbegian, who headed a commission to study the alternatives and make recommendations among them, made it clear to a Supreme Soviet committee on September 14 that the Shatalin plan must be taken as the major base of reform. More "radical" economically over the long run, it also allowed for the degrees of autonomy and sovereignty most union republics had already claimed, as the Ryzhkov plan did not.[196]

The two plans were indeed very different, but while the necessity of reform was accepted, the articulators of "working-class interests" qualified their acceptance and seemed to duck the issue of choice between the alternatives. Iarin, in a September 11 interview, asserted that the two plans *had* a good deal in common, and warned that the blue-collar workers were less well-placed to enter the new economy than other groups that had "taken advantage" of the legal confusion and economic chaos of recent times.[197] I. Klochkov, the chairman of the new Russian republic union federation (FNPR)—by name an independent body but in fact based on the old official union organizations in the RSFSR—"accepted" the Shatalin plan in principle, but then laid out an ambitious list of requirements with respect to guarantees on wages, pensions, and employment security that would surely be as hard to deliver under any reform variant as they were obviously eroding at present.[198]

On September 25, the Supreme Soviet gave Gorbachev the additional special presidential powers he had requested, and deferred the day of decision on the reform alternatives until October 15. Gorbachev's economic adviser Petrakov, somewhat frustrated, observed that even after discussion, the two plans seemed to be placed on an equal plane again. Thus, matters were at an impasse, even though the much-reformulated government plan still included the "command" food price increases for 1991, and 100 percent planned compensation for these that could only be delivered by printing more dubious rubles and inviting hyperinflation,[199] whereas the Shatalin plan allowed for a period of stabilization and price controls on essentials, while promising, via privatization, devaluation, and tough controls on the money supply, deeper surgery by far on the sick economy.

What emerged, finally, on October 16, was a compromise plan, adopting in principle more of the radicalism of the Shatalin strategy, but—in failing to impose any hard timetable for stages of the transition—giving eloquent testimony to the hesitations and fears of those who lacked confidence that any radical move could be other than destabilizing to society. October, thus, was not a month of choice, but of failure to choose, of failure to give perestroika the programmatic content appropriate to dealing with looming economic crisis.

A week later, the AUCCTU gathered for its Eighteenth Congress, and on October 24 voted to dissolve itself—but also for a "rebirth" as the General Confederation of Trade Unions of the USSR (VKP, or Vseobshchaia Konfederatsiia Profsoiuzov, SSSR). V. P. Shcherbakov, AUCCTU deputy chairman and acting head since Ianaev's departure for the Politburo, became head of the new VKP. Gorbachev and Ryzhkov both had addressed the congress, with speeches more notable for their rhetoric of alarm about economic crisis and their sober-yet-sympathetic tone on worker concerns than for any real specificity. The trade unionists' rhetoric was weighted as well with a "realism" about the likely pains of economic transition, but was here mixed with requests for state guarantees against some of the very pains that would realistically be expected in the areas of unemployment, wages, prices, and new, nonstate forms of ownership. The swiftness of the union's death and rebirth as the VKP, despite all the criticism of the old centralist, "transmission belt" AUCCTU and the pious profession of a new decentralized, autonomous spirit, was understandably reminiscent to some of a stubborn rearrangement of the deck chairs on a *Titanic* foundering in rough political seas. (Miners were largely absent, convening instead in their own congress far from Moscow in Kuznetsk. After some no-holds-barred debate, a majority voted to establish a quite independent miners' union.)

On the whole, 1990 had not, however, been a year of labor militancy to match 1989. Strikes were frequent, but the vast majority of the days lost to labor stoppages were attributable to national-ethnic, rather than class-economic, protest. No other branch of industry proved so radical as had the miners. Perhaps the organizational impulses of suffering and disgruntled blue-collar citizens were overwhelmed by the economic collapse all around them.

In this, they may have shared an experience with Gorbachev and his friends and foes in the political leadership. The slow but accelerating drift of the president and general secretary into a combination of defensiveness and assertiveness, a grim conviction that "the center must hold at all costs," looked like a reprise of other stories of failed reform. A decision to loosen the deadening hold of the state had unleashed social forces that drove the reformer backward into the arms of the "party of order." Gorbachev in December was a leader praised in the West, courted for Soviet solidarity in the front against Iraq's Saddam Hussein, while increasingly reviled at home by reformers and reactionaries alike. Still, it seemed to be more toward the latter, their perceptions and fears of nationalist secession and social chaos, that he tilted. A government reorganization effectively abolished the old Council of Ministers, concentrating more power in Gorbachev's hands. The hard-line Boris Pugo replaced the relatively liberal Bakatin at the interior ministry. The voices of the military and the KGB grew louder. Gorbachev's longtime ally Shevardnadze tendered a surprise resignation from the foreign minister's post, protesting the drift toward "dictatorship." The lackluster Ianaev proved Gorbachev's choice as vice-president and was pushed through on the second-try vote of an unenthusiastic and divided Congress of People's Deputies. Society as well seemed divided, demoralized, likely reflective of the workers' mood. The year 1990 ended on a note of continuing, never-ending crisis, but with a promise—or threat—that the crisis was coming to a head, and approaching some sort of resolution.

Epilogue _____

We do not trust the Soviet president or
government who have led the country to
collapse.
  (*A Donetsk strike leader*, April 6, 1991)

We are prepared today to cooperate with any
public forces and movements, especially the
trade unions. . . . We should like to be
clearly understood. The USSR Government,
with its fifty-three members, might be replaced or eliminated altogether if that is better for the country. I also admit that.
  (*Prime Minister V.S. Pavlov*, April 11, 1991)

MAY DAY, 1991, saw a subdued observance—it could hardly be called
a celebration—of the traditional workers' holiday in Red Square. Gorbachev, without the Politburo, stood on Lenin's tomb, flanked instead
mainly by representatives of the official trade union, the VKP. The
smallish number of those who marched past, having been organized
and issued signs by the VKP, bore slogans such as "No to Price Rises
and Unemployment" and "Out with the Sales tax." As civic ritual, it
was half-hearted and understated, and *obviously so*. The placards said
essentially no more than the union had been saying in its demands to
the Supreme Soviet: that reform was necessary, but that it should
somehow come without negative impact on security of employment
and the cost of living. There were few political signs (unlike on May 1,
1990, when, after the official parade, another spontaneous march had
coursed through the square with placards such as the wry one pro-
claiming, "Workers of the World, Forgive Us!"). But those that did
appear were Stalinist, anti-Semitic, xenophobic, and critical of both
Gorbachev and his rival, Yel'tsin.

Yel'tsin, after having met in a sort of "reconciliation" session with
Gorbachev the previous week, was in the Kuzbass coal region on that
same day, meeting striking miners in Novokuznetsk, ostensibly to
persuade them to end their eight-week strike. The popular Russian
politician received an enthusiastic welcome, but was also questioned
about why he had dealt with Gorbachev, whose resignation was a
prime strikers' demand. Yel'tsin made no call for a return to work,
leaving that to the miners, but signed an agreement offering the mines

of the Kuzbass more financial autonomy and a shift from USSR to Russian Republic jurisdiction—to a RFSFR whose first popularly-elected president Yel'tsin quite realistically expected to become on June 12. Whether Gorbachev, at the "center," had agreed to honor such a transfer remained to be seen.

The two scenes in Moscow and western Siberia showed contrasting aspects of the political and economic crisis that had gripped the workers, the leaders, and the whole country. It was a May Day unlike previous ones, and probably unlike any that might follow. But then, it had already been an extraordinary year.

The Year of Disintegration?

Early 1991 saw gloom deepening around an economy in crisis, a society nearly exhausted, a state increasingly the arena of unregulated conflict. Nationality tensions worsened; bloodshed in the Baltic came as a result of Gorbachev's increased tilt toward the reactionary end of the political spectrum. Gorbachev's harsher political face, whether a revelation of his own ideological limits, or an extension of his balancing act between reactionaries and reformers, still left him vulnerable to those who held him responsible for tolerating disorder too long, and to those of the opposite political persuasion who found Russia's leader, Boris Yel'tsin, an increasingly credible alternative. The referendum on March 17, asking the populace to vote, essentially, on whether the USSR should continue to exist—as the federation of sovereign states, guaranteeing citizen rights, that it had never been—was a statistical victory for Gorbachev and the "yes" party, but the results were sufficiently ambiguous to provide anything *but* an endorsement for a leader and a political course that were becoming increasingly unpopular.

On the political-economic front, the choice of Valentin Pavlov as new prime minister in Ryzhkov's place brought a classic high bureaucrat, a veteran of Gosplan, the ex-chairman of the State Committee on Prices, most recently Minister of Finance, to the highest "management" job. Nothing in Pavlov's curriculum vitae, in his own early statements, or in the near-contemptuous tones in which some of the press greeted his appointment,[1] could credibly establish his image as that of economic-reformer-by-conviction. He seemed, at best, a steady hand who would do as he was told by Gorbachev at a time when long-delayed elements of administered reform were finally on the agenda.

Wholesale prices on a span of goods had risen on January 1. In the early weeks of the year, it became clear that the much-discussed, deeply feared retail price hikes would follow. They could no longer be delayed. Were citizens, as the head of the State Committee on Prices asked in late February, "morally ready" for them?[2] Perhaps. But what had prepared them was not any fundamental psychological revolution regarding the popular views of the economy. (In a late 1990 poll, 40.2 percent of the respondents were against price rises on any basis, 33.9 percent found them acceptable if wages were raised proportionally, and only 11.9 percent were ready to see full decontrol.)[3] Rather, readiness could flow only from the fact that in many areas, for many people, for many foods and goods, state price control had already become a fiction. Fortunate workers in relatively favored plants might still buy some foods at state prices at the plants' internal distribution points; but for most people, food at state prices had disappeared from the stores and was available only at elevated prices on the free market. Factories in many branches were allowed to raise prices for their goods, and state retail outlets could pass these "exceptional" extra costs on to the consumer. Workers and their families were whipsawed by inflation and shortage.

The price reform plan, as it stood a few weeks before the April 2 date for its introduction, called for the freeing of prices on about 30 percent of all retail goods, continued control on others, and "administered" rises on other desubsidized items, including most foods. On the average, the cost of living would rise about 60 percent (though this estimate seemed modest, since so many foods would double or triple in price). A cut in taxes on enterprise profits would free funds for "compensation," to be delivered in workers' and employees' pay packets. The minimum wage rise was to be 60 rubles per month, with many provisions for larger raises. All in all, the compensation package was claimed to cover 85 percent of the impact of the average 60 percent cost-of-living increase. It was not "full" compensation but was nonetheless said to guarantee basic living standards[4]—though it seemed that the definition of basic might be proportioned to what the compensation would cover, rather than vice versa. It was no equivalent of the Polish "shock therapy" of early 1990. Prices were not freed to find their own levels; the "compensation" commitment carried the risk of the further printing of money (over which Pavlov had presided as minister of finance). It was as much, however, as a Gorbachev leadership from which virtually all reform economists had decamped was ready to do. Reviewing the plan against a background of "grave mistakes" made in 1988–90 in increasing the money in circulation while still vainly trying to control prices, an economist concluded that freeing prices completely, though "more effective economically," could "generate an extremely adverse reaction."[5] Short-term political realism thus dictated the path of controlled price hikes.

Labor reactions to the looming price increases and to the threat of unemployment if loss-making plants were closed were long, at least, on rhetoric; Shcherbakov, head of the VKP (the successor to the AUCCTU), and other leaders criticized the Supreme Soviet for slowness in acting on trade union rights, for contemplating unemployment, for failing sufficiently to guarantee payment and retraining schemes for the potentially unemployed, and for its less than 100 percent approach to price compensation.[6] At a February meeting of trade union leaders, he reminded Gorbachev that some industrial unions were calling for 70 to 100 percent wage increases as necessary compensation.[7] On January 3 the independent trade union federation of the Russian Republic (FNPR) threatened a strike call if employment was not protected and adjustment of wages to price increases was not guaranteed in two months.[8] The December 1990 first congress of "labor collective councils (STK) and workers' committees" established a "union" of these two bodies and sharply criticized any "new property forms" that would allow privatization of plants to *nomenklatura* bureaucrats (as had happened to some degree in Eastern Europe) or take away workers' rights to elect their own managers.[9] New legislation effective January 1, 1991, would take away from the STK its role—however poorly executed in the past—as an "organ of self-management," and its status would now be ambiguous, certainly weakened. Despite some reluctance, some common cause seemed to be emerging between STKs and the workers' committees, born of the 1989 strikes, that had so criticized them. This, though, was a "populism" that found it hard to come to grips with the notion that, should an enterprise cease to be state property, it could become the property of anyone but the workers themselves.[10] The Kuzbass Council of Workers' Committees, linked to the new independent coal miners' union and probably more authentic as an organ of worker representation than any of the above-mentioned bodies, encountered some confusion among workers in an unsuccessful call for a "general political strike" on January 18. Its new, *political* demands (which would resurface in the coalfield strikes that began in early March) included Gorbachev's resignation as president, the dissolution of the Congress of People's Deputies, and nationalization of party property.[11] It was, all in all, a scenario of disorder, adding to the "overload" that the beleaguered Gorbachev leadership faced in dealing with both national tensions and with the rising swell of public opinion in Moscow and elsewhere in favor of a vague but more charismatic Yel'tsin alternative.

On the factory floor, the dynamics of worker-management relations were complicated and ambiguous, neither good nor quite so conflictual overall as they might have been. A few possible reasons are worth exploring.

Factory managers, reluctant to honor their plan obligations or *gos-zakazy* for mere additions of rubles to their accounts, bargained and bartered directly with one another. While Gorbachev issued a decree against such practices,[12] a meeting of over three thousand industrial managers in December had shown managers to be angry, recalcitrant, and resistant to the very changes Gorbachev had brought earlier; one of them characterized parliamentary debates as "ugly shows" that made the country "nervous."[13] Many managers, it seemed, longed for a "strong hand," for order once more, but resisted Moscow's attempts to force *them* into line.

Workers were angry and frustrated. Rhetoric and opinion polls showed a failure of confidence in Gorbachev and the USSR government. But in fact no labor revolution had followed the hot summer of 1989 in the coalfields; what might be taken as moderation was probably linked to the further deterioration of the economic situation. It suggested an interesting reversion. As Andrew Walder argued in his stimulating study of authority relations in Chinese industry,[14] there were basic similarities in the worker-enterprise relationship in the USSR and PRC: employment was less a "market" transaction than one that provided a certain social identity and "rights to specific distributions and welfare entitlements"[15] to workers, while implying a greater degree of factory-exercised state control over them than under any variety of capitalism.

But in the richer USSR, in the post-Stalin period, worker dependency on the factory and factory control over the worker had eroded greatly when compared to China. China's vast labor surplus stood in sharp contrast to the USSR's labor shortage—Soviet workers' "tenure" was assured, while jobs in the Chinese state sector were pearls of some price. China's relative poverty subjected many foods and simple goods to factory-based rationing, while the USSR's relative affluence meant a larger supply of goods deployed into a larger retail sector, which reduced worker dependence on the factory.

The deterioration of 1990–91 suggested some reversal of those trends. The collapse of retail markets in a welter of scarcity and inflation increased the value of intraplant supply of meat and other goods at state prices (in those factories with sufficient clout to manage such provisioning), while the threat of plant closures and even temporary unemployment under various reform proposals weakened any confidence in job tenure. Workers had reason to be less militant and simply more worried than they otherwise might have been.

On the other hand, other changes that gave managers more options could increase their exposure to pressure from workers. In China, the post-Mao economic reforms since the late 1970s had given more autonomy to managers and more control over the distribution of bonuses and benefits—and thus increased the incidence of, and "stakes" in, amorphous worker-manager negotiation, resulting in "hidden baragining"or, as we have called a related phenomenon earlier, "negative control."[16] Chinese reform *had* gone deep, unshackled productive resources in the economy, increased supplies, and effected major improvements. The USSR had not yet, in early 1991, really experienced a reform. The 1987 enterprise law allowed many factories to raise prices. But indulgence in this practice by "strong" factories that could do so—criticized as "group egoism" in the press— also left managers more exposed than before to worker expectations of raises, in defense against the deterioration of living standards occasioned by shortages and inflation. If managerial independence was a necessary component of any reform, so were other elements still lacking—for example, demonopolization and other measures to put consumer goods on the market to give value to the ruble raises. If some realities pushed workers toward greater dependence on their enterprises, other realities of the larger economy limited the enterprises' ability to guarantee any consumer value for the rubles they put into wage packets. Some frustrated workers would still direct their ire at the factory. But more would take aim at Moscow and a system that no longer worked.

March–April 1991: Miners and Others

The strike that overwhelmed Soviet coal mines in March and April 1991 is still too close in time for us to establish much perspective on its ultimate political significance in the decline of the Soviet political system. Indeed we are still learning and have yet more to learn about many aspects of the 1989 coal strikes.[17] But its significance is undeniably large, for it involved a critical shift from economic to explicitly political issues.

At the end of February, the Donbass workers' committee leadership proposed a one-day strike on March 1, a ten-day wait, and then, if demands for a 100 to 150 percent pay increase were not met (in a coal region where mines were old, played out, and miners' wages below those of the Kuzbass), an all-out strike. The Kuzbass, however, took the lead. On March 4, its regional workers' committee launched a strike whose list of demands were headed by a call for Gorbachev's resignation from the presidency, the resignation of the Cabinet of Ministers, the Supreme Soviet, and the running of the country by the new Federation Council, composed of leaders of the republics. In this move, the miners in effect came over to the position of Yel'tsin and of those who sought a major devolution of power from the central government to the republics, and thereby underlined the deepening dissatisfaction with Gorbachev and his new team.

Initial reactions were harsh. Coal minister Shchadov threatened "no work, no pay" for the miners.[18] Prime Minister Pavlov's speech on March 5 was similarly tough, but, as it developed, not a deterrent to a gathering labor revolt. While Pavlov refused to meet with the strikers' representatives, Yel'tsin did so. The Kuzbass committee made it clear that their strike was "indefinite" and that the political objectives, including Gorbachev's ouster, were paramount.[19] While at the national level the official trade union federation, the VKP, had been demanding more compensation from the Cabinet of Ministers in the face of the price rises to come on April 2, its coal industry affiliate's head reverted to old practices, denouncing the strikes on March 13 as destructve and violative of working-class "unity."[20]

But the strikes were becoming broad and deep: pits were out in the Donbass and Kuzbass, in Vorkuta, Karaganda, and elsewhere. The Donbass miners added political demands, including (in a predominantly Russian work force) political and economic sovereignty for the Ukraine. (By March 22, Ukrainian Supreme Soviet chairman Kravchuk would, however, ask the miners to return to work, citing the economic effects of the strike on coal-consuming industries and the irreconcilability of that damage with the promotion of republican sovereignty.)[21] Perhaps 300,000 miners were striking by March 19, with demands growing to include abolition of a new 5 percent sales tax on many goods--a tax whose monstrous unpopularity would only increase with the coming price rises. By March 25, with the strikes now reaching the duration of the 1989 walkouts and idling about one-quarter of the country's 600 coalfields, the government found itself under great pressure. The Russian trade union (FNPR) leaders urged Gorbachev and Pavlov to meet the miners; the tough Vorkuta strikers demanded a meeting with Pavlov while rejecting *his* condition that they return to work before the talks.[22] The RSFSR Supreme Soviet had been urging Pavlov to talk, while the USSR Supreme Soviet's March 27 resolution calling for the Cabinet of Ministers to "examine" the miners' demands, but for the strikers to suspend their stoppage for two months and for the country to refrain from strikes for the rest of 1991,[23] was met with immediate rejection by the strikers.[24]

The miners were holding firm. Gas, oil, and metallurgical workers were raising demands as well and threatening strike actions. With the strikes effectively a month old, Pavlov did meet in the Kremlin with representatives of the workers' and strike committees and gave in on the economic demands, offering a 100 percent raise over one year, the

mines' rights to sell 5 to 7 percent of their coal on the world market, as
well as other concessions. Gorbachev too, addressed the miners after
the "agreement"—but it was far from clear that the miners viewed it
as such. Noting that the political demands had been refused, the miners continued the strike; more miners were out in the Kuzbass after
the Pavlov and Gorbachev meetings than before.[25]

This, then, was an eminently *political* crisis in an economic context
that was getting increasingly out of control. The GNP was dropping
precipitately versus the poor 1990 performance; the state budget deficit for the first quarter was around 31 billion rubles, already beyond
the 26.7 billion planned for the entire year. The republic governments
clung to their revenues, sending to Moscow in January and February
only 7 billion rubles instead of the 23.4 billion planned.[26] The government could print rubles, but it could not guarantee the production or
distribution of goods.

Nothing made this inability clearer than the April 2 price rises. Reactions were bitter. On the whole, the shelves in most locales remained bare and the expected emptying-out of warehouses which
had been stocked in anticipation of price hikes, did not eventuate. The
public mood viewed this all as *obman*—fraud, swindle. When prices
typically rose 100, 200, 300 percent, how was an "average" cost-of-
living rise of 60 percent derived—what sort of arithmetic considered
85 percent compensation of *this* low estimate adequate? In the Belorussian capital of Minsk, massive strikes began on April 3 against the
price increases and for wage increases—and this in a relatively well-
supplied city, generally quiescent in the past and thus the locus of a
Gorbachev "visit with workers" in a major tractor factory late in February, a factory that joined the strike in April. In the days that followed, the citizens of Minsk and other Belorussian cities would again
fill the streets with political demands similar to those of the miners,
directed at both the republican and central governments.

There were signs, then, that what had essentially been a *miners'*
movement was becoming a workers' movement, and there was
evidence that forces were gathering to push the country toward a political-economic abyss. Fears and tensions were evident, and organizations and personalities that had once claimed to speak for "the
workers" began to change their tunes. An OFTR spokesman in late
March denounced the disorders, crying "counterrevolution" and
claiming strikers were the unwitting victims of a new "bourgeoisie"
forming under the banner of perestroika, while "socialism, the CPSU,
Marxism, and the planned economy" were being blamed for the mis-
ery.[27] Teimuraz Avaliani, who had chaired the Kuzbass strike committee in 1989 and was now city party secretary in one of the region's

towns, accused the current strike leaders of trying to create "chaos," to use the workers' movement "to restore capitalism."[28]

The fears, then, were that there would be a total loss of the old order and worker support would be mobilized behind political movements such as "Democratic Russia" in the RSFSR, that aimed at a new political system. The evidence was growing that, unlike in 1989, the workers—or at least the miners—not only had the qualities of identity, opposition, and a certain "totalistic" view of their relationship to central state power, but now conceived of an alternative. If not clearly fleshed-out, the alternative was implicit in the rejection of the current forms of the USSR government and in the calls for "consultative" rule at the top via the Federation Council, with the devolution of a great deal of power to the republican governments.

History may mark the last week of April 1991 as the effective "end" of the USSR as the world had known it and assign a major role in forcing that end to the workers, the proletariat in whose name the system had been born seventy-three years earlier. Gorbachev faced down what seemed a half-hearted attempt to call him to account and precipitate his resignation from the General Secretaryship at a Central Committee plenum. The party still had clout, especially in the provinces, but it was unclear how the eventual elevation of any of the lackluster Politburo to replace him would advance the party's interests in order and control. On April 23, Gorbachev met with Yel'tsin and representatives of eight other republics in a dacha outside Moscow; the meeting was under the loose aegis of the Federation Council; but six other republics—the Baltics, Armenia, Georgia, and Moldavia—signaling their aim of independence, did not participate.

The details of the "pact" were vague, reflecting both a certain political realism and at the same time an economic desperation. It called for the negotiation, from the bottom up, of a new union treaty but recognized that the six republics missing from the meeting might well remain outside whatever new political entity emerged. Gorbachev had thus "conceded." But the more popular Yel'tsin, surely also realizing that he alone could not deliver the goods to the workers in the RSFSR itself, to say nothing of the eight other republics, conceded too, by his attendance, that political and economic order were at a critical point. Economically, the agreement called for moves to cancel the sales tax, "reexamine" the price rises, and move, within a month, on the matter of indexation of wages—decisions that had little relationship to other, tougher, elements of a new economic "crisis program" announced on April 22, and, if anything, seemed likely to speed the drift toward hyperinflation. All the representatives called for an end to the strikes, now nearing two months' duration. On April 29, two days before the workers' holiday of May 1, Yel'tsin headed for the Kuzbass to meet with the miners—with reason, perhaps, to wonder whether coming together with Gorbachev in a salvage operation had been politically well advised for a *Russian* leader, and what, after all, he could offer to those who awaited his arrival.

Class and Politics: A Final Look

All along, using Mann's categories, we have been holding up maximal criteria of a class in action—a class possessed of "truly revolutionary consciousness." The criteria have fit only partially—some Brezhnev-period and more Gorbachev-era evidence of identity and opposition and less reflection, at least until quite recent times, of the more elusive totality and consciousness of alternatives. The Soviet political arena was, until recently, too tightly controlled for classes or other groups to "act" at all. Until that arena's expansion under Gorbachev, we had been judging the presence of class elements that were only potential and not yet expressible in organized action (as opposed to episodic labor actions and "negative control" on the factory floor). We are in a new situation now, though it is anything but stabilized. To understand how far the working class and Soviet developments have gone, we will return to the question of class and class politics in the context of earlier Western analytic commentary on these matters, stretching from the earlier Khrushchev period to the late Brezhnev era.

Writing at the end of the 1950s, in the wake of the first few years of post-Stalin change, Jerzy Gliksman saw Soviet workers as constituting a proletariat, much like Soviet commentary so labeled the working masses under capitalism. Both were similar in "economic function," working "in a very similar factory environment, whose character is determined on both sides largely by the technology of mass production."[29] If from the Soviet viewpoint, the touchstone of the proletariat under capitalism was its lack of "real influence on the disposition of the means of production or on the distribution of 'surplus value',"[30] this was equally true of Soviet workers.

Of course, the technology of mass production has not been the sole determinant of factory environment; economic system counted, too. The Soviet party-state, as collective proprietor, in effect owned and managed the Soviet factory and the whole economy. Contemporary state-and-society theorists have reminded us that, in capitalist-market economies, "the state" is not simply an instrument of a ruling class of capitalists, nor just a referee among competing interests. The "state" can have its own interests and act on them as well as be acted upon by other interest groups. Crises within the state elite, "pacts" involving state and other actors, thus constitute parts of the drama of "transition"' from authoritarian to democratic orders, as has taken place in recent years in southern Europe and Latin America.

In the Soviet drama, however, the state-as-proprieter substituted for *all* sorts of propertied interests and the state as controller maintained a tighter grip on groups and their potential politics than authoritarian regimes managed, or even aspired to do. This fact colors the relations between state and proletariat in the Soviet context and makes for a very different politics of "transition." The omnicompetent state controlled so much and prevented so effectively the emergence of group politics that it subjected the workers to much greater domination than workers under capitalist owners backed by a state operating actively in their interests.

In the post-Stalin period, workers were surely a better-treated proleteriat. In these years of absolute and relative improvement, the process of hereditization reached its fruition and the heightening of educational levels and educational and occupational aspirations occurred, most markedly among the young who would become workers in large numbers. The workers were still a proletariat, but how much of a *class* were they?

Here, without getting into complicated semantics, we can say that analytic conclusions differed. At the end of an exhaustive review of Soviet writings on work authority and organization up to the early 1980s, Yanowitch saw a "class," or something very close to it: "This evidence . . . taken as a whole . . . suggests a working class conscious of its subordinate status, with a sense of distinct group interests and traditions which set it apart from its superiors (the *nachal'stvo*) at the workplace."[31] Yanowitch's evidence came largely from survey data on workers' assessments of their own degree of (non-)participation, efficacy in affecting decisions, and so forth in the plant. This focus, revealing workers conscious of their status as objects rather than subjects of authority, highlighted dimensions that were likely to suggest class identity and opposition.

Lane and O'Dell's 1978 perspective was rather different.[32] For them, the Soviet workers fit none of three "types" of workers they drew from Western social research. Workers were not "traditional," viewing themselves in a we-they relationship with their bosses that was shaped by a working-class counterculture; nor were they "deferential," since their "levels of participation in management and politics," and "higher levels of mobility"[33] ran against this attitude. Nor, finally, were they "privatized"—apathetic, isolated, totally instrumental (wage-oriented) in their relation to their jobs, non-solidary with their fellows. Instead, Lane and O'Dell proposed that the Soviet worker represented a fourth type—the "incorporated" worker:

> Many critics of the Soviet Union . . . have emphasized the role of coercion and repression. We would change the emphasis considerably to take into account socialization and incorporation of the working class. The "incorporated worker" shares many of the traits we have found in the above ideal types: he has certain forms of solidarity with the factory; he accepts the authority structure on the basis of its performance capacity; and he is closer to the administration both socially and politically than the worker in the capitalist society. But he does not actively shape the overriding values of his society, which are determined largely by the ruling political elites. While there are tendencies towards "privatization" of life in the sense that family orientation . . . and economistic attitudes are strengthening, the dominant ideology of Marxism-Leninism and the institutional forms of polity and economy place these attitudes in quite different context from the "privatized" worker in the West.[34]

This image of the "incorporated worker" is worth fleshing out, since it not only diverges so much from some of the earlier Brezhnev-era discussion, but also because it is so hard to recognize this worker in the radically changed context of the Gorbachev period:

> He accepts the authority structure of the industrial enterprise, he actively participates in the improvement of production and for him the factory is a focus of political and social life. Such a worker is closer to the values of the factory administration than the capitalist worker. He shares a general concern to promote the 'national interest.' Acceptance of the factory system entails acceptance of the whole social system: to work for the improvement of the enterprise is to work for the improvement of the Soviet system.[35]

Lane and O'Dell thus disagreed with those who saw "the development of a hereditary proletariat as leading to class-consciousness" and saw "no evidence of this tendency in the sense of a political counter-culture or . . . a "radical class-consciousness."[36] How much evidence was there for the greater closeness of the Soviet worker to the "values of the factory administration" than his Western counterpart? Judging such proximity was hardly easy for foreign observers in those years; as Lane and O'Dell rather delicately acknowledged, the "structural features of Soviet society undoubtedly severely inhibit opposition."[37] After the 1989 strikes, the same point was put more simply by a miner's union official: "Our social conditions were horrible even before Gorbachev came to power. . . . [But] earlier [miners] kept quiet about this. They feared to speak."[38]

Beyond taking the system a bit too much at its own claims, Lane and O'Dell also made too much of the state's solicitude toward workers as a social and economic reality, extending this to a claim that the state, though hardly controlled by it, ruled "on behalf of the working class."[39] We may allow that Khrushchev and Brezhnev showed some solicitude for workers—but they showed it for other groups as well. State policy might favor particular groups, or balance between them, without recognizing them as "class" claimants. Frank Parkin made the point cogently:

> The Communist party-state, it might be said, strives to maintain the uneven equilibrium between intelligentsia and proletariat through a conscious manipulation of the distributive system. That is to say, the party permits white collar experts and technocrats to accumulate a disproportionate share of social rewards, while at the same time ensuring that the gulf between this group and the workers does not widen to the extent that it might under an open market system.[40]

In such an interpretation, the state can be seen as actively

> inhibiting the intelligentsia from transforming itself into a dominant class, while simultaneously underwriting such privileges as it enjoys. Conversely, the state might be said to acquiesce in the subordination of the proletariat while also creating the conditions that shield labour from the harsh economic climate of market rationality and commodity exchange.[41]

The "conditions" amounted to the loose contract of employment security, pace of work, guaranteed bonuses and *vyvodilovka*, and subsidized prices—things perestroika found no longer supportable. The Brezhnevian state that did this, however, was not *pro*-working class. However its policies might benefit workers or others, it stood against classes as a whole and sought

> to make secure its own dominion and to preserve political stability by playing off one class against another. In Engels' schema the state succeeds in winning its independent power as a consequence of class stalemate or equilibrium; state power fills the vacuum created by the temporary suspension of class power. In the socialist reality, however, the causal sequence is reversed. It is state power that brings about the suspension of class power, and on anything but a temporary basis. The party-state strips away the capacity of social classes to organize in defense of their collective interests and replaces open distributive struggle by a centralized system of allocation.[42]

But did the party-state of the Brezhnev era always succeed? Some writers, certainly, were ready to see the workers of that time as a class—writers drawn toward this conclusion by the accumulation of the same class characteristics with which I have been concerned here. This was especially true of some left-wing critics of Soviet reality, one of whom, in 1982, asserted that the working class was "now a more hereditary social group than at any time in Soviet history, and it can be presumed more likely to respond if basic securities, like employment, are attacked."[43] For another writer in 1975, the prospect had been yet more dramatic:

> With the end of primitive accumulation and with the dramatic decline in social mobility over the past two decades, there has arisen for the first time in the Soviet Union a large hereditary proletariat. A hereditary proletariat raises the cultural level of the working class and the consciousness of itself as a social force. It is this proletariat which will lead the working class into the political arena—this time with redoubled force.[44]

If in 1975 this characterization was a bit premature, the use of the future tense would accomodate later developments that make it seem less overstated. Over the long run, from late Khrushchev to late Brezhnev times, workers had, at the very least, grown more and more important as a "quasi-group" with "latent interests," in Ralf Dahrendorf's terms, interests which became "politically relevant only through the perceptions of decision-makers."[45] Those perceptions focused increasingly on the workers.

Over the years, this "quasi-group" developed *social* characteristics that were critical in forming the basic potential for the emergence of a class. Shared second- (or third-) generation urban/worker status for the majority, a product of the self-reproductive force of hereditization, was not the whole picture. For what the Marxian criterion is worth, Soviet workers also shared the same relationship to the means of production, whatever their levels of skill, pay, education, and so on. There is plenty of diversity in these latter characteristics, but no large working class is homogenous with respect to them. The evidence at hand from emigré research, indicating that more skilled than unskilled workers are ready to opt for self-identification as *other* than "working class,"[46] need not reflect a differentiation that vitiates the many ways in which workers resemble, and understand that they resemble, each other. Wages differed, by skill, by branch—but less so as the long Brezhnev era proceeded. Work satisfaction differed as well, but here the general educational upscaling of the working class was probably a homogenizing factor: the younger, better-schooled workers, the emergent majority, found more and more of the jobs boring and empty and yielding less material satisfaction.

What had emerged, then, at the end of the Brezhnev era, was something rather more than a "quasi-group" and closer to a class in many of its characteristics (and, in the economic decline of Brezhnev's last years, more strike- prone). This was something new in Soviet history.

"Class," and "working class," had hitherto been talismanic terms, words to conjure with. Stalin and his successors had talked of the growth of the "working class," but a class was hardly what they sought: hereditary urban workers, better-educated workers, and more of them, formed in the Soviet system, seemed an attractive future prospect in the years when the typical "new hire" was a peasant, new to the city and near-illiterate.

It is likely that Soviet leaders of the past did not appreciate fully the politically stabilizing effect of having an industrial work force made up predominantly of ex-peasants: an "accidental" benefit. They anticipated positive returns from an enlarged supply of hereditary, educated worker urbanites, but tended to overlook the complications that might arise as the "quiet revolution" reached maturity and this supply came to dominate the workforce—and made it more of a class.

This, too, was an accidental result. Not that the various leaderships, in a general sense, were content to assume that "spontaneous" developments would work out the way they preferred: the organizations and mechanisms of Soviet politics, from the Kremlin to the factory, aimed to deny autonomy and self-regulation to all groups, workers among them; hence the obsession to control, and preempt, all independent organizational capacity. What the regime missed, it seems, was the emergence of "new" workers in large numbers, with capacities, aspirations, and claims different from workers of the past. (Interestingly, while some highly qualified Soviet sociologists were, in the early to mid-1980s, paying attention to the impact of hereditization, their published works at the time put a positive "gloss" on the process. This was different in emphasis from later commentary on the "new worker," typically identified as a factor complicating the old command-administrative management styles. There is every reason to conclude that the gloss was politically necessitated by pre-glasnost' conditions, rather than reflecting judgments that this trend carried no problematic consequences.)[47]

This, then, was the accidental proletariat, the legacy of the Brezhnev era to a Soviet history now being made in the Gorbachev times of political instability, ethnic conflict, and economic chaos. Old-style Soviet ideologues—or today, reactionaries, calling in 1991 for a restoration of "socialist order," condemning assaults on "the gains of October," condemning the rebirth of "capitalists" on Soviet soil—might still argue that the workers, after all, collectively own the means of production and cannot be a *proletariat*. But this is no longer a convincing or enforceable view. Workers are not owners and do not feel like owners. They have been, along with other Soviet citizens, alienated from property, from power, from authority. That they have exercised a certain amount of veto power ("negative control") in shop-floor situations, that they have been in a rough way taken "into account" in wage and price policies, testifies to their collective importance and possession of some resources, but not against their status as a proletariat.

Thus this proletariat was not unconsidered and uncared-for; the Soviet working class was not a proletariat "cut loose" by the state. Not only domination, but the state's welfare policies as well, marked its relationship to workers—employment security, subsidized prices, and other informal elements of the social contract. Such policies created a certain dependency on the proletariat's part, but one that was not at all irreconcilable with "oppositional" content in working-class consciousness. Populist legitimism allowed the two to balance, to a degree. In the situation that has been unfolding since 1985, populist legitimism has been losing its force.

What we have in the USSR today, then is a working class, making "working-class politics." There is evidence of class identity, of class opposition. If totality remains an elusive quality, it may be that it is hard to demonstrate on the basis of *any* data. But what was lacking before—worker awareness of a systematic alternative—finally emerged in the 1991 strikes. What else were the miners' political demands, touching not only personalities but institutions (the presidency, the Supreme Soviet, the Cabinet of Ministers, the Federation Council), but a radical rejection of the current system, the demand that a new one be put into operation? As the USSR approached May Day, 1991, not only miners but factory workers in Minsk and elsewhere added their voices in support of these demands. On April 26, fifty million workers, according to official sources,[48] joined one-hour work stoppages or meetings across the Russian Republic in response to calls by the "Democratic Russia" movement and the republic's union (FNPR) to support the miners and their demands.

Toward the Future

Thus, the working class has entered Soviet politics. This book is being completed at a time of full-blown crisis, and detailed predictions would be foolhardy for the author and of little utility to readers. It is possible to sketch alternative scenarios—a stabilization of workers' politics into a trade union mode not wholly unlike that in the West, a final breakthrough to a "real" perestroika via labor militancy, a workers' revolution that, in partial reprise of 1917, will seek a "third way" between capitalism and state socialism, or a descent of labor politics into a kind of Peronism, with workers exercising veto powers over various aspects of public policy via unions operating in an unstable politics of weak parties, political and economic institutions—these were four possibilities offered by Peter Rutland in late 1990.[49]

Given the developments of 1991, it is hard to see a clear way toward any of these, especially the first two alternatives. Class politics has emerged, but in the USSR it is anything but a politics of the "incorporation" of the working class as a political actor in a process that already accommodates a variety of other actors and their interests. It is thus not, and cannot be, a reprise of earlier Western experiences of "dealing in" labor at a table where landowners, the commercial bourgeoisie, and other groups already occupied places. Soviet class politics is being played out at a time when rules and institutions are in flux and in dispute: an old polity is in critical decline, a new one yet unborn. Economic crisis is so far advanced that even a well-rooted political system would be sorely pressed to contain its effect—and in the USSR this economic crisis is intensified by the current political confusion.

In such circumstances, *being* a class cannot determine how to *act* as a class. This depends on political and economic context as well—and here, developments in the Gorbachev period have been contradictory in several senses.

Political decompression, the loosening of the old bonds of repression, increased maneuvering room and expanded the political arena. In that arena, "class" action such as strikes, the formation of workers' and strike committees and their coordination, the founding of independent unions, became possible, with varying degrees of coordination and varying degrees of resistance from divided local and central authority. There is a similarity between Soviet state socialism in crisis and the situation of authoritarian capitalist regimes in their own early phases of transition to democracy, though it is potentially a misleading one. In the capitalist regimes there is an early "liberalization," which is aimed at maintaining much of what elites wish to preserve by relaxing some of their control. This nonetheless lowers "the costs—real and anticipated—of individual expression and collective action"[50] aimed against the prevailing order, including the things elites seek to conserve. Gorbachev's new dispensation in Soviet politics did this as well, but the low degree of class organization (real trade unions, political parties) that preceded the Soviet crisis period—essentially, the nonexistence of such entities—makes the road forward toward organized, legitimate class action all the more uncertain in the USSR.

The political-institutional context in the USSR is at present much too fluid and inchoate to conceive of the smooth cutting of a deal that would allow the working class to participate, in an organized way, in

making political and economic reforms. Even allowing for the Gor-
bachev-Yel'tsin pact of April 23 and taking its possibilities at their
maximum, the polity remains more accident- than compromise-
prone. Should the move toward the quite-unfamiliar market resume,
the coexistence of necessarily emergent "owners" and "workers,"
with conflicting interests but reason to moderate and regulate expression of those interests, will be all the more difficult in a context still
bereft of necessary organizations and institutions with a tradition of
recognized existence, a "history" of some duration. In contrast, the
scenarios of "democratic transition" from right-wing authoritarian
rule seem, for all their problems, easier. Consider O'Donnell and
Schmitter:

> To the extent that complex sets of collective actors have emerged to repre-
> sent the class, sectoral, and professional cleavages intrinsic to capitalist so-
> cial relations, it has become necessary to reach some agreement on how
> state agencies, business associations, trade unions, and professional organ-
> izations will behave during the transition and beyond it. Whether such a
> "social contract" can be agreed upon, and implemented, may have a major
> impact on the economy's performance at a time of considerable uncertainty
> over property rights, mobilized pressure for redistribution of benefits, and
> nervousness among external creditors, customers, and suppliers.[51]

In the USSR, class and other cleavages have emerged without a capitalist economy, or social relations, in place. The "collective actors,"
such as they are, have little history or experience in the new situation.
the uncertainty over property rights is over the very concept of such
rights, not just the question of "whose"? "Benefits" are less the issue
than is the distribution of scarcities, and hardy indeed is the "external
creditor" who does not flinch at what he sees in 1991.

If in the authoritarian-to-democratic transition the capacity of "class
and sectoral actors . . . to deliver the subsequent compliance of their
members is problematic, if only because the outgoing regime may
have systematically repressed unions and professional associations,"[52] the Soviet situation is much worse. Organizational support
and allegiances are fluid, unclear: "delivery" capacity is unpredictable; compromise is an unfamiliar art. Who, then, can credibly speak
for, "deliver" the workers? Who can deliver nonexistent business and
employers' associations, or for that matter, the "state," given the indeterminacy of the political future and the *rules* for determining that
future?

Does the future hold, then, a return to the political and economic
coercion of old? It seems unlikely that such a move could work to
stabilize the country as it did in the past, or for long. A return to the

ways of old cannot solve the economic crisis. Right-wing authoritarian coups and dictatorships of the Latin American or southern European sorts may stabilize economic crises, but these have been crises of already-operating market economies. Those who hope for a dictatorial transition toward the market in the USSR vastly underestimate the difficulties of such a course when a dictatorship would begin with so little.

Being aware that the events of weeks or months can readily outdate any speculations, let us nevertheless speculate on two broad scenarios—one nightmarish, one more positive. It is not impossible that the Soviet system could collapse before any emerging political and economic measures take hold. Ethnic-territorial tensions may assume forms too violent, in too many areas simultaneously, for any negotiated "withdrawal" of six republics or a new compact by which nine others—three Slavic, the rest "Moslem"—can associate themselves in a mutually satisfactory way. Production is declining in many industrial sectors, only partly due to the coal strike. Distribution of food and goods, such as there are, is hampered by a transport system that may be creaking to a halt. How far Moscow's writ will run under such circumstances, how readily deployable army, KGB, and MVD troops would be, is no longer clear. Disintegration rather than decentralization may spawn a diversity of uncertain territorial authorities, competing and cooperating, embargoing and bartering; politics will be local, possibly violent, certainly militant. Workers would have to seek their interests in militant fashion as well, from area to area.

On the positive side, it is possible that the strikes of 1991 will have forced the beginning of a turn away from the abyss. Workers need "things"; they also need hopes. A government that moves toward letting secessionist republics go, that understands that any new state pact must devolve power to the republics that remain, is moving in the right direction, whether Gorbachev, Yel'tsin, or someone else presides over it. Worker demands seem compatible with this. Such a government, to provide hope, must also be seen to be taking radical economic action. It may be unable to stem inflation, but it might take, *in extremis*, the undeniably risky course of Polish shock therapy, cease printing fictional rubles, and let all prices find their own level. Ultimately, the ruble would become convertible into goods at some stable rate. This would be brutal, but it might be bearable—at least as bearable as current conditions—in the context of further radical moves. State- and enterprise-owned apartments might be deeded, free, to their occupants: renters become owners. Demonopolization and privatization are hard, especially with respect to the large enterprises that dot the landscape. A swift privatization, through the issuance of free shares to the workers and employees is inelegant and problem-ridden: but it would recognize the fact that there are at present few likely purchasers of such shares, foreign or domestic, and would spread ownership, however unfamiliar it might be, across the accidental proletariat in a manner most would find more "just" than other alternatives. Each "owner" should be able to sell shares and buy shares; some would do each, and in so doing create an equity market. All this would be new and strange, but it would be a learning experience, with some chance of becoming self-sustaining, of a more positive sort than the one that has taught Soviet citizens bitter lessons over the past few years. It might be the beginning of a way out for the Soviet economy, for the workers—a rationale for the pains of adjustment to a new system that would replace the pains of life in the old, dying one.

Either scenario, as well as the one that actually occurs, will necessarily be the subject of books that remain to be written.

Notes

The following abbreviations are used in the notes:

AN SSSR   Akademiia Nauk SSSR
AON   Akademiia Obshchestvennykh Nauk
AS   *Arkhiv Samizdata*
CDSP   *Current Digest of the Soviet Press*
CHR   *A Chronicle of Human Rights in the USSR*
EKO   *Ekonomika i organizatsiia promyshlennogo proizvodstva*
FBIS   *Foreign Broadcast Information Service*
FT   *Financial Times*
JPRS   *Joint Publications Research Service*
NDVS   *Nauchnye doklady vysshei shkoly*
RKSM   *Rabochii klass i sovremennyi mir*
RLR   *Radio Liberty Research*
SI   *Sotsiologicheskie issledovaniia*
SIP   *Soviet Interview Project*
ST   *Sotsialisticheskii trud*

Introduction

1. "Reflections: The Triumph of Capitalism," *New Yorker*, January 23, 1989, p. 98.

2. See esp. Theda Skocpol, *States and Social Revolutions* (Cambridge, Eng.: Cambridge University Press, 1979), p. 32; also Walter D. Connor, *Socialism's Dilemmas: State and Society in the Soviet Bloc* (New York: Columbia University Press, 1988), pp. 5–20.

3. Irving Howe, "Sweet and Sour Notes: On Workers and Intellectuals," *Dissent* (Winter 1972), p. 266.

4. Ibid., p. 264.

5. Ralph Miliband, *The State in Capitalist Society* (New York: Basic Books/ Harper Colophon, 1969), p. 47.

6. See Norman Birnbaum, *Toward a Critical Sociology* (New York: Oxford University Press, 1971), p. 106.

7. Frank Parkin, *Marxism and Class Theory: A Bourgeois Critique* (New York: Columbia University Press, 1979), p. 24.

8. Michael Mann, *Consciousness and Action among the Western Working Class* (London: Macmillan, 1973), p. 13.

9. Ivan Szelenyi, "The Intelligentsia in the Class Structure of State-Socialist Societies," in Michael Burawoy and Theda Skocpol, eds., *Marxist Inquiries: Studies of Labor, Class, and States* (*American Journal of Sociology*, vol. 88, suppl. 1982) (Chicago: University of Chicago Press, 1982), p. 319.

10. Jack Barbash, "The Tensions of Work," *Dissent* (Winter 1972), p. 247.

11. Miklos Haraszti, *A Worker in a Worker's State* (New York: Universe Books, 1978); quotes are from pp. 70–71, 74, 75.

12. Szelenyi, "Intelligentsia," p. 320.

13. *Izvestiia*, December 24, 1988, p. 3 (*FBIS-Soviet Union*, January 19, 1989, p. 76).

14. At various points in the chapters to come, we will be returning to this matter.

15. Parkin, *Marxism*, pp. 320–21.

16. See Szelenyi, "Intelligentsia," pp. 319–20; also Jadwiga Staniszkis, *Poland: The Self-Limiting Revolution* (Princeton, N.J.: Princeton University Press, 1984).

17. Szelenyi, "Intelligentsia," pp. 320–21.

18. Blair Ruble, "The Soviet Union's Quiet Revolution," in George Breslauer, ed., *Can Gorbachev's Reforms Succeed?* (Berkeley: U.C. Center for Slavic and East European Studies, 1990), pp. 77–94.

19. See Walter D. Connor, "Social Policy under Gorbachev," *Problems of Communism* 35, 4 (July–August 1986); also Peter Hauslohner, "Gorbachev's Social Contract," *Soviet Economy* 3, 1 (1987).

20. See, e.g., Guillermo O'Donnell, Philippe C. Schmitter, and Laurence Whitehead, eds., *Transitions from Authoritarian Rule: Comparative Perspectives* (Baltimore: Johns Hopkins University Press, 1986).

21. See Gail W. Lapidus, "State and Society: Toward the Emergence of Civil Society in the Soviet Union," in Seweryn Bialer, ed., *Politics, Society and Nationality Inside Gorbachev's Russia* (Boulder, Colo.: Westview, 1989), pp. 121–47.

22. Available, with the contributions of others, in Z. Brzezinski, ed., *Dilemmas of Change in Soviet Politics* (New York: Columbia University Press, 1969).

23. See Walter D. Connor, "Dissent in a Complex Society: The Soviet Case," *Problems of Communism* 22, 2 (March–April 1973), p. 52.

24. Seweryn Bialer, "The Changing Soviet Political System: The Nineteenth Party Conference and After," in Bialer, ed., *Politics, Society, and Nationality*, pp. 202–203.

Chapter 1
Workers and Society

The opening quote is from D. Manuilskii, *Klassy, gosudarstvo, partiia v period proletarskoi diktatury* (Moscow and Leningrad, 1928), p. 87.

1. See Victoria Bonnell, *Roots of Rebellion: Workers' Politics and Organizations in St. Petersburg and Moscow, 1900–1914* (Berkeley: University of California Press, 1983); also, Bonnell, ed., *The Russian Worker: Life and Labor Under the Tsarist Regime* (Berkeley: University of California Press, 1983); Joseph Bradley, *Muzhik and Muscovite: Urbanization in Late Imperial Russia* (Berkeley: University of California Press, 1985); Laura Engelstein, *Moscow, 1905: Working-Class Organization and Political Conflict* (Stanford, Calif.: Stanford University Press, 1982); and Robert E. Johnson, *Peasant and Proletarian: The Working Class of Moscow in the Late Nineteenth Century* (New Brunswick, N.J.: Rutgers University Press, 1979); Diane Koenker, *Moscow Workers and the 1917 Revolution* (Prince-

ton, N.J.: Princeton University Press, 1981); S. A. Smith, *Red Petrograd: Revolution in the Factories, 1917–1918* (Cambridge, Eng.: Cambridge University Press, 1983); Reginald E. Zelnik, *Labor and Society in Tsarist Russia* (Stanford, Calif.: Stanford University Press, 1971). See also Rose L. Glickman, *Russian Factory Women: Workplace and Society, 1880–1914* (Berkeley: University of California Press, 1984).

2. Jerzy G. Gliksman, "The Russian Urban Worker: From Serf to Proletarian," in Cyril E. Black, ed., *The Transformation of Russian Society: Aspects of Social Change Since 1861* (Cambridge, Mass.: Harvard University Press, 1960), p. 312.

3. Ibid., pp. 312–13.

4. Ibid., p. 315.

5. Koenker, *Moscow Workers*, p. 45.

6. Gliksman, "Russian Urban Worker," pp. 314–15.

7. Bradley, *Muzhik*, p. 179.

8. Koenker, *Moscow Workers*, pp. 50–51.

9. Ibid., p. 29.

10. Smith, *Red Petrograd*, p. 19.

11. Johnson, *Peasant*, p. 63.

12. Ibid.

13. Koenker, *Moscow Workers*, pp. 44–46, poses this question with eloquence and conciseness.

14. See Bradley, *Muzhik*, p. 117; Smith, *Red Petrograd*, p. 29.

15. Engelstein, *Moscow*, p. 34.

16. Gliksman, "Russian Urban Worker," p. 317.

17. Johnson, *Peasant*, p. 65.

18. Engelstein, *Moscow*, p. 33.

19. See Teodor Shanin, *Russia 1905–1907: Revolution as a Moment of Truth* (New Haven and London: Yale University Press, 1986), p. 197, and sources cited therein.

20. S. L. Seniavskii and V. B. Tel'pukhovskii, *Rabochii klass SSSR (1938–1965)* (Moscow: Mysl', 1971), p. 94.

21. The following discussion of Petrograd/Leningrad is drawn from a classic article published in the Khrushchev period: O. I. Shkaratan, "Izmeneniia v sotsial'nom sostave fabrichno-zavodskikh rabochikh Leningrada (1917–1928 gg.)," *Istoriia SSSR*, no. 5 (1959), pp. 21–38 (trans. in *Soviet Sociology* 1, 3, Winter 1962–63, pp. 29–42).

22. Quoted in Geoffrey Hosking, *The First Socialist Society* (Cambridge, Mass.: Harvard University Press, 1985), pp. 130–31.

23. Isaac Deutscher, *The Unfinished Revolution: Russia, 1917–1967* (London, 1969), p. 29, quoted in J. D. Barber, *The Composition of the Soviet Working Class, 1928–1941* (Soviet Industrialization Project Series [SIPS], University of Birmingham, 1978, mimeo), p. 1.

24. See Barber, *Composition*, p. 3, table 1.

25. Shkaratan, "Izmeneniia."

26. Ibid., p. 33 (Russian version).

27. Ibid.

28. Ibid., p. 35 (Russian version).

29. See Barber, *Composition*, pp. 4–5.

30. Shkaratan, "Izmeneniia," p. 33 (Russian version).

31. Ibid., p. 35, and Smith, *Red Petrograd*, p. 20.

32. Note Smith's *caveat* (ibid., p. 269, n. 64) with respect to the underrepresentation of the peasantry in these figures: surveyed were workers in these industries in 1929, rather than at the periods of entry. Many peasants may have entered in each of these periods, and later left these industries (especially after 1917), not to return. Thus the degree to which the working class was "self-reproducing" at these points may well be overstated.

33. Barber, *Composition*, p. 3, table 1.

34. Ibid., p. 5.

35. See Frederick I. Kaplan, *Bolshevik Ideology and the Ethics of Soviet Labor, 1917–1920: The Formative Years* (New York: Philosophical Library, 1968); Jay B. Sorenson, *The Life and Death of Soviet Trade Unionism 1917–1928* (New York: Atherton Press, 1969).

36. Quoted in Sorenson, *Life*, p. 61.

37. Moshe Lewin, *The Making of the Soviet System: Essays in the Social History of Interwar Russia* (New York: Pantheon Books, 1985), p. 194.

38. See the essays by Cohen, Rigby, Tucker, and Lewin in Robert C. Tucker, ed., *Stalinism: Essays in Historical Interpretation* (New York: W. W. Norton, 1977).

39. Quoted by Sorenson, *Life*, p. 118, from Kollontai's *Rabochaia oppozitsiia* (Moscow, 1921), p. 6.

40. Smith, *Red Petrograd*, pp. 261–62.

41. Ibid., p. 261.

42. On Lenin as "Calvinist and Taylorist," see Sorenson, *Life*, pp. 163–64.

43. Quoted in Kaplan, *Bolshevik Ideology*, p. 200, from *Professional'nyi vestnik*, no. 8, December 20, 1917.

44. Quoted in ibid., p. 206, from *Pervyi vserossiiskii s"ezd professional'nykh soiuzov 7–14 Ianvaria 1918* (Moscow, 1918), p. 74.

45. Quoted in ibid., p. 220, from *IV Vserossiiskaia konferentsiia professional'nykh soiuzuv 12–17 marta 1918* (Moscow, 1923), p. 38.

46. Quoted in ibid., pp. 291–92, from V. I. Lenin, "O professional'nykh soiuzakh, o tekushchem momente i ob oshibkakh Trotskogo," in Lenin, *Sochineniia*, vol. 32 (Moscow: Gosudarstvennoe izdatel'stvo politicheskoi literatury, 1941–52), p. 11.

47. Quoted in Sorenson, *Life*, p. 114, from V. I. Lenin, *Selected Works*, vol. 9 (New York: International Publishers, n.d.), p. 36.

48. See Sorenson, *Life*, pp. 238ff.

49. M. P. Kim, "O nekotorykh osobennostiakh sovremennogo razvitiia rabochego klassa SSSR," in AON pri TsK KPSS, *Sovetskii rabochii klass na sovremennom etape* (Moscow, Mysl', 1964), pp. 6–7.

50. See Barber, *Composition*, p. 5, table 2, and sources cited.

51. A. Rashin, *Sostav fabrichno-zavodskogo proletariata* (Moscow, 1930), p. 20, and M. T. Gol'tsman, "Sostav stroitel'nykh rabochikh SSSR," in *Izmeneniia v chislennosti i sostave sovetskogo rabochego klassa* (Moscow, 1961), p. 137, cited in Barber, *Composition*, p. 6.

52. See *Sostav novykh millionov chlenov profsoiuzov* (Moscow, 1933), pp. 3–4, 16, cited in Barber, *Composition*, pp. 15–16.

53. Ibid., p. 80 (Barber, *Composition*, p. 15).

54. See *Profsoiuznaia perepis', 1932–1933 gg.* (Moscow: Profizdat, 1934), pp. 26–27, 29; also S. A. Gimatov, "Soderzhanie trudovykh traditsii sovetskogo rabochego klassa," in *Sotsial'no—klassovye problemy razvitiia sotsialisticheskogo obshchestva* (Moscow: Izdatel'stvo Moskovskogo universiteta, 1969), p. 112.

55. *Trud v SSSR: Spravochnik 1926–1930* (Moscow, 1930), p. 27, cited in Barber, *Composition*, p. 13.

56. See Barber, *Composition*, pp. 17–18, for a discussion.

57. This discussion follows that in Hiroaki Kuromiya, *Stalin's Industrial Revolution: Politics and Workers, 1928–1932* (Cambridge, Eng.: Cambridge University Press, 1988), pp. 200–20.

58. See ibid., p. 213, and sources cited therein.

59. Ibid., p. 209, citing *Sotsialisticheskoe stroitel'stvo SSSR: Statisticheskii ezhegodnik* (Moscow, 1936), p. 531.

60. See Peter A. Hauslohner, "Managing the Soviet Labor Market: Politics and Policymaking under Brezhnev," Ph.D. dissertation, University of Michigan, 1984, p. 118; on Stalin's consigning of recruitment and control of workers to ministries and enterprises, see pp. 115–18.

61. Ibid., p. 18.

62. Gliksman, "Russian Urban Worker," p. 318.

63. See Barber, *Composition*, pp. 18–19.

64. M. Ia. Sonin, *Vosproizvodstvo rabochei sily v SSSR*, cited in Barber, *Composition*, p. 19.

65. *Industrializatsiia SSSR 1938–1941 gg.* (Moscow, 1973), p. 248, cited in Barber, *Composition*, p. 20.

66. See Alex Inkeles and Raymond A. Bauer, *The Soviet Citizen: Daily Life in a Totalitarian Society* (Cambridge, Mass.: Harvard University Press, 1961), p. 81.

67. See Barber, *Composition*, p. 21.

68. L. A. Gordon and A. K. Nazimova, "Proizvodstvennyi potentsial sovetskogo rabochego klassa: Tendentsii i problemy razvitiia," *Voprosy filosofii*, no. 11 (1980), pp. 26–40 (trans. in *Soviet Sociology* 19, 4, Spring 1981, p. 30).

69. A. M. Panfilova, *Formirovanie rabochego klassa SSSR v gody pervoi piatiletki* (Moscow: Izdatel'stvo Moskovskogo universiteta, 1964), pp. 84–85.

70. John Scott, *Behind the Urals: An American Worker in Russia's City of Steel* (orig. pub. 1942; Bloomington: Indiana University Press, 1973), p. 13.

71. Ibid., p. 137.

72. Lewin, *Making*, p. 219, notes that the urban population grew 44 percent during the first FYP, and that the Moscow and Leningrad regions each added 3.5 million new residents in the same five years.

73. Alec Nove, *Stalinism and After* (London: George Allen and Unwin, 1975), p. 47.

74. Kuromiya, *Stalin's Industrial Revolution*, p. 81.

75. Ibid., pp. 231ff, 305.

76. Ibid., pp. 232–34.

77. Ibid., pp. 87–88.

78. Ibid., pp. 246–49.

79. Ibid., p. 251.

80. Ibid., pp. 114–15.

81. Ibid., pp. 133–35.

82. Ibid., pp. 283–84, quoting I. V. Stalin, *Sochineniia*, vol. 13 (Moscow, 1946–51), pp. 57–58.

83. Scott, *Behind*, p. 48.

84. Lewin, *Making*, p. 223.

85. Inkeles and Bauer, *Soviet Citizen*, p. 77.

86. The feeling of a massive, multifaceted revolution is well conveyed in a contemporary work by a generally sympathetic emigré witness to the times: Maurice Hindus, *The Great Offensive* (New York: Harrison Smith and Robert Haas, 1933), esp. chaps. 1–3.

87. George Urban, "Portrait of a Dissenter as a Soviet Man: A Conversation with Alexander Zinoviev," *Encounter*, April 1984, part 1, p. 21.

88. Ibid., p. 20.

89. Ibid., May 1984, part 2, p. 32.

90. Ibid.

91. Ibid.

92. I am not convinced that these *can* be separated. For anyone formed in the Western political-moral tradition, it seems to me that the judgment on this period—that of the Stalinization of an institutional system, one of whose most striking manifestations was the growth of the empire of the *gulag*—must be brutally negative. Even not considering the international dimension—the imposition of the Soviet system on Eastern Europe, the threat to the West from a USSR whose growth to military superpower began in the 1930s—the subjection of hundreds of millions to a regime that for so long locked them in a mesh of political repression and poverty and the deformation of human and state-society relations was catastrophic. Whatever the scale of social gains since 1917, the USSR is not their unique recipient—other countries have progressed, as well, and more than the USSR. The Soviet account will not balance. Since 1985 this has also been the conclusion drawn by many Soviet scholars and writers, who now have greater freedom to investigate the Soviet past. The writings of Afanas'ev, Seliunin, Tsipko, and others render a moral verdict on the evidence much more in line with that of "hard-line" students of Soviet reality than with that taken by Western "friends" of the Soviet Union for so many years.

93. The single best work remains Robert Conquest, *The Great Terror: Stalin's Purge of the Thirties* (New York: Macmillan, 1968).

94. Inkeles and Bauer, *Soviet Citizen*, p. 245.

95. On the dynamics of promotion, see Sheila Fitzpatrick, *Education and Social Mobility in the Soviet Union, 1921–1934* (Cambridge, Eng.: Cambridge University Press, 1979).

96. See esp. Robert A. Feldmesser, "Social Classes and Political Structure," in Black, ed., *Transformation*, pp. 235–52.

97. Donald Filtzer, *Soviet Workers and Stalinist Industrialization: The Formation*

of Modern Soviet Production Relations, 1928–1941 (London/New York: Pluto Press/M. E. Sharpe, 1986), p. 17.

98. I. I. Korotkov, "K proverke i chistke proizvodstvennykh iacheek," in E. M. Iaroslavskii, ed., *Kak provodit' chistku partii* (Moscow and Leningrad, 1929), p. 85, quoted in Kuromiya, *Stalin's Industrial Revolution*, p. 109.

99. Kuromiya, *Stalin's Industrial Revolution*, p. 132.

100. Filtzer, *Soviet Workers*, p. 21.

101. Ibid., p. 254.

102. Ibid., p. 255.

103. Ibid.

104. Neil Harding, "Socialism, Society, and the Organic Labour State," in Harding, ed., *The State in Socialist Society* (Albany: SUNY Press, 1984), pp. 29–30.

105. Ibid., p. 39.

106. Ibid., p. 42.

Chapter 2
A New Working Class?

The opening quote is from L. I. Brezhnev, *O konstitutsii SSSR: Doklady i vystupleniia* (Moscow, 1977), p. 11, quoted in M. E. Dobruskin, "Sodruzhestvo rabotnikov fizicheskogo i umstvennogo truda—vazhnaia cherta sotsialisticheskogo obraza zhizni," *Nauchnye doklady vysshei shkoly, Nauchnyi kommunizm*, no. 1 (1978), p. 40.

1. S. A. Gimatov, "Soderzhanie trudovykh traditsii sovetskogo rabochego klassa," in Moskovskii gosudarstvennyi universitet, *Sotsial'no-klassovye problemy razvitiia sotsialisticheskogo obshchestva* (Moscow: Izdatel'stvo MGU, 1969), p. 113.

2. M. P. Kim, "O nekotorykh osobennostiakh sovremennogo razvitiia rabochego klassa SSSR," in AON pri TsK KPSS, *Sovetskii rabochii klass na sovremennom etape* (Moscow: Mysl', 1964), p. 67.

3. A. V. Smirnov, "The Labor Force of the Heavy Machine-Building Industry of the USSR, 1946–1958," *Soviet Sociology* 2, 2 (Fall 1963), p. 24 (from *Istoricheskie Zapiski*, vol. 71, 1962).

4. Ibid., p. 22.

5. Akademiia Nauk SSSR (hereafter AN SSSR), Institut mezhdunarodnogo rabochego dvizheniia, *Sotsial'noe razvitie rabochego klassa SSSR* (Moscow: Nauka, 1977), pp. 22–23.

6. K. Z. Surblis, "Razvitie rabochego klassa Litovskoi SSR i izmeneniia v ego sostave," in AON pri TsK KPSS, *Sovetskii rabochii klass*, p. 147.

7. S. P. Zakharova, "Ob osnovnykh istochnikakh i formakh popolnenii rabochikh kadrov promyshlennosti Mariiskoi ASSR v gody chetvertoi i piatoi piatiletok," in *Iz istorii rabochego klassa SSSR* (Ivanovskii gosudarstvennyi pedagogicheskii institut, *Uchenye Zapiski*, vol. 71) (Ivanovo, 1970), pp. 126–27.

8. Jerzy G. Gliksman, "The Russian Urban Worker: From Serf to Proletarian," in Cyril E. Black, ed., *The Transformation of Russian Society* (Cambridge, Mass.: Harvard University Press, 1960), pp. 318–19.

9. AN SSSR, Institut filosofii, *Rabochii klass SSSR i ego vedushchaia rol' v stroi-tel'stve kommunizma* (Moscow: Nauka, 1975), p. 101.

10. L. A. Gordon and E. V. Klopov, "Sotsial'noe razvitie rabochego klassa SSSR," *Voprosy filosofii*, no. 2 (1972), p. 5, n. 8.

11. N. A. Aitov, *Sovetskii rabochii* (Moscow: Izdatel'stvo politicheskoi litera-tury, 1981), p. 25.

12. AN SSSR, Sibirskoe otdelenie, *Chislennost' i sostav rabochikh Sibiri v uslo-viiakh razvitogo sotsializma 1959–75* (Novosibirsk: Nauka, 1977), p. 113.

13. Kim, "O nekotorykh," p. 7.

14. F. G. Krotov, L. V. Fokin, and O. I. Shkaratan, *Rabochii klass: Ve-dushchaia sila stroitel'stva kommunizma* (Moscow: Mysl', 1965), pp. 23–25.

15. S. L. Seniavskii, *Rost rabochego klassa SSSR, 1951–1965 gg.* (Moscow: Nauka, 1969), p. 53.

16. AN SSSR, Institut istorii SSSR, *Rabochii klass SSSR, 1951–1965* (Moscow: Nauka, 1969), p. 89.

17. AN SSSR, *Rabochii klass SSSR*, p. 89; the same figures appear in AN SSSR, *Rabochii klass SSSR i ego vedushchaia rol'*, p. 101.

18. S. L. Seniavskii, "Nekotorye voprosy metodologii issledovaniia istorii rabochego klassa SSSR," in *Rabochii klass SSSR na sovremennom etape*, vol. 1 (Leningrad: Izdatel'stvo Leningradskogo universiteta, 1968), pp. 76–77.

19. AN SSSR, *Rabochii klass i ego vedushchaia rol'*, cites "340–350 thousand" (p. 102), while AN SSSR, *Rabochii klass SSSR, 1951–1965*, cites "350–400 thousand," p. 89.

20. AN SSSR, *Rabochii klass i ego vedushchaia rol'*, p. 102.

21. T. A. Babushkina, V. S. Dunin, and E. A. Zenkevich, "Sotsial'nye problemy formirovaniia novykh popolnenii rabochego klassa," *RKSM*, no. 3 (1981), p. 44.

22. See the data reported for three different surveys in Gordon and Klopov, "Sotsial'noe razvitie," p. 5, n. 8; Aitov, *Sovetskii rabochii*, p. 25; and AN SSSR, *Chislennost' i sostav*, p. 113.

23. AN SSSR, *Rabochii klass SSSR, 1951–1965*, pp. 101–102; see also M. P. Kim and S. L. Seniavskii, "The Growth of the Working Class of the USSR, 1953–61," *Soviet Sociology* 2, 2 (Fall 1963), pp. 3–20 (from *Voprosy istorii*, no. 3, 1963).

24. E. V. Klopov, *Rabochii klass SSSR (tendentsii razvitiia v 60–70-e gody)* (Moscow: Mysl', 1985), pp. 140–41.

25. Kim, "O nekotorykh," p. 8.

26. Klopov, *Rabochii klass*, pp. 138–41.

27. AN SSSR, *Rabochii klass SSSR, 1951–1965*, p. 89.

28. A. A. Amvrosov, "Vedushchaia rol' rabochego klassa v razvitii so-vetskogo obshchestva," in Vysshaia partiinaia shkola pri TsK KPSS, *Vedushchaia rol' rabochego klassa v sotsialisticheskikh stranakh* (Moscow: Mysl', 1974), p. 37.

29. Klopov, *Rabochii klass*, p. 140.

30. Ibid., p. 140.

31. E. V. Somova, "Ob istochnikakh popolneniia rabochego klassa i inzhenerno-tekhnicheskoi intelligentsii," in Ministerstvo vysshego i sredne-

spetsial'nogo obrazovaniia RSFSR, *Protsessy izmeneniia sotsial'noi struktury v sovetskom obshchestve* (Sverdlovsk, 1967), p. 112.

32. See Mervyn Matthews, *Class and Society in Soviet Russia* (New York: Walker and Company, 1972); Murray Yanowitch, *Social and Economic Inequality in the Soviet Union* (White Plains, N.Y.: M. E. Sharpe, 1977); Murray Yanowitch and Wesley A. Fisher, eds., *Social Stratification and Mobility in the USSR* (White Plains, N.Y.: International Arts and Sciences Press, 1973); see also, for a perspective on the USSR and the East European states, David Lane, *The End of Social Inequality? Status and Power under State Socialism* (London: Allen and Unwin, 1982), and Walter D. Connor, *Socialism, Politics and Equality: Hierarchy and Change in Eastern Europe and the USSR* (New York: Columbia University Press, 1979).

33. See Gur Ofer, *The Service Sector in Soviet Economic Growth: A Comparative Study* (Cambridge, Mass.: Harvard University Press, 1973).

34. N. Panteleev, "Razvitie ekonomiki i podgotovka molodezhi k trudu," *ST*, no. 9 (1983), p. 31.

35. Aitov, *Sovetskii rabochii*, p. 25.

36. AN SSSR, *Chislennost' i sostav*, p. 113.

37. M. N. Rutkevich and F. R. Filippov, *Sotsial'nye peremeshcheniia* (Moscow: Mysl', 1970), p. 89.

38. F. R. Filippov, "Sotsial'nye peremeshcheniia v sovetskom obshchestve," *SI*, no. 4 (1975), p. 16.

39. Both L. A. Gordon and E. V. Klopov, *Chelovek posle raboty* (Moscow: Nauka, 1972), and Klopov's *Rabochii klass* are based on studies in Taganrog.

40. See AN SSSR, Institut mezhdunarodnogo rabochego dvizheniia, *Sotsial'noe razvitie*, pp. 26–27.

41. Klopov, *Rabochii klass*, p. 136.

42. G. Bliakhman, "Sotsial'nyi portret sovremennogo molodogo rabochego," *ST*, no. 10 (1979), p. 63.

43. Rutkevich and Filippov, *Sotsial'nye peremeshcheniia*, p. 89.

44. G. A. Slesarev, *Demograficheskie protsessy i sotsial'naia struktura sotsialisticheskogo obshchestva* (Moscow: Nauka, 1978), p. 116.

45. F. R. Filippov, "Nauchno-tekhnicheskii progress i sovershenstvovanie sotsial'noi struktury sovetskogo obshchestva," *SI*, no. 4 (1985), p. 5.

46. O. I. Shkaratan, O. V. Stakanova, and O. V. Filippova, "Cherty sotsial'nogo rosta sovetskogo rabochego," *SI*, no. 4 (1977), pp. 33–44 (trans. in *JPRS* 70514, January 20, 1978, pp. 7–22, 12–13).

47. A. V. Smirnov, "Labor Force," p. 33.

48. AON pri TsK KPSS, *Rabochii klass razvitogo sotsialisticheskogo obshchestva* (Moscow: Mysl', 1974), p. 79.

49. The discussion which follows draws on a number of sources: Mervyn Matthews, *Education in the Soviet Union: Policies and Institutions Since Stalin* (London: George Allen and Unwin, 1982), esp. pp. 24ff; Robert J. Osborn, *Soviet Social Policies: Welfare, Equality, and Opportunity* (Homewood, Ill.: Dorsey, 1970), pp. 95–135; Joel J. Schwartz and William R. Keech, "Public Influence and Educational Policy in the Soviet Union," in Roger E. Kanet, ed.,

The Behavioral Revolution and Communist Studies (New York: Free Press, 1971), pp. 151–86, as well as those cited in the footnotes that follow.

50. Warren W. Eason, "Labor Force," in Abram Bergson and Simon Kuznets, eds., *Economic Trends in the Soviet Union* (Cambridge, Mass.: Harvard University Press, 1963), pp. 66–67.

51. Osborn, *Soviet Social Policies*, p. 96.

52. Nicholas De Witt, "Upheaval in Education," *Problems of Communism* 8, 1 (January–February 1959), pp. 28–29.

53. Schwartz and Keech, "Public," note the first explanation, while Matthews, *Education*, emphasizes the latter.

54. See A. A. Kissel', "K voprosu o motivakh povysheniia obshcheobrazovatel'nogo urovnia molodogo rabochego," *Chelovek i obshchestvo*, vol. 2 (1967), pp. 67–68.

55. See M. N. Rutkevich, "Reforma obrazovaniia, potrebnosti obshchestva, molodezh', " *SI*, no. 4 (1984), pp. 22–23.

56. Here, I follow the general argument of Schwartz and Keech, "Public," but emphasize the labor-supply factor they regarded as marginal to Khrushchev's motives.

57. I emphasize the broader professional strata here. The narrow, "super-elite" of several thousand high party, state, and military leaders were still, of course, able to preserve *their* advantage for their children, so far as we can tell.

58. F. R. Filippov, "Srednaia shkola kak faktor sotsial'noi mobil'nosti," in M. N. Rutkevich and Iu. E. Volkov, eds., *Izmeneniia sotsial'noi struktury sotsialisticheskogo obshchestva* (Sverdlovsk; Ural'skii gosudarstvennyi universitet, 1965), pp. 101–102.

59. Ibid., p. 103.

60. *Istoriia rabochego klassa razvitogo sotsialisticheskogo obshchestva (Rabochii klass SSSR na sovremennom etape)*, vol. 10 (Leningrad: Izdatel'stvo Leningradskogo universiteta, 1983), p. 173.

61. T. V. Riabushkin, "Pokazateli sotsial'nogo razvitiia rabochego klassa," *SI*, no. 4 (1980), p. 23.

62. Filippov, "Nauchno-tekhnicheskii progress," p. 7.

63. I. S. Kon et al., *Obshchestvo i molodezh'*, 2d ed. (Moscow: Molodaia gvardiia, 1973), p. 122.

64. Rutkevich, "Reforma obrazovaniia," p. 23.

65. See Yanowitch, *Social and Economic Inequality*, p. 80.

66. See Gregory Grossman, "An Economy at Middle Age," *Problems of Communism* 25, 2 (March–April 1976), pp. 18–33.

67. Filippov, "Nauchno-tekhnicheskii progress," p. 5.

68. F. R. Filippov, L. G. Gaft, E. D. Igitkhanian, and V. I. Molchanov, "Trudovye biografii pokolenii (nekotorye rezul'taty vsesoiuznogo issledovaniia)," *SI*, no. 4 (1986), p. 33.

69. Ibid.

70. Ibid., p. 34.

71. Ibid., p. 33.

72. Ibid.

73. V. N. Shubkin, ed., *Trudiashchiasia molodezh': Obrazovanie, professiia, mobil'nost'* (Moscow: Nauka, 1984). The figures cited here are drawn directly, calculated, or interpolated from data in tables 86–91, pp. 171ff.

74. Ibid.

75. Ibid., table 93, p. 179.

76. My calculations are based on ibid., tables 95–97, pp. 182–184.

77. N. A. Aitov, V. G. Mordkovich, and M. Kh. Titma, eds., *Sovetskii gorod: Sotsial'naia struktura* (Moscow: Mysl', 1988), p. 175, table 41. Long-term trends would further intensify hereditization, in that the data indicate a good number of non-manual-origin children with first jobs as workers. These are often short-term "parking spaces" for youth who will later connect with educational opportunities providing exit from the worker stratum and reentry into the stratum of origin.

78. Ibid., p. 176, table 42.

79. Ibid.; see comments about this on pp. 133–35, and table 29, p. 135.

80. L. A. Gordon and A. K. Nazimova, "Sotsial'no-professional'naia struktura sovremennogo sovetskogo obshchesta: Kharakter i napravlenie peremen," *RKSM*, no. 3 (1983), pp. 59–72 (trans. in *Soviet Sociology* 24, 1–3, Summer-Fall-Winter 1985–86, pp. 33–61, 53–54).

81. See Donna Bahry, "Politics, Generations and Change in the USSR," *SIP, Working Paper No. 20* pp. 37–38 and fig. 8 (Urbana-Champaign: University of Illinois, March 1986, mimeo).

82. For an emphasis on differentiation among Soviet workers, see Alex Pravda, "Is There a Soviet Working Class?" *Problems of Communism* 21, 6 (November–December 1982), pp. 1–24.

83. See the argument, which was to some degree later echoed by Soviet writers who questioned the benefits of general education for most kinds of work, in Ivar Berg, *Education and Jobs: The Great Training Robbery* (New York: Praeger, 1970).

Chapter 3
Forming Workers

The opening quote, by an official of the Moldavian SSR, is taken from "Proforientatsiia i trudoustroistvo molodezhi v respublike," *ST*, no. 7 (1983), p. 75.

1. See V. V. Ksenofontova, "Career Plans of 8th and 9th Grade Students and Their Realization," in M. N. Rutkevich, ed., *The Career Plans of Youth* (White Plains, N.Y.: International Arts and Sciences Press, 1969), p. 48.

2. V. S. Gendel', "Problemy sotsial'noi podvizhnosti molodezhi pri sotsializme," *kandidat* dissertation, Leningrad State University, 1971, p. 175, cited in Richard B. Dobson, "Education and Opportunity," in Jerry G. Pankhurst and Michael P. Sacks, eds., *Contemporary Soviet Society* (New York: Praeger, 1980), p. 121.

3. M. N. Rutkevich, "Reforma obrazovaniia, potrebnosti obshchestva, molodezh'," *SI*, no. 4 (1984), p. 24.

4. F. R. Filippov, "Srednaia shkola kak faktor sotsial'noi mobilnosti," in

M. N. Rutkevich and Iu. E. Volkov, eds., *Izmenenie sotsial'noi struktury sotsialisticheskogo obshchestva* (Sverdlovsk: Ural'skii gosudarstvennyi universitet, 1965), p. 103.

5. E. K. Vasil'eva, *The Young People of Leningrad: School and Work Options and Attitudes* (White Plains, N.Y.: International Arts and Sciences Press, 1976), p. 51.

6. See Ia. M. Tkach, "Career Plans of Graduates of Complete Secondary Schools," in Rutkevich, ed., *Career Plans*, pp. 57–62.

7. V. N. Shubkin, "Molodezh' vstupaet v zhizn'," *Voprosy filosofii*, no. 5 (1965) (trans. in *Soviet Sociology* 4, 3, Winter 1965–66, p. 10).

8. Adapted from Ia. M. Tkach, "Roditeli o sud'bakh svoikh detei," in *Protsessy izmeneniia sotsial'noi struktury v sovetskom obshchestve* (Sverdlovsk: Ministerstvo vysshego i sredne-spetsial'nogo obrazovaniia RSFSR, 1967), pp. 147–50.

9. B. G. Rubin and Iu. S. Kolesnikov, *Student glazami sotsiologa: Sotsial'nye problemy vosproizvodstva rabochei sily vysshei kvalifikatsii* (Rostov: Izdatel'stvo Rostovskogo universiteta, 1968), p. 70, and A. V. Isaiko, "Nekotorye sotsial'nye problemy vysshego zaochnogo i vechernego obrazovaniia," in Iu. Leonavichius, ed., *Effektivnost' podgotovki spetsialistov* (Kaunas: Kaunas politekhnicheskii institut, 1969), p. 224, cited in Dobson, "Education," p. 127.

10. L. I. Sennikova, "Vechernoe i zaochnoe obuchenie v vysshei shkoly kak faktor izmeneniia sotsial'nogo polozheniia," in *Protsessy izmeneniia*, p. 135.

11. See David Lane and Felicity O'Dell, *The Soviet Industrial Worker: Social Class, Education, and Control* (New York: St. Martin's Press, 1978), pp. 101–105.

12. See, e.g., Vera S. Dunham, "The Waning Theme of the Worker as Hero in Recent Soviet Literature," in Arcadius Kahan and Blair A. Ruble, eds., *Industrial Labor in the USSR* (New York: Pergamon Press, 1979), pp. 401–403.

13. Murray Yanowitch, *Social and Economic Inequality in the Soviet Union* (White Plains, N.Y.: M. E. Sharpe, 1977), p. 80, and sources cited therein in n. 38.

14. F. R. Filippov, "Rol' vysshei shkoly v izmenenii sotsial'noi struktury sovetskogo obshchestva," *SI*, no. 2 (1977), p. 48.

15. Slesarev, *Demograficheskie protsessy*, pp. 136–37.

16. I. Bolotin and V. Chizhov, "Trudovye resursy i sistema narodnogo obrazovaniia," *Planovoe khoziaistvo*, no. 8 (1981), p. 104.

17. E. V. Belkin, "Professional'no-tekhnicheskoe obrazovanie v zhiznennykh planakh molodezhi," *SI*, no. 2 (1981), p. 107.

18. Slesarev, *Demograficheskie protsessy*, pp. 135–36.

19. V. Potapovich, "Trudoustroistvo vypusknikov obshcheobrazovatel'nykh shkol," *ST*, no. 5 (1983), p. 87.

20. V. Gentvainite, A. Matulenis, and M. Taliunaite, "Sotsial'naia orientatsiia vypusknikov srednykh shkol," *SI*, no. 2 (1977), p. 75.

21. V. N. Turchenko, "Vazhneishaia sostavliaiushchaia proizvoditel'nykh sil," *EKO*, no. 12 (1983), pp. 87–88.

22. Ibid., p. 88.

23. Ibid.; see sources cited by Turchenko (notes 19, 20).

24. I. E. Zaslavskii, V. A. Kuz'min, and R. T. Ostrovskaia, "Sotsial'nye i

professional'nye ustanovki moskovskikh shkolnikov," *SI*, no. 3 (1983), p. 131.

25. N. A. Aitov, "Vlianie obshcheobrazovatel'nogo urovnia rabochikh na ikh proizvodstvennuiu deiatel'nost'," *Voprosy filosofii*, no. 11 (1966), p. 24.

26. A. Maikov, "Trudovye resursy i proizvoditel'nost' truda," *ST*, no. 10 (1971) (trans. in *Problems of Economics* 15, 3, July 1972, p. 64).

27. M. Ia. Sonin, "Effektivno ispol'zovat' trudovye resursy," *EKO*, no. 4 (1977), pp. 3–12 (trans. in *Problems of Economics* 20, 12, April 1978, pp. 5–6); see also T. Baranenkova, "Rezervy ekonomii rabochei sily," *Voprosy ekonomiki*, no. 5 (1980), pp. 51–62 (trans. in *Problems of Economics* 23, 10, February 1981, p. 6).

28. Maikov, "Trudovye," p. 64.

29. See Murray Feshbach, "The Structure and Composition of the Industrial Labor Force," in Kahan and Ruble, eds., *Industrial Labor*, p. 8, and sources cited therein.

30. See A. Solov'ev, "Vo vsem li prav Kulagin?" (a discussion of G. Kulagin, "Sootvetstvuet li sistema obrazovaniia potrebnostiam narodnogo khoziaistva?" *ST*, no. 1, 1980), in *ST*, no. 7 (1980), p. 105, cited in *RLR* 308/80, August 29, 1980.

31. K. Karpukhin and I. Oblomskaia, "Sotsial'no-ekonomicheskie problemy truda na etape razvitogo sotsializma," *Planovoe khoziaistvo*, no. 2 (1980), pp. 90–100 (trans. in *Problems of Economics* 23, 6, October 1980, pp. 65–66).

32. E. V. Foteeva, *Kachestvennye kharakteristiki naseleniia SSSR* (Moscow: Finansy i statistika, 1984), pp. 93–94.

33. V. Kostakov, "Ekonomnoe ispol'zovanie truda zaniatogo naseleniia," *Planovoe khoziaistvo*, no. 7 (1974), pp. 72–77 (trans. in *Problems of Economics* 18, 1, May 1975, p. 79).

34. N. A. Aitov, "O nekotorykh diskussionykh voprosakh izucheniia sovetskoi intelligentsii," *SI*, no. 3 (1979), pp. 29–34 (trans. in *Soviet Sociology* 20, 2, Fall 1981, p. 31).

35. Iu. P. Sosin, "Faktory ukrepleniia trudovoi distsipliny," *EKO*, no. 5 (1975), pp. 66–174 (trans. in *CDSP*, February 18, 1976, p. 8).

36. *Pravda*, June 28, 1983, p. 3 (trans. in *CDSP*, July 27, 1983, p. 25).

37. A. E. Kotliar and M. I. Talalai, "Kak zakrepit' molodye kadry," *EKO*, no. 4 (1977), pp. 26–43 (trans. in *CDSP*, September 21, 1977, pp. 1–3).

38. V. A. Smirnov, "Problema formivovaniia v rabochei molodezhi soznatel'nogo otnosheniia k trudu," *SI*, no. 4 (1978), p. 85, table 3.

39. See Rutkevich in *Sovetskaia Rossiia*, September 21, 1983, p. 3 (*CDSP*, November 2, 1983, pp. 1–4).

40. *Izvestiia*, January 29, 1977, p. 5 (*CDSP*, February 23, 1977, p. 31).

41. Iu. Averichev, "Proforientatsiia molodezhi i prestizh rabochei professii," *ST*, no. 6 (1977), pp. 130–32.

42. E. V. Belkin, "Professional'no-tekhnicheskoe obrazovanie," p. 106.

43. I. E. Zaslavskii, V. A. Kuz'min, and R. T. Ostrovskaia, "Sotsial'nye i professional'nye," p. 132.

44. Kotliar and Talalai, "Kak zakrepit'," pp. 1–3.

45. I. N. Ryndia, "Proizvodstvennaia aktivnost' molodykh rabochikh," *SI*, no. 4 (1983), p. 94.

46. *Sovetskaia kul'tura,* January 4, 1986 (*CDSP,* February 19, 1986, pp. 1–4).

47. TASS interview, January 16, 1986 (cited in *RLR* 35/86, January 17, 1986, p. 11).

48. See, e.g., *New York Times,* July 4, 1987, pp. 1–2.

49. The discussion that follows is based on the following sources: Matthews, *Education,* pp. 67–87; Michael Swafford, "The Socialization and Training of the Soviet Industrial Labor Force," in Kahan and Ruble, eds., *Industrial Labor,* pp. 19–41; Osborn, *Soviet Social Policies,* pp. 116–25.

50. Matthews, *Education* p. 70.

51. E. V. Somova, "Ob istochnikakh popolneniia rabochego klassa i inzhenerno-tekhnicheskoi intelligentsii," in *Protsessy izmeneniia,* pp. 111–12.

52. See Matthews, *Education,* pp. 82–84.

53. Somova, "Ob istochnikakh," p. 112.

54. Swafford, "Socialization," pp. 27–29.

55. V. P. Tomin, *Uroven' obrazovaniia naseleniia SSSR* (Moscow: Finansy i statistika, 1981) (trans. in *Soviet Education* 26, 7–8, May–June 1984, pp. 53–54).

56. E. G. Antosenkov, "Raznye grani odnoi problemy," *EKO,* no. 3 (1977), p. 103.

57. L. N. Dmitrieva, "Zabota partii o povyshenii obrazovatel'nogo urovnia molodogo pokoleniia rabochego klassa," in *Rabochii klass SSSR v sovremennom etape,* vol. 2 (Leningrad: Izdatel'stvo Leningradskogo universiteta, 1973), p. 136.

58. V. Bilibin and I. Kocheryzhkin, "S uchetom trebovanii sovremennogo proizvodstva," *Professional'no-tekhnicheskoe obrazovanie,* no. 6 (1969), pp. 6–7.

59. N. P. Konstantinova, O. V. Stakanova, and O. I. Shkaratan, "Peremeny v sotsial'nom oblike rabochikh v epokhu razvitogo sotsializma," *Voprosy istorii,* no. 5 (1978), pp. 3–18 (trans. in *Soviet Sociology* 17, 4, Spring 1979, p. 11).

60. Matthews, *Education,* p. 84.

61. Reprinted as "Molodaia smena rabochego klassa," *Professional'no-tekhnicheskoe obrazovanie,* no. 5 (1969), p. 3.

62. See Matthews, *Education,* p. 84; Swafford, "Socialization," pp. 24ff; V. F. Finogenov, "Vlianie podgotovki i vospitaniia rabochikh na izmeneniia struktury rabochego klassa," in *Podgotovka i vospitanie kadrov rabochego klassa SSSR v usloviiakh razvitogo sotsializma* (*Rabochii klass SSSR v sovremennom etape*), vol. 5 (Leningrad: Izdatel'stvo Leningradskogo universiteta, 1977), pp. 31–32.

63. See, e.g., E. Morozov, "Voprosy organizatsii uchebnoi raboty v prof-tekhuchilishchakh novogo tipa," *Professional'no-tekhnicheskoe obrazovanie,* no. 8 (1969), pp. 8–10.

64. A. Bulgakov, "Novye rubezhi sovetskoi professional'noi shkoly," *Professional'no-tekhnicheskoe obrazovanie,* no. 5 (1971), p. 1.

65. I. Bolotin and V. Chizhov, "Trudovye resursy i sistema narodnogo obrazovaniia," *Planovoe khoziaistvo,* no. 8 (1982), p. 103.

66. George Avis, "Access to Higher Education in the Soviet Union," in J. J. Tomiak, ed., *Soviet Education in the 1980s* (London/New York: Croom Helm/St. Martin's Press, 1983), p. 203.

67. F. R. Filippov and V. A. Malova, "O nekotorykh napravleniiakh povysheniia effektivnosti obrazovaniia," *SI*, no. 2 (1984), pp. 62–71 (trans. in *Soviet Education* 28, 4, February 1986, pp. 92–93).

68. D. I. Ziuzin, "Orientatsiia shkolnikov na razlichnye formy srednego obrazovaniia," *SI*, no. 1 (1977), p. 97.

69. Ibid., p. 99.

70. Avis, "Access," p. 207.

71. N. Novoselov, "Schools for a Totalitarian-Technocratic Utopia," *RLR* 115/84, March 13, 1984, p. 2.

72. *Uchitel'skaia gazeta*, February 4, 1973, p. 3.

73. E. V. Belkin, "Professional'no-tekhnicheskoe obrazovanie," p. 103.

74. I. S. Poltorak and Iu. E. Shul'ga, "Adaptatsiia vypusknikov proftekhuchilishch na proizvodstve," *SI*, no. 2 (1984), pp. 79–80.

75. E. Zhil'tsov, "Sovershenstvovanie kompleksnogo planirovaniia obrazovaniia i podgotovki kadrov," *NDVS, Ekonomicheskie nauki*, no. 1 (1980), pp. 61–70 (trans. in *Problems of Economics* 23, 6, October 1980, p. 45).

76. Ibid.

77. F. R. Filippov, *Sotsiologiia obrazovaniia* (Moscow: Nauka, 1980) (trans. in *Soviet Education* 26, 12, October 1984, p. 50).

78. Ibid., pp. 51–52.

79. Zhil'tsov, "Sovershenstvovanie," p. 46.

80. Ibid.

81. Ibid., p. 47.

82. *Pravda* and *Izvestiia*, January 4, 1984, pp. 1–2 (trans. in *CDSP*, February 1, 1984, pp. 1–9).

83. The official compilation is *O reforme obshcheobrazovatel'noi i professional'noi shkoly: Sbornik dokumentov i materialov* (Moscow: Izdatel'stvo politicheskoi literatury, 1984). Much of the contents of that volume is also available in English in *USSR: New Frontiers of Social Progress: Documents of the First Session of the USSR Supreme Soviet (Eleventh Convocation), April 11–12, 1984* (Moscow: Novosti Press Agency Publishing House, 1984). The final reform document is also translated in *CDSP*, May 30, 1984, pp. 12–20 (but see n. 85, below).

84. *Pravda*, June 16, 1983 (trans. in *CDSP*, July 20, 1983, p. 6).

85. My translation is from *O reforme*, p. 42. However, the *CDSP* (May 30, 1984, p. 13) translation of this section renders approximate "doubling" as increasing by one-and-a-half times.

86. *CDSP*, February 1, 1983, p. 4.

87. *CDSP*, May 30, 1984, p. 13.

88. An alternate calculation works this way for 1980 estimates (total equals 100%): to academic school, 52.0%; to SPTU, 19.6%; to PTU, 17.7%; to *tekhnikum*, 10.7%. Then, assuming (1) stability in *tekhnikum* entrance, (2) merger of SPTU and PTU, and (3) "doubling" of the intake of (2), the reform line yields (total 100%): to academic school, 28.6%; to SPTU, 60.7%; to *tekhnikum* 10.7%. Basic figures for academic school ninth grade, SPTU, and PTU adapted from Felicity O'Dell, "Vocational Education in the USSR," in Tomiak, ed., *Soviet Education*, pp. 127–28. Data on enrollments in *tekhnikums*, and on the shares of entrants from eighth and tenth grades, were derived from a combination of Filippov,

Sotsiologiia obrazovaniia, pp. 5, 50–52, and Bolotin and Chizhov, "Trudovye resursy," pp. 101–104).

89. Filippov and Malova, "O nekotorykh napravleniiakh," pp. 96–97.

90. B. A. Efimov, "Obrazovanie i sotsial'no-professional'noe podvizhenie molodykh rabochikh," *SI*, no. 3 (1977), p. 50.

91. V. G. Aseev, L. A. Gorchakov, and N. E. Kogan, "Kakim ty pridesh v rabochii klass?" in E. K. Vasil'eva et al., *Sovetskaia molodezh: Demograficheskii aspekt* (Moscow: Finansy i statistika, 1981), pp. 62–63.

92. Foteeva, *Kachestvennye kharakteristiki*, p. 148.

93. Ibid., p. 145, citing B. E. Levanov, "Semeinoe vospitanie: Sostoianie i problemy," *SI*, no. 1 (1979), p. 118.

94. G. A. Aliev, "Ob osnovnykh napravleniiakh reformy obshcheobrazovatel'noi i professional'noi shkoly," *Uchitel'skaia gazeta*, April 13, 1984 (trans. in *Soviet Education* 27, 6–7 April–May 1985, p. 141).

95. M. Zimianin, "Sleduia Leninskim printsipom razvitiia," *Kommunist*, no. 7 (1984), pp. 18–34 (trans. in *Soviet Education* 28, 1, November 1985, p. 59).

96. Ibid.

97. "Reforma obshcheobrazovatel'noi i professional'noi shkoly—sostavnaia chast' sovershenstvovaniia razvitogo sotsializma," *Politicheskoe samoobrazovanie*, no. 9 (1984), pp. 69–75 (trans. in *Soviet Education* 28, 1, November 1985, pp. 88–89).

98. *Sovetskaia Belorussiia*, February 4, 1984, p. 3 (trans. in *CDSP*, March 28, 1984, pp. 14–17).

99. *Izvestiia*, January 7, 1984, p. 2 (trans. in *CDSP*, February 15, 1984, pp. 7–9).

100. *Izvestiia*, January 27, 1984, p. 3 (trans. in ibid.).

101. *Sovetskaia Belorussiia*, February 4, 1984, p. 3 (trans. in *CDSP*, February 15, 1984, pp. 7–9).

102. *Literaturnaia gazeta*, March 7, 1984, p. 10 (trans. in *CDSP*, May 2, 1984, p. 13).

103. See I. N. Nazimov, "V sootvetstvii s vozmozhnostiami cheloveka i potrebnostiami obshchestva," *EKO*, no. 3 (1977), p. 91.

104. V. D. Voinova and V. S. Korobeinikov, "Obshchestvennoe mnenie o reforme shkoly—edinstvo i mnogoobrazie," *SI*, no. 4 (1984), p. 100.

105. A. V. Kinsburskii, "Vseobshchee professional'noe obrazovanie molodezhi: Mneniia, otsenki," *SI*, no. 4 (1984), p. 103.

106. Zimianin, "Sleduia," p. 60.

107. See *Uchitel'skaia gazeta*, August 22, 1985, pp. 1–2.

108. See, e.g., A. Gladkii, "Uchilishche v . . . nagruzku," *Professional'no-tekhnicheskoe obrazovanie*, no. 4 (1986), pp. 34–35.

109. Jerry F. Hough, "Policy-Making and the Worker," in Kahan and Ruble, eds., *Industrial Labor*, p. 381.

110. *Sovetskaia Rossiia*, October 24, 1986, p. 2.

111. See *Izvestiia*, September 22, 1987, p. 3 (*FBIS*, October 21, 1987, pp. 18–19).

112. See *Pravda*, December 29, 1987, p. 3 (*CDSP*, January 27, 1988, pp. 29–30).

113. *Pravda*, September 12, 1987, p. 2 (*CDSP*, October 21, 1987, p. 20).

114. *Pravda* and *Izvestiia*, February 18, 1988, pp. 1–4 (*CDSP*, March 23, 1988, p. 9).

115. Radio Moscow (Russian), 1000 GMT, March 8, 1988 (*FBIS*, March 8, 1988).

116. See *Uchitel'skaia gazeta*, August 22, 1987.

117. Radio Moscow, World Service (English), 0310 GMT, March 26, 1988 (*FBIS*, April 25, 1988, p. 49).

118. See Albert O. Hirschmann, *Exit, Voice and Loyalty* (Cambridge, Mass.: Harvard University Press, 1970).

Chapter 4
Work, Wages, and Welfare

The opening quote is from E. V. Klopov, *Rabochii klass SSSR (Tendentsii razvitiia v 60–70-e gody)* (Moscow: Mysl', 1985), pp. 260, 261.

1. For 1932 and 1940, see L. A. Gordon and E. V. Klopov, "Sotsial'noe razvitie rabochego klassa SSSR," *Voprosy filosofii*, no. 2 (1972), p. 12, table 5. For 1978, see M. N. Rutkevich, "Sblizhenie rabochego klassa i inzhenerno-tekhnicheskoi intelligentsii," *SI*, no. 4 (1980), pp. 25–34 (trans. in *JPRS 77574*, March 12, 1981, p. 28). For other years, see Janet C. Chapman, "Recent Trends in the Soviet Industrial Wage Structure," in Kahan and Ruble, eds., *Industrial Labor*, p. 173, and sources cited therein.

2. Chapman, "Recent Trends," pp. 169, 172.

3. Rutkevich, "Sblizhenie," p. 28.

4. See Connor, *Socialism, Politics and Equality*, passim.

5. As a distinguished economist noted, by the later 1970s it was very low pay levels in the "nonproduction" sphere, not simply the supply of jobs rated "unskilled," that produced a category of very poorly paid people. Women, of course, are heavily overrepresented in the "nonproductive" sector, and the difficulties of single mothers with a dependent or two in this area must be great indeed. See, on these matters, N. M. Rimashevskaia, "Strukturnye izmeneniia v tendentsiiakh rosta blagosostoianiia," *SI*, no. 4 (1985), p. 29.

6. See, e.g., Rutkevich, "Sblizhenie," p. 28.

7. See Abram Bergson, *The Economics of Soviet Planning* (New Haven and London: Yale University Press, 1964), p. 115, and sources cited therein.

8. Ibid.

9. Ibid., p. 117.

10. The major works are Alastair McAuley, *Economic Welfare in the Soviet Union: Poverty, Living Standards, and Inequality* (Madison: University of Wisconsin Press, 1979); and Leonard J. Kirsch, *Soviet Wages* (Cambridge, Mass.: MIT Press, 1972).

11. See McAuley, *Economic Welfare*, pp. 184–91, for a discussion of the logic of skill differentials.

12. Ibid., p. 192.

13. See ibid., pp. 192–94, on working-condition differentials.

14. See ibid., pp. 119–21, on regional differentials.

15. Alec Nove, *An Economic History of the USSR* (Harmondsworth, U.K.: Penguin Books, 1982), pp. 347–48.

16. Gosudarstvennyi komitet Soveta Ministrov SSSR po voprosam truda i zarabotnoi platy, *Trud i zarabotnaia plata v SSSR* (2d rev. ed.) (Moscow: Ekonomika, 1974), p. 241.

17. Ibid.

18. See McAuley, *Economic Welfare*, p. 188, and sources cited therein.

19. See Chapman, "Recent Trends," p. 155.

20. McAuley, *Economic Welfare*, p. 207.

21. V. Maier, "Aktual'nye problemy povysheniia narodnogo blagosostoianiia," *Voprosy ekonomiki*, no. 11 (1977), pp. 47–56 (trans. in *Problems of Economics* 20, 12, February 1978, p. 13).

22. McAuley, *Economic Welfare*, pp. 206–207.

23. Maier, "Aktual'nye problemy," p. 13.

24. See McAuley, *Economic Welfare*, p. 210, on this matter.

25. Maier, "Aktual'nye problemy," p. 13.

26. O. I. Shkaratan, "Peremeny v sotsial'nom oblike gorozhan," in AN SSSR, Institut sotsiologicheskikh issledovanii, *Sovetskaia sotsiologiia*, vol. 2 (Moscow: Nauka, 1982), pp. 39–52 (trans. in *Soviet Sociology* 24, 1–3, Summer-Fall-Winter 1985–86, pp. 104–19, table 2).

27. See the comments on this in L. S. Bliakhman and T. S. Zlotnitskaia, "Differentsiatsiia zarabotnoi platy kak faktor stimulirovaniia truda," *SI*, no. 1 (1984), pp. 39–47 (trans. in *Soviet Sociology* 23, 4, Spring 1985, p. 46).

28. See Connor, *Socialism, Politics, and Equality*, pp. 259–66.

29. See A. A. Ovsiannikov, "Vzaimosviaz' truda i potrebleniia: Opyt tipologicheskogo analiza," *SI*, no. 1 (1984), pp. 84–87 (trans. in *Soviet Sociology* 24, 1–3, Summer-Fall-Winter 1985–86, pp. 120–25, table 1).

30. See Aaron Vinokur and Gur Ofer, "Family Income Levels for Soviet Industrial Workers, 1965–75," in Kahan and Ruble, eds., *Industrial Labor*, p. 198, for a discussion of "adult equivalent units" and dependency.

31. Ovsiannikov, "Vzaimosviaz'," p. 85.

32. Ibid.

33. Ibid.

34. Vinokur and Ofer, "Family Income," p. 191.

35. E. I. Romanovskii, "Sem'i trudiashchikhsia v SSSR: Dokhod i blagosostoianie," *RKSM*, no. 6 (1986), p. 76.

36. I. Gladkii, "Vazhneishee sotsial'no-ekonomicheskoe meropriiatie piatiletki," *ST*, no. 1 (1987), p. 11.

37. See V. Shcherbakov, "Povyshenie stimuliruiushchei roli zarabatnoi platy," *ST*, no. 1 (1987), p. 30.

38. Romanovskii, "Sem'i trudiashchikhsia," p. 77.

39. Ibid., pp. 80–82.

40. Numerous people classified as "workers," of course, are to be found outside industry, predominantly in transport, communications, construction, and several other sectors. Similarly (see chap. 2) in the service sector, some low-level functionaries whose work lies at the boundary of mental and manual labor were reclassified from "employee" to "worker" in the past two decades.

41. See E. Kapustin, "Ekonomicheskii aspekt sotsialisticheskogo obraza zhizni," *Voprosy ekonomiki*, no. 6 (1975), pp. 38–47 (trans. in *Problems of Economics* 18, 11, March 1976, p. 15).

42. Ibid.

43. L. T. Volchkova, "Osnovnye tendentsii differentsiatsii zarabotnoi platy na sovremennom etape razvitiia sotsializma," *Vestnik Leningradskogo universiteta*, no. 23 (1980) (seriia ekonomiki-filosofii-prava, vyp. 4), p. 13.

44. I. A. Gomberg and L. Sushkina, "Osnovnye napravleniia differentsiatsii zarabotnoi platy rabotnikov promyshlennosti," *NDVS, Ekonomicheskie nauki*, no. 1 (1982), pp. 60–67 (trans. in *Problems of Economics* 25, 1, March 1983, p. 37).

45. Maier, "Aktual'nye problemy," p. 8.

46. McAuley, *Economic Welfare*, p. 46.

47. Ibid., p. 44.

48. See D. Karpukhin, review of *Narodnoe khoziaistvo SSSR v 1959 godu* (Moscow, 1960), in *Planovoe khoziaistvo*, no. 1 (1960), pp. 87–91 (trans. in *Problems of Economics* 3, 2, July 1960, p. 28).

49. V. Maier, "Narodnoe blagosostoianie i potrebitel'skii spros," *Voprosy ekonomiki*, no. 2 (1981), pp. 54–63 (trans. in *Problems of Economics* 24, 10, February 1982, p. 46).

50. "Sotsial'nyi progress i programma povysheniia narodnogo blagosostoianiia," *EKO*, no. 5 (1981), pp. 3–19 (trans. in *Problems of Economics* 25, 1, May 1982, p. 33).

51. See Allen Kroncher, "Is Socialist Economics Giving Birth to a New Leisured Class?" *RLR* 300/82, July 26, 1982, citing Sh. B. Sverdlik, "Rost sberezhenii naseleniia: Prichiny i sledstviia," *EKO*, no. 6 (1982) pp. 115–30.

52. See A. P. Gnutov and M. A. Naidis, "Struktura i stabil'nost' ukladov," *Den'gi i kredit*, no. 4 (1975), pp. 67–74 (trans. in *Problems of Economics* 18, 9, January 1976, p. 80).

53. See Kroncher, "Is Socialist?"

54. Ibid.

55. *Ekonomicheskaia gazeta*, no. 35 (August 1981), p. 9.

56. See, e.g., on services, V. I. Dmitriev, "Vyezdnaia forma obsluzhivaniia naseleniia," *SI*, no. 1 (1975), pp. 106–12; V. M. Rutgaizer, "Chelovek truda v sfere raspredeleniia i potrebleniia," *EKO*, no. 9 (1981), pp. 46–62.

57. See Mervyn Matthews, *Poverty in the Soviet Union* (New York: Cambridge University Press, 1986).

58. Figures from Nove, *Economic History*, pp. 381–82, and *Pravda*, November 16, 1981, as cited in *RLR* 6/82, January 4, 1982.

59. Arcadius Kahan, "Some Problems of the Soviet Industrial Worker," in Kahan and Ruble, eds., *Industrial Worker*, p. 297.

60. See the readers' letters and responses in *Sovetskaia Rossiia*, February 5, 1988, p. 3.

61. See James R. Millar, "Life in the USSR on the Eve of the Gorbachev Era: Some Results of the Soviet Interview Project," *SIP Working Paper No. 41* (Urbana-Champaign: University of Illinois, October 1987, mimeo), p. 13 and table 3.

62. Ibid.

63. See Janet Chapman, "Consumption," in Abram Bergson and Simon Kuznets, eds., *Economic Trends in the Soviet Union* (Cambridge, Mass.: Harvard University Press, 1963), pp. 235–82.

64. Ibid., p. 251.

65. Ibid., pp. 252–53.

66. Ibid., pp. 238–39.

67. Ibid.

68. Ibid.

69. Ibid.

70. Ibid., p. 240.

71. Some of the sociopolitical consequences of such a fact were discussed, in the context of later large-scale mobility processes in Eastern Europe, in Walter Connor, "Social Change and Stability in Eastern Europe," *Problems of Communism* 26, 6 (November–December 1977), pp. 16–32.

72. See Chapman, "Consumption," pp. 256–57.

73. Ibid., pp. 262–63.

74. See Mervyn Matthews, "The Soviet Worker at Home," in Kahan and Ruble, eds., *Industrial Labor*, p. 214.

75. Ibid.

76. Data for 1965–71 from ibid., p. 220.

77. See ibid., pp. 209–13, on workers' housing.

78. See, e.g., Alfred John DiMaio, Jr., *Soviet Urban Housing: Problems and Policies* (New York: Praeger, 1974), pp. 122–25; Mervyn Matthews, *Privilege in the Soviet Union: A Study of Elite Life-Styles under Communism* (London: George Allen and Unwin, 1978), pp. 43–46; Henry W. Morton, "Who Gets What, When, and How? Housing in the Soviet Union," *Soviet Studies* 32, 2 (April 1980), p. 241.

79. Matthews, "Soviet Worker," p. 211.

80. Data from Arcadius Kahan, "Some Problems," pp. 284–86.

81. Ibid., p. 284.

82. Discussions of methodology and assumptions are available in the original reports by Keith Bush: "Retail Prices in Moscow and in Four Western Cities in November 1971," *RLR Paper*, no. 49 (1972); "Retail Prices in Moscow and Four Western Cities in May 1976," *RLR Supplement*, June 16, 1976; "Retail Prices in Moscow and Four Western Cities in March 1982," *RLR Supplement*, June 4, 1982; "Retail Prices in Moscow and Four Western Cities in October 1986," *RLR Supplement*, January 21, 1987.

83. Bush, "Retail . . . 1986," p. 31.

84. See Keith Bush, "Supplement: Retail Prices in Moscow and Four Western Cities in March 1982," in Leonard Schapiro and Joseph Godson, eds., *The Soviet Worker from Lenin to Andropov*, 2d ed. (New York: St. Martin's Press, 1984), p. 318, appendix 3, n. 8.

85. See Gertrude E. Schroeder and Imogene Edwards, *Consumption in the USSR: An International Comparison* (Washington, D.C.: Joint Economic Committee, U.S. Congress, 1981).

86. Richard Pipes, *Survival Is Not Enough: Soviet Realities and America's Future* (New York: Simon and Schuster, 1984), p. 127. Pipes (see his n. 16, p. 287) cites another version of the Schroeder study noted above.

87. See Aaron Vinokur, *Material'naia zainteresovannost' rabochikh sotsialisticheskoi promyshlennosti v trude i ego resultatakh* (Novosibirsk, 1970), esp. pp. 108–109, for original data.

88. Aaron Vinokur and Gur Ofer, "Family Income Levels for Soviet Industrial Workers, 1965–1975," in Kahan and Ruble, eds., *Industrial Labor*, p. 197.

89. Ibid., pp. 196, 198.

90. For a general description of the project, see James R. Millar, "The Soviet Interview Project: History, Method, and the Problem of Bias," *SIP, Working Paper No. 22* (Urbana-Champaign: University of Illinois, July 1986, mimeo).

91. Paul R. Gregory, "Productivity, Slack and Time Theft in the Soviet Economy: Evidence from the Soviet Interview Project," *SIP, Working Paper No. 15* (Urbana-Champaign: University of Illinois, February 1986, mimeo), p. 21 and table 3.

92. Ibid., p. 9 and table 1. While "decline" in absolute labor productivity is rare, and the object of the research involves *declining rates* of labor productivity *growth*, the question was phrased in the former sense, as a less technical formulation to which interviewee response was solicited.

93. James R. Millar and Elizabeth Clayton, "Quality of Life: Subjective Measures of Relative Satisfaction," *SIP, Working Paper No. 9* (Urbana-Champaign: University of Illinois, February 1986, mimeo), figs. 12B–12D.

94. V. D. Sitnikova and A. A. Michurin, "Sub"ektivno-otsenochnoe vopriiatie obraza zhizni," *SI*, no. 4 (1986), p. 90.

95. Millar and Clayton, "Quality," p. 10.

96. See Millar, "Life in the USSR," esp. tables 1, 2.

97. N. E. Rabkina and N. M. Rimashevskaia, "Raspreditel'nye otnosheniia i sotsial'noe razvitie," *EKO*, no. 5 (1978), pp. 17–32 (trans. in *Problems of Economics* 22, 3, July 1979, pp. 40–58).

98. Ibid., p. 47.

99. Ibid., p. 42.

100. L. T. Volchkova, "Osnovnye tendentsii," pp. 14–15.

101. Ibid., p. 15.

102. G. Sarkisian, "Ekonomicheskii rost i narodnoe blagosostoianie," *Voprosy ekonomiki*, no. 5 (1981), pp. 3–15 (trans. in *Problems of Economics* 25, 1, May 1982, p. 18).

103. Ibid.

104. E. L. Manevich, "Khoziaistvennyi mekhanizm i ispol'zovaniia trudovykh resursov," *EKO*, no. 12 (1985), p. 34.

105. L. S. Bliakhman and T. S. Zlotnitskaia, "Differentsiatsiia zarabotnoi platy," pp. 49–50.

106. Ibid., p. 44.

107. Ibid., pp. 40–41.

108. Maier, "Aktual'nye problemy."

109. Ibid., pp. 9–10.

110. Ibid., p. 14.

111. Ibid., p. 18.

112. See Jerry F. Hough, "Policy-Making and the Worker," pp. 382ff.

113. Ibid.

114. See Bliakhman and Zlotnitskaia, "Differentsiatsiia," p. 40.

115. Oleg Bogomolov, "Centrally Planned Economies in the Period up to the Year 2000" (UNESCO Economic Commission for Europe, November 19, 1985, mimeo), p. 14.

116. Peter Hauslohner, "Gorbachev's Social Contract," *Soviet Economy* 3, 1 (1987), p. 83.

117. Ibid., p. 71.

118. *Nepszabadsag*, January 24, 1987, p. 5 (*FBIS*, February 6, 1987, pp. 51–61).

119. *Izvestiia*, November 1, 1986, p. 1.

120. TASS (Russian), 1230 GMT, November 26, 1986 (*FBIS*, November 28, 1986, p. R8).

121. *Pravda*, February 17, 1987, pp. 3, 6.

122. *Pravda*, November 16, 1986, p. 1.

123. Ibid.

124. Moscow Television, 1600 GMT, November 20, 1986 (*FBIS*, No. 25, 1986, pp. R4–6).

125. *Izvestiia*, December 4, 1986; see also Elizabeth Teague, "Stormy Protests at Soviet Truck Plant," *RLR* 461/86, December 4, 1986.

126. *RLR* 476/86, p. 18 (citing TASS, December 29, 1986).

127. *Sovetskaia Rossiia*, January 16, 1987, cited in *RLR* 28/87, January 16, 1987, p. 12.

128. TASS (English), 1210 GMT, March 4, 1987 (*FBIS*, March 11, 1987, p. S13).

129. TASS (English), 1712 GMT, March 5, 1987 (*FBIS*, March 13, 1987, p. S1).

130. Andreas Tenson, "State Acceptance Commissions" (*RLR* 113/87, March 24, 1987), gives a good account of the early *gospriemka* experience. V. Antosenkov, of *Goskumtrud*'s research arm, estimated that about half the workers in affected plants experienced wage cuts in the first six months of 1987 (interview with author, Moscow, January 1988).

131. *Sotsialisticheskaia industriia*, March 10, 1987, p. 1.

132. *Trud*, June 9, 1987, pp. 1–2.

133. Ibid.

134. *Sovetskaia Rossiia*, June 6, 1987, p. 1 (*FBIS*, June 18, 1987, pp. S4–5).

135. *Trud*, June 9, 1987.

136. *Sotsialisticheskaia industriia*, August 9, 1987, p. 1.

137. Moscow Television, 1430 GMT, July 26, 1986 (*FBIS*, July 28, 1986, p. R7).

138. Moscow Television, 1500 GMT, July 27, 1987 (*FBIS*, August 12, 1987, p. S18).

139. "Raziasniaet otdel zarabotnoi platy Goskomtruda SSSR," *ST*, no. 10 (1987), p. 41.

140. See, e.g., "Ne vse idet gladko," *ST*, no. 7 (1987), p. 48.

141. L. Kostin, "Perestroika sistemy oplaty truda," *Voprosy ekonomiki*, no. 11 (1987), p. 42.

142. See, e.g., three pieces in *ST*, no. 1 (1987): I. Gladkii, "Vazhneishee sotsial'no-ekonomicheskoe meropriiatie piatiletki," pp. 7–13; V. Shcherbakov, "Povyshenie stimuliruiushchei roli zarabatnoi platy," pp. 19–32; L. Kunel'skii, "Sotsial'no-ekonomicheskie predposylki vvedeniia novykh tarifnykh uslovii oplaty truda," pp. 32–34.

143. See "Rekomendatsii po sovershenstvovaniiu organizatsii zarabotnoi platy i vvedeniiu novykh tarifnykh stavok i dolzhnostnykh okladov rabotnikov proizvodstvennykh otraslei narodnogo khoziaistva," *ST*, no. 2 (1987), pp. 57–96.

144. Kostin, "Perestroika," p. 41.

145. See the editorial, "Perestroika ekonimiki nabiraet tempy," *ST*, no. 1 (1987), p. 4, and Iu. Shatyrenko, "Kak oplachivat' trud rukovoditelei," in ibid., pp. 48–52.

146. A ten-article, branch-by-branch review appeared in *ST*, no. 3 (1987), pp. 7–50.

147. Editorial, "Pervye rezul'taty reformy zarabotnoi platy," *ST*, no. 9 (1987), pp. 8–9.

148. K. Pashkevich and A. Konovalov, "Povyshat' stimuliruiushchuiu rol' premii," *ST*, no. 10 (1987), p. 34.

149. Ibid.

150. G. Vladimirov, "Problemy perestroiki organizatsii zarabotnoi platy," *ST*, no. 12 (1987), p. 68.

151. *Sotsialisticheskaia industriia*, June 19, 1988, p. 3 (*FBIS*, June 28, 1988, p. 74).

152. See, e.g., *Ekonomicheskaia gazeta*, no. 41 (October 1986), p. 8 (*CDSP*, December 10, 1986, pp. 7–8).

153. TASS (Russian), 0855 GMT, September 17, 1987 (*FBIS*, September 24, 1987, p. 64).

154. *Izvestiia*, September 11, 1987, p. 2.

155. L. A. Gordon, "Sotsial'naia politika v sfere oplaty truda," *SI*, no. 4 (1987), pp. 3–19.

156. Ibid., esp. pp. 14–17.

157. For a pro-differentiation argument, especially on managers and professionals, see M. Klimenko, "Povyshat' rol' tarifa," *ST*, no. 7 (1986), p. 74.

158. See *Izvestiia*, December 19, 1987, p. 2.

159. *Sotsialisticheskaia industriia*, June 1, 1988, p. 3; see also Aaron Trehub, "Poverty in the Soviet Union," *RLR* 256/88, June 20, 1988, p. 1.

160. Trehub, "Poverty," p. 2.

161. G. Sarkisiants, "Sotsial'nye aspekty perestroiki upravleniia," *ST*, no. 12 (1987), p. 6.

162. Aaron Trehub, "Tough Talk About Soviet Living Standards," *RLR* 438/88, September 26, 1988, p. 3, citing A. Zaichenko, *Moskovskie novosti*, no. 34 (1988).

163. L. A. Gordon pointed this out to me in January 1988.

164. For a general and detailed treatment, see Matthews, *Poverty in the Soviet Union*.

Chapter 5
Labor, Authority, Autonomy

1. Alec Nove, *An Economic History of the U.S.S.R.* (Harmondsworth, U.K.: Penguin Books, 1982), pp. 261–64.

2. Ibid., p. 264.

3. Ibid., pp. 263–64.

4. Jerzy Gliksman, "Recent Trends in Soviet Labor Policy," *Problems of Communism* 5, 4 (July–August 1956), pp. 22–23.

5. Nove, *Economic History*, pp. 348–49.

6. Paul Barton, "The Current Status of the Soviet Worker," in Abraham Brumberg, ed., *Russia Under Khrushchev* (New York: Praeger, 1962), p. 265.

7. See Leon Herman, in "Discussion: Towards a 'Communist Welfare State'?" *Problems of Communism* 9, 3 (May–June 1960), p. 45.

8. Nove, *Economic History*, p. 349.

9. Emily Clark Brown, *Soviet Trade Unions and Labor Relations* (Cambridge, Mass.: Harvard University Press, 1966), p. 168.

10. Of prime importance is Murray Yanowitch, *Work in the Soviet Union: Attitudes and Issues* (Armonk, N.Y.: M. E. Sharpe, 1985), with excellent coverage of Soviet empirical research since the early 1960s and of Soviet policy debates. Also by the same author is chap. 5 (pp. 134–64) in *Social and Economic Inequality in the Soviet Union* (White Plains, N.Y.: M. E. Sharpe, 1977), and, edited by Yanowitch, *Soviet Work Attitudes* (White Plains, N.Y./Oxford: M. E. Sharpe/Martin Robertson, 1979). See also Robert Conquest, ed., *Industrial Workers in the U.S.S.R.* (New York: Praeger, 1967), esp. pp. 95–149.

11. A. G. Zdravomyslov, V. P. Rozhin, and V. A. Iadov, *Chelovek i ego rabota* (Moscow: Nauka, 1967); English version, *Man and His Work*, ed. and trans. by Stephen P. Dunn (White Plains, N.Y.: International Arts and Sciences Press, 1970).

12. The argument here follows Yanowitch, *Work*, pp. 38ff.

13. See Zdravomyslov et al., *Chelovek*, p. 177; see also Yanowitch, *Work*, p. 37.

14. See Yanowitch, *Work*, p. 43, citing an interview with Iadov in *Znaniesila*, no. 10 (1979).

15. Ibid., p. 39, table 2.6, and sources cited therein.

16. Adapted from ibid., p. 42, table 2.7.

17. N. A. Aitov, "Izuchenie struktury rabochego klassa promyshlennogo tsentra," *SI*, no. 1 (1974), pp. 60–65 (trans. in *JPRS* 65631, September 9, 1975, pp. 54ff).

18. N. B. Bindiukov, "Sotsial'nye faktory povysheniia kachestva produktsii," *SI*, no. 1 (1983), pp. 134–36.

19. These are summarized in Yanowitch, *Work*, pp. 28–29, table 2.1; see also pp. 165–68. My averages are derived from the fourteen studies listed on p. 28.

20. Ibid.

21. See James R. Millar and Elizabeth Clayton, "Quality of Life: Subjective Measures of Relative Satisfaction," *SIP, Working Paper No. 9* (Urbana-Champaign: University of Illinois, February 1986, mimeo), table 2E.

22. Yanowitch, *Work*, p. 31, and sources cited in his n. 20.

23. *Izvestiia*, February 27, 1988, p. 1.

24. This is especially true with regard to working *conditions*, to judge by studies reported in A. E. Kotliar and V. V. Trubin, *Problemy regulirovaniia pereraspredeleniia rabochei sily* (Moscow: Ekonomika, 1978), p. 134, table 32.

25. *Izvestiia*, February 27, 1988, p. 1.

26. Z. I. Kalugina, "Vliianie trudovogo statusa na uroven' zhizni rabotnikov," in *Problemy sovershenstvovaniia sotsial'no-klassovykh otnoshenii v sovetskom obshchestve* (Tezisy nauchnoi konterentsii, Khar'kov 22–24 sent. 1987 g.) (VI, 2) (Khar'kov: KhU, 1987), pp. 16–18.

27. Basile Kerblay, *Modern Soviet Society* (New York: Pantheon Books, 1983), p. 194.

28. Ibid., p. 188.

29. See the summary and discussion in Yanowitch, *Social and Economic Inequality*, pp., 136–40.

30. B. P. Kutyrev, "Distsiplina truda: Orientatsiia na konechnyi rezul'tat," *SI*, no. 3 (1982), pp. 119–24 (trans. in *JPRS* 82075, October 25, 1983, p. 91); also see Iu. P. Sosin, "Faktory ukrepleniia trudovoi distsipliny," *EKO*, no. 5 (1975), pp. 167–70.

31. Sosin, "Faktory," pp. 169–70.

32. R. B. Gitel'makher, "Master v otsenkakh rabochikh," *EKO*, no. 6 (1981), p. 122.

33. Ibid.

34. Ibid., pp. 123–24.

35. G. V. Morozov and V. N. Pushina, "Otsenka rabotnitsami deiatel'nosti neposredstvennogo rukovoditelia," *SI*, no. 1 (1983), pp. 136–39 (trans. in *JPRS* 83368, April 29, 1983, p. 151).

36. See the excellent discussion in Yanowitch, *Work*, pp. 48–57.

37. Ibid., p. 53, citing A. G. Kharchev and S. I. Golod, *Professional'naia rabota zhenshchin i sem'ia* (Leningrad, 1971), pp. 45–49.

38. See, on the employment of women, Connor, *Socialism, Politics, and Equality*, pp. 238–43; also Gail Warshofsky Lapidus, *Women in Soviet Society: Equality, Development, and Social Change* (Berkeley and Los Angeles: University of California Press, 1978), esp. chap. 5.

39. See Yanowitch, *Work*, pp. 54–56.

40. Kerblay, *Modern*, p. 198, and source cited.

41. V. P. Klimonov, "Put' proizvodstvennogo mastera," *EKO*, no. 5 (1980), pp. 133–38.

42. See A. A. Dregalo and O. V. Ovchennikov, "Mesto mastera na proizvodstve," *RKSM*, no. 4 (1987), pp. 63–76.

43. Ibid., p. 71.

44. Yanowitch, *Social and Economic Inequality*, p. 146.

45. See Yanowitch, *Work*, pp. 111–13, esp. p. 112, table 5.2.

46. Ibid.

47. Iu. N. Dorozhkin, "Sotsial'naia aktivnost' i rasshirenie uchastiia trudiashchikhsia v upravlenii delami proizvodstvennogo kollektiva," *NDVS, Nauchnyi Kommunizm*, no. 1 (1983), p. 45, table 2.

48. See Russell Bova, "On *Perestroyka*: The Role of Workplace Participation," *Problems of Communism* 36, 4 (July–August 1987), pp. 70–86.

49. *Literaturnaia gazeta*, December 2, 1987, p. 11 (*FBIS*, December 17, 1987, pp. 65–67).

50. *Sotsialisticheskaia industriia*, December 1, 1987, p. 2 (*FBIS*, December 15, 1987, pp. 69–71).

51. *Izvestiia,* January 31, 1988, p. 2.

52. Nazimova, in "Perestroika i rabochii klass (Uchenie sotsialisticheskiich stran obmenivaiutsia mneniiami)," *RKSM,* no. 5 (1987), p. 58.

53. Ferenc Gazso and Vladimir Shubkin, *Trudiashchiasia molodezh': Orientatsii i zhiznennye puti* (Budapest: Institute for the Social Sciences, 1984), p. 147.

54. Yanowitch, *Work . . . ,* p. 63, n. 38.

55. Paul R. Gregory and Janet Kohlhase, "The Earnings of Soviet Workers: Human Capital, Loyalty and Privilege (Evidence from the Soviet Interview Project), *SIP, Working Paper No. 13* (Urbana-Champaign: University of Illinois, February 1986, mimeo), p. 22.

56. S. P. Goriunov and F. M. Aev, "Obshchestvennoe mnenie o proizvodstvennoi situatsii," *SI,* no. 2 (1986), p. 123.

57. L. A. Gordon and A. K. Nazimova, "Sotsial'no-professional'naia struktura sovremennogo sovetskogo obshechstva: kharakter i napravlenie peremen," *RKSM,* no. 3 (1983), pp. 59–62 (trans. in *Soviet Sociology* 24, 1–3, Summer-Fall-Winter 1985–86, p. 57).

58. Ibid., p. 58.

59. See Elizabeth Teague, "Labor Discipline and Legislation in the USSR: 1979–85," *RLR Supplement* 2/85, October 16, 1985, p. 8.

60. Anthony Giddens, *The Class Structure of the Advanced Societies* (New York: Harper and Row, 1975), p. 250.

61. See the review in Yanowitch, *Work,* pp. 119–35.

62. Ia. S. Kapeliush, "Public Opinion on Electing Managers," in Yanowitch, ed., *Soviet Work Attitudes,* pp. 60–80 (trans. from "Obshchestvennoe mnenie o vybornosti na proizvodstve," *Informatsionnyi biulleten* 39, 54, Institut konkretnykh sotsiologicheskikh issledovanii AN SSSR, Moscow, 1969, pp. 4–24); See also, by Kapeliush, "Vybornost' rukovoditelei: Vchera i segodnia," *SI,* no. 2 (1988), pp. 44–49.

63. Ibid., pp. 68–69.

64. Ibid., pp. 70–73.

65. See Joel C. Moses, "Worker Self-Management and the Reform Alternative in Soviet Labour Policy, 1979–1985," *Soviet Studies* 39, 2 (April 1987), pp. 222–23.

66. *Pravda,* November 16, 1987, p. 5 (see *RLR* 473/87, November 20, 1987, p. 5).

67. Several of the specialists on labor policy with whom I spoke in Moscow in January 1988 expressed these reservations.

68. See the excellent piece by L. A. Gordon and A. K. Nazimova, "Proizvodstvennyi potentsial sovetskogo rabochego klassa: Tendentsii i problemy razvitiia," *Voprosy filosofii,* no. 11 (1980), pp. 26–40; also Gordon and E. V. Klopov, "Rabochii klass v stranakh sotsialisticheskogo sodruzhestva: Tendentsii vozrastaniia sotsial'nogo potentsiala," *RKSM,* no. 5 (1984), pp. 46–57.

69. See Yanowitch, *Work,* pp. 128–29, citing *Literaturnaia gazeta,* August 31, 1977.

70. Ibid., p. 97, citing D. P. Kaidalov and E. I. Suimenko, *Psikhologiia edinonachaliia i kollegial'nosti* (Moscow, 1979), p. 171.

NOTES TO CHAPTER 5

71. *Pravda*, August 28, 1981, quoted in Iu. N. Dorozhkin, "Sotsial'naia aktivnost'," p. 43.

72. Gordon and Nazimova, "Sotsial'no-professional'naia struktura," pp. 59–60.

73. See *Komsomol'skaia pravda*, February 9, 1988, p. 2.

74. Iu. P. Sosin, "Faktory ukrepleniia trudovoi distsipliny," *EKO*, no. 5 (1975), p. 172.

75. M. Ia. Sonin, "Zametki o trudovoi distsipline," *EKO*, no. 5 (1981), pp. 65–79 (trans. in *Problems of Economics* 24, 12, April 1982, p. 6).

76. M. Ia. Sonin, "Effektivno ispol'zovat' trudovye resursy," *EKO*, no. 4 (1977), pp. 3–12 (trans. in *Problems of Economics* 20, 12, April 1978, p. 10).

77. Bob Arnot, "Soviet Labour Productivity and the Failure of the Shchekino Experinement," *Critique*, no. 15 (1982), p. 46.

78. Kutyrev, "Distsiplina truda," p. 92.

79. *Trud*, December 29, 1982, cited in Teague, "Labor Discipline," p. 4.

80. *Pravda*, December 28, 1982, cited in ibid.

81. Sonin, "Zametki," p. 15.

82. See Teague, "Labor Discipline," pp. 15–18.

83. Iu. P. Sosin, "Rabochee vremia: Istochniki poter," *EKO*, no. 10 (1984), p. 160.

84. See P. P. Reznikov, "Distsiplina truda kak faktor sotsial'nogo razvitiia proizvodstvennogo kollektiva," *SI*, no. 2 (1978), pp. 58–63 (trans. in *JPRS* 71856, September 13, 1978, pp. 44–52).

85. Ibid., pp. 48–49.

86. V. G. Karpov, "Distsiplina truda kak tema gazetnykh publikatsii," *SI*, no. 1 (1986), pp. 124–27.

87. Ibid., p. 125.

88. V. M. Iakushev, "Raspredelenie po trudu: Vzaimosviaz' khoziaistvennogo mekhanizma i sorevnovanie," *SI*, no. 3 (1982), pp. 68–78 (trans. in *JPRS* 82075, October 25, 1982, pp. 35–36).

89. Filtzer, *Soviet Workers and Stalinist Industrialization*, p. 150.

90. See, e.g., David E. Powell, "Labor Turnover in the Soviet Union," *Slavic Review* 36, 2 (June 1977), pp. 268–85.

91. The discussion of turnover here follows Teague, "Labor Discipline," pp. 5ff, and sources cited therein.

92. *Pravda*, March 25, 1982; Radio Moscow, August 24, 1983, cited in Teague, "Labor Discipline," p. 5.

93. A. Kotliar and M. Talalai, "Adaptatsiia vypusknikov srednykh shkol na proizvodstve," *ST*, no. 10 (1975), pp. 133–34.

94. *Pravda*, January 12, 1980; see Teague, "Labor Discipline," pp. 9–10.

95. See, e.g., the studies done in 1978 in the Altai Krai; D. I. Ziuzin, "Vlianie dinamiki truda na mobil'nost' trudovykh resursov," *SI*, no. 3 (1981), pp. 72–78.

96. Kotliar and Talalai, "Adaptatsiia," pp. 127–29.

97. See Hauslohner, "Managing the Soviet Labor Market," chap. 7, esp. pp. 600–39.

98. "The Novosibirsk Report," *Survey* 28, 1 (Spring 1984), pp. 88–108.

99. Ibid., p. 91.

100. Ibid., p. 90.

101. This discussion draws on Darrell Slider, "The Brigade System in Soviet Industry: An Effort to Restructure the Labor Force," *Soviet Studies* 39, 3 (July 1987), pp. 388–405, and on Yanowitch, *Work*, pp. 135–55.

102. See Slider, "Brigade System," and G. Ibragimov, "Brigadnaia organizatsiia kak sistema," *ST*, no. 6 (1986), pp. 59–63.

103. See, e.g., Slider, "Brigade System," p. 390.

104. See the editorial, "Perestroika i tvorcheskaia aktivnost' trudiashchiksia," *ST*, no. 8 (1987), p. 5.

105. Slider, "Brigade System," pp. 395–96, 401; Yanowitch, *Work*, p. 153.

106. See the important piece, L. A. Gordon, G. A. Monousova, and A. K. Nazimova, "Novye formy brigadnoi organizatsii truda: Problemy, protivorechiia, perspektivy," *RKSM*, no. 1 (1987), pp. 120–21.

107. Ibid.

108. See, e.g., three indicative pieces in *Sotsialisticheskii trud*: V. Khlevetskii and V. Peshkov, "Kollektivnyi podriad v deistvii," no. 3 (1987), pp. 90–93; V. Kolosov, "Ot brigadnogo podriada—k kolletivnomu," no. 9 (1987), pp. 39–42; G. Melikian, "Tendentsiia razvitiia kollektivnogo podriada," no. 10 (1987), pp. 9–17.

109. See *Sovetskaia Rossiia*, January 7, 1986, p. 1 (*CDSP*, February 12, 1986, pp. 1–2).

110. *Pravda*, October 24, 1986, pp. 2–3 (*CDSP*, November 26, 1986, pp. 7, 14).

111. See Gordon et al., "Novye formy," p. 128; see also the discussion of the contribution of legal experts, notably B. P. Kurashvili, to the same line in policy discussions in Moses, "Worker Self-Management," pp. 209–10.

112. Gordon reemphasized this point in a conversation with me in Moscow in January 1988.

113. See Yanowitch, *Work*, pp. 151–52.

114. See, e.g., Filtzer, *Soviet Workers*, pp. 103–104. The balance between egalitarian/cohesive responses and more conflictual ones was, however, complex. See also Kuromiya, *Stalin's Industrial Revolution*, pp. 236ff.

115. Slider, "Brigade System," p. 191.

116. See, e.g., E. Posadkov, "Raspredelenie obshchego zarabotka v podriadnykh kollektivakh," *ST*, no. 3 (1987), p. 86.

117. Slider, "Brigade System," p. 398.

118. Posadkov, "Raspredelenie," p. 87.

119. Slider, "Brigade System," p. 398.

120. See, e.g., N. Maksimova, "Brigady na pereput'e: Zametki ob ekonomike i nravstvennosti," *EKO*, no. 8, (1985), pp. 151–99.

121. Gordon et al., "Novye formy," p. 126.

122. See V. P. Kutyrev, comp., "Razvitie brigadnykh form (zaochnaia konferentsiia)," *EKO*, no. 12 (1986), pp. 46–47.

123. See C. Shkurko and A. Moshcherin, "Eksperiment i posle eksperimenta," *ST*, no. 6 (1987), pp. 102–103.

124. See Slider, "Brigade System," p. 397; also E. I. Khrishchev and L. I. Kozhokar', "Svet i teni kollektivnogo podriada," *SI*, no. 4 (1986), p. 47; Khlevetskii and Peshkov, "Kollektivnyi podriad," p. 91; Melikian, "Tendentsiia," p. 14.

125. Slider, "Brigade System," p. 396; Khrishchev and Kozhokar, "Svet i teni," p. 48.

126. Slider, "Brigade System," p. 402.

127. Ibid., pp. 394–95.

128. See Gur Ofer and Aaron Vinokur, *Private Sources of Income in the Soviet Urban Household* (Report R-2359-NA, August 1980) (Santa Monica, Calif.: Rand, 1980).

129. Data and discussion here are drawn from ibid., pp. 10–25, esp. tables 2–5. Later analyses by Ofer and Vinokur of data on Soviet emigrés of more recent times—though without some of the relevant figures here—are available in "Inequality of Earnings, Household Income and Wealth in the Soviet Union in the 70s," *SIP, Working Paper No. 25* (Urbana-Champaign: University of Illinois, June 1986, mimeo).

130. Brian D. Silver, "Political Beliefs of the Soviet Citizen: Sources of Support for Regime Norms," *SIP, Working Paper No. 6* (Urbana-Champaign: University of Illinois, December 1985, mimeo), p. 33, n. 46.

131. David Granick, *Job Rights in the Soviet Union: Their Consequences* (Cambridge, Eng.: Cambridge University Press, 1987).

132. Hauslohner, "Managing," pp. 293, 311ff.

133. *Sovetskaia kul'tura*, January 4, 1986 (*CDSP*, February 19, 1986, pp. 1–4).

134. TASS interview, January 16, 1986, cited in *RLR* 35/86, January 17, 1986, p. 11.

135. *Neue AZ* (Vienna), June 6, 1987, pp. 4–5 (*FBIS*, June 15, 1987, pp. 45–56).

136. *New York Times*, July 4, 1987, pp. 1–2.

137. *Pravda* and *Izvestiia*, November 23, 1985, pp. 1–2.

138. On dismissals of personnel in Moscow ministries, see *Sotsialisticheskaia industriia*, November 10, 1987, pp. 2–3 (*FBIS*, November 12, 1987, pp. 62–65). See also several articles: *Moskovskie novosti*, March 6, 1988, p. 9; *Izvestiia*, February 27, 1988, p. 2; *Izvestiia*, March 2, 1988, p. 3; *Moskovskie novosti*, March 13, 1988, p. 4; *Moskovskaia pravda*, March 2, 1988, p. 2; *Nedelia*, February 29–March 6, 1988, p. 8; *Pravda*, March 4, 1988, pp. 1–2 (trans. or abst. in *CDSP*, April 6, 1988, pp. 1–8).

139. James R. Millar and Elizabeth Clayton, "Quality of Life: Subjective Measures of Relative Satisfaction," *SIP, Working Paper No. 9* (Urbana-Champaign: University of Illinois, February 1986, mimeo), figs. 12A–D.

140. Ia. Tairov, "Pervye uroki," *ST*, no. 2 (1987), p. 31.

141. "Povyshenie smennosti—vazhnyi faktor uskoreniia," *ST*, no. 12 (1986), p. 6.

142. See *RLR* 347/87, August 27, 1987, via TASS.

143. *Izvestiia*, August 25, 1987, p. 2.

144. TASS (Reuters), July 15, 1987, in *RLR* 279/87, p. 9.

145. See *RLR* 318/86.

146. See *RLR* 101/86 (Aaron Trehub, "Gorbachev's Speech to the Twenty-Seventh Party Congress: Social Issues"), February 27, 1986, pp. 1–2, for the General Secretary's comments on employment issues.

147. TASS, March 26, 1987, cited in *Soviet Labour Review*, nos. 5–6 (February–April 1987), p. 11.

148. *Trud*, January 28, 1988, pp. 1–2 (*FBIS*, February 9, 1988, p. 63).

149. V. Konstantinov, "Problemy trudoustroistva," *ST*, no. 4 (1987), p. 34.

150. E. Afanas'ev and O. Medvedeva, "Organizatsionno-pravovye voprosy pereraspredeleniia vysvobozhdennykh rabotnikov," *ST*, no. 1 (1987), p. 68.

151. V. Bachilo, "Trudoustroistvo vysvobozhdennykh rabotnikov," *ST*, no. 2 (1987), p. 53.

152. Kostin in *Izvestiia*, September 11, 1987, p. 2 (*CDSP*, October 14, 1987, p. 24).

153. See *RLR* 109/86, p. 2.

154. See n. 133.

155. N. Shmelev, "Avansy i dolgi," *Novyi mir*, no. 6 (1987).

156. *RLR* 237/87 (Philip Hanson, "The Reform Debate: What Are the Limits?"), June 23, 1987, p. 2.

157. TASS (Russian), 1426 GMT, June 29, 1987 (*FBIS*, July 1, 1987, p. 44).

158. TASS (English) September 2, 1987, in *RLR* 357/87, September 4, 1987, p. 9.

159. TASS, June 19, 1987, cited in *Soviet Labour Review*, no. 2 (August 1987), p. 12.

160. *RLR* 339/87, August 21, 1987, p. 9, citing UPI, August 19, 1987.

161. *RLR* 294/87, July 24, 1987, p. 6 (citing *Newsweek*, July 20, 1987).

162. *Sovetskaia Rossiia*, July 1, 1987, p. 3.

163. Prague Television, 2015 GMT, July 1, 1987 (*FBIS*, July 15, 1987, p. R-19).

164. Moscow Television, 1615 GMT, February 12, 1988 (*FBIS*, February 19, 1988, pp. 78–79).

165. V. G. Kostakov, "Polnaia zaniatost': Kak my ee ponimaem," *Kommunist*, no. 14 (1987), pp. 16–25 (trans. in *Problems of Economics* 30, 10, February 1988, p. 97).

166. *Izvestiia*, February 13, 1988, p. 3 (*FBIS*, February 26, 1988, pp. 59–61).

167. As told to me in January 1988 in Moscow by V. Antosenkov of Goskumtrud's Scientific Research Institute on Labor.

168. See James R. Millar, "Life in the USSR on the Eve of the Gorbachev Era: Some Results of the Soviet Interview Project," *SIP, Working Paper No. 41* (Urbana-Champaign: University of Illinois, October 1987, mimeo), p. 18.

169. See *RLR* 38/87, p. 2, citing TASS, January 27, 1987.

170. *Izvestiia*, July 1, 1987, p. 1; the earlier draft version had appeared on February 8, 1987.

171. See, e.g., *Izvestiia*, December 19, 1987, p. 2.

172. See *Pravda*, September 22, 1988, p. 3, on a case of managerial "election" that, clearly, goes in a direction other than that envisioned by perestroika.

173. See Bova, "On *Perestroyka*."

174. Ibid., pp. 84–85.

175. A very solid review of the problem is available in Elizabeth Teague, "Workers' Self-Management and the Enterprise Law," *RLR* 486/88, November 9, 1988.

176. Several of the specialists with whom I spoke in the USSR in January 1988 saw this development as possible.

177. See *Trud*, September 15, 1988, p. 2 (*FBIS*, September 20, 1988, pp. 55–56).

178. *Argumenty i fakty*, August 6–12, 1988, pp. 1–2 (*FBIS*, August 12, 1988, pp. 50–52).

179. *Sotsialisticheskaia industriia*, May 9, 1988, p. 2 (*FBIS*, May 16, 1988, pp. 54–55).

180. Mann, *Consciousness and Action*, pp. 20, 29–30.

181. Ibid., pp. 20–23.

182. Ibid., pp. 32–33.

183. Ibid., p. 20.

Chapter 6
Regime Control and Worker Opposition

The first opening quote is from the account by N. Alekseev, "Zametki rabochego," *Materialy samizdata*, no. 34/81 (1981), *AS* 4413; the second, from ibid., no. 28/83 (1983), *AS* 4985.

1. Blair A. Ruble, "Industrial Trade Unions in the USSR," in Alex Pravda and Blair A. Ruble, eds., *Trade Unions in Communist States* (Boston: George Allen and Unwin, 1986), p. 28.

2. Typical of the genre are two works, both collective products of the Institute of the History of the USSR, Soviet Academy of Sciences: *Rabochii klass SSSR, 1951–1965* (Moscow: Nauka, 1969), and *Rabochii klass SSSR, 1966–1970* (Moscow: Nauka, 1979).

3. V. M. Khmelevskii, "Partiinoe rukovodstvo trudovymi kollektivami proizvodstvennykh ob"edinenii," *NDVS, Nauchnyi kommunizm*, no. 4 (1984), pp. 48–49.

4. See Jerry F. Hough and Merle Fainsod, *How the Soviet Union Is Governed* (Cambridge, Mass.: Harvard University Press, 1979), pp. 335–39.

5. See Mervyn Matthews, "The Soviet Worker at Home," in Kahan and Ruble, eds., *Industrial Labor*, p. 226, and sources cited therein.

6. Klopov, *Rabochii klass SSSR*, p. 208.

7. Ibid., pp. 198, 200; *Rabochii klass SSSR, 1966–1970*, p. 207; "KPSS v tsifrakh," *Partiinaia zhizn'*, no. 21 (1987), pp. 8–9.

8. On the matter of party "saturation," see Jerry F. Hough, *The Soviet Union and Social Science Theory* (Cambridge, Mass.: Harvard University Press, 1977), pp. 125–39.

9. N. P. Konstantinova, O. V. Stakanova, and O. I. Shkaratan, "Peremeny v sotsial'nom oblike rabochikh v epokhu razvitogo sotsializma," *Voprosy istorii*, no. 5 (1978), pp. 3–18 (trans. in *Soviet Sociology* 17, 4, Spring 1979, pp. 25–26).

10. N. K. Petrova, *Obshchestvenno-politicheskii oblik sovetskoi rabochei molodezhi (70-e gody)* (Moscow: Nauka, 1986), p. 66, table 20.

11. V. A. Smirnov, *Sotsial'naia aktivnost' sovetskikh rabochikh* (Moscow: Izdatel'stvo politicheskoi literatury, 1979), p. 142.

12. Matthews, "Soviet Worker," p. 226.

13. *Rabochii klass SSSR, 1951–1965*, p. 403.

14. *Rabochii klass SSSR, 1966–1970*, p. 283.

15. Figures from 1973 are taken from the periodic volume, *Itogi vyborov i sostav deputatov mestnykh sovetov narodnykh deputatov* (Moscow: Izdatel'stvo "Izvestiia Sovetov Narodnykh Deputatov SSSR," various cited years).

16. See A. N. Kushnikov, "Uchastie rabochikh v upravlenii pri sotsializme," *NDVS, Nauchnyi kommunizm*, no. 3 (1975), p. 41; *Rabochii klass SSSR, 1966–1970*, p. 282; Charles E. Ziegler, "Worker Participation and Worker Discontent in the Soviet Union," *Political Science Quarterly* 98, 2 (Summer 1983), p. 237; *Narodnoe khoziaistvo SSSR za 70 let* (Moscow: Finansy i statistika, 1987), p. 382.

17. Ziegler, "Worker Participation," p. 237.

18. *Rabochii klass SSSR, 1966–1970*, pp. 283, 291.

19. Paul R. Gregory and Janet Kohlhase, "The Earnings of Soviet Workers: Human Capital, Loyalty, and Privilege (Evidence from the Soviet Interview Project)," *SIP, Working Paper No. 13* (Urbana-Champaign: University of Illinois, February 1986, mimeo), pp. 18–19.

20. Ibid.

21. See William Zimmerman, "Mobilized Participation and the Nature of the Soviet Dictatorship," *SIP, Working Paper No. 19* (Urbana-Champaign: University of Illinois, April 1986, mimeo), p. 30.

22. Ibid., and tables 3–6, 8–9.

23. Rasma Karklins, "Soviet Elections Revisited: The Significance of Voter Abstention in Non-competitive Balloting," *SIP, Working Paper No. 8* (Urbana-Champaign: University of Illinois, n.d., mimeo), pp. 12–13.

24. Zimmerman, "Mobilized Participation," table 11.

25. Victor Zaslavsky, *The Neo-Stalinist State: Class, Ethnicity, and Consensus in Soviet Society* (Armonk, N.Y./Brighton, U.K.: M. E. Sharpe/The Harvester Press, 1982), pp. 27–32.

26. Gregory, "Productivity, Slack and Time Theft," table 1.

27. See Scott, *Behind the Urals*, p. 84.

28. Alex Pravda and Blair A. Ruble, "Communist Trade Unions: Varieties of Dualism," in Pravda and Ruble, eds., *Trade Unions*, pp. 2–3.

29. Ibid., p. 16.

30. Ruble, "Industrial," p. 27.

31. See Mary McAuley, *Labour Disputes in Soviet Russia, 1957–1965* (Oxford: The Clarendon Press, 1969), pp. 40–41, 48–56.

32. Ibid., pp. 72–73.

33. Ibid., p. 106.

34. Blair A. Ruble, *Soviet Trade Unions: Their Development in the 1970s* (Cambridge, Eng.: Cambridge University Press, 1981), p. 109; see also McAuley, *Labour*, pp. 69–71.

35. On overwork and inefficiency, see Bernice Q. Madison, "Trade Unions and Social Welfare," in Kahan and Ruble, eds., *Industrial Labor*, pp. 60–63.

36. See McAuley, *Labour*, pp. 171–80.

37. Ibid., pp. 212–13; see also Ruble, "Factory Unions and Workers' Rights," in Kahan and Ruble, eds., *Industrial Labor*, pp. 60–63.

38. Ruble, *Soviet Trade Unions*, pp. 109–14.

39. Ibid., pp. 106–107.

40. See Ruble, "Factory Unions," pp. 72–75.

41. Emily Clark Brown, *Soviet Trade Unions and Labor Relations* (Cambridge, Mass.: Harvard University Press, 1966), p. 173.

42. See Ruble, *Soviet Trade Unions*, p. 99.

43. On AUCCTU "advocacy" of workers' interests and its politicking with Gosplan, the State Committee on Labor and Social Questions, and party departments, see Jerry F. Hough, "Policy-Making and the Worker," in Kahan and Ruble, eds., *Industrial Labor*, pp. 373ff.

44. The evocative phrase is from J. M. Montias, "Observations on Strikes, Riots, and Other Disturbances," in Jan F. Triska and Charles Gati, eds., *Blue-Collar Workers in Eastern Europe* (London: George Allen and Unwin, 1981), pp. 173–86.

45. Alex Pravda, "Political Attitudes and Activity," in ibid., p. 56.

46. Vadim Belotserkovsky, "Workers' Struggles in the USSR in the Early Sixties," *Critique*, nos. 10–11 (1979), pp. 37–50.

47. Betsy Gidwitz, "Labor Unrest in the Soviet Union," *Problems of Communism* 31, 6 (November–December 1982), pp. 25–42.

48. M. Holubenko, "The Soviet Working Class: Discontent and Opposition," *Critique*, no. 4 (Spring 1975), pp. 5–25.

49. Liudmila Alekseeva, "Zabastovki v SSSR (poslestalinskii period)," *SSSR: Vnutrennie protivorechiia*, no. 15 (1986), pp. 80–145.

50. This discussion generally follows ibid.

51. Though Alekseeva, "Zabastovki," identifies the individual strikes in some of her categories, this is not always the case, and I cannot reproduce her results here with a full accounting of which strikes fall under which rubric.

52. See ibid., pp. 90–93.

53. The head of the AUCCTU, Shibaev, lost his job in 1981, in moves perhaps related to this increased strike activity; see also ibid., pp. 88, 126.

54. Alex Pravda, "Spontaneous Workers' Activities in the Soviet Union," in Kahan and Ruble, eds., *Industrial Labor*, p. 351.

55. Alekseeva, "Zabastovki," p. 84.

56. See Montias, "Strikes," p. 180.

57. See Holubenko, "Soviet Working Class," pp. 7–8.

58. Geoffrey Hosking, *The First Socialist Society* (Cambridge, Mass.: Harvard University Press, 1985), p. 388.

59. Holubenko, "Soviet Working Class," p. 7.

60. See Gidwitz, "Labor Unrest," p. 169; Pravda, "Spontaneous," pp. 350–55; and Holubenko, "Soviet Working Class," p. 9.

61. Belotserkovsky, "Workers' Struggles," p. 48.

62. On this, see Montias, "Strikes," pp. 177–78.

63. Millar and Clayton, "Quality of Life," p. 10.

64. Belotserkovsky, "Workers' Struggles," pp. 47–48.

65. Ibid., p. 48.

66. Ibid.

67. Ibid., p. 14.

68. Ibid., p. 22.

69. For the development of the free trade unions, see Gidwitz, "Labor Unrest"; Gleb Vysotin and Valentin Sereda, "The Past, Present and Future of Independent Trade Unions," CHR, no. 39 (July–September 1980), pp. 27–42.

70. Vysotin and Sereda, "The Past," p. 32.

71. Ibid.

72. Gidwitz, "Labor Unrest," p. 37, n. 84.

73. Ibid., pp. 37–38, and sources cited therein.

74. Ibid., p. 38.

75. David K. Shipler, Russia: Broken Idols, Solemn Dreams (New York: Times Books, 1983), p. 207.

76. Ibid.

77. Anatoly Marchenko, "Live as Others Live," CHR, no. 43 (July–September 1981), p. 40.

78. Ibid., p. 41.

79. Ibid.

80. Ibid.

81. "Oleg Alifanov: The Workers' Life," Soviet Analyst 14, 21, October 23, 1985, p. 8.

82. Ibid.

83. Ibid., p. 7.

84. "Kiev Workers Protest to the Central Committee," Critique, no. 2 (1973), p. 76.

85. Ibid.

86. Ibid., p. 77.

87. Alekseeva, "Zabastovki," p. 84.

88. Evgeny Nikolaev, "A Note on the Origins of the Free Trade Unions," CHR, no. 35 (July–September 1979), p. 12.

89. Vysotin and Sereda, "The Past," pp. 28–29.

90. Materialy samizdata, no. 16/84 (1984); AS 5207 (Munich: Radio Liberty, 1984, mimeo).

91. Walter D. Connor, "Dissent in a Complex Society: The Soviet Case," Problems of Communism 22, 2 (March–April 1973), p. 50.

92. Reinhard Bendix, Nation-Building and Citizenship: Studies of Our Changing Social Order (Garden City, N.Y.: Doubleday Anchor Books, 1969), p. 55.

93. Ibid.

94. Ibid.

95. Vysotin and Sereda, "The Past," pp. 34–35.

96. Liudmila Alekseeva, "Workers' Participation in the Dissident Movement," CHR, no. 39 (July–September 1980), p. 52.

97. Ibid., pp. 53–54.

98. Vysotin and Sereda, "The Past," p. 35.

99. "K trudiashchimsia S.Sh.A.," *Materialy samizdata*, no. 6/79 (1979); *AS* 3474.

100. George Miller, "SMOT Challenge to Andropov," *Soviet Analyst* 12, 4 (February 23, 1983), pp. 7–8.

101. "Passive Workers Condemned," *Soviet Analyst* 10, 20 (October 7, 1981), p. 6.

102. See Riga Domestic Service (Russian), 0729 GMT, February 19, 1987 (*FBIS*, February 25, 1987, pp. R5–22).

103. Radio Moscow, World Service (English), 0700 GMT, July 27, 1988 (*FBIS*, July 27, 1988, p. 61).

104. *Sotsialisticheskaia industriia*, September 28, 1988 (*FBIS*, September 29, 1988, pp. 79–81).

105. *Izvestiia*, September 24, 1988, p. 2; September 10, 1988, p. 1.

106. *Pravda* and *Izvestiia*, July 1, 1988, p. 1; see excerpts in *CDSP*, August 31, 1988, pp. 8–9.

107. *Sovetskaia kul'tura*, June 7, 1988, pp. 1, 4 (*FBIS*, June 19, 1988, p. 79).

108. *Pravda*, January 7, 1981, p. 3.

109. V. Kashin, "Po normam sotsial'noi spravedlivosti," *ST*, no. 10 (1986), p. 97.

110. *Sotsialisticheskaia industria*, January 5, 1988, p. 2.

111. *Moscow News*, July 3, 1988, pp. 10–11 (*FBIS*, July 28, 1988, pp. 53–55).

112. See I. Gladkii, "Sovetovat'sia s trudovymi kollektivami," *ST*, no. 2 (1986), pp. 17–21.

113. Ibid., p. 21, and see also K. Turysov, "Otvetstvennye zadachi prof-soiuzov," *ST*, no. 1 (1987), p. 17.

114. K. Turysov, "Po puti perestroiki," *RKSM*, no. 4 (1987), pp. 4, 7.

115. *Pravda*, July 3, 1988, p. 2.

116. TASS (English), 1807 GMT, August 24, 1988 (*FBIS*, August 25, 1988, pp. 39–40).

117. *Pravda*, September 12, 1988, p. 2.

118. *Izvestiia*, August 18, 1986, p. 4.

119. *Izvestiia*, December 4, 1986; see also Elizabeth Teague, "'Stormy Protests' at Soviet Truck Plant," *RLR* 461/86, December 4, 1986.

120. *Moscow News*, no. 16 (1987), p. 9.

121. *Moscow News*, no. 38 (1987), p. 9.

122. See articles translated or summarized in *CDSP*, January 27, 1988, pp. 7–10: *Moskovskie novosti*, December 27, 1987, p. 4; *Izvestiia*, December 26, 1987, p. 3; *Sovetskaia Rossiia*, December 20, 1987, p. 2; *Izvestiia*, January 7, 1988, p. 2.

123. *Moskovskie novosti*, October 18, 1987, pp. 8–9 (*CDSP*, January 27, 1988, pp. 30–31).

124. *Sotsialisticheskaia industriia*, February 24, 1988, p. 2; (*FBIS*, February 26, 1988, pp. 56–57).

125. *Pravda*, March 30, 1988 (see also *RLR* 139/88, April 1, 1988, p. 7).

126. TASS (English), 1239 GMT, December 28, 1987 (*FBIS*, January 5, 1988, p. 52).

127. *Pravda*, May 22, 1988, p. 6 (*CDSP*, June 22, 1988, pp. 26–27).

128. *Pravda*, July 18, 1988, p. 4.

129. Ibid.

130. Ibid.

131. TASS, cited in *RLR* 412/88, September 16, 1988, p. 10; see also *RLR* 432/88, September 16, 1988.

132. *Sotsialisticheskaia industriia*, February 24, 1988, p. 2.

133. Radio Moscow (Russian), 0800 GMT, September 15, 1988 (*FBIS*, September 16, 1988, pp. 35–36).

134. *Pravda*, August 6, 1988; *Izvestiia*, August 7, 1988 (*CDSP*, August 31, 1988, p. 5).

135. *Pravda*, July 18, 1988, p. 4.

136. *Moscow News*, no. 16 (1987), p. 9.

137. *Izvestiia*, August 18, 1986, p. 4.

138. *Moscow News*, no. 16 (1987), p. 9.

139. *Pravda*, September 25, 1988, p. 1.

140. *RLR* 412/88, September 16, 1988, p. 11, cited a Reuters report that Shalaev expressed this to an unnamed Finnish paper.

141. "Generally accepted" in the sense that most of the Western analytic writing on Soviet trade unions, before the wave of strikes in 1989 and the bitterness they revealed, took this line on the unions. There was little direct evidence to back the more radical critical conclusions that now appear to be more generally accepted.

142. See Mann, *Consciousness and Action*, p. 13.

Chapter 7
Worker Politics and Economic Crisis

The opening quote is from *Sotsialisticheskaia industriia*, April 6, 1989, p. 1 (trans. in *CDSP*, May 31, 1988, p. 15).

1. Thus the chapter combines a "longer" perspective on issues of entrepreneurship, equality, and "social contract" concerns with a shorter (1989–90) one on strikes.

2. *New York Times*, June 18, 1989, p. 8.

3. *Ekonomika sel'skogo khoziaistva*, no. 3 (1986), pp. 59–64, cited in *RLR* 295/86, August 4, 1986, p. 1.

4. *Sovetskaia kul'tura*, March 20, 1986, p. 3.

5. See *Trud*, August 22, 1986, cited in *RLR* 321/86, August 22, 1986, p. 6.

6. *Izvestiia*, September 19, 1987, p. 3 (*FBIS*, September 25, 1987, pp. 51–52).

7. *Izvestiia*, November 19, 1987, p. 2 (*FBIS*, December 7, 1987, p. 71).

8. *Literaturnaia gazeta*, January 20, 1988, p. 10 (*FBIS*, January 26, 1988, pp. 66–68).

9. *Izvestiia*, November 19, 1987, p. 2.

10. *Izvestiia*, March 14, 1989, p. 2 (*FBIS*, March 22, 1989, pp. 75–77).

11. *Literaturnaia gazeta*, October 5, 1988, p. 10 (*FBIS*, October 5, 1988, pp. 65–68).

12. *Der Spiegel*, July 6, 1987, pp. 98–103 (*FBIS*, July 15, 1987, p. S-4).

13. What follows draws upon *Sovetskaia Rossiia*, October 18, 1987, p. 3 (deputy chairman Komin of *Goskomtsen*); *Trud*, November 22, 1987, p. 2, and

Sotsialisticheskaia industriia, April 1, 1988, pp. 1–2 (both from Pavlov, head of Goskomtsen); *Trud*, October 5, 1988, pp. 1–2 (from Rimashevskaia).

14. V. Antosenkov, director of Goskomtrud's Scientific Research Institute on Labor, predicted this to me in January 1988 in Moscow.

15. For phases of this "retreat," see Aganbegian in *Svenska Dagbladet*, February 2, 1988, sec. 3, p. 2 (*FBIS*, February 12, 1988, p. 67); and in *L'Unita*, May 5, 1988, p. 24 (*FBIS*, May 13, 1988, p. 60); *Sotsialisticheskaia industriia*, March 2, 1988, p. 3; Radio Moscow World Service (English), 1600 GMT, October 23, 1988 (*FBIS*, October 25, 1988, p. 84); *Argumenty i fakty*, December 24–30, 1988, p. 8 (*FBIS*, December 28, 1988, p. 49).

16. *Moscow News*, no. 50 (December 11, 1988), p. 10.

17. Radio Moscow, World Service (English), 0210 GMT, March 26, 1989 (*FBIS*, March 30, 1989, p. 69).

18. *Literaturnaia gazeta*, January 25, 1989, p. 11 (*FBIS*, January 31, 1989, p. 78).

19. See *Izvestiia*, April 10, 1990, p. 1 (*CDSP*, May 9, 1990, pp. 5–6).

20. *Narodnoe khoziaistvo SSSR v 1985 godu* (Moscow: Finansy i statistika, 1986), p. 478; and *Narodnoe khoziaistvo SSSR za 70 let* (Moscow: Finansy i statistika, 1987), p. 480.

21. *Literaturnaia gazeta*, September 16, 1987, p. 12.

22. V. Rutgaizer et al., "Sovershenstvovanie sistemy planovykh pokazatelei dokhodov naseleniia," *Voprosy ekonomiki*, no. 1 (1988), p. 33.

23. *Sotsialisticheskaia industriia*, November 12, 1988, p. 3 (*FBIS*, November 18, 1988, pp. 82–84).

24. Radio Moscow World Service (English), 1100 GMT, January 17, 1988 (*FBIS*, January 13, 1989, pp. 68–69).

25. See, e.g., Radio Moscow, World Service (Russian), 1900 GMT, January 8, 1989 (*FBIS*, January 9, 1989, p. 89); *Izvestiia*, January 12, 1989, p. 2 (*FBIS*, January 13, 1989, pp. 68–69).

26. Philip Hanson, "Inflation versus Reform," RL, *Report on the USSR*, no. 16 (1989), pp. 13–18.

27. *Sotsialisticheskaia industriia*, June 1, 1988, p. 3 (*FBIS*, June 24, 1988, pp. 67–69).

28. See, *Trud*, April 28, 1989, p. 1 (*FBIS*, May 11, 1989, p. 41).

29. See Aaron Trehub, "Soviet Economist on US and Soviet Living Standard," *RLR, Report on the USSR*, no. 6 (1989), pp. 4–7.

30. See, e.g., V. Krivosheev, "O zavisimosti khoda idei ot khoda veshchei," *Druzhba narodov*, no. 10 (1988), pp. 200–201.

31. *Pravda*, June 9, 1989, p. 2 (*FBIS*, June 9, 1989, supp. p. 26).

32. *Sovetskaia kul'tura*, December 13, 1988, p. 3 (*FBIS*, December 15, 1988, p. 69).

33. *Izvestiia*, January 1, 1989, p. 4 (*FBIS*, January 4, 1989, pp. 45–46).

34. *Argumenty i fakty*, May 20–26, 1989, pp. 4–5 (*FBIS*, May 24, 1989, pp. 64–66).

35. *Izvestiia*, April 20, 1989, p. 3 (*FBIS*, April 26, 1989, p. 100).

36. V. V. Kulikov, "Struktura i formy realizatsii sotsialisticheskoi sobstvennosti," *RKSM*, no. 5 (1987), pp. 17–18.

37. TASS, March 12, 1988, cited in *RLR* 120/88 (March 18, 1988), p. 3.

38. *Pravda*, May 28, 1986, pp. 1–2.

39. N. Shmelev, "Avansy i dolgi," *Novyi mir*, no. 6 (1987), pp. 142–58 (trans. in *Problems of Economics* 30, 10, February 1988, pp. 7–43), p. 17.

40. *Ekonomicheskaia gazeta*, no. 43 (October, 1986), pp. 15–16.

41. *Pravda*, November 1, 1986, pp. 1, 3.

42. See, e.g., *Izvestiia*, December 12, 1987, p. 5; *Izvestiia*, May 16, 1987, p. 2.

43. *Izvestiia*, September 10, 1987, p. 3.

44. *Pravda*, December 20, 1986, p. 3.

45. *Pravda*, June 8, 1986, pp. 2–5; see also John Tedstrom, "The New Law on Cooperatives," *RLR* 246/88, June 10, 1988.

46. See, generally, John Tedstrom, "Soviet Cooperatives: A Difficult Road to Legitimacy," *RLR* 244/88, May 31, 1988; and idem, "New Draft Law on Income Taxes," *RLR, Report on the USSR*, no. 24 (1989), pp. 8–10.

47. *Sotsialistcheskaia industriia*, February 21, 1989, p. 2 (*FBIS*, March 6, 1989, p. 93).

48. *Moscow News*, no. 10 (1989), p. 4 (*FBIS*, March 16, 1989, pp. 85–86).

49. *Ekonomicheskaia gazeta*, no. 17 (1989), p. 3.

50. Tedstrom, "New Draft Law."

51. *Pravda*, April 23, 1983, cited in *RLR, Report on the USSR*, no. 18 (1989), p. 26.

52. *Izvestiia*, July 27, 1988, p. 1 (*FBIS*, August 4, 1988, p. 63).

53. February 27, 1988, p. 3 (*FBIS*, March 11, 1988, p. 42).

54. *Izvestiia*, December 12, 1987, p. 5.

55. *Trud*, April 24, 1988, p. 1.

56. *Argumenty i fakty*, March 28–April 3, 1987, pp. 4–5.

57. *Izvestiia*, February 27, 1988, p. 3 (*FBIS*, March 11, 1988, p. 42).

58. *Argumenty i fakty*, June 18–24, 1988, pp. 1–2 (*FBIS*, June 28, 1988, p. 79).

59. V. Z. Rogovin, "Sotsial'naia spravedlivost' i sotsialisticheskoe raspredelenie zhiznennykh blag," *Voprosy filosofii*, no. 9 (1986), p. 17.

60. G. Lisichkin, "Liudi i veshchi," *Druzhba narodov*, no. 1 (1988), pp. 214–15.

61. See *RLR* 337/88, July 29, 1988, p. 4, citing *Novosti*.

62. L. A. Gordon and A. K. Nazimova, "Proizvodstvennyi potentsial sovetskogo rabochego klassa: Tendentsii i problemy razvitiia," *Voprosy filosofii*, no. 11 (1980), pp. 26–40 (trans. in *Soviet Sociology* 19, 4, Spring 1981, p. 50).

63. *Izvestiia*, March 30, 1989, p. 1 (*FBIS*, April 4, 1989, pp. 73–74).

64. *Izvestiia*, November 6, 1985, p. 3.

65. *Pravda*, October 12, 1989, p. 1 (*FBIS*, October 19, 1988, pp. 87–88).

66. *Moscow News*, no. 40 (October, 1987), p. 12.

67. Conversation with V. Shastitko, deputy director of the Academy of Sciences' Institute on the Economics of the World Socialist System, Moscow, January 1988.

68. *Pravda*, April 5, 1989, p. 3 (*FBIS*, April 12, 1989, pp. 75–78).

69. *Izvestiia*, January 7, 1989, p. 3 (*FBIS*, January 11, 1989, pp. 78–80).

70. *Pravda*, December 17, 1988, cited in *RLR* 552/88, December 16, 1988, pp. 9–10.

71. *Pravda*, February 16, 1989, p. 3 (*FBIS*, February 16, 1989, p. 44).

72. *Trud*, May 19, 1989, p. 2 (*FBIS*, June 5, 1989, pp. 50–54).

73. *Pravda*, February 16, 1989, p. 3 (*FBIS*, February 16, 1989, p. 47).

74. *Ekonomicheskaia gazeta*, no. 27 (July 1989), wrote of "about 100" strikes thus far in that year.

75. TASS (English), 1549 GMT, February 24, 1989 (*FBIS*, March 10, 1989, p. 27).

76. *Trud*, March 10, 1989, p. 2 (*FBIS*, March 29, 1989, p. 63).

77. Jerusalem Radio (Hebrew), 1700 GMT, March 24, 1989 (*FBIS*, March 27, 1989, pp. 70–71).

78. Radio Moscow (Russian), 1400 GMT, March 7, 1989 (*FBIS*, March 8, 1989, p. 63).

79. Coverage of the Noril'sk strikes is drawn from TASS (Russian), 0753 GMT, April 13, 1989; and *Pravda*, April 13, 1989, p. 6 (both *FBIS*, April 14, 1989, pp. 65–66); *Trud*, April 25, 1989, p. 2 (*FBIS*, May 9, 1989, pp. 73–77).

80. *Trud*, April 20, 1989, p. 2 (*FBIS*, April 28, 1989, pp. 71–74).

81. *Komsomol'skaia pravda*, February 26, 1989, p. 1 (*FBIS*, March 10, 1989, pp. 87–88).

82. *RLR, Report on the USSR*, no. 21 (1989), p. 38, citing TASS.

83. *Trud*, February 11, 1989, p. 2.

84. *Wochenpresse* (Vienna), February 10, 1989, p. 34 (*FBIS*, February 14, 1989, p. 75).

85. See the "platform" in *Trud*, March 25, 1989, pp. 1–2 (*FBIS*, April 13, 1989, pp. 57–61).

86. Radio Moscow (Russian), 1045 GMT, March 4, 1989 (*FBIS*, March 15, 1989, pp. 90–92).

87. *Trud*, April 19, 1989, p. 1.

88. Radio Moscow (Russian), March 4, 1989 (*FBIS*, March 15, 1989, pp. 90–92).

89. *Noorte haal*, February 17, 1989 (*FBIS*, March 1, 1989, pp. 48–49).

90. See the draft law text in *Trud*, April 29, 1989, pp. 2–3 (*FBIS*, May 9, 1989, pp. 48–58).

91. *Trud*, May 3, 1989, pp. 1–2 (*FBIS*, May 9, 1989, p. 61).

92. *Trud*, May 5, 1989, p. 2 (*FBIS*, May 11, 1989, p. 47).

93. *Sotsialisticheskaia industriia*, May 1, 1989, p. 2.

94. *Pravda*, February 16, 1989, pp. 1–3 (trans. in *CDSP*, March 15, 1989, p. 19).

95. See *RLR, Report on the USSR*, no. 23 (1989), p. 7.

96. *Leningradskaia pravda*, April 25, 1989, pp. 1–2 (*FBIS*, May 5, 1989, p. 46).

97. *Pravda*, April 27, 1989, p. 4.

98. *Sovetskaia Rossiia*, May 7, 1989, p. 1 (*FBIS*, May 15, 1989, p. 65).

99. *Pravda*, April 27, 1989, p. 6.

100. Ibid., p. 7.

101. *Trud*, April 7, 1989, pp. 1–2.

102. *Sotsialisticheskaia industriia*, May 1, 1989, p. 1.

103. This narrative draws on a variety of Soviet press and media sources. Valuable summaries and appraisals are available in Elizabeth Teague, "Min-

ers' Strike in Siberia Winds Down, Strikes in Ukraine Spread to Other Areas: A Status Report," *RLR Report*, no. 30, July 28, 1989, pp. 15–18; and idem, "Embryos of People's Power," *RLR Report on the USSR*, no. 32 (August 11, 1989), pp. 1–4.

104. *Anteni* (Sofia), August 1, 1989, p. 11 (*FBIS*, August 10, 1989, p. 45).

105. The sociologists Gordon and Klopov report this figure in *Pravda*, January 18, 1990, p. 4 (*FBIS*, January 24, 1990, p. 81).

106. Radio Kiev (Ukrainian), 1845 GMT, September 8, 1989 (*FBIS*, September 12, 1989, pp. 44–45).

107. *Izvestiia*, September 6, 1989, p. 3 (*FBIS*, September 15, 1989, pp. 61–63).

108. Agence France Presse (English) 1540 GMT, October 3, 1989 (*FBIS*, October 4, 1989, p. 82).

109. Moscow Television, 1530 GMT, October 25, 1989 (*FBIS*, October 26, 1989, pp. 79–80).

110. Mainz ZDF Television, 1800 GMT, October 25, 1989 (*FBIS*, October 26, 1989, p. 86).

111. Moscow Television, 1230 GMT, November 19, 1989 (*FBIS*, November 20, 1989, p. 66).

112. *Izvestiia*, December 1, 1989, p. 3 (*FBIS*, December 4, 1989, pp. 107–108).

113. *Izvestiia*, December 14, 1989, p. 1.

114. There is some confusion about this, however; see *Izvestiia*, July 15, 1989 (*FBIS*, July 18, 1989, p. 80), but also Theodore Friedgut and Lewis Siegelbaum, "The Soviet Miners' Strike, July 1989: Perestroika from Below," Carl Beck Papers, no. 804 (University of Pittsburgh, Center for Russian and East European Studies, 1990). Much of what follows on the strike in Donetsk is drawn from this excellent work.

115. Nina Maksimova, "Zabastovka," *EKO*, no. 11 (1989), p. 70.

116. Ibid., p. 67.

117. Ibid., p. 70.

118. Radio Moscow (Russian), 0500 GMT, July 26, 1989 (*FBIS*, July 27, 1989, pp. 59–60).

119. *Trud*, July 13, 1989, p. 1 (*FBIS*, July 14, 1989, p. 37).

120. Maksimova, "Zabastovka," p. 70, and TASS (English), 1654 GMT, July 18, 1989 (*FBIS*, July 19, 1989, p. 65).

121. See *Izvestiia*, July 15, 1989, p. 3 (*FBIS*, July 17, 1989, pp. 37–38); *Sotsialisticheskaia industriia*, August 8, 1989, p. 2 (*FBIS*, August 17, 1989, p. 70); and Radio Moscow (Russian), 1500 GMT, July 22, 1989 (*FBIS*, July 24, 1989, p. 57).

122. *Trud*, August 3, 1989, p. 3 (*FBIS*, August 18, 1989, p. 40).

123. Moscow Television, 1700 GMT, July 27, 1989 (*FBIS*, July 28, 1989, p. 58).

124. *Sotsialisticheskaia industriia*, August 8, 1989, p. 2 (*FBIS*, August 17, 1989, p. 71).

125. *Pravda*, August 21, 1989, p. 3 (*FBIS*, August 25, 1989, p. 46).

126. Such numbers seem consistent with an earlier study of "informal groups" among workers; see V. Korshunova and M. Novosel'tsev, "Rabochie-neformaly," *ST*, no. 3 (1989), pp. 68–73.

127. *Trud*, July 18, 1989, p. 1 (*FBIS*, July 18, 1989, p. 76).

128. *Pravda*, July 31, 1989, pp. 1–2 (*FBIS*, August 11, 1989, pp. 75–78).

129. *Moscow News*, no. 32 (August 6, 1989), p. 8 (*FBIS*, August 22, 1989, p. 38).

130. TASS (English), 1756 GMT, September 6, 1989 (*FBIS*, September 7, 1989, p. 69).

131. Ken Jowitt, "Soviet Neotraditionalism: The Political Corruption of a Leninist Regime," *Soviet Studies* 35, 3 (July 1983), pp. 275–97.

132. Friedgut and Siegelbaum, "Soviet Miners' Strike," p. 15.

133. See Elizabeth Teague, "Draft Law on Trade Unions Published," *RLR Report on the USSR*, no. 20 (May 19, 1989), pp. 1–2.

134. Radio Moscow (Russian), 1600 GMT, October 2, 1989 (*FBIS*, October 3, 1989, pp. 57–58).

135. Radio Moscow (English), 1000 GMT, October 3, 1989 (*FBIS*, October 3, 1989, p. 61).

136. *Izvestiia*, October 5, 1989, p. 1 (*FBIS*, October 5, 1989, pp. 49–50).

137. Elizabeth Teague, "Worker Unrest in 1989," *RLR Report on the USSR*, no. 4 (1990), pp. 12–13.

138. Anders Aslund, *Gorbachev's Struggle for Economic Reform* (Ithaca, N.Y.: Cornell University Press, 1989), esp. chap. 5.

139. *Komsomol'skaia pravda*, July 14, 1989, p. 1 (*FBIS*, August 7, 1989, p. 72).

140. *Trud*, July 26, 1989, p. 1 (*FBIS*, August 10, 1989, p. 44).

141. *Financial Times* (hereafter *FT*), September 13, 1989, p. 3.

142. *FT*, July 21, 1989, p. 2.

143. *FT*, October 2, 1989, p. 1.

144. *FT*, September 12, 1989, p. 20; September 13, 1989, p. 3.

145. See TASS (English), 1831 GMT, July 17, 1989 (*FBIS*, July 18, 1989, pp. 73–74), on Makeevka; *Sotsialisticheskaia industriia*, July 26, 1989, p. 3 (*FBIS*, August 18, 1989, p. 44), on Karaganda; and *Trud*, August 3, 1989, p. 3 (*FBIS*, August 18, 1989, pp. 38–39), on the overall Kuzbass characterization.

146. *New York Times*, July 21, 1989, p. 1.

147. TASS (English), 1831 GMT, July 17, 1989 (*FBIS*, July 18, 1989, pp. 73–74).

148. *Komsomol'skaia pravda*, November 2, 1989, p. 2 (*FBIS*, November 28, 1989, pp. 95–98).

149. Moscow Television, 0722 GMT, July 24, 1989 (*FBIS*, July 25, 1989, p. 44).

150. See Friedgut and Siegelbaum, "Soviet Miners' Strike," and *FT*, July 24, 1989, p. 1.

151. See *Sovetskaia Rossiia*, July 13, 1989, p. 2 (*FBIS*, July 13, 1989, p. 49), on Mezhdurechensk; TASS (English), 0940 GMT, July 20, 1989 (*FBIS*, July 20, 1989, p. 47), on Dnepropetrovsk; *Trud*, July 22, 1989, p. 1 (*FBIS*, August 2, 1989, p. 68), on Karaganda; and *Izvestiia*, August 6, 1989, p. 6 (*FBIS*, August 7, 1989, p. 70), on Vorkuta.

152. Radio Moscow (Russian), 0800 GMT, July 19, 1989 (*FBIS*, July 20, 1989, p. 55).

153. Moscow Television, 1430 GMT, July 26, 1989 (*FBIS*, July 27, 2989, p. 62).

154. *Sovetskaia Rossiia*, July 30, 1989, p. 2 (*FBIS*, August 22, 1989, p. 44).

155. See Friedgut and Siegelbaum, "Soviet Miners' Strike," pp. 27ff.

156. *Pravda*, August 14, 1989, pp. 1, 2 (*FBIS*, August 15, 1989, p. 45).

157. *Sotsialisticheskaia industriia*, August 8, 1989, p. 2 (*FBIS*, August 17, 1989, p. 73).

158. TASS (English), 1756 GMT, September 6, 1989 (*FBIS*, September 7, 1989, p. 69).

159. See *FT*, September 29, 1989, p. 2; and TASS (Russian), 1742 GMT, September 26, 1989 (*FBIS*, September 27, 1989, p. 104).

160. *Trud*, December 2, 1989, p. 2 (*FBIS*, December 15, 1989, pp. 98–100).

161. *Trud*, January 24, 1990, p. 1 (*FBIS*, January 30, 1990, p. 109).

162. Radio Kiev (Ukrainian to North America), 2200 GMT, February 1, 1990 (*FBIS*, February 6, 1990, p. 91).

163. *Pravda*, February 11, 1990, p. 2 (*FBIS*, February 15, 1990, pp. 113–14).

164. See *Pravda*, February 5, 1990, p. 3; and February 11, 1990, p. 2; also Radio Kiev (Ukrainian to North America), 2200 GMT, February 2, 1990 (*FBIS*, February 6, 1990, p. 91).

165. *Izvestiia*, October 4, 1989, p. 1 (*FBIS*, November 1, 1989, p. 27).

166. TASS (English), 1356 GMT, April 5, 1990 (*FBIS*, April 6, 1990, p. 41).

167. *Izvestiia*, April 18, 1990, p. 1.

168. *Izvestiia*, May 3, 1990, p. 1 (*FBIS*, May 4, 1990, p. 44); also *Rabochaia tribuna*, April 26, 1990, p. 1 (*FBIS*, May 10, 1990, p. 50).

169. *Rabochaia tribuna*, April 24, 1990, pp. 1–2 (*FBIS*, April 26, 1990, pp. 71–72).

170. *Pravda*, May 16, 1990, pp. 1–2 (*FBIS*, May 21, 1990, pp. 55–58).

171. V. S. Dunin and I. Iu. Var'iash, "Inzhener—podruchnyi v rabochego," *SI*, no. 1 (1989), pp. 50–54.

172. *Literaturnaia gazeta*, August 2, 1989 (*FBIS*, August 11, 1989, p. 85); see also *RLR Report on the USSR*, no. 30 (July 28, 1989), pp. 51–52.

173. See Vera Tolz, "Politics in Leningrad and the Creation of Two Popular Fronts," *RLR Report on the USSR*, no. 29 (1989), pp. 38–40.

174. TASS (English), 1439 GMT, October 26, 1989 (*FBIS*, October 27, 1989, p. 60).

175. See *FT*, October 26, 1989, p. 2; also Kathleen Mihalisko, "Reaching for Parliamentary Democracy in Belorussia and Ukraine," *RLR Report on the USSR*, no. 50 (1989), p. 17; and *Leningradskaia pravda*, November 29, 1989, pp. 1–2 (*FBIS*, December 21, 1989, p. 78).

176. TASS (English), 1439 GMT, October 26, 1989 (*FBIS*, October 27, 1989, p. 60).

177. *Izvestiia*, December 3, 1989, p. 2 (*FBIS*, December 11, 1989, pp. 109–10).

178. TASS (English), 1723 GMT, September 6, 1989 (*FBIS*, September 7, 1989, p. 70).

179. See *Trud v SSSR* (Moscow: Finansy i statistika, 1988), pp. 19, 20 (the population figure is from the 1979 census; the "workers and employees" figure is dated 1987).

180. *Sovetskaia Rossiia*, September 13, 1989, p. 2; also Moscow Television,

1430 GMT, September 17, 1989 (*FBIS*, Sep. 18, 1989, pp. 75–76); *FT*, September 14, 1989, p. 2.

181. Moscow Television (see n. 180).

182. *Izvestiia*, November 1, 1989, p. 3 (*FBIS*, November 2, 1989, p. 76).

183. *Izvestiia*, December 27, 1989 (*CDSP*, January 24, 1990, pp. 34–35).

184. *Pravda* and *Izvestiia*, September 25, 1989, pp. 1–2 (*CDSP*, October 25, 1989, p. 4).

185. *Literaturnaia Rossiia*, December 29, 1989, pp. 2–3 (*CDSP*, February 7, 1990, pp. 1–4, 23).

186. See John B. Dunlop, "Moscow Voters Reject Conservative Coalition," *RLR Report on the USSR*, no. 16 (April 20, 1990), pp. 15–17.

187. *RLR Report on the USSR*, no. 16 (April 20, 1990), p. 29.

188. See the interviews in *Rabochaia tribuna*, March 27, 1990, p. 1; and *Izvestiia*, April 7, 1990, p. 2.

189. *Sobesednik*, April 1, 1990, pp. 4–5 (*FBIS*, May 11, 1990, p. 31).

190. *Izvestiia*, November 21, 1989, p. 6; *Rabochaia tribuna*, April 26, 1990, p. 1 (*FBIS*, May 10, 1990, pp. 50–52); and *Izvestiia*, May 3, 1990, p. 1 (*FBIS*, May 4, 1990, p. 44).

191. *Moscow News*, no. 13 (April 1, 1990), p. 8.

192. *RLR Report on the USSR*, no. 14 (April 6, 1990), pp. 31–32.

193. *Rabochaia tribuna*, April 24, 1990, pp. 1, 2 (*FBIS*, April 26, 1990, p. 101).

194. Radio Moscow (Russian), 1500 GMT, April 25, 1990 (*FBIS*, April 26, 1990, p. 101).

195. *Izvestiia*, April 6, 1990, p. 1 (*CDSP*, May 9, 1990, p. 4).

196. TASS (English), 1358 GMT, September 14, 1990 (*FBIS*, September 17, 1990, p. 47).

197. *Pravda*, September 11, 1990, p. 1.

198. *Trud*, September 19, 1990, pp. 1–2.

199. *Izvestiia*, September 15, 1990, p. 1.

Epilogue

The opening quotes are from the *Financial Times*, April 9, 1991, p. 2 (strike leader), and Moscow Radio 1600 GMT, April 11, 1991; *FBIS*, April 12, 1991, p. 45 (Pavlov).

1. *Moscow News*, January 27—February 3, 1991, p.11.

2. *Pravda*, February 15, 1991, p. 2; *FBIS*, February 20, 1991, p. 57.

3. *Trud*, November 27, 1990, p. 3; *FBIS*, December 12, 1990, pp. 49–50.

4. *Sel'skaia zhizn'*, February 5, 1991, p. 2; *FBIS*, February 12, 1991, pp. 55–57.

5. *Izvestiia*, February 16, 1991, p. 2; *FBIS*, February 21, 1991, pp.55–58.

6. See *Trud*, February 5, 1991; *FBIS*, February 8, 1991, pp. 38–40.

7. *Trud*, February 21, 1991, p. 1; *FBIS*, February 21, 1991, pp. 51–52.

8. TASS (English), 1420 GMT, January 3, 1991; *FBIS*, January 4, 1991, p. 44; also *Sovetskaia Rossiia*, January 4, 1991, p. 2; *FBIS*, January 7, 1991, p. 56.

9. See *Komsomol'skaia pravda*, December 9, 1990, p. 1; *FBIS*, December 17, 1990, pp. 55–58.

10. See *Izvestiia*, December 12, 1990, p. 2; *FBIS*, January 11, 1991 (suppl.),

pp. 19–20; also *Sovetskaia Rossiia*, December 13, 1990, p. 2; *FBIS*, January 25, 1991, pp. 52–54.

11. Moscow Radio (Russian), 1500 GMT, January 15, 1991; *FBIS*, January 22, 1991, p. 33; see also *Trud*, January 18, 1991, p. 1; *FBIS*, January 24, 1991, p. 43.

12. See *RL Report on the USSR*, no. 51, December 21, 1990, p. 41, citing TASS, December 14, 1990.

13. TASS (English), 1827 GMT, December 6, 1990; *FBIS*, December 7, 1990, pp. 40–41.

14. Andrew G. Walder, *Communist Neo-Traditionalism: Work and Authority in Chinese Industry* (Berkeley and Los Angeles: University of California Press, 1986).

15. Ibid., p. 16.

16. Ibid., p. 239, citing Charles Sabel and David Stark, "Planning, Politics, and Shop-Floor Power: Hidden Forms of Bargaining in Soviet-Imposed State-Socialist Societies," *Politics and Society* 11, 4 (1982), pp. 439–75.

17. See e.g., Peter Rutland's thought-provoking analysis, "Labor Unrest and Movements in 1989 and 1990," *Soviet Economy* 6, 3 (1990), pp. 345–84; see also Linda J. Cook, "Lessons of Soviet Coal Miners' Strike of Summer 1989," *Harriman Institute Forum*, 4, 3 (March 1991), pp. 1–10. Months after the events of 1989, several Soviet articles also provide analytic context on the strikes and the emergent workers' committees. See, e.g., L. L. Mal'tseva and O. N. Puli-aeva, "Chto privelo k zabastovke," *SI*, no. 6, (1990), pp. 38–42, and in the same issue, V. G. Britvin, "Zabastovki na predpriiatiiakh s pozitsii trudi-ashchikhsia," pp. 49–53, and the round-table discussion, "Razgovor u barri-kady," pp. 66–76. See also V. N. Shalenko, "Proizvodstvennye zabastovki kak ob"ekt sotsiologicheskogo analiza," *SI*, no. 7 (1990), pp. 107–11.

18. Moscow Television, 1200 GMT, March 5, 1991; *FBIS*, March 5, 1991, p. 4.

19. TASS (Russian), 0734 GMT, March 12, 1991; *FBIS*, March 12, 1991, p. 63.

20. Moscow Television, 1200 GMT, March 13, 1991; *FBIS*, March 25, 1991, p. 42.

21. TASS (Russian), 1313 GMT, March 22, 1991; *FBIS*, March 25, 1991, p. 42.

22. *Komsomol'skaia pravda*, March 23, 1991, p. 1; *FBIS*, March 26, 1991, p. 49.

23. *Pravda*, March 27, 1991, p. 2; *FBIS*, March 27, 1991, p. 13.

24. *Izvestiia*, March 28, 1991, p. 1; *FBIS*, March 28, 1991, p. 29ff.

25. *Izvestiia*, April 8, 1991, p. 1; *FBIS*, April 8, 1991, p. 44.

26. *FT*, April 4, 1991, p. 1.

27. *Literaturnaia gazeta*, no. 11, March 20, 1991, p. 3; *FBIS* (suppl.), March 26, 1991, pp. 31–32.

28. Moscow Radio (English), 1200 GMT, March 28, 1991; *FBIS*, March 28, 1991, p. 30.

29. Gliksman, "The Russian Urban Worker," p. 321.

30. Ibid., p. 322.

31. Yanowitch, *Work in the Soviet Union*, p. 157.

32. This discussion draws on David Lane and Felicity O'Dell, *The Soviet*

Industrial Worker: Social Class, Education, and Control (New York: St. Martin's Press, 1978), pp. 46–52.

33. Ibid., p. 47.
34. Ibid., p. 50.
35. Ibid., p. 137.
36. Ibid., p. 49.
37. Ibid., p. 50.
38. "Razgovor u barrikady," p. 70.
39. Lane and O'Dell, *Soviet Worker*, p. 136.
40. Frank Parkin, *Marxism and Class Theory: A Bourgeois Critique* (New York: Columbia University Press, 1979), p. 136.
41. Ibid., p. 137.
42. Ibid.
43. Arnot, "Soviet Labour Productivity," p. 55.
44. Holubenko, "Soviet Working Class," p. 25.
45. Ralf Dahrendorf, *Class and Class Conflict in Industrial Society* (Stanford, Calif.: Stanford University Press, 1961), p. 126.
46. Emigré research of the late 1970s–early 1980s showed a tendency for skilled workers, to a greater degree than unskilled, to claim identity as "employee" or "intelligentsia" in traditional Soviet categories, or to elect "middle" class status (an alternative not found in the Soviet categories), as alternatives to assumption of a "working class" identity (which 38 percent of the skilled, versus 61 of the unskilled, elected in one study at the beginning of the 1980s); see Alex Pravda, "Is There a Soviet Working Class?" *Problems of Communism* 31, 6 (November–December, 1982), p. 15 (table 6), for a discussion of data from the research of Zvi Y. Gitelman of the University of Michigan on class self-identification.
47. E. V. Klopov's major work, *Rabochii klass SSSR*, takes the predominance of worker social origin among those entering the plants as a "very important (positive) objective factor," "since those who come from worker families rather than from the peasantry, hereditary urbanites rather than migrants from rural locales, are better prepared to fulfill the demands of an industrially organized society; they have, as a rule, a shorter period of adaptation to the production and social-psychological situation in their corresponding collectives, they are generally more rapidly included in their social life. Therefore data on the share of hereditary workers also reflect the process of the broadening of the social nucleus of the working class, the intensification of the preparedness of the whole class for the resolution of the diverse tasks of perfecting developed socialism" (p. 128).

This is the "conventional" view; still, Klopov, along with L. A. Gordon, authored in 1984 a much more detailed article-length treatment of hereditization in the working classes of the USSR and the six other European CMEA member states, still taking an "upbeat" perspective (see "Rabochii klass v stranakh sotsialisticheskogo sodruzhestva: tendentsii vozrastaniia sotsial'nogo potentsiala," *RKSM*, no. 5 [1984], pp. 46–57); in a related article at the outset of 1985, they looked in more detail at the emergence of a better-educated youth "draft"to the industrial labor force, and addressed the problem of developing training as well, and the "lag," discussed earlier, between the two. See "Rabochii klass v stranakh sotsialistischeskogo sodruzhestva: tendentsii kul'turno-kvalifikatsionnogo rosta," *RKSM*, no. 1 (1985), pp. 7–16.

48. *Radio Liberty Daily Report*, April 29, 1991, citing TASS.

49. Rutland, "Labor Unrest," pp. 379–382.

50. Guillermo O'Donnell and Phillippe C. Schmitter, *Transitions from Authoritarian Rule: Tentative Conclusions about Uncertain Democracies* (Baltimore and London: The Johns Hopkins University Press, 1986), p. 7.

51. Ibid., p. 46.

52. Ibid.

Index

Abalkin, Leonid, 188, 191, 258, 261, 262
Aganbegian, Abel, 189, 191, 300
Aitov, N. A., 82, 83
Alekseeva, Liudmila, 214, 215, 216, 220, 233, 234
All-Union Trade Union Congress, 157
Andropov, Iu., 92, 169, 173, 175–76
Apparats, 271, 280, 283
Association of Free Trade Unions. *See* Free Trade Unions
AUCCTU, 142, 200, 219, 226, 237, 238; as an advocate, 212; effort to redefine as "populist," 281; at plenum, 290, 292, 295; protest of price hikes, 291; as "servant of the State," 274; and strikes, 273; support of coal miners' union, 282; threatens use of strike, 299; turnover in leadership, 292; vote to dissolve, 301

Barkar, A., 73
Belotserkovsky, Vadim, 213, 214
Bergson, Abram, 106
Bialer, Seweryn, 16
Bloc of Russian Public-Patriotic Movements, 297
Blue-collar differentiation, 105–11
Bogomolov, Oleg, 143, 258, 262
Bolsheviks, 26, 27, 28, 42, 43, 45, 208, 234
Bonner, Elena, 227
Brest-Litovsk Treaty, 24
Brezhnev, Leonid, 48, 137, 219; Brezhnev era, 70, 71, 77, 188, 124, 136, 144, 153, 161, 162, 238, 248; construction programs under, 124; and growth of strike activities, 218; and political integration of workers, 201; wage policies under, 153, 215, 225
Brigades, 163, 179–84, 192, 197, 235, 236
Bunich, Pavel, 269

Cadres, 22, 25, 70, 92
Capitalism, 3, 27, 247
Central Committee, 61, 233, 275, 286, 297, 299; delegation visits Novo-

cherkassk, 214; Gorbachev delivers pep talk to, 145; grievances sent to, 230; plenums, 92, 99; on SPTU, 96
Chapman, Janet, 120–21, 122, 123
Chernenko, Konstantin, 92, 235
Class, working; and aftermath of war, 48, 125; alternatives, 10–12, 245–47; defined, 7–8; and economic reward, 152; identity, 10–11, 13, 41, 42, 44, 45, 70–71, 153, 154, 245–48; ideological debate, 28; limitations of analysis, 13; and militancy, 245; and opposition, 10–11, 41, 44, 45, 70, 153, 154, 197, 200, 245–47; political control over, 44; reverse mobility, 57; and second economy, 184–87; and Stalin, 43; totality, 10–11, 45, 72, 102, 154, 245–46
Coal miners, 107, 109, 111, 136, 189, 271–72, 107, 109, 111, 136, 189, 271–72, 277–78
Collectivization: death of peasants, 40; effects of, 121; harshness of regime, 49; in *kolkhoz*, 52, 116, 117, 153, 264
Commissriats of Labor, 29
Communist Party. *See* CPSU
Confederation of Labor, 292, 297
Congress of Free Trade Unions. *See* ICFTU
Congress of People's Deputies, 275, 277, 281, 286, 287, 293, 294, 302
Conservatism, "Proletarian," 293–96
Cooperatives, 264–66, 290; liquidation of, 51
Council of Ministers, 61, 263, 279, 291, 302
Council of the Labor Collective. *See* STK
CPSU, 157, 158, 200, 282, 283

"Decree No. 608," 279
Democratic centralism, 130, 170
Dynamism, 40

Economy, Soviet: "commercial" stores opened, 35; and consumption, 120–21, 124; cost of goods and services, 125;

Workers, Soviet (*cont.*)
  repression of, 219, 225; and politics,
  201- 207, 258; and power, 288; and
  quality control, 146; reaction to economic reforms, 154; reclassification of,
  52; recruitment of, 31, 38, 49, 50, 52,
  86; regime control of, 200–201; resistance from, 15, 37, 38, 43, 91, 182; rural
  migration of, 46, 49; and *samizdat*, 206–
  207; social mobility of, 39–40, 42, 65,
  70; and society, 19; and strikes, 249–57;
  textile workers, 22; and theft, 16, 172,
  196; and unemployment, 190–91; unskilled, 34, 35, 44, 62, 67, 84; and

wages, 36, 103, 104–20, 137, 162; white
collar, 31, 38, 61, 65, 66, 67, 77, 83,
104, 111, 112, 118, 135, 136, 137, 144,
148, 152, 185, 188, 212; women, 33, 48,
67, 105, 112, 153, 156, 164–65, 185, 216;
in the workplace, 162–71

Yakovlev, Aleksandr, 270
Yanowitch, Murray, 79, 160, 166

Zaslavskaia, Tatiana, 11, 144, 178–79,
  182, 188
Zaslavsky, Victor, 207
Zinoviev, Alexander, 28, 39